THEIR MARYLAND

The Army of Northern Virginia from the
Potomac Crossing to Sharpsburg in September 1862

Alexander B. Rossino

Savas Beatie
California

Library of Congress Cataloging-in-Publication Data

Names: Rossino, Alexander B., 1966-author.
    Title: Their Maryland: The Army of Northern Virginia from the Potomac
       Crossing to Sharpsburg in September 1862 / Alexander B. Rossino.
    Description: California: Savas Beatie, [2021] | Includes bibliographical
       references and index. | Summary: "Their Maryland. The Army of Northern Virginia
       From the Potomac Crossing to Sharpsburg in September 1862 charts the course
       of the Confederate military campaign in Maryland during the American Civil War.
       The book is organized into seven comprehensive chapters that examine Robert E. Lee's
       motive for launching the campaign, what he hoped to accomplish, the interaction between
       Maryland civilians and Confederate soldiers, and explains why Lee fought the Battle of
       Sharpsburg/Antietam"—Provided by publisher.
    Identifiers: LCCN 2021013959 | ISBN 9781611215571 (hardcover) |
       ISBN 9781611215588 (ebook)
    Subjects: LCSH: Maryland—History—Civil War, 1861-1865—Campaigns. |
       Confederate States of America. Army of Northern Virginia. | Lee, Robert
       E. (Robert Edward), 1807-1870. | United States—History—Civil War,
       1861-1865—Regimental histories. | Virginia—History—Civil War,
       1861-1865—Regimental histories.
    Classification: LCC E474.61 .R67 2020 | DDC 973.7/452—dc23
    LC record available at https://lccn.loc.gov/2021013959

First Edition, First Printing

Savas Beatie
989 Governor Drive, Suite 102
El Dorado Hills, CA 95762
916-941-6896 / sales@savasbeatie.com / www.savasbeatie.com

All of our titles are available at special discount rates for bulk purchases in the United States. Contact us for information.

Proudly published, printed, and warehoused in the United States of America.

FOR MY FATHER, ALLEN ROSSINO,
WHO FIRST TOOK ME TO ANTIETAM.

(Confidential)

Hd Qrs Army of Northern Va
Sept 9th 1862

Special Orders }
No 191 }

~~III~~ The army will resume
its march to-morrow taking the Hagerstown road Gen Jackson's command
will form the advance and after
passing Middletown with such portion
as he may select take the route towards
Sharpsburg. Cross the Potomac at the
most convenient point & by Friday
morning take possession of the
Baltimore & Ohio R.R. capture such
of the Enemy as may be at Martinsburg
and intercept such as may attempt
to Escape from Harpers Ferry

IV Gen Longstreets command will
pursue the main road as far as Bo-
ons when it will halt, with reserve supply and baggage trains of the army

V Gen McLaws with his own
division and that of Gen R. H. Anderson
will follow Gen Longstreet. on reaching
Middletown will take the route

Table of Contents

Table of Contents (continued)

List of Maps

Photos have been placed throughout the book
for the convenience of the reader.

Acknowledgments

As it is with every book, there are too many people to thank who helped me along the way than I can possibly name here. Please know that I appreciate your efforts on my behalf.

Historical research is an arduous process under normal circumstances. When conducted amidst a global health emergency such as that attending the novel coronavirus (COVID-19) it becomes nearly impossible. Archives and libraries closed for months (some are still shuttered) as I was completing the final stages of research for this book, potentially eliminating the chance that I might get to see several key sources and collections before going to press. It is only due to the service provided by several key individuals that I found it possible to retrieve important materials and access some collections.

Rebecca Smith, Head of Reader Services and Technical Processing at The Historic New Orleans Collection, sent me an electronic copy of Alfred R. Waud's diary and sketch book, which clarified the date when Waud created his drawing of the Army of Northern Virginia crossing the Potomac River. Anita Hoffman, the Archivist at Heritage Frederick, assisted me with several weeks of digging through their records for information on Elias Delashmutt, Jr. when I could not access the facility. Similarly, Kathleen Shoemaker, the Reference Coordinator of Research Services at the Stuart A. Rose Manuscript, Archives, & Rare Book Library of Emory University, went out of her way to ensure that a reel of microfilm containing the diary of James Blackshear made it to the Western Maryland Room of the Washington County Free Library for me to examine the contents. My sincere thanks to Kathy and to Robin Vance of the Interlibrary Loan office at the Washington County Library for helping me coordinate access to the reel. I'm also grateful to Stephanie Gray of the Antietam National Battlefield Library in Keedysville, and to the archivists at the Wilson Library of the University of North Carolina at Chapel Hill, for helping to provide me with material from the Southern Historical Collection. To all of the other archivists and staff at other sites I may have forgotten, I offer my deepest thanks.

Certain crucial individuals also helped my research by supplying copies of sources and references that provided excellent insight into specific subjects. Douglas J. Ashton, a specialist on Confederate Brig. Gen. William Barksdale, shared several sources concerning Rebel operations in Maryland. D. Scott Hartwig and Steven R. Stotelmyer offered support by providing scans of historical sources I never would have been able to see due to the COVID-19 emergency.

My thanks as well to those who took time to read this book in manuscript form, including Thomas G. Clemens, James M. McPherson, Ethan S. Rafuse, Bradley M. Gottfried, and Gene M. Thorp. M. Keith Harris and Cory M. Pfarr took an early look at the first chapter and encouraged me to continue with the effort. John Foskett, Esq. gave this a careful proofreading and offered thoughtful content suggestions. I value and appreciate all their help very much.

Theodore Savas at Savas Beatie deserves a big mention here for his unflagging support. Without his help the book in your hands might have never seen the light of day. Kudos as well to his fine staff at Savas Beatie, including "The Sarahs" (Sarah Keeney and Sarah Closson), Donna Endacott, Lisa Murphy, and Lois Olechny. I am humbly grateful for the time they invest in bringing quality history to the people. All of them are to be applauded.

Alexander B. Rossino, Ph.D.
Boonsboro, Maryland
May 2021

Introduction

THIS book grew out of research I started in 2011 for my first work of historical fiction, *Six Days in September* (Savas Beatie, 2017), a novel about Lee's Army in Maryland in 1862. *Six Days* explored two dimensions of the September 1862 Maryland Campaign via the medium of a first-person narrative: the experience of Rebel soldiers in the run-up to the clash at Sharpsburg, and the reasons why Robert E. Lee chose to fight such a dangerous battle there despite the weakness of his army. My original research uncovered information I never had the opportunity to use in *Six Days*; ongoing research conducted after the book's publication added to the unused source material.

Faced with this growing collection of material, it occurred to me that an audience interested in the history of Lee's army in Maryland might want to read some of my findings in a non-fiction format rather than in a work of historical fiction. Many readers hold biases in both directions: some will not read historical fiction under any circumstances, no matter how closely it is sourced, while others prefer fiction over footnoted scholarly accounts. Being a historian by training and inclination, I can relate to each type of reader. Finding myself with a foot in both worlds, I decided to write this set of loosely related chapters about the Confederate experience in Maryland. They focus equally on General Lee and on the men of his army. I hope they satisfy non-fiction readers I have not yet had the opportunity to reach.

In addition to examining the usual sources (the *Official Records, Battles and Leaders, Southern Historical Society Papers*, and so on), my research included extensive collections of accounts written by men in the Army of Northern Virginia. This body of material grew over time into hundreds of pages of notes on different aspects of the Southern experience. It soon became clear that the histories of the campaign published thus far captured only a portion of the rich story found within these sources. Sometimes these sources offered very different takes on a variety of aspects of the campaign than those related in the aforementioned histories. As a result, I found myself questioning some of the premises and conclusions penned by other historians.

These seven chapters represent my findings on specific aspects of the Confederate experience during the Maryland Campaign. My hope is that my interpretation of these sources enhances our knowledge on some subjects, and corrects the record on others. My intent is not to supplant the work of those who have come before me. It is simply to offer a different take on specific topics based on what I believe these sources tell us.

Interpreting the past using contemporary documents is the historian's fundamental task, but it is not always as simple as it sounds. Over time, every historical subject accumulates what I call the intellectual equivalent of moss. This "moss" manifests itself in the persistence of timeworn, but poorly documented, ideas. For example, it has long been accepted that Lee's army camped almost exclusively in the area between Frederick City and John T. Best's rented farm on the west bank of the Monocacy River. Newly examined evidence suggests otherwise. Historians and others add fresh layers of this interpretive "moss" based on their flawed readings of sources. For instance, a major newspaper article claimed (incorrectly) that a recent examination of the famous photograph of Confederate troops on the march in Frederick concluded the photo depicts Jubal Early's men in July 1864 rather than Thomas J. "Stonewall" Jackson's men in September 1862. Both types of information—the poorly documented and the poorly interpreted— continue to plague the history of Robert E. Lee's Maryland Campaign. These chapters attempt to set the record straight on a number of issues, be it correctly identifying where the various portions of Jeb Stuart's cavalry crossed the Potomac River on September 5, establishing where Lee's army camped several days later near Frederick, Maryland, or explaining what Lee sought to accomplish by fighting at Sharpsburg.

Four of the chapters in this book focus exclusively on the first week of the Confederate operation, specifically the dates of September 4-10, 1862. Chapter 1, "Rebel Revolutionary: Did Robert E. Lee Hope to Foment Rebellion in Maryland in September 1862," explores the general's motives for embarking on the campaign. His reasons for doing so have long been described as the result of a pragmatic dilemma: because of a lack of viable options, Lee was forced to do so in order to supply his army. In fact, I believe the sources show that Lee sought to achieve both a political aim (i.e., Maryland's secession from the Union) and a military objective (i.e., defeating Federal forces above the Potomac) at the same time. Feeding his men loomed large in Lee's thinking, but the general considered it secondary to the potentially war-winning blow that successfully encouraging rebellion in Maryland could have struck against the Northern foe. What might have happened to Washington, D.C., if Maryland seceded? Would the Lincoln administration have been forced to vacate the capital? Lee was playing for high stakes. Achieving such an outcome could have ended the war in 1862.

The next chapter, "High Hopes for Liberating Maryland: The Army of Northern Virginia Crosses the Potomac River, September 4-7, 1862," examines the opinions of the campaign held by Lee's men while documenting their movements across the Potomac into Maryland. The more I have studied this period, the more I have come to realize its uniqueness in the history of the Civil War. Entering Maryland represented the first time that Lee pressed an offensive beyond the boundaries of Virginia, and it was the first time a Confederate army actively sought by its presence to encourage rebellion against the national government in a fellow "Southern" state. The result was a series of exceptional experiences that captured the attention of Southern troops who never imagined they would see such things—events rendered even more extraordinary because they were not battle-related.

Most soldiers who wrote about the war tended to focus on two types of experiences: their daily life in the army, and the engagements in which they fought. As might be expected, many Confederates who participated in the Battle of Sharpsburg/Antietam wrote about it in some fashion. The same cannot be said for many of the campaign's other mundane experiences—except for the army's march into Maryland. These events were so unique that many Southern troops felt compelled to write about them. In doing so, they revealed little distance between what they believed about the campaign and what General Lee hoped to achieve by embarking on it.

The third chapter, "Four Days on the Monocacy: Confederate Encampments Near Frederick City and the Implications for the Lost Orders Debate," follows the Confederate army's columns to the doorstep of Frederick, Maryland, the first city that Rebel troops visited outside of their own country. Only two scholars, Joseph Harsh and D. Scott Hartwig, have tried to determine specifically where Lee's men camped around Frederick. I noticed discrepancies between where these historians placed some of the Army of Northern Virginia's formations, and where the sources say about where those men actually camped. I also discovered that no scholar seems to have questioned whether evidence exists that Maj. Gen. D. H. Hill's division camped at the place where men with the 27th Indiana later found the lost copy of Lee's Special Orders No. 191. This seemed especially significant because historians have long debated the importance of the "Lost Orders," as they have come to be known, without confirming if Hill's men ever camped at that location. As it turns out, Hill's men did not camp where the "Lost Orders" were discovered, which forces us to contemplate other possibilities regarding who may have lost them where they were eventually found.

Chapter 4, "Dreams Dashed On The Rocks of Reality: The Army of Northern Virginia's Mixed Reception in Maryland," delves into the subject of relations between Lee's men and Maryland's people during the Rebel army's two weeks in the state. Entering Frederick caused many in Lee's army to openly wonder at the material plenty they encountered in a city located so close to the desolation that was war-torn northern Virginia. Lee's troops dreamt of a Confederate Maryland waiting to greet them with open arms; some people in Frederick and elsewhere did indeed offer such warmth. But in an example of just how politically divided Maryland was at this time, an even larger portion of the populace either shunned their Rebel "saviors" or aggressively insulted them. Confederate troops recorded both experiences. The delusions that many of Lee's men carried with them evaporated in the face of hard evidence that, in general, most Marylanders wanted nothing to do with the new Confederacy.

Almost a sub-part of the previous chapters, Chapter 5, "Rebels Photographed in Frederick, Maryland: The Case for September 1862," investigates the historical context surrounding the well-known photograph of a column of Confederate troops halted in the streets of Frederick, Maryland. Poorly documented claims surfaced in 2018 that this image may have been taken on July 9, 1864, when Jubal Early's Valley Army marched through Frederick en route to the fighting along the Monocacy River. The Internet helped circulate this claim far and wide. It continues to be argued by enthusiasts without anyone offering real proof for the later date. Unwilling to allow such an extraordinary claim to pass unexamined, and thereby turn into yet another example of the "moss" previously described, I review the available evidence for both dates in an effort to get to the truth. The existing sources do not definitively prove one date or the other, but they more firmly place the photograph in 1862 rather than 1864.

The final two installments—Chapter 6, "The Army of Northern Virginia Makes A Stand: A Critical Assessment of Robert E. Lee's Defensive Strategy at Sharpsburg on September 15-16, 1862," and Chapter 7, "A Very Personal Fight: The Role of Robert E. Lee on the Field at Sharpsburg, September 17, 1862"—

explore Robert E. Lee's actions and decision-making during the run-up to, and fighting at, Sharpsburg. These chapters evolved from my efforts in producing *Six Days* to understand Lee's motives for fighting north of the Potomac, and to discern where the general was during the battle. A deep dive into the questions of timing and motivation demonstrate that Lee decided to stand and fight very early on the morning of September 15. He never wavered in his decision or tried to move his army from its position, and once the battle commenced, he played an important personal role in ensuring that George McClellan's troops did not drive his army from the field. These findings, particularly those outlined in Chapter 6, offer a new interpretation of Lee's intentions that combines larger strategic considerations with developments on the tactical level, providing in the process an explanation for the long unanswered questions of why Lee fought at Sharpsburg and what he hoped to accomplish there.

ONE

REBEL REVOLUTIONARY

⟨⟨⟨

Did Robert E. Lee Hope to Foment Rebellion
in Maryland in September 1862?

F EW songs have exercised as much influence over the beliefs of an army as John Ryder Randall's *Maryland! My Maryland*. Written in the aftermath of the April 1861 riots in Baltimore, when Federal troops threatened by a secessionist mob opened fire on the crowd, Randall's anthem captured the outrage of pro-Confederacy Southerners while spreading the idea that one day the downtrodden Old Line State would rise up and claim its independence from the despotic rule of Abraham Lincoln's presidential administration.[1]

> The despot's heel is on thy shore, Maryland!
> His torch is at thy temple door, Maryland!

---

1 An anonymous author using the pseudonym "Baltimorean" provided this description of the night when John R. Randall composed *Maryland! My Maryland:* "In April 1861, Colonel Randall read in the *New Orleans Delta* news of the attack on the Massachusetts troops as they passed through Baltimore. 'This account greatly excited me,' said Randall. 'I had long been absent from my native city, and the startling event there influenced my mind. That night I could not dismiss what I had read in the paper. About midnight I arose, lit a candle, and went to my desk. Some powerful influence seemed to possess me, and almost involuntarily I proceeded to write the song of 'My Maryland.' Some wild air that I cannot now recall took shape, and the whole poem was dashed off rapidly. No one was more surprised than I was at the widespread and instantaneous popularity of the poem I had been so strangely stimulated to write. The poem 'wrote itself.'" Randall died on Jan. 15, 1908. See Baltimorean, "Great War Song Was Cheap," in *Confederate Veteran*, Vol. 16, No. 5 (May 1908), 231-232.

Avenge the patriotic gore
That flecked the streets of Baltimore,
And be the battle queen of yore,
Maryland! My Maryland!

Hark to an exiled son's appeal, Maryland!
My mother State! to thee I kneel, Maryland!
For life and death, for woe and weal,
Thy peerless chivalry reveal,
And gird thy beauteous limbs with steel,
Maryland! My Maryland!

Dear Mother! burst the tyrant's chain, Maryland!
Virginia should not call in vain, Maryland!
She meets her sisters on the plain—
"Sic semper!" 'tis the proud refrain
That baffles minions back amain,
Maryland! My Maryland!

I hear the distant thunder-hum, Maryland!
The Old Line's bugle, fife, and drum, Maryland!
She is not dead, nor deaf, nor dumb—
Huzza! She spurns the Northern scum!
She breathes! She burns! She'll come! She'll come!
Maryland! My Maryland.[2]

Little did it matter that most of Maryland's people remained steadfast in their support of the national government. Many in the ranks of Robert E. Lee's Army of Northern Virginia thought Randall's hymn expressed the belief that Maryland remained a lost sister state that belonged in the new Confederacy—a destiny prevented only by onerous Federal military occupation. Marylanders in Lee's army encouraged this impression among their comrades, and many who served with them accepted it as the truth. This, in turn, fired the rank and file's desire to cross the Potomac River in September 1862, and may have provided some motivation for Lee's decision to launch the expedition.

Of course, to speak of the Confederate offensive in Maryland as an "invasion" would have been anathema to Lee and his men. Liberation was their watchword at

---

2 *Maryland! My Maryland* (abridged version) by James Ryder Randall, 1861.

the time and, following a long summer of hard marching and severe clashes that some in the Army of Northern Virginia referred to as the Green Corn Campaign, the victorious Rebel general found himself at the end of August with an opportunity to test the sentiment expressed in Randall's lyrics.[3]

Any analysis of the Maryland Campaign must begin with an exploration of what Lee intended to do at the beginning of September 1862. The moment when he decided to turn his army north and cross the Potomac has been a matter of some debate. The lengthiest discussion to date is that provided by Joseph L. Harsh, who argues that Lee faced a "strategic dilemma" after his victory at Second Manassas.[4] Unable to directly attack the fortifications of Washington, D.C., Lee could not remain where he was due to a dearth of food for his men and fodder for the army's animals. Withdrawing south to the Rapidan River remained an option, but doing so would have relinquished all of the territory Lee's men had shed blood to free from Federal occupation. A shift west into the fertile Shenandoah Valley offered yet another option, but making that choice would have left uncovered a direct route for the enemy to advance on Richmond.

According to Harsh and several other authors, Lee contemplated each of these possibilities before deciding as late as September 4 to move north across the Potomac. It is Harsh who makes the most of the "strategic dilemma" thesis, claiming Lee pondered multiple alternatives after speaking with Maj. Gen. Thomas J. "Stonewall" Jackson, "who advised him to move north through the Valley and cross the Potomac at or above Harpers Ferry, clearing out the [enemy's] forces at Winchester &c." Lee opposed this movement "because it took him too far from McClellan, and might not induce the latter to cross over [the river], which was his main object," an aim he confirmed in his post-campaign report of August 1863.[5]

---

3   William M. Owen, *In Camp and Battle with the Washington Artillery of New Orleans* (Boston, MA, 1885), 130.

4   See Chapter 2 of Joseph L. Harsh, *Taken at the Flood: Robert E. Lee and Confederate Strategy in the Maryland Campaign of 1862* (Kent, OH, 1999), and Appendices A-F, Joseph L. Harsh, *Sounding the Shallows: A Confederate Companion for the Maryland Campaign of 1862* (Kent, OH, 2000).

5   Stephen W. Sears, *Landscape Turned Red: The Battle of Antietam* (Boston, MA, 1983), 64 and Lenoir Chambers, *Stonewall Jackson, Vol. II: Seven Days to Last March* (New York, NY, 1959), 178, each pay lip service to the idea by sparing a page for the subject. Neither cites any source; Harsh, *Sounding the Shallows*, 137. Harsh points out Lee's poor memory here, as Pope, and not McClellan, was still the commander of the Federal field army in Virginia at the time. The quote is from a memorandum written by William Allan of a conversation with Gen. Lee on Feb. 15, 1868. See William Allan, "Memoranda of Conversations with General Robert E. Lee," in Gary

Elsewhere, Harsh quotes a second conversation on April 15, 1868, between Lee and former Confederate officer William Allan concerning the potential for a movement to the northwest. Telling Allan that "To have retired up into Loudoun [County] was giving the enemy possession of Fairfax &c.," Lee argued pursuing such a course was "inviting him to flank towards Richmond." Similarly, on February 15, 1868, during an earlier conversation with Allan, Lee stated flatly "that after Chantilly [about Sept. 1] he found he could do nothing more against the Yankees unless he attacked them in their fortifications around Washington, which he did not want to do, and therefore [he] determined the cross the river into Maryland."[6]

Nowhere in these statements does one find Lee discussing strategic alternatives beyond those supporting his intention to maintain direct pressure on Washington. Jackson urged moving through the Shenandoah Valley as an alternative to advancing above the Potomac east of the Blue Ridge, which is not the same thing as retiring to feed the army or moving west to await the next enemy advance because it still involved a northward offensive. Lee's comment about moving into Loudoun County made no sense and perhaps should be considered the statement of a man with declining mental faculties; advancing to Leesburg, the seat of Loudoun County, was in fact precisely the decision the Confederate commander eventually made.

The discussion of a strategic dilemma facing Lee seems to have originated with the general's aide-de-camp, Col. Charles Marshall, whose papers did not appear publicly until 1927.[7] As Sir Frederick Maurice, the English editor of the papers,

---

W. Gallagher, ed. *Lee the Soldier*, (Lincoln, NE and London, 1996), 7. Lee confirmed in his post-campaign report that he crossed his army east of the Blue Ridge "in order, by threatening Washington and Baltimore, to cause the enemy to withdraw from the south bank, where his presence endangered our communications and safety of those engaged in the removal of our wounded and the captured property from late battle-fields." Robert E. Lee, "Report of the Capture of Harper's Ferry and the Operations of the Army in Maryland (1862)," Aug. 19, 1863, in *The War of the Rebellion: A Compilation of the Official Records of the Union and Confederate Armies*, 128 vols. (Washington, DC, 1880-1901), Series 1, Vol. 19, Part 1, 145. Cited hereafter as *OR*.

6 Allan, "Memoranda," in Gallagher, ed., *Lee the Soldier*, 7. Allan later summarized these statements in his unfinished history of the war. At no time did Allan suggest Lee faced a strategic dilemma similar to that described by Charles Marshall. William Allan, *The Army of Northern Virginia in 1862* (Boston, MA, 1892), 322.

7 Marshall died in 1902. Sir Frederick Maurice, ed., *Charles Marshall: An Aide-De-Camp of Lee, Being the Papers of Colonel Charles Marshall Sometime Aide-De-Camp, Military Secretary, and Assistant Adjutant General on the Staff of Robert E. Lee, 1862–1865* (Boston, MA, 1927). Not all students of

explained, Marshall wrote his thoughts on Lee's post-Second Manassas strategic situation in the early 1870s as part of a response to the Prince Philippe of d'Orléans, otherwise known as the Comte de Paris, who had written Marshall for information he intended to publish in the second volume of his history of the American Civil War.[8] The Count, stated Maurice, "questioned the wisdom of Lee's first invasion of Maryland," prompting Colonel Marshall to "correct" the count's impression by launching into a passionate defense of Lee's decision. Marshall noted the lack of provisions around Manassas and Lee's fear of a second water-borne Federal invasion of eastern Virginia. Lee also assessed the detrimental "moral effect" that a southward withdrawal by the Virginia army would have had following the successful campaign that summer. "General Lee," Marshall concluded, "had nothing left to do after the battle [Second Manassas] except to enter Maryland."[9]

Subsequent scholars picked up Marshall's exposition, ensuring it would have a lasting effect on at least some interpretations of Lee's motives for the Maryland Campaign. The most important of these was Douglas Southall Freeman, who incorporated Marshall's theme in his exhaustive four-volume biography of Lee published in 1934. Freeman summarized the situation thusly:

> If manoeuvre had to be undertaken promptly in a country where the army could be subsisted, whither should it be directed? Not eastward, for that would carry the army under the very shadow of the Washington defenses. Not southward to any great distance, for that would take the army into a ravaged land and would bring the war back toward Richmond. Withdrawal a slight distance southward, to Warrenton, for instance, might be considered. That would put the Army of Northern Virginia on the flank of any force advancing to Richmond, and would give it the advantage of direct rail communication with the capital, once the bridges across the Rapidan and the Rappahannock were reconstructed. Carrying

---

the Maryland Campaign agree that Lee faced a strategic dilemma at the beginning of Sept. 1862. James V. Murfin, *The Gleam of Bayonets: The Battle of Antietam and the Maryland Campaign of 1862* (New York, NY, 1965) dedicated no space to Lee's dilemma, and D. Scott Hartwig, *To Antietam Creek: The Maryland Campaign of September 1862* (Baltimore, MD, 2012), 50 placed much less emphasis on it than Harsh, harkening back to Ezra A. Carman, *The Maryland Campaign of September 1862: Volume 1, South Mountain*, Thomas G. Clemens, ed. (El Dorado, CA, 2010), and Francis W. Palfrey, *The Antietam and Fredericksburg* (New York, NY, 1893), neither of which discussed the subject.

8 Louis Philippe d'Orléans-Comte de Paris, *History of the Civil War in America*, Louis F. Tasistro, trans., 2 Vols. (Philadelphia, PA, 1876).

9 Maurice, *Charles Marshall*, Chapter VII. Available online at https://leefamilyarchive.org/reference/books/marshall2/07.html.

the army westward would put it in the Shenandoah Valley, a terrain of many strategical possibilities, but one in which a retreat would force the army steadily back toward the line of the Virginia Central Railroad. By elimination, then, destiny beckoned northward, across the Potomac.[10]

The authority Freeman lent to Marshall's conjecture ensured that the notion of Lee pragmatically pondering strategic alternatives prior to the invasion of Maryland would remain in at least a portion of the historical literature. The problem is that no documentary evidence has surfaced confirming it. The closest Lee himself came to expressing anything similar to Marshall's thoughts appeared in his August 1863 report on the Maryland Campaign: "To prolong a state of affairs in every way desirable, and not to permit the season for active operations to pass without endeavoring to inflict further injury upon the enemy, the best course appeared to be the transfer of the army into Maryland."[11] Lee's mention of a "best course" suggests other alternatives existed, but he used the phrase strictly within the context of maintaining pressure on the Federals and not of moving the army elsewhere.

Another detail that militates against the notion of Lee pondering a strategic dilemma after Second Manassas is the fact that before he moved his army north to confront John Pope, Lee consulted with Jefferson Davis about the place of Maryland in Confederate military and diplomatic strategy. Joseph Harsh notes that a "third Confederate war aim, also present from the start, was the expansion of national boundaries. The Southern founding fathers envisioned their country stretching north to the Mason-Dixon Line."[12]

Accordingly, in its May 6, 1861, declaration of war upon the United States, the Confederate Congress did not name Maryland as a belligerent state because Southerners believed Northern military occupation had forced it to stay in the old Union. President Davis himself even informed Great Britain and France in

---

10 Douglas Southall Freeman, *R. E. Lee: A Biography*, 4 Vols. (New York, NY, 1934), 2:351.

11 OR 19, 1:144.

12 Joseph L. Harsh, *Confederate Tide Rising: Robert E. Lee and the Making of Southern Strategy, 1861-1862* (Kent, OH and London, 1998), 9. The works referenced by Harsh concerning Confederate war aims are E. Merton Coulter, *The Confederate States of America, 1861-1865: A History of the South* (Baton Rouge, LA, 1950), and Emory M. Thomas, *The Confederate Nation, 1861-1863* (New York, NY, 1979.)

February 1862 that Richmond would not accept any peace treaty "which does not secure the independence of the Confederate States, including Maryland."[13]

Therefore, concluded Harsh, "Lee knew, when he entered field command, that Jefferson Davis expected him to go on the offensive to save Richmond and to reclaim Virginia. He also knew Davis was ready for even wider applications of the offensive, if the opportunities presented themselves." To that end, Lee proposed sending Stonewall Jackson reinforcements on June 5, 1862, so that Old Jack might "cross Maryland into Pennsylvania." Such an action, wrote Lee, "would change the character of the war" by forcing McClellan to abandon his fortified works outside of Richmond and fight a battle out in the open where Lee's army could get at him. "Lee chose the offense," declared Harsh, "because he wanted to win the war, and he thought it offered the only chance. He believed the defensive was the sure path to defeat."[14]

By Harsh's own reckoning, if Lee intended (with Davis's blessing) to pursue an offensive policy from June 1862 onward, then as of the end of August Lee knew he must either move north to draw the Federals out of their works around Washington, or he must attack those works directly. And those are the two options we find Lee pondering before he makes the decision that his army should enter Maryland. Choosing a movement in any other direction represented the defensive tactics that he and Davis had already rejected. Therefore, not only does the suggestion that Lee faced a dilemma about what to do before September 2 make no sense, the idea that the Rebel commander would even consider retreating in the wake of a major victory also flies in the face of stated Confederate war aims. A victorious general on the verge of accomplishing objectives established by the civilian authorities simply does not contemplate withdrawal unless duress forces him to choose it.

The only authoritative sources outlining Lee's thoughts prior to his army's crossing of the Potomac are his three letters to President Davis. Contrary to Marshall's assertions, these missives reveal the general's singular focus on entering Maryland following a brief hiatus in Loudoun County to gather provisions. Writing to Davis on September 3, 1862, Lee stated "the present seems to be the most

---

13 *Official Records of the Union and Confederate Navies in the War of the Rebellion*, 31 vols. (Washington, DC, 1922), Series 2, Vol. 3, 333.

14 Harsh, *Confederate Tide Rising*, 62.

propitious time since the commencement of the war for the Confederate Army to enter Maryland," and argued the moment had come to "give material aid to Maryland and afford her an opportunity of throwing off the oppression to which she is now subject." Continuing on, Lee pointed out how

> the two grand armies of the United States that have been operating in Virginia, though now united, are much weakened and demoralized. Their new levies, of which I understand 60,000 men have already been posted in Washington, are not yet organized, and will take some time to prepare for the field. [Moreover,] after the enemy had disappeared from the vicinity of Fairfax and Washington, I did not think it would be advantageous to follow him farther. I had no intention of attacking him in his fortifications, and am not prepared to invest them. If I possessed the necessary munitions, I should be unable to supply provisions for the troops. I therefore determined, *while threatening the approaches to Washington, to draw the troops into Loudoun, where forage and some provisions can be obtained, menace their possession of the Shenandoah Valley, and, if found practicable, to cross into Maryland* [emphasis added].[15]

Nowhere in this letter does one find Lee considering any move other than one preparatory to an advance north of the Potomac. Like a wrestler grappling with an opponent, the Confederate chieftain sought nothing less than to maintain as much pressure on Washington as his army could bring to bear.

Lee hammered the point home for a second time in a letter he dictated to Davis on the following day. Writing from his new headquarters in Leesburg, Virginia, Lee emphasized the salutary impact that entering Maryland could have on the Southern cause. "Since my last communication to you, with reference to the movements which I propose to make with this army, I am more fully persuaded of the benefit that will result from an expedition into Maryland," declared the general, "and I shall proceed to make the movement at once, unless you signify your disapprobation."[16]

Lee initially pointed to securing subsistence as the primary benefit his army would derive from entering Maryland, and to that end he requested "the services of someone known to, and acquainted with, the resources of the country;" a man like the secessionist ex-governor of Maryland, Enoch Louis Lowe, who resided at the time in Richmond, Virginia. Lee's request for Lowe is fascinating because the

---

15 *OR* 19, 2:590. According to Lee's former military secretary, the general composed this letter on Sept. 2. See Armistead L. Long, *Memoirs of Robert E. Lee* (New York, NY, 1886), 204.

16 *OR* 19, 2:591-592.

general seems to have thought the presence of the ex-governor would make his army's stay in western Maryland more palatable to the local populace upon which the Confederates would depend for food. Lee may have also wished to lend the expedition political credibility. "As I contemplate entering a part of the State with which Governor Lowe is well acquainted," he wrote, "I think *he could be of much service to me in many ways* [emphasis added]." This vague expression of his expectations suggests that Lee had more in mind for Lowe than to have him act as the Army of Northern Virginia's chief commissary officer. It reveals that the general knew Lowe hailed from Frederick County and that Lowe had made regular public appeals for "the young men of Maryland . . . to rally in support of the Confederacy."[17]

It was no coincidence, therefore, that when his army arrived in the vicinity of Frederick on September 6, Lee made his headquarters in a grove of trees on the grounds of the Hermitage (also known as the Best farm) where Lowe had been born. There, Lee could wait for Lowe to join him and lend political clout to the secessionist cause in Maryland. The Confederate commander was subtly leveraging the symbolic continuity between Enoch Lowe's prewar governorship and the situation as it stood in September 1862 to help fan the flames of rebellion. As Lee wrote to President Davis in his final pre-Potomac crossing letter on September 5: "I have already had the honor to inform you [that] this army is about entering Maryland, *with a view of affording the people of that State an opportunity of liberating themselves* [emphasis added]. Whatever success may attend that effort, I hope, at any rate, to annoy and harass the enemy."[18]

Lee's latter statement probably referred to plans for an eventual advance into Pennsylvania, but at this point his immediate objective for the campaign appeared to be convincing Marylanders to secede, a development that would have taken the state out of the Union and cut off Washington from the North. Had such an event come to pass, it would have created immense difficulties for the Lincoln administration's continued prosecution of the war. Above all, a Confederate

17 Lowe's father, a Mexican War veteran, is mentioned by name in the fourth verse of John Ryder Randall's *Maryland! My Maryland.* "Come! 'tis the red dawn of the day, Maryland! Come with thy panoplied array, Maryland! With Ringgold's spirit for the fray, With Watson's blood at Monterey, With fearless Lowe and dashing May, Maryland! My Maryland!"; *The Rome* (GA) *Weekly Courier,* Sept. 5, 1862.

18 Thomas J. C. Williams and Folger McKinsey, *History of Frederick County, Maryland,* 2 Vols. (Baltimore, MD, 1997), 2:1338; *OR* 19, 2:593.

Maryland might compel the national government to abandon the District of Columbia in favor of Philadelphia, Boston, or New York, thereby achieving one of Lee's cherished goals: to remove the war from Virginia by pushing the fight north. In addition, bringing Maryland into the Confederate states might draw Great Britain and France into the conflict, strike a blow at the will of the Northern populace to continue prosecuting the war, and give the South the breathing space it needed to recover from the taxing campaigns of that year. Lee may have imagined he could accomplish all of these things without his men firing another shot if his plan to foster rebellion in Maryland, something James Ryder Randall had promised would occur, proved successful. Facing no real dilemma, Lee determined on September 2 to carry the war north to whatever beneficial outcome he might be able to achieve, be it political, military, or a combination of both.[19]

Despite Lee's own statements affirming it, the fact that he sought to encourage revolt among Maryland's people is not a commonly accepted hypothesis. Indeed, various other interpretations have appeared over the years. Francis W. Palfrey argued in the 1890s, for example, that while Lee did not anticipate "'My Maryland' would breathe or burn in any exceptional fashion, or 'be the battle-queen of yore,'" he might "Without indulging in the illusions of audacious hope . . . fairly count upon great and certain gains from transferring his army to the soil of Maryland."[20]

Stephen W. Sears echoed Palfrey a century later by briefly noting Lee's statement to Davis about helping Marylanders "throw off the Yankee yoke" before laying aside the issue in favor of discussing the general's plans to invade Pennsylvania.[21] Douglas Southall Freeman, on the other hand, cautiously expressed the belief that Lee at least entertained the idea of fomenting of rebellion in Maryland: "The presence of a large Confederate force above the Potomac . . .

---

19 That Lee could have entertained such an idea is not idle speculation, for it appears to have been a commonly held opinion. For instance, according to David Clough, a Maryland man, "Some said that within a short time the armies of the South would enter Maryland and then Maryland would secede and the war would have to come to an end, because Washington would then be within the Confederacy." Leighton Parks, *Turnpikes and Dirt Roads* (New York, NY, 1927), 250. President Lincoln's general-in-chief, Henry Halleck, voiced exactly this concern in a message to George McClellan on Sept. 13: "You attach too little importance to the capital. I assure you that you are wrong. The capture of this place will throw us back six months, if it should not destroy us." *OR* 19, 2:280. Armistead Long notes that the general decided to enter Maryland "On the 2d of September succeeding Pope's defeat." See Long, *Memoirs*, 204.

20 Palfrey, *The Antietam and Fredericksburg*, 16-17.

21 Sears, *Landscape*, 65.

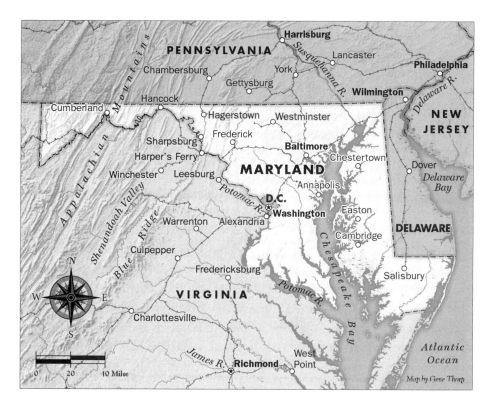

would not assure revolt against Federal authority, but it would give the people of Maryland what they had never had—a chance to express their will." Joseph Harsh devoted even-handed attention to the subject as well, granting, "It may be that at this early stage in his thinking, [Lee] did somewhat naively believe Marylanders would rise up in large numbers to cast off the 'despot's heel.' . . . Yet, it may be doubted that such a political aim would have held much weight with Lee had it not coincided with his assessment of both military objectives and realities."[22]

Elsewhere, Harsh describes Lee's September 4 "I am more fully persuaded" statement to Davis as expressing the general's tentativeness rather than as evidence of his growing conviction. Regarding a September 5 conference in Leesburg with Jackson and Col. Bradley T. Johnson, a native Marylander in Confederate service and former resident of Frederick City who allegedly warned Lee of western Maryland's divided loyalties, Harsh concluded, "It is doubtful Lee was much dismayed by what he heard, *since his primary reason for entering the state had always been*

22 Freeman, *R. E. Lee*, 2:351; Harsh, *Taken*, 58.

military and not political [emphasis added] . . . it is even less likely he placed much reliance on substantial support from the state."[23] Scott Hartwig agreed for the most part with this depiction of Lee as the ultimate pragmatist, arguing "No doubt, Lee hoped his invasion might stir trouble for the Union government among dissenters in Maryland, but he was not so naive as to think the brief entry and exit of his army across the state would trigger an uprising."[24]

Perhaps, but prior to entering Maryland, Lee voiced no doubt about the potential for attracting popular support—a fact that aligned his sentiments with those held by observers both north and south of the Potomac. The notion of a Maryland patiently waiting its chance to revolt manifested itself not only in the lyrics of James Ryder Randall's poem, it also appeared regularly in Confederate political discourse and newspapers. Even the Confederate Congress famously declared, "never to cease this war until Maryland has the opportunity to decide for herself, her own fate, untrammeled and free from Federal bayonets."[25]

Similarly, historian William A. Blair noted that newspapers like the *Richmond Examiner* argued "entering Maryland would not be an invasion at all 'but, on the contrary, going where we shall meet hosts of warm and true friends'."[26] Such rhetoric continued during the Confederate incursion itself. On September 17, while the Army of Northern Virginia fought for its life near Sharpsburg against the Army of the Potomac, the *Edgefield Advertiser* of South Carolina published an opinion piece replete with references to the secessionist myth:

> The hopes and expectations of the Confederacy cluster for the moment around the people of Maryland; because upon their course in a measure depends the success of the new onward movement. Surely there cannot be a doubt of Maryland's southern affinities. And if not, we shall soon hear that she has 'burst the tyrant's chain,' and that her sons by tens of thousands are flocking to the standard of Lee. How glorious her opportunity of disenthrallment and of revenge! It is the turning point in the destiny of a noble people. Will they sink to the degradation of slaves or will they 'remember Howard's warlike thrust,' and

23 Harsh, *Taken*, 75, 82.

24 D. Scott Hartwig, "Robert E. Lee and the Maryland Campaign," in Gallagher, ed., *Lee the Soldier*, 334.

25 Clement A. Evans, ed., *Confederate Military History*, 12 Vols. (Atlanta, GA, 1899), 2:90.

26 William A. Blair, "Maryland, Our Maryland: Or How Lincoln and His Army Helped to Define the Confederacy," in Gary W. Gallagher, ed., *The Antietam Campaign* (Chapel Hill, NC, 1999), 86.

while they 'Avenge the patriotic gore that flow'd the streets of Baltimore,' place another bright and glowing star in the Southern Cross.[27]

A voracious reader of newspapers, General Lee must have been exposed to these opinions as frequently as any of his other literate countrymen. Many in the North held them as well, with some writing openly of their suspicion that Marylanders sought merely an opportunity to erupt against the national government. The *New York Herald* published precisely this opinion on August 26, 1862, claiming, "The condition of affairs in Maryland is not satisfactory to loyal Union men. It is well known that the rebels there are openly organized in every county in the State, and there is reason to believe they are fully prepared with arms, and only wait an opportunity to raise the black flag of rebellion. The military authorities are strongly urged to require the disarming immediately of all who will not take the oath of allegiance."[28]

The Baltimore correspondent of the *Philadelphia Ledger* believed the same, writing in an article published after the Confederate advance had already begun: "private accounts from Maryland are not such as the loyal men of the nation would desire, for it is boldly stated that, should Jackson succeed in getting his army into the State, he will be joined at once by no less than 60,000 of its inhabitants. The aim is said to be to make Baltimore the Headquarters of the Confederate army, cut off the northern communication with Washington, and maintain a threatening attitude towards that city to result finally in its capture and destruction."[29]

Returning specifically to General Lee, his few statements before crossing the Potomac reveal the hope, if not the outright belief, that Maryland's people would rally to the Confederate cause. Some historians of the campaign have nevertheless tended to minimize this fact in favor of the view promoted by Lee and others after the reverse at Sharpsburg that they had never expected Maryland's people to rebel. Gary W. Gallagher has identified the motivation behind this revisionist tendency. "Maryland's anemic response to Lee's army," he wrote, "engendered feelings of

27 *Edgefield Advertiser*, Sept. 17, 1862. Readers will note the language borrowed from Randall's *Maryland! My Maryland.*

28 *New York Herald,* Aug. 26, 1862.

29 *Philadelphia Ledger* text reprinted in the *Mobile Advertiser and Register*, Vol. XXX, No. 141, Sept. 12, 1862. Northerners commonly believed that Jackson commanded his own army independent of Lee.

disappointment and anger. Many Confederates were torn between an inclination to criticize Maryland for not doing more, and a desire to give residents of a sister slave state the benefit of the doubt. . . . Conditioned by newspaper accounts to believe that only Federal bayonets held Maryland in the Union, many Confederates had invested considerable hope in the prospect of wooing another state to their slaveholding republic."[30]

General Lee's post-campaign writings display after-the-fact excuses along these lines, which is why his comments must be scrutinized with some care. Achieving clarity is problematic because of exculpatory rationalizations written by certain ex-Confederates after the war. The most famous of these is an address given by former general Bradley Johnson before the Reunion of the Virginia Division Army of Northern Virginia Association in October 1884.[31] Both Joseph Harsh and D. Scott Hartwig rely heavily on Johnson's comments as evidence that Lee could not have entered Maryland with the hope of sparking a rebellion within the state. What they do not point out is that the veracity of Johnson's remarks is highly suspect.[32]

A native Marylander and a son of Frederick City, Johnson had risen to the rank of colonel by the time of the Maryland Campaign. Stonewall Jackson trusted him implicitly, and prior to the campaign Johnson was one of those in Lee's army who perpetuated the myth of a Maryland ready to burn with secession. Johnson commanded the brigade of Jackson's troops that entered Frederick City as the army's vanguard, an action pregnant with symbolic meaning. He established the provost marshal's office in Frederick, an assignment intended to not only smooth relations between the army and Frederick's inhabitants, but also to demonstrate that Maryland's leading secessionists had returned to rescue their allegedly oppressed countrymen. Johnson also retained the authority to publish a proclamation to the people of Maryland on September 8 (the same day that Lee

---

30 Gary W. Gallagher, "The Net Result of the Campaign Was in Our Favor: Confederate Reaction to the Maryland Campaign," in Gallagher, ed., *The Antietam Campaign*, 15.

31 Bradley T. Johnson, "Address on the First Maryland Campaign," at the Reunion of the Virginia Division Army of Northern Virginia Association, Oct. 23, 1884, in *Southern Historical Society Papers*, 52 Vols. (1884), 12:503-509. Referred to hereafter as *SHSP*.

32 Other scholars have also used Johnson's comments uncritically. See, for example, James I. Robertson, Jr., *Stonewall Jackson: The Man, The Soldier, The Legend* (New York, NY, 1997), 586.

issued a proclamation of his own) calling on them to "rise at once in arms, and strike for liberty and right."[33]

Johnson performed all of these duties in the belief that Marylanders would rebel against the national government, and yet in his 1884 comments claimed to have advised Lee in Leesburg on September 5 that "a large portion of the people [of Maryland] were ardent Unionists; that perhaps an equal number were equally ardent sympathizers with the Confederate cause, still, they had been since June, 1861, so crushed beneath the overwhelming military force, that they could not be expected to afford us material aid until we gave them assurance of an opportunity for relief, by an occupation promising at least some permanence." What is more, Johnson claimed rather ambiguously, "I believe that I know that the Maryland campaign was not undertaken by General Lee under any delusive hope that his presence there would produce a revolution in Maryland, and such a rising as would give a large force of reinforcements to him."[34]

Believing that one knows something, and actually knowing it, are not the same thing, and in this case amount to little more than speculation along the same lines of Charles Marshall's comments concerning Lee's alleged strategic dilemma before the campaign. Did Johnson truly tell Lee not to count on rebellion in Maryland, or is this a case of a former Confederate officer and native Marylander covering his hindquarters after claiming before the campaign that the people would rise? Would Jackson have selected Johnson to lead the advance into Frederick, and then allow him to issue exhortations for revolution, if Johnson had told his senior commanders that they should not count on popular support? Johnson himself provided the answer to this question in his 1884 address:

> This incident I relate to prove what, *in my judgment* [emphasis added], was the real objective of General Lee in the Maryland campaign. It was not as the Count of Paris states in his history of the civil war, or as General Palfrey, in his well-considered and elaborate memoir of Antietam says, that by the transfer of the seat of war to the north banks of the Potomac

33 Jackson named Johnson commander of the Second Brigade in the Stonewall Division after a wound at Malvern Hill knocked John R. Jones out of action. Upon his return to the army on Sept. 7, 1862, Jones retook command of Jackson's old division, while Johnson returned to Richmond to take a post as provost marshal. Captain John Edmund Penn took command of the Second Brigade at Frederick and led it until being wounded and captured at Sharpsburg. See Johnson's proclamation in Evans, ed., *Confederate Military History*, 2:90-91.

34 Johnson, "Address," 503-504.

the secessionists of Maryland would be afforded an opportunity to rise, and by revolution, supported by Lee's army, transfer Maryland to the Confederation of States. General Lee knew perfectly well that a people who had been under military rule for fifteen months, who had been subjugated by every method known to military and relentless force, could not organize resistance or revolution until confidence in themselves and their cause was restored by the presence of an abiding and permanent power. Therefore it seems beyond dispute that the first Maryland campaign was undertaken by General Lee solely and *entirely as part of his defensive operation for the protection of Virginia* [emphasis added].[35]

Here we see the Comte de Paris causing trouble for another ex-Confederate officer as the mythology of the Lost Cause is in the process of being constructed. Johnson's comments, which he admitted were based on his judgment alone and not on any real knowledge or cited document, absolved himself of the failure to stoke rebellion in Maryland, and of Robert E. Lee for ever having hoped to achieve such an outcome. The Comte de Paris, by contrast, wrote that Lee

did not look upon Maryland as a hostile country. Being a slave State, Southern politicians considered her as belonging by right to their Confederacy, and military men relied upon meeting with the same sympathy which had so powerfully aided them in Virginia. Emigrants from Maryland who had taken refuge in the ranks of Lee's army had induced [the general] to believe, notwithstanding his perspicacity, that thousands of volunteers would rally around him as soon as he should appear on the soil of their State, and that this region, yet untouched by the horrors of war, would revictual his army much more effectually than the distant depots of Richmond.[36]

Johnson took issue with these claims because they cast his and Lee's failed expectations in a poor light, a fact that should raise suspicions about Johnson's motives. His comments about the Comte de Paris's analysis also differ significantly from those of Charles Marshall, himself a Maryland man, who never denied the potential importance of rebellion and recruiting to Lee even though the colonel had plenty of opportunity to take issue with the Comte de Paris's characterization of those issues. Could this be because the Comte de Paris was right and it embarrassed men like Johnson, whose efforts during the war had resulted in failure, but who

35 Ibid., 504.

36 Comte de Paris, *History of the Civil War in America*, II:310.

sought after the conflict's end to maintain their reputations by posing as the prophets of that failure rather than as its instigators?[37]

There is credible evidence to support the view expressed by the Comte de Paris as opposed to the "we never expected to succeed" perspective offered by Bradley Johnson. Take, for instance, what Armistead Long, Lee's military secretary during the Maryland Campaign, wrote in his *Memoirs of Robert E. Lee*, published in 1886:

> On the 2d of September succeeding Pope's defeat, Colonel Long wrote from the dictation of General Lee to President Davis in substance as follows: As Virginia was free from invaders, the Federal army being within the defences of Washington, shattered and dispirited by defeat, and as the passage of the Potomac could now be effected without opposition, the present was deemed a proper moment, with His Excellency's approbation, to penetrate into Maryland. The presence of the victorious army could not fail to alarm the Federal authorities and make them draw forces from every quarter for the defence of their capital, thus relieving the Confederacy from pressure and—for a time, at least—from the exhaustion incident to invasion. *The presence of a powerful army would also revive the hopes of the Marylanders, allow them a free exercise of their sympathies, and give them an opportunity of rallying to the aid of their Southern friends* [emphasis added]. Above all, the position of the army, should it again be crowned with victory, would be most favorable for seizing and making the best use of the advantages which such an event would produce.   In anticipation of the President's concurrence, General Lee immediately began the preparation for the invasion of Maryland.[38]

Here is Long, a man who often wrote out the general's correspondence and therefore as good a witness as one could hope for, confirming that Lee never faced a strategic dilemma, and that by September 2 the general had already decided to enter Maryland. Long also states that Lee made his decision for two reasons: to draw Federal forces out of war-weary Virginia, and to encourage secessionist tendencies among Maryland's people. James Longstreet also agreed with this

---

37 The English editor of Charles Marshall's papers shared the Comte de Paris's understanding of Gen. Lee's motives, writing "A success gained in Maryland might have the effect of making decisive the influence of those in the North who thought that the attempt to maintain the Union by force was not worth the cost, and would almost certainly bring considerable reenforcements from that State to the Confederate cause. Sir Frederick Maurice, *Robert E. Lee the Soldier* (New York, NY, 1925), 147. It is instructive to note that foreign writers not influenced by Lost Cause literature offer a more dispassionate view of how Maryland fit into Lee's plans than do American authors.

38 Long, *Memoirs*, 204-205.

assessment. A leading participant in the campaign and a close confidant of Lee, Longstreet described no strategic dilemma entertained by Lee in the days leading up to the Maryland operation. Instead, he asserted: "The commercial, social, and blood ties of Maryland inclined her people to the Southern cause. A little way north of the Potomac were inviting fields of food and supplies more plentiful than on the southern side; and the fields for march and manoeuvre, strategy and tactics, were even more inviting than the broad fields of grain and comfortable pasture-lands. *Propitious also was the prospect of swelling our ranks by Maryland recruits* [emphasis added]."[39]

Additional proof may be found in the pages of contemporary newspapers. The *Philadelphia Inquirer* reported in October 1862 that during the stay of Lee's army near Frederick City,

> A number of rebel officers, among them the Adjutant General of General Lee's staff . . . took lodging with a very worthy Union farmer, by the name of [Joseph] H. Finney, residing some three miles below Frederick. While here, they conversed freely among themselves . . . [and] came to the conclusion that they had no friends in Maryland. This was a positive fact, as the very men who had invited them turned their backs to them. One of Gen. Lee's Aides took a paper from his pocket with over one hundred names thereon, at the same time stating, 'these men wrote to us, and *it was by their assurances we came here* [emphasis added], and now they are our worst enemies, they will do nothing for us.' . . . Most named were residents of Baltimore, a few were from Hagerstown, and eleven from Frederick. A pin hole had been placed opposite each Fredericktonian. The officer was particularly severe about these men.[40]

The *New York World* also reported after the war, based on the comments of a former (and unnamed) member of Lee's staff, that sources in Maryland specifically told the general that a move by the Southern army into the state would generate "untold numbers of recruits." Likewise, the *Baltimore American* wrote that just before Lee's army began traversing the Potomac River, "a number of prominent secessionists had whispered to some of their loyal relatives and acquaintances that

---

39 James Longstreet, *From Manassas to Appomattox: Memoirs of the Civil War in America* (Philadelphia, PA, 1886), 279.

40 *Philadelphia Inquirer*, Oct. 6, 1862. Also quoted in Paul and Rita Gordon, *Frederick County, Maryland: Never the Like Again* (Frederick, MD, 1995), 41.

Frederick would be in possession of the Confederate troops before twenty-four hours; that they had positive information of the fact."[41]

Finally, there is the statement of a "Virginia captain" alleged to have "told a relative in Leesburg, during the passage of Lee's army through it, that the Rebel force was eighty-four thousand, though *Lee expected it would be increased thirty or forty thousand by Secessionists of Maryland* [emphasis added]." Taken together, these stories support the idea that secessionists north of the Potomac made efforts to induce Lee to enter the state with his army by giving him the impression that its people would revolt and flock to the Army of Northern Virginia's standards.[42]

Other prominent veterans echoed this belief in their postwar writings. Robert L. Dabney, a personal acquaintance of General Lee and a major on the staff of Stonewall Jackson until the end of August 1862, wrote the following in his wartime biography of Old Jack: "Wise policy dictated that the soil of Virginia should, if possible, be relieved of the burden of the invading and the patriot armies, which it had so long borne, and that their ravages should be retorted upon the aggressor. Maryland, it was known, had succumbed reluctantly to his yoke, and *the hope was entertained that the presence of the southern army would inspirit its people to attempt something in aid of their own liberation* [emphasis added]."[43]

Fitzhugh Lee, Robert E. Lee's nephew and the commander of a brigade of cavalry in James Ewell Brown "Jeb" Stuart's division, published a biography of General Lee in 1898 in which he claimed that his uncle

> believed if he could win a decisive victory the fall of Washington and Baltimore would follow, with far-reaching results. Second, because it (crossing into Maryland) would relieve

---

41 *Baltimore American* quoted in *Alexandria Gazette*, Sept. 8, 1862. Also see the *Frederick Examiner*, Sept. 24, 1862. "Friday, Sept. 5th. After noon rumors became rife that the Rebels had crossed into Maryland. . . . Their coming was undoubtedly known beforehand to the Secession sympathizers in our midst, some of whom had admonished their particular Union friends to leave."

42 Marylanders crossing the Potomac to encourage a northward march by the Confederate army appears to have been a relatively common occurrence. For example, in Aug. 1861, Pvt. Robert A. Moore of the 17th Mississippi, then stationed near Leesburg, recalled meeting a gentleman from Maryland who swam the river to say that fifty thousand Marylanders were waiting to revolt. Robert A. Moore and J. W. Silver, eds., *A Life for the Confederacy, as Recorded in the Pocket Diaries of Pvt. Robert A. Moore. Co. G. 17th Mississippi Regiment, Confederate Guards, Holly Springs, Mississippi* (Wendell, NC, 1987), 55.

43 Robert L. Dabney, *Life and Campaigns of Lieut.-Gen. Thomas J. Jackson* (Richmond, VA, 1866), 543. Dabney completed this biography during the war.

Virginia and the Confederate quartermasters and commissary departments at Richmond of the support of his army for a time. Third, because *it was hoped that large accessions to his decimated ranks would be obtained from those who sympathized with his cause in Maryland . . . .* The sons of Maryland in the Confederate army were splendid soldiers, enthusiastic in the cause, and brave in battle, and *they knew, as the Southern commander did, that a battle fought and won in western Maryland, followed by a rapid march in the direction of Baltimore and Washington, would be attended with immense results* [emphasis added], and that nothing would be accomplished, so far as Maryland was concerned, till then.[44]

Fitz Lee conflated General Lee's military and political goals, hinting that a rapid march on Baltimore would have achieved "immense results." He did not clarify what these results might have been, but Confederate troops and politicians imagined that Maryland's people would "breathe and burn" per Randall's lyrics if a victorious Southern army moved among them. In short, should the mere presence of the Army of Northern Virginia on Maryland's soil prove insufficient to prompt rebellion, then securing a military victory north of the Potomac might accomplish the same result.

Prussian-born Major Heros von Borcke, Jeb Stuart's chief of staff, held a similar view of General Lee's objectives in Maryland. In his memoirs, published in 1866, von Borcke wrote,

General Lee had now decided not to attack the enemy in their strong fortifications around Alexandria, but boldly to carry the war into the enemy's territory, or at least into the fertile plains of Maryland. Many advantages, it was hoped, might be secured by this policy. For a considerable period he would be able there to subsist his army, relieved from the necessity of protecting his lines of communication for supplies. *The confident belief was also entertained that our army would be increased by 20,000 to 25,000 recruits, who were supposed to be only awaiting the opportunity of taking up arms against the Federal Government* [emphasis added]. Being so reinforced our commander-in-chief doubted not that he might easily strike a blow against Baltimore, or even Washington, or transfer the theatre of military operations across the border into the rich agricultural region of Pennsylvania.[45]

Clearly, von Borcke believed that Lee thought advancing into Maryland would be attended by both military and political benefits, including vast numbers of

---

44 Fitzhugh Lee, *General Lee* (New York, NY, 1898), 197, 200.

45 Heros von Borcke, *Memoirs of the Confederate War for Independence*, 2 Vols. (Edinburgh and London, 1866), 1:181-182.

recruits for the Army of Northern Virginia derived from a populace supposedly seething with anger against the national government. No less authoritative a source than Lee's own aide, Maj. Walter H. Taylor, also wrote in the later years of his life that, "In his proclamation to the people of Maryland, General Lee clearly shows . . . he hoped for some movement of the people to the Confederate standards, with the view of regaining the rights of which they had been despoiled. This view was also held by the authorities at Richmond."[46]

James Murfin picked up this theme of fomenting rebellion in his classic *The Gleam of Bayonets*: "Lee labored under the false impression that the central and western counties [of Maryland] . . . shared these same sentiments" of Southern sympathy as the eastern portions of the state. William Blair concurred, writing in 1999, "Besides the military and logistical value of an offensive, [Lee] understood the potential political gain and warmed to this thinking as he corresponded with [Davis] . . . The march of the liberators was on."[47]

Convincing evidence points to General Lee pursuing political and military goals in Maryland that he saw as closely aligned. While noting his logistical and military objectives to Jefferson Davis before the campaign, and elaborating on them after his army had returned to Virginia in late September, Lee also gave ready expression to political considerations, especially during the early phase of his operation. It could be said in this sense that Lee pursued parallel courses—the political, centered on fostering secession, and the military, focused on drawing the Federal army away from Washington for a final, decisive clash in western Maryland or southern Pennsylvania. Fitzhugh Lee claimed that his uncle thought of those goals as one and the same—try first to stoke the smoldering coals of rebellion into a conflagration or, failing that, blow them into life by winning a decisive military victory and moving on Baltimore. Most modern scholars, however, have chosen to leave aside the political considerations in order to give predominance to Lee's military goals. This makes sense given the general's position as the commander of the Confederacy's largest army in the east, but it also overlooks the evidence that Lee pursued demonstrable secessionist goals as military objectives. Indeed, Lee

---

46 Walter H. Taylor, *General Lee: His Campaigns in Virginia, 1861-1865 with Personal Reminiscences* (Norfolk, VA, 1906), 119.

47 Blair, "Maryland, Our Maryland," in Gallagher, ed., *The Antietam Campaign*, 88.

appears to have believed that encouraging rebellion and fighting the Federal army were complementary, not competing, aims.

In addition to his letters to President Davis, there are the orders Lee issued concerning the desired conduct of his troops within the state. On September 4, as his plans evolved in Leesburg, Lee wrote out General Orders No. 102:"This army is about to engage in most important operations," he explained, "where any excesses committed will exasperate the people, lead to disastrous results, and enlist the populace on the side of the Federal forces in hostility to our own." The general ordered that "quartermasters and commissaries will make all arrangements for the purchase of supplies needed by our army, to be issued to the respective commands upon proper requisitions, thereby removing all excuse for depredations." He also noted that Brig. Gen. Lewis A. Armistead, who would suffer a mortal wound in the Pickett-Pettigrew-Trimble Charge on the third day at Gettysburg, would act as provost marshal of the army with the power to arrest and punish stragglers (i.e., men who left their commands without authorization). On the following day, Lee issued Special Orders No. 188, which stated that "Brigade commanders will arrest all stragglers, without regard to their commands, who may fall back from preceding commands, retaining them until arrival in camp, where they may be restored to their respective commands."[48]

Straggling on the march to forage across the countryside had long presented a discipline problem for Lee. Now, with his men in Maryland and dependent on what they could procure from the locals for food, the general sought to mitigate the friction that could arise from hordes of Southern troops taking as they pleased from fields, barns, and chicken coops. As one witness who passed through Frederick during the Confederate occupation explained to readers of the *Washington Republican*, "The soldiers are not allowed, under a penalty of death, to touch a thing or take articles without the consent of the owner, and then pay liberally for it (in Confederate scrip). The orders are strictly enforced," he continued, "and as a consequence, not an ear of corn or a fence rail is disturbed. This forbearance is shown because, as they say, Maryland belongs to the Confederacy, and is a part of their country."[49]

---

48 OR 19, 2:595.

49 Letter to the *Washington Republican* reprinted in the *Rockingham Register and Advertiser*, Harrisonburg, Virginia, Sept. 19, 1862.

Lee shared this opinion, fully believing that measures against straggling were essential in a state whose supposedly restive populace was said to await the opportunity to rise up against the national government. Of this he effusively reminded his men in General Orders No. 103: "Soldiers, press onward! Let each man feel the responsibility now resting on him to pursue vigorously the success vouchsafed to us by Heaven. Let the armies of the East and the West vie with each other in discipline, bravery, and activity, *and our brethren of our sister States will soon be released from tyranny* [emphasis added], and our independence be established upon a sure and abiding basis."[50]

The first elements of Lee's army, belonging to the infantry division of Maj. Gen. Daniel Harvey Hill, crossed the Potomac River on September 4 to cut the Chesapeake and Ohio Canal and secure a bridgehead at Noland's Ferry. Jackson's divisions began crossing the next day at White's Ford with Jeb Stuart's cavalry brigades screening their right flank from Poolesville to Urbana. James Longstreet's command followed these columns, bringing up the army's rear. For the next two days, Confederate infantry marched toward Frederick with Jackson and Hill in the lead. "From the Potomac, General Lee advanced to Frederick, at which place he arrived on the 6th, and established himself behind the Monocacy," recounted Armistead Long. Furthermore,

> As the principal object of the present advance into Maryland was to create a diversion in her favor in order that if so disposed she might array herself beside her sister Southern States [emphasis added], General Lee determined to remain at Frederick a sufficient time to allow the Marylanders to rally to his support. At the commencement of hostilities many brave Marylanders had flocked to the Confederacy, and there were soon seen in the Southern ranks [Arnold G.] Elzey, G. H. Steuart, Bradley Johnson, McLean, Marshall, Andrews, and a host of others of a like noble and generous spirit. Many of these gallant gentlemen were now with the army, anxious to assist in rescuing their State from the Federal authority.[51]

On the afternoon of September 6, General Lee arrived at the rented farm of John T. Best about four miles south of Frederick City. After establishing his headquarters in a grove of oaks to watch for Enoch Lewis Lowe, Lee had himself

---

50 OR 19, 2:596. Mention of an army in the West refers to a force under the command of Gen. Edmund Kirby Smith that had won a victory at the Battle of Richmond, Kentucky, on Aug. 30, 1862.

51 Long, *Memoirs,* 207.

driven by ambulance into Frederick City to attend dinner that evening. Major Heros von Borcke, who also happened to be in Frederick, described the city as being "in a tremendous state of excitement" at the time, recalling how

> The Unionists living there had their houses closely shut up and barred, but the far greater number of the citizens, being favourably disposed to the Confederate cause, had thrown wide open their doors and windows, and welcomed our troops with the liveliest enthusiasm. Flags were floating from the houses, and garlands of flowers were hung across the streets. Everywhere a dense multitude was moving up and down, singing and shouting in a paroxysm of joy and patriotic emotion, in many cases partly superinduced by an abundant flow of strong liquors.[52]

If von Borcke's account is to be believed, a good number of Fredericktonians greeted Confederate troops with open arms. It was into this jubilant setting that Robert E. Lee and his staff traveled. Fortunately, a corporal in the Rockbridge Artillery and aide to General Jackson, James Powers Smith, also happened to be a friend of the family hosting the meal to which Lee had been invited.[53] Smith had the uncomfortable experience of joining the event in his tattered uniform. "I found myself seated in the parlor I had known in childhood," recalled Smith many years later, when to "my surprise and chagrin . . . there came in to dine no less a party than General Robert E. Lee and his staff, well-dressed and toileted. The private soldier made an effort to escape, but was captured and brought back; and, seated for

---

52 Lee was unable to ride a horse at this time due to injuries to his hands. James P. Smith, "With Stonewall Jackson in the Army of Northern Virginia," in *SHSP*, Vol. 43, No. 5 (1920), 16; Von Borcke, *Memoirs*, 189.

53 According to Leighton Parks, "What a Boy Saw of the Civil War" in *The Century Magazine*, Vol. 70, No. 2 (1905), 259, Lee received multiple invitations to dinner from prominent sympathizers in Frederick. He declined all of them save one, allegedly out of concern that the host family would face persecution after the Army of Northern Virginia left the vicinity. Why he chose to accept one of the invitations is not known. The host family in question was probably that of Reverend Dr. John B. Ross, the pastor of Frederick's First Presbyterian Church. A well-known Southern sympathizer, Ross now led "the church where my father had once been pastor," recalled Smith, "and where, in my childhood, I had slept with my head in my mother's lap." The night of the dinner Smith also remembered sitting "in the parlor I had known in childhood," suggesting Ross's family lived in the parsonage (i.e., the residence of the pastor) next door to the First Presbyterian Church, the same house where Smith's family had lived when his father was minister. Smith, "With Stonewall Jackson in the Army of Northern Virginia," 15-16.

protection by the side of the lady of the home, he permitted the generals and colonels to do the talking and ate a dinner not yet forgotten."[54]

Details of the night's conversation have been lost, but it is probable that those in attendance suggested Lee announce his army's intentions to Maryland's populace. As the general admitted in a missive to Davis dated September 12, upon reaching Frederick he found "the citizens embarrassed as to the intentions of the army." Lee referred the president to the proclamation to the people of Maryland that he composed on September 7 (the day after the dinner) and which he had printed and distributed on Monday morning (September 8). Lee confessed to Davis that he had "waited on entering the State for the arrival of ex-Governor Lowe; but finding that he did not come up . . . I determined to delay no longer in making known our purpose." Lee had hoped Lowe would join him to further Confederate political objectives during this early stage of the expedition, but when the ex-governor did not arrive, Lee was forced into the awkward position of issuing the proclamation himself.[55]

As of September 6, Lee still hoped that his army's march into Maryland would spark a secessionist rebellion in the state, but after discussing the issue with a sympathetic audience in Frederick he began to see the situation in a different light. This change in Lee's thinking is evident in the letter he dictated to Davis on September 7. "Notwithstanding individual expressions of kindness that have been given," he wrote, "and the general sympathy in the success of the Confederate States, *situated as Maryland is* [emphasis added], I do not anticipate any general rising of the people in our behalf. Some additions to our ranks will no doubt he received, and I hope to procure subsistence for our troops."[56]

Here, for the first time, Lee expressed doubt that a spontaneous uprising in favor of the Southern cause would take place in Maryland. This did not mean that he believed a rebellion could not be provoked. Rather, Lee's thinking on the subject

---

54 Smith, "With Stonewall Jackson in the Army of Northern Virginia," 16. Smith told this same story thirteen years earlier, adding then that General Lee had "put a crippled hand on his shoulder and spoke with pride of the fine service the boy's battery had rendered." Freeman, *R. E. Lee*, 2:356, and the *Richmond Times-Dispatch*, Jan. 20, 1907.

55 *OR* 19, 2:605; "Monday, 8th inst. Lee's, Johnson's, Philpot's, White's, Heard's and Kilgour's pronunciamientoes were published in handbill form." *Frederick Examiner*, Sept. 24, 1862.

56 *OR* 19, 2:596. This dispatch to Davis is of particular interest because it illustrates how Lee sometimes withheld information from the Confederate president until he could present that information in the desired light.

moved in a different direction. Until the dinner he attended on September 6, the general seems to have assumed that the mere presence of his troops in Maryland would be sufficient to incite revolt. Now he concluded that fomenting a rebellion against the Union would be possible only after his army had won another battle. The key phrase "situated as Maryland is" reveals the change in Lee's thinking. Thanks to the opinions expressed by well-wishers in Frederick, Lee came to understand that Maryland, hemmed in between fortified Washington and much larger pro-Union Pennsylvania, faced invasion at multiple points. This hard reality intimidated the pro-Southern portion of its populace into believing that they alone could never free themselves through armed rebellion. The Army of Northern Virginia would need to fight for their support.

That Lee reached this conclusion on September 7 comes through clearly in his August 1863 report on the campaign:

> The condition of Maryland (i.e., occupied by Federal troops and under martial law) encouraged the belief that the presence of our army . . . would induce the Washington Government to retain all its available force to provide against contingencies (i.e., popular rebellion) which its course toward the people of that State (i.e., military occupation) gave it reason to apprehend, *it was [therefore] hoped that military success might afford us an opportunity to aid the citizens of Maryland in any efforts they might be disposed to make to recover their liberties* [emphasis added].[57]

Lee and other staunch Confederates believed that martial law in Maryland caused public outrage, generating the fear of a popular uprising that forced the Lincoln administration to keep large numbers of troops in the state. It followed that pro-secession Marylanders might be prompted to revolt if a military success, meaning a victory by the Confederate army, could reassure the people of protection from Federal retaliation. As Lee explained to Davis, he "fully appreciated . . . the difficulties that surrounded Maryland's people," and as a result he did not expect any "active demonstration on the part of the people, *unless success should enable us to give them assurance of continued protection* [emphasis added]. Influenced by these considerations, the army was put in motion."[58]

---

57 *OR* 19, 1:144.

58 *OR* 19, 2:596. I have rewritten some of Lee's tortured language to clarify his point and avoid the passive voice as much as possible. Here is the original passage: "The condition of Maryland

There is an additional piece of evidence that suggests Lee shared his new sense of things with others. Shortly after a visit to Lee's headquarters in mid-October 1862, Lt. Col. Garnet Joseph Wolseley, an Irishman and observer from the British Army, recorded the following: "It is generally stated that the Confederate authorities calculated upon a rising in Maryland directly after their army entered that State [but] everybody to whom I spoke on the subject ridiculed the idea of ever having thought that any such rising would take place, until either Baltimore was in their hands, *or they had at least established a position in that country* [emphasis added]."[59]

Despite being rife with the kind of post-campaign revisionism identified by Gary Gallagher, Wolseley's comment betrays the fact that some of Lee's senior officers, and perhaps even the general himself, had voiced the belief that a rebellion in Maryland might have resulted if the Army of Northern Virginia had proven its ability to remain north of the Potomac. Some thirty years later Wolseley concluded, "Lee thought his best plan to accomplish the end he had in view was to invade Maryland, where the Southern cause had thousands of sympathizers."[60]

September 6 thus proved to be a pivotal date in the history of the Maryland Campaign. That evening, Lee learned from sympathetic Fredericktonians that the only way Maryland's people could be induced to revolt was if the Army of Northern Virginia won a signal victory in the state or in Pennsylvania. Lee apparently agreed with this reasoning and dutifully reported the change in his thinking to Davis on September 7. It was then that he began planning the operation against Harpers Ferry, which he needed to capture before the Army of Northern Virginia could move farther north. In short, the nebulous military and political objectives that Lee had pursued since the beginning of the month came fully

---

encouraged the belief that the presence of our army . . . would induce the Washington Government to retain all its available force to provide against contingencies, which its course toward the people of that State gave it reason to apprehend. At the same time it was hoped that military success might afford us an opportunity to aid the citizens of Maryland in any efforts they might be disposed to make to recover their liberties. The difficulties that surrounded them were fully appreciated, and we expected to derive more assistance in the attainment of our object from the just fears of the Washington Government than from any active demonstration on the part of the people, unless success should enable us to give them assurance of continued protection. Influenced by these considerations, the army was put in motion."

59 James A. Rawley, ed., *The American Civil War: An English View, The Writings of Field Marshal Viscount Wolseley* (Mechanicsburg, PA, 2002), 32.

60 Ibid., 143.

together on the night of September 6; after this date he began working toward their accomplishment with a reinforced sense of purpose.

Clarifying the connection between military victory and winning popular support made it doubly important to Lee that he nurture confidence in the Confederate cause among Maryland's people. Hence his effort to deal with the scourge of straggling. In a second letter to Davis composed on September 7, Lee again raised the issue of discipline in his army while linking it directly with the objectives of his campaign. Arguing that most stragglers left the army "by design," Lee called them "cowards . . . [who] desert their comrades in times of danger." He requested the formation of a "military commission of men known to the country" to handle disciplinary actions as quickly as possible, and advised Davis of the need for an Inspector General. "I assure you some remedy is necessary," he concluded, "especially now, when the army is in a State *whose citizens it is our purpose to conciliate and bring with us* [emphasis added]. Every outrage upon their feelings and property should be checked."[61]

Lee also began writing his proclamation to Maryland's people that same day, which he published on Monday, September 8. This announcement sought to convince Marylanders of the righteousness of the Confederate cause and explain why the Army of Northern Virginia had crossed the Potomac. Lee appears to have instructed Maryland officers under his command to issue proclamations of their own at the same time, resulting in a coordinated release of calls for support and recruits. Beginning his proclamation with "It is right," a phrase lifted straight out of the Episcopal Church's *Book of Common Prayer*, Lee contended that the people of Maryland

> should know the purpose that has brought the army under my command within the limits of your State, so far as that purpose concerns yourselves. The people of the Confederate States have long watched with the deepest sympathy the wrongs and outrages that have been inflicted upon the citizens of a Commonwealth allied to the States of the South by the strongest social, political, and commercial ties. They have seen with profound indignation their sister-State deprived of every right and reduced to the condition of a conquered province. Under the pretense of supporting the Constitution, but in violation of its most valuable provisions, your citizens have been arrested and imprisoned upon no charge and contrary to all forms of law; the faithful and manly protest against this outrage made by the

61 OR 19, 2:597-598.

venerable and illustrious Marylander to whom in better days no citizen appealed for right in vain was treated with scorn and contempt; the government of your chief city has been usurped by armed strangers; your legislature has been dissolved by the unlawful arrest of its members; freedom of the press and of speech has been suppressed; words have been declared offences by an arbitrary decree of the Federal executive, and citizens ordered to be tried by a military commission for what they may dare to speak.[62]

In a telling turn of phrase, and in terms that revealed no daylight between his beliefs and those of his men, Lee went on to explain the rationale behind his decision to march north of the Potomac River:

Believing that the people of Maryland possessed a spirit too lofty to submit to such a government, the people of the South have long wished to aid you in throwing off this foreign yoke, to enable you again to enjoy the inalienable rights of freemen and restore independence and sovereignty to your State. *In obedience to this wish our army has come among you, and is prepared to assist you with the power of its arms in regaining the rights of which you have been despoiled* [emphasis added]. This, citizens of Maryland, is our mission, so far as you are concerned.[63]

Coercion would not be employed, explained Lee in conclusion, juxtaposing the operations of his army to those of the old national government against which it struggled:

No constraint upon your free will is intended; no intimidation will be allowed. Within the limits of this army at least, Marylanders shall once more enjoy their ancient freedom of thought and speech. We know no enemies among you, and will protect all, of every opinion. It is for you to decide your destiny freely and without constraint. This army will respect your choice, whatever it may be; and, while the Southern people will rejoice to

---

62 As a practicing Episcopalian, Robert E. Lee would have been intimately familiar with the administration of the Holy Eucharist. A portion of the language during that rite involves a type of call and response interaction between the minister and his congregation with the minister saying, "Let us give thanks unto our Lord God," which the people respond to with, "It is meet and right to do so." Some editions of the *Book of Common Prayer* record the phrase as, "It is right to give him thanks and praise." *The Book of Common Prayer, and Administration of the Sacraments* (New York, NY, 1854), 296.

63 *OR* 19, 2:601-602.

welcome you to your natural position among them, they will only welcome you when you come of your own free will.[64]

Bradley Johnson published his proclamation on the same day, using high-sounding language that bore little or no resemblance to his supposed September 5 warning about Maryland's unionist tendencies. Calling explicitly for Marylanders to rise up and rebel against the tyranny of the national government, Johnson claimed

> After sixteen months of oppression more galling than the Austrian tyranny, the victorious army of the South brings freedom to your doors. Its standards now wave from the Potomac to Mason and Dixon's line. The men of Maryland, who during the last long months have been crushed under the heel of this terrible despotism, now have the opportunity for working out their own redemption, for which they have so long waited and suffered and hoped. The government of the Confederate States is pledged by the unanimous vote of its Congress, by the distinct declaration of its President, the soldier and statesman Davis, never to cease this war until Maryland has the opportunity to decide for herself, her own fate, untrammeled and free from Federal bayonets. The people of the South, with unanimity unparalleled, have given their hearts to our native State, and hundreds of thousands of her sons have sworn with arms in their hands that you shall be free. You must now do your part. We have the arms here for you. I am authorized immediately to muster in for the war, companies and regiments, the companies of one hundred men each, and the regiments of ten companies. Come, all who wish to strike for their liberties and homes! Let each man provide himself with a stout pair of shoes, a good blanket and a tin cup. Jackson's men have no baggage. Officers are in Frederick to receive recruits, and all companies formed will be armed as soon as mustered in. Rise at once. Remember the cells of Fort McHenry! Remember the dungeons of Fort Lafayette and Fort Warren! The insults to your wives and daughters! The arrest! The midnight searches of your houses! Remember these wrongs! and rise at once in arms, and strike for liberty and right.[65]

Captain Elijah Viers "Lige" White, the owner of the land along the south bank of the Potomac River containing White's Ford, and the commander of a battalion of cavalry serving as scouts and Brig. Gen. Alexander Lawton's bodyguard during the Maryland Campaign, published a call of his own on September 8. Crying "Marylanders to the rescue!" White identified himself as a Maryland man in

64 Ibid.

65 Evans, ed., *Confederate Military History*, 2:90-91.

"service eighteen months opposing the tyranny which would have made of the South a subjugated and ruined country."[66] White announced that he had resolved to do what he could to carry Maryland "where she belongs—to the Southern Confederacy," and asked patriotic Marylanders to join him in raising a regiment of cavalry. "I have no recruiting office," explained White, and "can be found at General Lawton's headquarters, where I will be happy to receive recruits. Come at once, or make up your minds to be slaves to the Northern despotism forever."[67]

Sergeant J. Mortimore Kilgour, the quartermaster of White's battalion, also published a recruiting handbill stating he had been "detailed to recruit for Captain White's Cavalry Regiment . . . All persons desiring to join this far-famed corps will apply to me at the Provost Marshal's."[68]

Lastly, John W. Heard, the former editor of the *Frederick Herald*, a secessionist newspaper, made a desperate plea for recruits:

Men of Old Frederic Arouse—Defend your Homes! Under the authority of the Confederate Government, I am now engaged in raising a company of infantry. The great Army of the South, unconquered and unconquerable, is now in your midst, and has determined that Maryland shall be free. What say you, Marylanders? Are you willing to fight for the liberties for which you have so long been clamorous, or are you so abject as to accept them as a boon at the hands of others? No! no! sons of Maryland—inheritors of her revolutionary glory—by your own right arm achieve the independence of your own State. Falter not, hesitate not, now that the opportunity is offered you–but rally at once and vindicate your history. Recruiting-Office next door to the Provost Marshal's, where there will always be found an officer in attendance.[69]

---

66 White was born in Poolesville, Maryland, in 1832. Frank M. Myers, *The Comanches: A History of White's Battalion, Virginia Cavalry* (Baltimore, MD, 1871), 8.

67 Reprinted in *Report of Lewis H. Steiner, Inspector of the Sanitary Commission Containing a Diary Kept During the Rebel Occupation of Frederick, MD, and an Account of the Operations of the U.S. Sanitary Commission During the Campaign in Maryland, September, 1862* (New York, NY, 1862), 16. Referred to hereafter as the *Steiner Report*.

68 *Steiner Report*, 16. G. B. Philpot also recalled being asked by Gen. John R. Jones to enlist recruits on the grounds that he hailed from Maryland, writing, "Jack West and I were invited by an old gentleman to be his guests while in the city, and we gladly accepted. I had been detailed by General Jones to recruit for my company, which had been very much depleted. I had circulars distributed calling on the young men to rally to our flag, in which I quoted a line from the Maryland song, 'She bleeds, she burns; she'll come, she'll come, Maryland, my Maryland'." I recruited fifteen men, who were ever after called the "Bleeders." See G. B. Philpot, "A Maryland Boy in the Confederate Army," in *Confederate Veteran*, Vol. 24, No. 7 (July 1916), 314.

69 *Steiner Report*, 16-17.

Although reports about the success of Confederate recruiting efforts varied at the time, in the end Marylanders did not respond to these calls, either in state-wide rebellion or in large numbers as volunteers for the army. At that moment, however, no one could fully judge the success or failure of the appeals because the Army of Northern Virginia did not linger at Frederick City.

By September 8, Lee had set aside proclamations in order to focus on achieving the military objectives that might help him realize the Confederacy's political aims. This planning resulted in the distribution of Special Orders No. 191 on September 9 outlining the operation against Harpers Ferry. On September 10, Lee set the army in motion. Nothing more remained for him to accomplish in Frederick City. Ex-Governor Enoch Lowe had not materialized, some of Frederick's shopkeepers had proven themselves "unwilling, while overrun by members of this army, to open their stores," the populace of Maryland remained quiescent, and recruits only trickled in. More important, reports had arrived that the Federal army was advancing toward Frederick, once again under the command of George McClellan. This was a development Lee had not expected given his assumption that it would take weeks after Second Manassas for the enemy to field another army against him.[70]

Joseph Harsh has argued "there is no contemporaneous evidence that Lee knew as early as the 9th [of September] it would be McClellan" in command of Union forces. It is true that only three questionable sources specifically mention Lee knowing of McClellan's return, but this does not mean the general had not heard of it, especially because evidence abounds that Fredericktonians, Southern newspaper correspondents, and the men in Lee's army had already learned the news.[71]

---

70 On Sept. 9, "I was sent from Frederick City Maryland to meet his Ex. the President & Ex Govr Lowe. Failing to meet them at Leesburg, I proceeded to Winchester & there learned that his Ex. had returned to Richmond & the Govr had left for this place." See Lockwood Tower, ed., *Lee's Adjutant: The Wartime Letters of Colonel Walter Herron Taylor, 1862-1865* (Columbia, SC, 1995), 43. Special Orders No. 191, Sept. 9, 1862, reprinted in Dowdey and Manarin, eds., *The Wartime Papers of Robert E. Lee*, 301. "From reports that have reached me, I believe that the enemy are pushing a strong column up the Potomac River by Rockville and Darnestown, and by Poolesville toward Seneca Mills. I hear that the commands of Sumner, Sigel, Burnside, and Hooker are advancing in the direction above mentioned." OR 19, 2:602.

71 Harsh, *Taken*, 130, 141. One of the sources is John G. Walker, "Jackson's Capture of Harper's Ferry," in Robert Underwood Johnson and Clarence Clough Buel, eds., *Battles and Leaders of the Civil War*, 4 Vols. (New York, NY, 1885), 2:605. The second source is Lee himself, who stated to William Allan after the war: "Stuart reported McClellan near Rockville. . . . He

In its attempt to appeal to the Southern patriotism of Maryland's people, the Army of Northern Virginia allowed visitors to come and go from Frederick with relative freedom.[72] As a result, information passed from travelers to Confederate troops and from Confederate troops to the outside world. One story originating in this fashion appeared in the September 18 pages of the Cumberland, Maryland, *Civilian and Telegraph* recounting the experience of a man who had stayed in Frederick from September 6 to September 9. This gentleman, who preferred to remain anonymous, reported:

> when I left Frederick on Tuesday evening (September 9) it was under the conviction that they (the Rebels) were about to leave. . . . There was every indication that they had become alarmed to the systematic movements General McClellan, and were looking to secure a safe line of retreat back to Virginia. The starting of Jackson with his immense division, estimated at from 15,000 to 20,000 men of all arms towards Hagerstown was looked upon as the first indication of a backward movement. There were also evidences of trepidation among the troops who began to think they were not on safe ground.[73]

(Lee) then retired from Frederick as McClellan advanced." Allan, "Memoranda," in Gallagher, ed. *Lee the Soldier*, 9. It is impossible to conclude from Lee's comments if he recalled the events accurately, or if he simply inserted McClellan's name into his memory after the fact. The third source is Dabney, *Life and Campaigns of Lieut.-Gen. Thomas J. Jackson*, 549 which stated that as of Sept. 7, "Two . . . plans remained [to Lee]: the one was to leave Harper's Ferry to itself for the present, and fight McClellan as he advanced. The other was to withdraw the army west of the mountains, as at first designed . . . and then to re-assemble the whole at some favorable position in that region for a decisive struggle with McClellan. The former was advocated by Jackson; he feared lest the other system of movements should prove too complex for realizing that punctual and complete concentration which sound policy required." Dabney did not cite a source for these comments. An indefatigable collector of material for his biography of Jackson, he likely picked it up from those who had known the general, particularly during a visit he made to the Army of Northern Virginia in Aug. 1863. Thomas C. Johnson, *Life and Letters of Robert Lewis Dabney* (Richmond, VA, 1903), 282. Additionally, the newspaper in small and far-away Milledgeville, Georgia, reported on Sept. 9 that "General McClellan . . . is now actually performing the duties of General Commanding." *Southern Recorder*, Sept. 9, 1862. Similarly, a correspondent from Georgia traveling with the Army of Northern Virginia reported home on Sept. 1, "McClellan, who, it is reported has been assigned chief command in the field. . . . It is not improbable that McClellan, who is now in command, will seek to conduct the retreat as he did at Richmond." *Savannah Republican*, Sept. 10, 1862.

72 A report from the *New York Tribune* reprinted in the *Richmond Dispatch* noted of the Confederate occupation, "So far as we can ascertain they (the Rebels) allowed free ingress and egress to and from the town. The pickets on the road appear to have been stationed merely to watch military movements, and paid no attention to civilians." *Richmond Dispatch*, Sept. 15, 1862.

73 "Four Days Experience with the Rebels in Frederick," in the *Civilian and Telegraph*, Sept. 18, 1862.

John Robson of the 52nd Virginia, part of General Lawton's division, expressed this unease in his reminiscences of the war, writing that while near Frederick, "we soon learned . . . 'Little Mac' was again at the head of the army, and then the idea occurred to 'us generals' that our Maryland business had better be attended to promptly."[74]

A letter Brig. Gen. Dorsey Pender wrote to his wife on September 7 inferred that John Robson's information had probably come from the people of Frederick. As Pender explained, "It was rumored here before we came that four of the six members of the [Lincoln] Cabinet were against McClellan's being again placed in command of the army, but that the soldiers refused to fight unless he was."[75]

William McClendon, a soldier with the 15th Alabama, also learned of McClellan's return to command, recalling, "in a few days it was known that . . . McClellan had been placed in command of his old army again." In other words, Fredericktonians already knew as of September 6 that McClellan had returned to command the Army of the Potomac, and within days, if not hours, afterward so did the lowliest Rebel private.[76]

The spread of this news inspired sufficient disquiet in the Confederate ranks for a civilian bystander to have learned of it. How likely is it, then, that the commanding general of the army did not also catch wind of George McClellan's return, particularly given his visit to the city on September 6? In this respect at least Brig. Gen. John G. Walker's notoriously skewed postwar writing may have been correct when he recalled Lee asking him on September 8 whether he was "acquainted with General McClellan."[77]

---

74 John S. Robson, *Reminiscences of the Civil War* (Durham, NC, 1898), 119.

75 William W. Hassler, ed., *One of Lee's Best Men: The Civil War Letters of General William Dorsey Pender* (Chapel Hill, NC, 1965), 172.

76 After initially being placed in command of the Washington defenses on Sept. 2, McClellan received verbal authorization from President Abraham Lincoln on Sept. 7 to take the forces around Washington into the field. This differentiation of responsibility meant nothing to observers from afar. They knew only that McClellan's name had been discussed in connection with returning to command at the beginning of September, information that had clearly reached Frederick City by Sept. 7. Two days earlier on Sept. 5, for example, the men of the 10th Maine "were told that the entire army of the Potomac, with McClellan again in command, was moving to drive Lee out of Maryland." John M. Gould, *History of the First–Tenth–Twenty–Ninth Maine Regiment* (Portland, ME, 1871), 223. Also see Hartwig, *To Antietam Creek*, 703, Note 4, and *OR* 19, 1:25.

77 Walker, "Jackson's Capture of Harper's Ferry," 605.

Eleven days later, the battered Army of Northern Virginia re-crossed the Potomac River with Lee's hope of fomenting Maryland's rebellion shattered. The general wrote a letter shortly after this to Confederate Secretary of War George W. Randolph expressing frustration that his army's stay "in Maryland was so short as to *prevent receiving the aid I had expected from that State* [emphasis added]. Some few recruits joined us, and others are finding their way across the river to our lines."[78]

This telling statement reveals that one of Lee's key assumptions for embarking on the campaign—receiving material support from the people of Maryland, including supplies, recruits, and even civil unrest—had never left his mind. The Confederate commander thought that as of September 3 he would have sufficient time to turn Marylanders in his favor. After all, as he had written Jefferson Davis, "The two grand armies of the United States . . . are much weakened and demoralized. Their new levies . . . are not yet organized, and will take some time to prepare for the field."[79]

George McClellan's impressive success in quickly re-constituting the Army of the Potomac, followed by the chance discovery of a copy of Special Orders No. 191 near Frederick on September 13 prompting him to attack the fragmented Rebel force at South Mountain, had thoroughly thwarted Lee's devices, dooming his effort to pry Maryland from the Union.[80]

As for the Old Line State's failure to revolt, Lee blamed martial law for cowing the populace. "Maryland," he wrote Davis on October 2, "is so tightly tied that I fear nothing but extraneous aid can relieve her." Lee nevertheless still believed that thanks to "recent proclamations of President Lincoln," a clear reference to the preliminary Emancipation Proclamation of September 22, 1862, "and civil liberty so completely trodden under foot," the fires of revolt smoldered among Maryland's people just waiting to be stoked into life.[81]

---

78 *OR* 19, 2:636-637.

79 Ibid., 590.

80 For a detailed treatment of McClellan's handling of Lee's orders on Sept. 13, 1862, see Gene M. Thorp and Alexander B. Rossino, *The Tale Untwisted: George McClellan and the Discovery of Lee's Lost Orders, September 13, 1862* (El Dorado, CA, 2019). See also the first chapter in Steven R. Stotelmyer, *Too Useful to Sacrifice: Reconsidering George B. McClellan's Generalship in the Maryland Campaign from South Mountain to Antietam* (El Dorado, CA, 2019).

81 "The conservative portion of that people, unless dead to the feelings of liberty, will rise and depose the party now in power," concluded Lee. See *OR* 19, 2:644.

Given this evidence, Robert E. Lee's decision to stand and fight at Sharpsburg on September 16-17 must be seen as the culmination of his design to incite a secessionist revolt in Maryland. As Lee explained to Davis in August 1863, "it was hoped that military success might afford us an opportunity to aid the citizens of Maryland in any efforts they might be disposed to make to recover their liberties." Lee's reference to a "military success" could mean nothing other than fighting and winning a battle north of the Potomac River. By September 7, Lee had come to believe it essential that he deliver a military victory to solve the crippling geographic position of pro-Confederate supporters in Maryland. Difficulties surrounded them, he wrote in 1863, meaning Marylanders would not rise to recover their liberties and offer support for the Southern cause "unless success should enable us to give them assurance of continued protection." Overwhelming Federal military power in Washington, Baltimore, and Pennsylvania threatened Maryland's would-be rebels, but if the Army of Northern Virginia could win a victory north of the Potomac River, those secessionist forces might be encouraged to revolt. Hence Lee's willingness to risk everything at Sharpsburg when the more prudent military course would have been to retire to Virginia and defend the line of the Potomac River. As Jackson's friend Robert Dabney put it, "The battle of Sharpsburg was fought by the Confederates . . . to redeem their offers of aid to oppressed Maryland."[82]

With all this in mind, Lee cannot rightfully be criticized for fighting an unnecessary or vainglorious battle in Maryland. He knew exactly what he was doing and he did everything in his power to accomplish the objective he set out to achieve in early September. That Lee failed was due more to his misunderstanding of popular sentiment in Maryland and to the competence of George McClellan than to any shortcoming on the part of himself or of his army. Fitzhugh Lee understood this about his uncle when he argued that he knew "a battle fought and won in western Maryland, followed by a rapid march in the direction of Baltimore and Washington, would be attended with immense results, and that nothing would be accomplished, so far as Maryland was concerned, till then."[83]

Artillerist Edward Porter Alexander agreed. Lee's September 8 proclamation, he argued, "compelled [him] to appear as a deliverer who had come to free the

82 OR 19, 1:144; Dabney, *Life and Campaigns of Lieut.-Gen. Thomas J. Jackson*, 570.

83 Fitzhugh Lee, *General Lee*, 200.

Marylanders from a yoke. [Days later,] there was an opportunity for him (Lee) to avoid a great risk of grave disaster by withdrawal into Virginia, without serious loss of men or impairment of prestige. . . . In his decision to stand his ground and fight, his attitude as deliverer probably had a large share."[84]

Colonel (later lieutenant general) John Gordon of the 6th Alabama entertained a similar notion. "[T]here was still a prevalent belief among Southern leaders [in 1862] that Southern sentiment was strong in Maryland," he wrote after the war, "and that an important victory within her borders might convert the Confederate camps into recruiting-stations, and add materially to the strength of Lee's army."[85]

Regardless of where he had imagined the war's next battle might be fought, one thing seems clear: Robert E. Lee stood at Sharpsburg in the hope that a victory won by his army would spark Maryland's secession from the Union. Securing Maryland for the Confederacy and deriving the benefits that might attend such an outcome were the true objectives of his campaign.

Lee the revolutionary thought the Old Line State a potentially war-ending prize and he believed himself to be the man who could win it.

---

84 Edward Porter Alexander, *Military Memoirs of a Confederate: A Critical Narrative* (New York, NY, 1907), 224.

85 John B. Gordon, *Reminiscences of the Civil War* (New York, NY, 1904), 138.

Two

HIGH HOPES FOR LIBERATING MARYLAND

ᒧᑌᑭᓅ

The Army of Northern Virginia
Crosses the Potomac River, September 4-7, 1862

IF Robert E. Lee expressed a firm but quiet belief in the ripeness of Maryland for the South's picking, the men of his army fairly shouted their convictions to heaven.

After months of hard service culminated in the rout of John Pope's Federal Army of Virginia near the old battlefield of Manassas, Lee's men set their sights on the Old Line State. They believed it was a prize that, as more than a year of newspaper stories and campfire tales had told them, would fall easily into their hands. Maryland was a slaveholding state thought by some in the South to possess as many loyal men as Virginia; a state said to be as firm in its secessionist convictions as South Carolina; a state whose sons had shed blood on the cobbled streets of Baltimore before any state in the Confederacy had done the same; a state waiting patiently for an army of Southern brothers to set her free from the bondage of Federal military occupation.

Many of Lee's men believed all of these things. The notion of entering a friendly state fired their imaginations and filled them with self-righteous justification. Reflecting a fundamental characteristic of romantic antebellum chivalry, many of the soldiers in the Army of Northern Virginia considered themselves to be the saviors of lost "Southern" Maryland, a metaphorical damsel in distress certain to be faithful until the war was won, or the bitter final blow of defeat had been dealt to the dream of Confederate independence. And thus on September 3, Lee's weary but confident columns turned north.[1]

"The well known song of 'Maryland. My Maryland,' greeted the ear at every camp," recalled Marshall Hurst, a musician with the 14th Alabama. "Soon the road from Manassas to Leesburg was swarming with rebel soldiers." Billy Wood of the 19th Virginia fondly recalled the same enthusiasm among his fellows: "We left the plains of Manassas . . . and when Tiltow struck up 'Maryland, My Maryland,' a shout went up from the Nineteenth which proved the popularity of a Northern tour upon which dame rumor said we were entering."[2]

Lee's tattered ranks appreciated their proximity to the Potomac River. The fact that they had successfully fought their way so far north justified the sacrifices made en route. All of the suffering and hardship would be worthwhile if they could rescue Dame Maryland from the clutches of her Yankee oppressors. This spirit helped Lee's troops endure empty bellies and exhaustion as they turned toward the green fields beyond the Potomac beckoning to them with promises of late summer bounty, friendship, warm welcome, and thousands of citizen soldiers waiting to replace their fallen comrades.

After a brief overnight hiatus near the late battlefield at Manassas, on September 3 Maj. Gen. Lafayette McLaws's unattached division and three of the five brigades under Maj. Gen. Daniel Harvey Hill marched first from the vicinity of Groveton, Virginia.[3] With McLaws's troops in the lead, the combined column took the Little River Turnpike northwest before turning up the road to Gum Spring to reach Leesburg around sunset. "Very fatiguing marching," recalled McLaws in a letter home to his wife. Even before they had spied Leesburg's steeples, noted

---

1 A letter home from Pvt. Benjamin H. Watkins of the 12th Battalion, Georgia Light Artillery, dated Aug. 30, 1862, is typical of the euphoric sentiment predominating in the army: "We will be in Maryland in less than a week, if everything works like it does now—and then we will have some fun." *Augusta* (GA) *Weekly Chronicle and Sentinel*, Sept. 9, 1862.

2 William Nathaniel Wood, *Reminiscences of Big I* (Charlottesville, VA, 1909), 45.

3 For reasons that remain unclear, Gen. Lee decided to divide D. H. Hill's command for the march on Leesburg. Hill took three brigades—Robert Rodes, Samuel Garland, and George B. Anderson—while the other two under Alfred Colquitt and Roswell Ripley marched with the main body of the army via Chantilly and Dranesville. See, for example, Hartwig, *To Antietam Creek*, 92, and Harsh, *Taken at the Flood*, 52. Harsh wrote that Hill's command led the column, but Hartwig establishes that McLaws's division marched first and arrived in Leesburg around 5:00 p.m. All of the sources from Hill's command mention moving through the town after dark.

William Hill of the 13th Mississippi, "Many of the citizens met us several miles from town . . . [offering] a cordial welcome home." Hill's allusion to home was a reference to the sojourn William Barksdale's brigade had made near Leesburg while defending the Confederacy's northern frontier during the autumn of 1861. Moving through the cheering town as the sun slipped behind the Catoctin range to their west, McLaws's infantrymen set up camp at their former bivouac on the grounds of the Big Spring farm, owned by the prominent local landowner George Washington Ball.[4]

Roughly 3,000 of D. H. Hill's men came after them, passing "through the town a little after dark, the moon shining bright as day, lending a yellow tinge," recalled James W. Shinn of the 4th North Carolina. John Tucker of the 5th Alabama echoed Shinn's memory of "passing through a delightful Country & . . . through the Town after dark." Despite the late hour, Leesburg's people stood outside their houses to applaud Hill's troops moving north on King Street. "The Moon shown brightly & the Ladies & Citizens crowded the side walks," continued Tucker, "cheering us up & seemingly perfectly delighted to see us which was duely appreciated judging from the deafning yells that went up with each regt as they filed by." The warm greeting also made a moving impression on an anonymous Alabama soldier in Robert Rodes's brigade. On "Wednesday night we reached Leesburg," he recorded, and were "welcomed in the most enthusiastic manner. Cheer after cheer rent the air; brave men and fair women wept tears of joy at our return; the houses of the citizens were thrown open to the hungry soldier, and their ability was the only limit to their hospitality. Long shall we remember the people of Leesburg, than whom there is not a more loyal people in the Southern confederacy."[5]

Rodes's brigade, and probably that of Samuel Garland, appear to have marched straight through the town, moving out "2 miles" before camping for the night with McLaws's command at Big Spring. The brigade of George Burgwyn Anderson seems to have taken a different route, however, turning west on Market Street and marching to a "high hill about one mile distant" before settling down to rest. That Anderson's men found a campsite away from the balance of D. H. Hill's

---

4 John C. Oeffinger, ed. *A Soldier's General: The Civil War Letters of Major General Lafayette McLaws* (Chapel Hill, NC, 2002), 154; William H. Hill Diary, Sept. 3, 1862, in the Mississippi Department of Archives and History (MDAH), Jackson, MI. Referred to hereafter as Hill Diary. My thanks to Scott Hartwig for this source. See also, Hartwig, *To Antietam Creek*, 94.

5 Letter from Maryland, Camp of Rhodes' [sic] Brigade in *Columbus* (GA) *Sun*, Oct. 1862, copy in Alabama Vertical File at the Antietam National Battlefield Library (ANBL). Referred to hereafter as Letter from Maryland.

command is borne out by the fact that on the following day (September 4) Hill allowed Anderson's men to rest before ordering them to proceed "along the pike toward Harper's Ferry" on September 5. James Shinn, who provided the evidence for this movement, was a careful diarist. His notes make no mention of marching back through Leesburg to reach the turnpike leading to the ferry. By September 5, Maj. Gen. James Longstreet's divisions also packed the roads through town, which Shinn probably would have mentioned had he and his comrades been required to retrace their steps to reach the turnpike.[6]

The main body of Lee's army approached Leesburg from the direction of Dranesville, Virginia, with Maj. Gen. Thomas J. Jackson's troops in the vanguard. Starting "at an early hour" on September 4, Jackson's men "marched on through Leesburg and out to Ball's [farm], to the Big Spring, for the night," confided the general's topographer Jedediah Hotchkiss to his diary. "All are in fine spirits, being sure that we are on the way to Maryland." John Worsham of the 21st Virginia echoed Hotchkiss's enthusiasm on September 4, despite the fact that neither he nor his comrades had eaten a hot meal in days. "We started on the march early in the morning," recalled the foot soldier, and "Soon it was passed from lip to lip along the line that we were going into Maryland. This created great excitement among the men, and they stepped off so briskly as to give no suggestion that these men had had only one night's rest and none during the day, for more than a week! At night we halted, and were allowed another good rest. Our wagons joined us during the night, and the next morning we were given time to cook rations, the first that the men had cooked since Aug. 25th." By "the afternoon of the 4th," wrote Brig. Gen. Jubal Early, Jackson's command had passed through Leesburg, "and bivouacked near Big Springs, two or three miles from the latter place."[7]

---

6 Wilson, "The Diary of John S. Tucker," 19. No source could be located for Samuel Garland's brigade. The assumption made here is that it marched with Rodes and Anderson to maintain divisional integrity. Shinn Diary, Sept. 3, 1862. Another participant in these events named Walter Battle, who served as a clerk on the headquarters staff of Gen. Anderson, wrote to his mother on Sept. 5 that the brigade had reached the south bank of the Potomac on that day "after a march of about twenty miles," which is roughly the distance from Leesburg to the point opposite Berlin (Brunswick), Maryland. Laura E. Lee, *Forget-Me-Nots of the Civil War: A Romance Containing Original Letters of Two Confederate Soldiers* (St. Louis, MO, 1909), 74.

7 Archie P. McDonald, ed., *Make Me a Map of the Valley: The Civil War Journal of Stonewall Jackson's Topographer* (Dallas, TX, 1973), 78; Worsham, *One of Jackson's Foot Cavalry*, 137; Jubal A. Early, *Autobiographical Sketch and Narrative of the War Between the States* (Philadelphia, PA, 1912), 134.

The nearness of the men to the Potomac kept spirits high and "'Maryland, My Maryland' was in the air," explained James Nisbet of the 21st Georgia. By now everyone in the ranks anticipated crossing the river, which led Nisbet to indulge in a wishful flight of fancy. "The defeat of Pope's Army, and our proximity to Washington, gave 'Old Abe' such a scare," wrote Nisbet emphatically, "that he sent his household goods board a transport, which was kept steamed up ready for departure at a moment's notice."[8]

Although PERSONNE reported in a letter printed by the *Charleston Daily Courier* that Leesburg's residents greeted Jackson's column with "yells and screeches," none of the accounts from Jackson's men mentioned receiving the same enthusiastic greeting that troops under McLaws and Hill had experienced when they marched through Leesburg.[9] What makes this doubly unusual is that the town's citizens emerged in large numbers to cheer Longstreet's column when it marched through on September 5. Longstreet's troops had moved slowly on the road to the town, maybe as a result of the time it took for Jackson's men to file through the narrow streets, or perhaps because, as Scott Hartwig suggests, General Lee had not yet decided on September 4 which fords over the river his army would use as crossing points.[10]

Jackson's position north of Leesburg made crossing at Noland's Ferry, Cheek's Ford, or the more obscure White's Ford, logical choices, but with Longstreet's command south of Leesburg, the crossing at Edwards' Ferry may have made more sense. Whatever caused the delay, "For some reason our command was very late going into camp," explained William Wood of the 19th Virginia, a regiment with Richard Brooke Garnett's brigade. "It was pitch dark, and the march was slow." George Wise of the 17th Virginia, serving with James Kemper's brigade, described confusion on the road: "On the afternoon of the fourth, we again passed over a part of the route traveled the day before, and about night halted near Mr. Robert Harper's farm, two miles south of Leesburg." When the column finally settled down, "green corn [was] served out," remembered Alexander Hunter. The appearance of friendly faces from Leesburg eased the hardship of at least some of the men, wrote Randolph Abbott Shotwell of the 8th Virginia, also of Garnett's brigade. Two miles from town, the column met "scores of citizens on horseback and in vehicles—including many ladies whose pride and

8   James C. Nisbet, *Four Years on the Firing Line* (Chattanooga, TN, 1914), 149.

9   J. Cutler Andrews, *The South Reports the Civil War* (Princeton, NJ, 1970), 204.

10 Hartwig, *To Antietam Creek*, 92.

affection for the war-worn veterans was hardly greater than their surprise at the ragged dilapidated appearance of their favorites. And in truth we were a hard-looking set!"[11]

At some point on September 4, General Lee transmitted a verbal order to D. H. Hill directing him to send two brigades of his division across the Potomac at Noland's Ferry and Cheek's Ford. Their mission entailed seizing a bridgehead in Maryland, wrecking the riverside berm of the Chesapeake and Ohio Canal, and destroying the aqueduct that enabled the canal to pass over the mouth of the Monocacy River where it flowed into the Potomac.[12]

Whether Lee issued this order in person, via a courier, or through an intermediary is unknown as neither Hill nor the commanding general mentioned the circumstances under which it was given. The most important factor to Lee appears to have been that Hill's brigades around Leesburg were the only sizeable units ready to march. Accordingly, Hill got Robert Rodes's Alabama brigade and the North Carolinians under Brig. Gen. Samuel Garland moving north on the Noland's Ferry road. They stepped off on a cool sunny day. "All the soldiers that could sing, struck up 'Maryland, My Maryland,'" remembered Capt. Jonathan Whitehead Williams of the 5th Alabama. Turning northeast toward Cheek's Ford, Rodes's men "marched to a point about five miles above Leesburg, where we halted, sent out a party of skirmishers to the bank of the river, and a couple of pieces of artillery. A few shots from our skirmishers and a few shells from the guns caused the Yankee pickets to 'skedaddle' in hot haste." Robert Rodes led his horse

---

11 Wood, *Reminiscences of Big I*, 34. George Pickett, the official commander of the brigade, had been wounded outside of Richmond during the Seven Days' Battles and would not return to command until that October. Richard Garnett led the brigade in his stead. Harsh, *Sounding the Shallows*, 56; George Wise, *History of the Seventeenth Virginia Infantry* (Baltimore, MD, 1870), 107; Alexander Hunter, "A High Private's Account of the Battle of Sharpsburg," in *SHSP*, Vol. 10, Nos. 10-11 (1882), 507; J. G. De Roulhac Hamilton, ed., *The Papers of Randolph Abbott Shotwell*, Vol. 1 (Raleigh, NC, 1929), 308.

12 "With two brigades, we drove away the Yankee forces near the mouth of the Monocacy, and crossed the Potomac." D. H. Hill's Report in *OR* 19, 1:1020. Hill later wrote of this operation: "My division was the first to cross the Potomac, which it did at Cheek's ford, upon a verbal order, and with no knowledge whatever of the object of the expedition." Daniel Harvey Hill, "The Lost Dispatch," in *The Land We Love*, Vol. IV (Charlotte, NC, 1868), 274. Hill's recollection of this event suffered from either poor memory or a dab of mendacity because the men with him at the time immediately began wrecking the banks of the Chesapeake and Ohio Canal and attempted to destroy the aqueduct over the Monocacy River, indicating that Hill's mission from Lee was to cut the flow of commerce and communications on the Maryland side of the Potomac.

Old John to the riverbank and ordered his men into the water, telling them to "move up" as they approached.[13]

According to Col. Cullen Andrews Battle, "a detachment of two companies of the Third Alabama under Capt. John R. Simpson, of the Gulf City Guards," led the regiment, "clearing the way" forward as skirmishers. Battle's men removed their ragged trousers and stepped into the water "four men abreast holding each others hand to keep from falling over the rocks." As the sun descended in the western sky, recalled Capt. John Williams, he and his comrades slogged through the "nearly waist-deep" tide until they reached the far shore, where the half-naked color-bearer of the 3rd Alabama splashed out of the river "and stuck his colors firmly in the ground."[14]

Colonel John Brown Gordon, commander of the 6th Alabama, took it upon himself to congratulate the brigade on being the first to plant "our battle flag—the Southern Cross—upon the soil of Maryland." The news elicited heavy cheers before word of a nearby canal boat "laden with flour and bacon" sent Rodes's famished troops into a frenzy. Still other Alabamians discovered a small general store in the vicinity (probably owned by a man named Thomas Walter) and quickly bought out the entire stock of boots, sugar, and coffee with Southern currency, which was an encouraging sign considering Maryland's official status as a neutral state. General Hill ordered Rodes's men to start digging out the C&O Canal's berm while he sought a farm to purchase provisions.[15]

---

13   Jonathan Whitehead Williams, *His Life and Times with the 5th Alabama, C.S.A. Company "D" Greensboro Guards* (Greensboro, AL, 1903), entry of Dec. 17. A copy of this manuscript may be found at the ANBL. The Federal pickets belonged to the First Regiment of the Maryland Potomac Home Brigade; Letter from Maryland, Oct. 1862; Williams, *Life and Times*, entry of Dec. 17, 1903.

14   Brandon H. Beck, ed., *Third Alabama! The Civil War Memoir of Brigadier General Cullen Andrews Battle, C.S.A.* (Tuscaloosa, AL, 2000), 42. One source claims the 12th Alabama was the first to cross the Potomac, but the preponderance of evidence weighs in favor of the 3rd Alabama. See, for example, Robert E. Park, *Sketch of the Twelfth Alabama Infantry of Battle's Brigade, Rodes' Division, or Early's Corps of the Army of Northern Virginia* (Richmond, VA, 1906), 6, and Hartwig, *To Antietam Creek*, 94. A man serving with the 13th Georgia observed how Confederate troops tended to cross "all streams where there is no bridge by wading, in four ranks." Harrison Wells to Mollie Long, Oct. 2, 1862, Harrison Wells Papers #5422-z, Southern Historical Collection, The Wilson Library, University of North Carolina at Chapel Hill. Available online at https://finding-aids.lib.unc.edu/ 05422/#folder_2#. Referred to hereafter as Wells Letter; Williams, *Life and Times*, entry of Dec. 17, 1903, and Letter from Maryland, Oct. 1862. ANBL. Hartwig, *To Antietam Creek*, 94.

15   Letter from "A," *The Alabama Beacon*, Oct. 17, 1862. Some details for this episode are taken from Hartwig, *To Antietam Creek*, 94. The Martenet and Bond map of Montgomery County from 1865 shows "Walter's Store" in the vicinity of the location where Rodes's infantry brigade

Thomas Nast's depiction of D. H. Hill's Division crossing the Potomac River at Noland's Ferry. See Appendix A for more information. LOC

General Garland's command, Hill's second brigade in Maryland, crossed the river that same day one mile upstream at Noland's Ferry. "With what bounding hearts did we climb the opposite banks of the Potomac, looking eagerly for the support of 'Maryland, My Maryland,'" remembered Capt. Vines Turner of the event. Word of the Rebel incursion passed quickly to Federal authorities. Spotting Garland's foray from Sugarloaf Mountain, the Union army signal station communicated to Federal Second Corps headquarters:

The enemy crossed the Potomac at Noland's Ferry last evening. Pickets of [Col. William P.] Maulsby's [1st Maryland] regiment [Potomac Home Brigade] stationed at the aqueduct. After firing off their ammunition, [they] passed here en route to Frederick. They report that pickets of an Ohio regiment at the ferry retreated without firing a gun. The river is easily fordable at that point. I can see about 2,000 of the enemy upon this side, scattered along from the aqueduct to Noland's Ferry.[16]

crossed the Potomac River. Simon J. Martenet & Isaac Bond, *Martenet and Bond's Map of Montgomery County* (Baltimore, MD, 1865). This is available online at www.loc.gov/item/2002620533/.

16 V. E. Turner and H. C. Wall, "Twenty-Third Regiment," in Walter Clark, ed., *Histories of the Several Regiments and Battalions from North Carolina in the Great War, 1861-'65*, 5 vols. (Goldsboro, NC, 1901), 5:216; *OR* 19, 2:184-185. Colonel Banning of the 87th Ohio at Point of Rocks also

Nightfall interrupted the canal's destruction, but Hill had at least found food for those not fortunate enough to have plundered the bacon-laden canal boat. "One of General Hill's first acts after crossing the Potomac into Maryland, was to buy a large field of corn," wrote men with the 23rd North Carolina, while Capt. Williams of the 5th Alabama recalled "rations of green corn, which was all we had for several days, except for a few Irish potatoes." Williams and his comrades consumed their meager provisions after going "into camp in [a] thick piece of woods. The division doubled so thick that when we spread our blankets, we almost covered the ground." Temperatures fell into the high 50s that night, so the men had little choice but to huddle together for warmth until the following morning.[17]

September 5 dawned bright and cool as Rodes's and Garland's men moved back to the towpath of the C&O Canal. They dug out the culvert over the Little Monocacy River to drain the Seven Mile Level of the canal and cut down the canal berm and towpath banks before corduroying the muddy bed to permit the passage of artillery and wagons. The men burned canal boats marooned in the bed before turning their attention to wrecking the aqueduct over the Monocacy River. The aforementioned Thomas Walter, keeper of Lock No. 27, pleaded with General Hill to spare the aqueduct, and the discussion quickly escalated into an argument with the hot-tempered North Carolinian. Hill finally brushed Walter aside and ordered his engineers to proceed. Much to Walter's chagrin, when they discovered "the aqueduct could not be destroyed for want of powder and tools," Hill elected to wreck Lock No. 27 by using a small powder charge to disable the gates.[18]

The fact that Hill's men did not have the proper tools necessary to complete their mission is perplexing in light of the fact that Lee specifically sent them to destroy transportation infrastructure. This failure may have come about because Lee embarked quickly on the Maryland operation, with Hill moving too fast for proper arrangements to be made; the Army of Northern Virginia lacked tools such as pick-axes; or Hill simply did not have time to get his wagon train over the river before his division needed to move on. General Orders No. 102, issued by Lee on September 4 (the day of Hill's departure) directed all commanders to "reduce their

---

reported to Dixon Miles at Harpers Ferry that the enemy had "passed the Potomac south of him in force." OR 19, 2:180. See also, Carman, *The Maryland Campaign of September 1862*, 1:89.

17 Turner and Wall, "Twenty-Third Regiment," 217; Williams, *Life and Times*, Dec. 17, 1903.

18 Williams, *Life and Times*, Dec. 17, 1903; Harsh, *Sounding the Shallows*, 6-7, for meteorological observations; Harlan D. Unrau, *Historic Resource Study: Chesapeake & Ohio Canal* (Hagerstown, MD, 2007), 735; "The enemy . . . that have crossed the Potomac at Noland's Ferry have cut the canal at Seven-mile level, and [are] running off the water." OR 19, 1:790, 1019.

transportation to a mere sufficiency to transport cooking utensils and the absolute necessities of a regiment." In Hill's case, the trains of Garland's and Rodes's regiments made it into Maryland only on the evening of September 5, which was too late in the day for Hill to complete his mission given the tools he required.[19]

Hill learned on the afternoon of September 5 that Jackson had crossed "probably a division on the Maryland side" of the river by 2:00 p.m. Thus, per Old Jack's instructions, Hill set off late in the day to combine their commands. Jackson had written Hill of his intention to "reach the Baltimore & Ohio Railroad bridge over the Monocacy this evening (September 5)," which required a forced march of some nine miles to Monocacy Junction. This objective proved impractical, however, because Hill's remaining three brigades had not yet come up. Colonel Alfred Colquitt's and Brig. Gen. Roswell Ripley's commands reached Leesburg on September 4, just as Rodes's and Garland's men were making their way across the Potomac. According to James Folsom of the 28th Georgia, part of Colquitt's brigade, they "again took up the line of march, and, passing through Leesburg to the Point of Rocks, crossed the Potomac river on the night of the 5th of September." The fact that it took Colquitt and Ripley's men all day to march to Point of Rocks attests to the congestion in Leesburg caused by Longstreet's divisions as they moved to the campground at Big Spring recently evacuated by Jackson's men.[20]

Fortunately for George B. Anderson, his men had camped on the west side of Leesburg, which enabled them to avoid the crowded streets of town. "The morning of the 5th broke clear and cool upon us," recalled James Shinn, and "morning reveille soon roused the sleeping camp. At an early hour our brigade took up the line of march and proceeded along the pike toward Harper's Ferry." Reverend Alexander Betts of the 30th North Carolina took time that morning to "Call and buy eggs and butter from a man in Morrisonville, [Virginia], for which he would receive no pay," providing good evidence that Anderson's men took the Berlin Turnpike north from the Wheatlands crossroads to Lovettsville. Anderson halted his men at the latter place for an hour, where "many of the boys bought hats, shoes, coffee, etc." before marching "down by the river, opposite Berlin, Md." At about 10:00 p.m., Anderson ordered his men to cook rations before the brigade's

19 Williams, *Life and Times*, entry of Dec. 17, 1903. John Tucker of the 5th Alabama: "Came back after the wagon train at Camp. Riding all night & getting no sleep at all and crossing back into Md." Wilson, ed., "The Diary of John S. Tucker," 19.

20 James M. Folsom, *Heroes and Martyrs of Georgia* (Macon, GA, 1864), 55.

planned river crossing the next day. Exhausted from their march, however, the men refused to draw rations, preferring instead to eat what little remained in their haversacks. Anderson left his soldiers in peace until the next morning, when he ordered them to retrace their steps to Lovettsville. According to Private Shinn, pickets along the river had heard enemy activity all night on the Maryland side, including the arrival and departure of rail cars that could contain reinforcements, all of which had prompted Anderson to order his retrograde movement. The wisdom of his decision to do so was confirmed when a section of howitzers with the 5th New York Heavy Artillery, Co. A, fired on his men.[21]

With the Federals determined to contest the crossing at Berlin (Brunswick), Anderson had no choice but to locate another ford farther east. He took advantage of the change in plan by ordering the brigade's baggage train in Leesburg to meet the column near Cheek's Ford on September 6. Once there, the brigade camped for the night. "Early this morning," wrote Private Shinn on September 7, "we took up the line of march for the river," which the 4th North Carolina reached after sunrise. As other regiments before them had done, the 4th's band waded across first. Once over, the soggy musicians took up a spot on the northern bank where they could serenade their comrades as crossed. "Soon we heard the moving melting notes of 'My Maryland' sounding upon the still air and sending a thrill of emotion through every heart," confided Shinn to his journal. "The scene was one of grand and magnificent interest. By 10 our brigade was in Maryland. Forward or for woe we would soon know what Maryland would do, whether she was so thoroughly tired of Lincoln's rule as many would have us believe."[22]

During their march into the Old Line State, the Tarheels encountered "a different country" compared to the nearly complete desolation they had left behind in Virginia. To William Alexander Smith of the 14th North Carolina, Maryland appeared to offer the wealth and resources that more than a year of stories and song had promised:

> The untrodden green grass, horses in every lot; large, well kept; cattle fat and sleek; barns full to bursting; farms well tilled and set to grass and clover. They did not fear us, did not expect the Rebels to take, consume and devastate! The children going to school were

---

21 Shinn Diary, Sept. 5-6, 1862; Rev. Alexander D. Betts, *Experience of a Confederate Chaplain, 1861-1865* (Piedmont, SC, 1904), 16; "September 6—Turn and march down the river, and camp near Cheek's Ford." Betts, *Experience*, 16. According to OR 19, 1:534, the 5th New York Heavy Artillery, Co. A, was assigned to the 87th Ohio Infantry.

22 Shinn Diary, Sept. 5, 1862, and Betts, *Experience*, 16.

unmolested. The farmers along the roadside unmolested, stood gazing at the ragged, foot-sore Johnnies clad in anything but uniforms, a motley of color, and fearlessly, without trepidation, they asked to see Generals Lee and Jackson. [They] did not seem to know or care for other generals.[23]

By the time Anderson got across the Potomac, most of D. H. Hill's division had already reached Frederick. Before his command departed from Virginia, however, Hill appears to have ordered his subordinates to communicate the sense of Gen. Lee's General Orders No. 102 to their men. Section II of those orders stipulated good behavior: "This army is about to engage in most important operations, where any excesses committed will exasperate the people, lead to disastrous results, and enlist the populace on the side of the Federal forces in hostility to our own." The duty of announcing this message to Rodes's brigade fell to Col. Edward Asbury O'Neal of the 26th Alabama, who told the troops that "the people of Maryland [are] a people held in subjugation, but [are] believed to be our friends." O'Neal closed with the hope that nothing "would occur to discredit . . . the army or tarnish the honor of Alabama."[24]

At least one historian has argued that D. H. Hill's crossing of the Potomac River was a raid, while Hill later recalled it as a single unified event. In truth, it was neither a raid nor a well-coordinated single event. According to formal United States military doctrine, a raid is defined as follows: "an operation to temporarily seize an area to secure information, confuse an enemy, capture personnel or equipment, or to destroy a capability *culminating with a planned withdrawal* [emphasis added]." Clearly D. H. Hill's operation did not exhibit these characteristics. Having neither contemplated, nor ordered, a withdrawal, Lee sent Hill "in anticipation" of an advance by the whole army to capture and hold certain points along the north bank of the Potomac until Jackson instructed him to do otherwise once he had crossed the river.[25]

---

23 William Alexander Smith, *The Anson Guards: Company C, Fourteenth Regiment North Carolina Volunteers, 1861-1865* (Charlotte, NC, 1914), 150.

24 Letter from "A," Oct. 17, 1862. Also see *OR* 19, 2:592.

25 Joseph Harsh referred to D. H. Hill's operation as a "raid" into Maryland, writing: "Lee may have decided to undertake a raid by Hill before deciding fully to enter Maryland with the [army's] main body . . . Certainly Lee's later report and postwar testimony implies otherwise, but it would not be the only time his memory telescoped two events into one." Harsh, *Sounding the Shallows*, 154 and *Taken*, 71; U. S. Department of Defense, "Joint Publication 3-0: Joint Operations," Jan. 17, 2017, GL-14, available online at www.jcs.mil/Portals/36/Documents/Doctrine/pubs/jp3_0ch1.pdf?ver=2018-11-27-160457-910. The modern definition aptly

Instead of a hit-and-run raid, Hill's operation bore a closer resemblance to the Allied assault on Arnhem in 1944, where the objective was the seizure of a bridgehead intended to be held until reinforced. Hill himself is responsible for creating the false impression that his operation was in fact a unified historical event. After the campaign ended, General Hill wrote, "On the 4th, Anderson's brigade was sent to fire on the Yankee trains at Berlin, and, with two brigades, we drove away the Yankee forces near the mouth of the Monocacy, and crossed the Potomac." In actuality, only two of Hill's brigades crossed the Potomac River on September 4.[26]

The brigades of Alfred Colquitt and Roswell Ripley, still on the march from Dranesville, had not even made it to Leesburg by the time Rodes and Garland stepped off. G. B. Anderson had his brigade on hand but, contrary to Hill's report, it did not get moving until the next day. James Shinn recalled September 4 thusly: "About 7 o'clock this morning our brigade had orders to be ready to march by 9 o'clock with nothing but guns and accoutrements, canteens and haversacks and that we would make a silent and rapid march . . . they took care not to tell us where we would march, but before the hour of 9 arrived, the order was countermanded and we were permitted to rest."[27]

General Anderson did not leave for Berlin, Maryland, until the following day, presumably around the same time that Colquitt and Ripley departed for the river crossing at Point of Rocks. These movements, undertaken by Hill after Jackson had already started his command into Maryland, seem more like afterthoughts than a coordinated pre-invasion maneuver.

Lee appears to have sent D. H. Hill into Maryland with four objectives. His first task was the destruction of the aqueduct over the Monocacy, a job the North Carolinian failed to accomplish. Lee also directed Hill to wreck portions of the canal so that it would not be navigable for commercial traffic, which Hill managed to achieve. Lee ordered Hill to disrupt the Baltimore and Ohio Railroad, something George Anderson's men did not accomplish before the Army of Northern Virginia captured Monocacy Junction on September 6 and cut the line at that point. Finally and most importantly, Lee seems to have sent Hill to secure the key Potomac

---

describes numerous operations undertaken by both Confederate and Federal cavalry commanders during the Civil War, so it is appropriate in this case to apply a modern military term to an historical event; Gallagher, ed., *Lee the Soldier*, 7.

26 *OR* 19, 1:1019.

27 Shinn Diary, Sept. 4, 1862.

crossing point at Noland's Ferry. Reports surfaced days later that the Rebels placed a captured Federal pontoon bridge at Noland's Ferry for the army's wagon train to use, and the crossing point was also sheltered behind the Monocacy, which Lee had selected as his first defensive line in Maryland.[28] The Rebel commander did not intend for Hill to raid the Potomac crossing points and then withdraw. He intended that Hill capture and hold Noland's Ferry until Jackson crossed into Maryland the next day and assumed command of Confederate operations north of the river.[29]

From the moment General Lee began planning his army's operation in Maryland, he seems to have intended an outsized role for Stonewall Jackson. Long an advocate of sending Confederate troops north of the Potomac to destroy transportation infrastructure, Jackson provided Lee with advice before the operation began and field leadership once the army's columns finally stirred into motion. It was Jackson who had brought Frederick City native Bradley Johnson to Lee's headquarters at the stately home of Henry Harrison in Leesburg on September 4 to discuss the lay of the land north of the Potomac and, allegedly, the tepid reception Lee could expect to receive there.[30]

Lee also selected Jackson to lead the army's formal advance into Maryland, including the choice of the ford most of it would use, and to exercise command over all Confederate forces north of the Potomac until Lee himself traversed the river on September 6. Eventually, Jackson would also establish the route that most

28 "A man has just come into our picket lines, who left Leesburg last Saturday. He says that he crossed Noland's Ferry with Longstreet's wagon train. . . . The artillery crossed upon a pontoon bridge captured on the Peninsula." *Philadelphia Inquirer*, Sept. 9, 1862. *Harper's Weekly*, Sept. 27, 1862, 618, reported: "The rebels appear to have begun their crossing on 4th, and to have thrown bodies of men steadily forward ever since. The artillery crossed on a pontoon bridge, the cavalry and infantry forded the stream, the water being knee and thigh deep." Additionally, the Richmond correspondent for the Columbus, Georgia, *Daily Sun* reported: "The present location of the two armies is not definitely known, though the transportation of pontoon bridges for the past day or two from this city is significant of the very close proximity of our army to the shores of Maryland and the intention of the Commander-in-Chief to carry the war beyond the Potomac. These pontoon bridges were captured from the enemy on James River some time since." *The Daily Sun*, Sept. 9, 1862. See the third chapter of this study for more details on Lee's selection of the Monocacy River as a defensive position.

29 Lee described his immediate campaign objectives to William Allan in 1868, although he garbled some of the details, stating: "he therefore ordered Jackson to take command in advance & cross in Loudoun and move towards Frederick, destroying the canal &c. He sent Stuart with him, and had just ordered D. H. Hill . . . to White's Ferry in anticipation of this. He told Jackson to take Hill with him. He came on with remainder of the army as soon as he could." Allan, "Memoranda," in Gallagher, ed., *Lee the Soldier*, 7.

30 See the first chapter of this study for a critical assessment of Johnson's meeting with Lee at Harrison Hall in Leesburg.

of the Army of Northern Virginia would take from the Potomac to Frederick, and it was his command that would later besiege Harpers Ferry before rejoining Lee to defend the army's left flank in the fighting at Sharpsburg on September 16-17. From the beginning of the campaign to its end a fortnight later, Maj. Gen. Thomas Jonathan Jackson featured prominently in the Confederate effort to pry Maryland loose from the Union and secure its resources for the South.

Following an early conference at Harrison Hall, during which Lee authorized Jackson, Stuart, and Longstreet to initiate the army's river crossing, Old Jack got his command moving "about sunrise" on Friday, September 5. "All the officers and men of our command were joyous at the prospect [of going into Maryland] and marched with a light step—fewer straggling than I almost ever saw," recalled Jed Hotchkiss.[31]

Troops under Brig. Gen. William E. Starke, who temporarily commanded Jackson's old division while John R. Jones recuperated from the wound he had received at Malvern Hill, led the column toward the river on a private road through farmland owned by Lige White. According to Hotchkiss, Jackson rode on the column's left front alongside the 10th Virginia, the regiment leading the way to the sparkling line of the Potomac visible in the distance. After calling up engineers to level the Virginia shore for his wagons and artillery to pass, Jackson sent the 10th Virginia's regimental band ahead. The men waded in with a shout under the watchful guns of Maj. William Nelson's artillery battalion, followed by the balance of the regiment marching in a column of four abreast.[32]

Hotchkiss described this remarkable scene in a letter to his wife. "The 10th Regiment was in the advance (only a small cavalry escort of Marylanders being in front)," he began,

31 For Jackson's departure time, see McDonald, ed., *Make Me a Map of the Valley*, 78. Concerning the Harrison House conference, see "General Lee's Visit to Leesburg and Harrison Hall, Aug. 2, 1927," Collection SC 0048 at the Thomas Balch Library in Leesburg, Virginia, and Von Borcke, *Memoirs*, 182-183. Von Borcke notes that prior to departing for the Potomac, "It was necessary . . . for the General [i.e., Jeb Stuart] to repair for final instructions to the headquarters of General Lee in the town, and in this ride he was accompanied by his Staff." Von Borcke provided the confirmation of Longstreet's presence at the meeting, whereas only Jackson and Stuart are mentioned in the "General Lee's Visit" document.

32 According to an unsourced comment in W. Cullen Sherwood and Richard L. Nicholas, *Amherst Artillery, Albemarle Artillery, and Sturdivant's Battery* (Lynchburg, VA, 1996), 22, Nelson's battalion stood guard on the Virginia side of White's Ford from Sept. 5-7 while the rest of the army crossed into Maryland.

with the Virginia Flag proudly streaming out in a gentle breeze and under an unclouded sun, and then followed other regiments and there were 3 Confederate flags and the Virginia one in the river at once and a dense column of infantry banding the stream— fully a quarter of a mile wide—Gen Jackson and his staff in front—he on a cream colored horse, more than usually attentive to all that passed—and men on reaching the opposite shore the band struck up "Maryland, My Maryland" and the troops shouted in response— the scenery was in keeping—all grand and glorious.[33]

Crossing the river from southwest to northeast, and close to the northern tip of Mason's Island, the column made its way across the water. Captain Thomas Pollock of General Starke's staff reached the far bank, turned his horse about, and "looked back at the long dark line stretching across the broad shallow river. I felt I was beholding what must be the turning point of the war," he later admitted. Pollock confessed that he never again expected to witness such a spectacle.[34]

William McClendon of the 15th Alabama also found the scene impressive. "We see the Virginians who are leading the division crossing," he wrote after the war. "I have learned since that it was done for effect, as Virginia and Maryland joins, it was as a voice from Virginia speaking to her sister State, saying, here we are, we have come at last to assist you in throwing off the yoke of tyranny that have held you down since the riot in Baltimore in 1861." The powerful influence of John Ryder Randall is palpable here. Crying in his poem for Marylanders to "burst the tyrant's chain" so that "Virginia should not call in vain," Jackson's selection of Virginians to cross the river first, and McClendon's rendering of it afterward, illustrate the influence of Randall's mythology on both Confederate perceptions and military operations.[35]

Meanwhile, an enthusiastic crowd of civilians gathered on the towpath of the C&O Canal to greet the arriving Rebel column. In all likelihood, Lige White had orchestrated their presence. Born in Poolesville, Maryland, White maintained contacts on both sides of the river while commanding a battalion of border cavalry from Loudoun County. He had married a woman from the Trundle family in

---

33 Jedediah Hotchkiss to Sara A. Hotchkiss, Sept. 8, 1862, in Hotchkiss Family Letters, Augusta County, Virginia Collection, Center for Digital History, University of Virginia, Charlottesville, VA. Available online at https://valley.lib.virginia.edu/VoS/personalpapers/documents/augusta/p2hotchkissletters.html. Referred to hereafter as Hotchkiss Letters.

34 Robertson, *Stonewall Jackson*, 587.

35 McClendon, *Recollections*, 128.

Montgomery County, Maryland, several members of which owned land near Mason's Island and Lock No. 26 along the C&O Canal.[36]

It makes sense to assume that White passed word of the pending Confederate incursion to his Maryland contacts because the locals collected at the right time near a ford that few people knew about (compared to other crossing points in the vicinity). Furthermore, no bridge over the canal existed at White's Ford, the closest crossing being a foot bridge at Lock No. 26, roughly one-third of a mile north. In addition to arranging a local welcome for Jackson's troops, White guided the general to the river through his own farmland after informing Jackson of the "obscure" ford adjacent to his property that the army could utilize. General Lee could just as easily have ordered Jackson to use the crossing at Noland's Ferry taken by D. H. Hill the day before, but in what appears to have been a characteristic effort to "mystify" the Federals, Jackson chose to use White's Ford because it was inconspicuous and because it allowed him to cross the Potomac at a place hidden from direct Federal observation. Indeed, local legend in Leesburg holds that "Jackson rose early in the morning from his bed in the Harrison house to examine the several suggested points for the Southern Army to cross the Potomac. He is locally credited with the decision that the place known as White's Ford was best for the purpose and it was there, on the 5th September, that much of the Army crossed."[37]

Collecting sympathetic Marylanders to greet the army as a liberating force created the joyful backdrop painted by Randall's poem. When it reached the opposite bank, the 10th Virginia's band "stopped and played 'Maryland, my Maryland,'" reported a war correspondent from Harrisonburg, Virginia, traveling with the men. "Whilst the Marylanders and hardy soldiers shouted and wept tears of joy. Oh, it was a wild scene!" he continued. "The people flocked around great Jackson, and it is said, ladies greeted the hero with the nectar of their rosy lips." Lige White, who had crossed the river with Jackson, took part in the production by

---

36 George W. Diehl, *A True Confederate Soldier: Col. Elijah Viers White*, 3, unpublished manuscript in the Thomas Balch Library, Leesburg, VA.

37 A National Park Service Ranger once described Lock No. 26 as "so obscure" that he could not find any photos of it in the NPS database. See https://www.canaltrust.org/discovery area/lock-26/; "This ford was an obscure one on the road through the farm of Capt. Elijah White." Early, *Autobiographical Sketch*, 134. Jackson's design appears to have worked; no source identifying direct Federal surveillance of White's Ford has been found. Robertson, *Stonewall Jackson*, 586. White's Ford was "not generally known to the Federals" at this point in the war. Harrison Williams, *Legends of Loudoun: An Account of the History and Homes of a Border County of Virginia's Northern Neck* (Richmond, VA, 1938), 210.

throwing himself from his horse "among a group of mothers and daughters [to kiss] such a lot of them in five minutes, that I venture to say the record was never broken," recalled Henry Kyd Douglas. Jed Hotchkiss also found himself carried away by the moment. The crossing, he wrote, was "a noble spectacle, the broad river, fringed by the lofty trees in full foliage; the exuberant wealth of the autumnal wild flowers down to the very margin of the stream and a bright green island stretched away to the right." A another witness was similarly "transported to the times of ancient history . . . whilst observing the passage . . . The whole river seemed alive with troops pressing forward, each eager to place his foot on the soil of Maryland before his comrades."[38]

The rest of Brig. Gen. William Booth Taliaferro's Third Brigade, under the temporary command of Col. Edward T. H. Warren, followed the 10th Virginia and completed the crossing ahead of the Second Brigade. The Second Brigade reached the Potomac "about 9 or 10 o'clock" in the morning and forded it "with great enthusiasm—bands playing, men singing and cheering."[39]

Not all of Jackson's men exhibited the same level of excitement. Brigadier General Dorsey Pender, for example, "sent for the officers of the brigade to report at his headquarters" on the morning of September 5 to communicate a sobering message about discipline. Pender "made them a speech," recorded George Mills, "telling them that we were now going to cross the Potomac and going into the enemy's country, and that they must act as officers and gentlemen, keeping a firm hand on the men of their commands, and that he would hold them responsible for their conduct."[40]

In fact, only a few accounts of the passage by Jackson's subsequent divisions mention the same level of cheering and shouting exhibited by the Virginians. "Every regiment singing and as happy as if going to a ball" until the men reached the river, reported Sam Buck of the 13th Virginia, part of Jubal Early's brigade. Then they were given no time to take off their shoes or trousers before their

---

38 *Rockingham Register and Virginia Advertiser*, Sept. 19, 1862; Henry Kyd Douglas, *I Rode with Stonewall* (Chapel Hill, NC, 1940), 147; McDonald, ed., *Make Me a Map of the Valley*, 78; Letter from "A. T." printed in the *Richmond Dispatch*, Sept. 20, 1862.

39 Worsham, *One of Jackson's Foot Cavalry*, 137. No information could be found concerning the crossing of Jackson's Fourth Brigade, which was at that time under the command of Brig. Gen. William Starke.

40 George H. Mills, "Supplemental Sketch Sixteenth Regiment," in Clark, ed., *Histories of the Several Regiments and Battalions from North Carolina*, 4:164. Pender's comments echoed those of Col. O'Neal to Robert Rodes's troops on that same day.

officers drove them into the water like cattle. The men "waded through singing 'Maryland, My Maryland'" anyway, he remembered, but many resented having to march the rest of the day with wet footwear. John Robson of the 52nd Virginia, also a part of Early's brigade, noted with some bitterness, "On the 5th September we crossed the Potomac at White's Ford, and stood on Maryland soil, but it was only a remnant of the 'Army of Northern Virginia' that went over. Thousands of our boys had lagged, worn out, bare-footed, sick, hungry; they could not keep up, and so, from actual necessity, twenty thousand men of Lee's army staid in Virginia and crept, as best they could, to the rendezvous indicated to them by the General for a rallying point—Winchester."[41]

General Branch's column came up last, making "a forced march and crossing of the Potomac just as the sun was setting," confided Draughton Haynes of the 49th Georgia to his diary.[42] Wayland Dunaway confirmed the late hour of the crossing when he and his comrades in the 40th Virginia, Brig. Gen. Charles Field's brigade, reached the shoreline. "[W]e came to the Potomac river, which was then about four feet deep, with its bottom covered with rounded stones of many sizes." He continued:

> We were not so favored as Joshua's host at the Jordan, but we just walked from shore to shore as if there were no water there. Beautiful was the scene. As I approached the river I beheld those who had crossed ascending the hill on the farther shore; in the water a double line of soldiers stretching from side to side, their guns held high above the current and gilded by the beams of the westering sun.[43]

41 Robson, *Reminiscences*, 117-118. David E. Johnston, *The Story of a Confederate Boy in the Civil War* (Portland, OR, 1914), 132, also notes the establishment of Winchester as the rallying point for invalid and barefooted soldiers. "Winchester was made the rendezvous for all the sick, lame, shoeless and others who remained as we passed Leesburg." Lieutenant Alexander S. Erwin of Company C, Philips Legion, Thomas Drayton's brigade, D. R. Jones's division, Longstreet's command, recalled the same thing: "General Longstreet issued an order here [Leesburg] that all the barefooted, weak and inefficient troops of each regiment be left with the baggage in charge of an officer. I was detained for that purpose and left at Leesburg with about one hundred and fifty of our regiment. The detail suited me very well as I had blistered my feet so that I had been riding in the wagon for several days and could not march—so I took charge of them and have a good deal of trouble attending to my present duties. They then ordered all that were left, about five thousand (5,000) in all, to Winchester where we now are." Letter of Alex Erwin, Sept. 15, 1862, *Athens Watchman*, Oct. 1, 1862. Text available online at www.angelfire.com/ga2/Phillips Legion/erwin.html. My thanks to Steven Stotelmyer for this source.

42 Draughton Stith Haynes, *The Field Diary of a Confederate Soldier* (Darien, GA, 1963), 15.

43 Wayland F. Dunaway, *Reminiscences of a Rebel* (New York, NY, 1913), 47. Fields was wounded at Second Manassas, so brigade was under the command of John Brockenbrough.

Allen C. Redwood's depiction of Stonewall Jackson's men crossing the Potomac River at White's Ford. See Appendix A for more details. *LOC*

The late hour meant Branch's men could expect to spend the night in damp clothing. Still, Haynes derived some amusement from the situation: "Never did I behold so many naked legs in my life. The river was about 1/2 mile wide and many were the jokes passed between the boys as we were going through the stream." With the infantry across, Jackson's artillery and wagons followed well into the night.[44]

The crossing afforded William Mercer Otey of William Poague's Rockbridge Artillery an opportunity to stop and wash his underclothing while the cool river water cleansed his "battle-begrimed body." Branch's wagon train made slow

44 Haynes, *Field Diary*, 15; "We marched until 12 ½ last night." John Hampden "Ham" Chamberlayne, *Virginian: Letters and Papers of an Artillery Officer in the War for Southern Independence, 1861-1865* (Richmond, VA, 1932), 102. The marching order noted comes from a combination of sources that put Starke's division across the Potomac in the morning. An Alabama soldier with Lawton's division recalled, "We see the Virginians who are leading the division crossing . . . the Virginians were first to cross, and I have learned since that it was done for effect," indicating that Lawton's division came second. McClendon, *Recollections of War Times*, 127-128.

progress, encountering difficulty late in the afternoon when the mules pulling the wagons found standing in the cool water more to their liking than hauling their loads down a hot and dusty road. Coming back to find the ford "completely blocked," Jackson lashed out at Maj. Gen. A. P. Hill, an officer he had already placed under arrest for not marching his troops efficiently on September 4. Hill snarled bitterly in reply that "it was no part of his business to get tangled wagons out of the river," which was true given that General Branch was in command of the division at the time. Jackson called in frustration for his quartermaster, Maj. John A. Harman, to untangle the mess and clear the ford. Harman "dashed in among the wagoners, kicking mules [while he] poured out a volume of oaths that would have excited the admiration of the most scientific mule-driver . . . The mules caught the inspiration from a chorus of familiar words, and all at once made a break for the Maryland shore, and in five minutes the ford was cleared." Despite his disdain for profanity, Jackson thanked Harman for the assistance before riding off to rejoin the head of the column traveling up the towpath to Lock No. 26.[45]

Earlier in the day Jackson had ordered two canal boats lashed together at the lock and planked over to make a bridge. In the meantime, the men loitering near the lock had encountered a third canal boat laden with watermelons. These they eagerly purchased from the boat's captain and presented the general with a "noble melon."[46]

Jackson directed his column toward the Furnace Road that would take them to the night's bivouac near Three Springs with part of D. H. Hill's command. The general had hoped to make better time than he did on his first day in Maryland, writing to D. H. Hill of his desire to march all the way to Frederick City. In the end, Old Jack's command made it only one mile north of Noland's Ferry. Near Three Springs, Jackson allowed his men to get corn for their rations, while those who could begged food from nearby houses. Their trousers and shoes still damp from the cool water of the Potomac, Jackson's men let themselves drop down to sleep,

45 John D. Imboden, "Incidents of the Battle of Manassas," in *The Century Magazine*, Vol. 30 (1885), 97-98. Imboden would later confuse the details of the mule affair told to him by Maj. Harman, when he claimed that the "Hill" Jackson rebuked was Daniel Harvey Hill. Because D. H. Hill was waiting to meet Stonewall Jackson near the Monocacy River, Imboden probably meant Ambrose Powell Hill, who maintained a bitterly antagonistic relationship with Jackson. I have corrected Imboden's telling of the tale to reflect the presence of A. P. Hill, and not D. H. Hill.

46 McDonald, ed., *Make Me a Map of the Valley*, 78. Hotchkiss Letters, Sept. 8, 1862.

the prospect of bringing Maryland into the Confederacy looking brighter than ever.[47]

Two brigades of Jeb Stuart's cavalry division also crossed the Potomac on September 5. Their story is the most confused of any Confederate command to do so. In his history of the event, Joseph Harsh has Stuart traversing the river at White's Ford late on the afternoon of September 5, after detaching Beverly Robertson's brigade to remain in Virginia as a rear guard, ordering Wade Hampton to cross his brigade "when possible," and sending Fitzhugh Lee's brigade on an "easterly detour" of Leesburg to cross at Edwards' Ferry. Historian D. Scott Hartwig likewise describes Stuart going over the river on September 5, and adds that both Hampton's and Lee's brigades crossed late in the afternoon at Edwards' Ferry, while Robertson's brigade remained in the vicinity of Leesburg until the following day.[48]

A careful reading of the sources reveals that these descriptions are only partially correct. Rather than crossing his entire command at Edwards' Ferry, Jeb Stuart appears to have made a two-pronged advance across the Potomac at Conrad's Ferry and Edwards' Ferry. Stuart crossed personally with Hampton's brigade at the former location late in the day on September 5, while Fitz Lee's brigade crossed at the latter place a short time earlier. Fitz Lee also appears to have made it across the Potomac with relative ease, whereas the traffic in and around Leesburg held up Hampton's advance for several hours. Finally, Robertson's brigade, now under the command of Col. Thomas T. Munford, brought up the cavalry's rear on September 6, it being the only portion of Stuart's division to cross the river at White's Ford.[49]

News confirming that "the army would cross the Potomac and test the sympathy of Northwestern Maryland with the Confederate cause," reached Stuart's troopers on September 4 while they were enjoying a rare day of rest. According to Maj. Heros von Borcke, Gen. Stuart mustered his men for the day's advance at around 1:00 a.m. on September 5. "The Confederate camps presented a scene of

47 For comments on bridging the lock see Early, *Autobiographical Sketch*, 134; Worsham, *One of Jackson's Foot Cavalry*, 137; and the *Rockingham Register and Virginia Advertiser*, Sept. 19, 1862. Thomas H. White, "About the Shelling of Leesburg," in *Confederate Veteran*, Vol. 21, No. 1 (Jan. 1913), 582 stated the army "camped on Carroll's Manor in Frederick County, Md." which is in the vicinity of Adamstown, Maryland, and Three Springs.

48 Hartwig, *To Antietam Creek*, 103.

49 George M. Neese, *Three Years in the Confederate Horse Artillery* (New York, NY, 1911), 111-112.

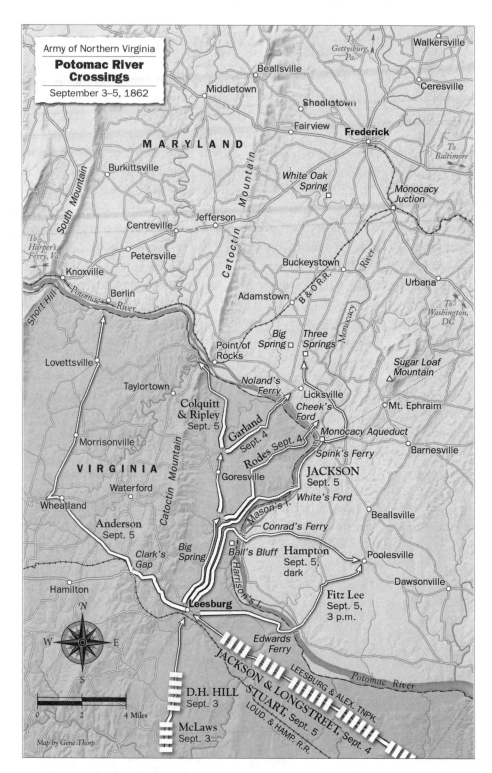

Army of Northern Virginia
Potomac River Crossings
September 3–5, 1862

bustling activity," observed the Prussian-born Confederate. "Every regiment was preparing for the march, officers were riding to and fro, and the long artillery-trains were moving off along the turnpike, their rumbling noise combining with the rattle of the drums and the roll of the bugles to wake the echoes for miles around. Our direction was northward, and . . . we rode onward towards the little town of Leesburg, inspirited by this fact, our horses exhibiting new life from yesterday's repose."[50]

George M. Neese of Capt. Roger Chew's battery of horse artillery recorded similar sights, although he took a less literary approach to what was transpiring. "The road was crowded with wagons and consequently we made slow progress," noted Neese. "We were detained three hours at Goose Creek, a small stream two miles from Leesburg, where the ford was deep and miry, and the water came near running over our guns" thanks to torrential rains that had battered northern Virginia a few days earlier.[51]

The mounted column slogged on, finally approaching Leesburg after the sun had risen. Von Borcke remembered "The streets of the village [being] . . . compactly filled with troops, artillery, and waggon-trains" from James Longstreet's command as it moved up to occupy the campground at Big Spring then being vacated by Jackson's men. The traffic jam proved so impassable that Stuart "halted [his command] about a mile distant [from Leesburg], instead of proceeding through the place." Locating a spring near their temporary bivouac, Stuart's men watered their horses and "breakfasted on roasted corn and apples" while the general himself went with von Borcke and several others of his staff to find Gen. Lee.[52] Stuart arrived at Harrison Hall while the conference with Jackson and Longstreet was already underway. There he learned from Lee that his orders were to enter Maryland and screen the army's right flank as it moved north from White's Ford. Lee appears to have ordered Stuart to advance his command into Maryland at Edwards' Ferry and Conrad's Ferry. Both of the vaunted cavalier's brigades were then directed to sweep north from Poolesville to Barnesville, Urbana, and New Market.[53]

50 Von Borcke, *Memoirs*, 182.

51 Neese, *Three Years in the Confederate Horse Artillery*, 111.

52 Beale, *History of the Ninth Virginia Cavalry*, 37.

53 Von Borcke, *Memoirs*, 182-184.

While meeting with Lee, Stuart received approval for his September 4 decision to replace the disappointing Brig. Gen. Beverly Robertson, commander of the cavalry's third brigade, with Col. Thomas Munford. Munford found his new command scattered at the time due to assignments that had sent portions of it in opposite directions. As Robertson himself later reported, "In compliance with instructions received on the morning of September 4, with the Seventh and Twelfth Regiments Virginia Cavalry and three pieces of Chew's battery I proceeded in the direction of Falls Church, to make a demonstration against the enemy and hold him in check while our army was crossing the Potomac above."[54]

In the meantime, Stuart had ordered Munford on September 2 to take the 2nd Virginia Cavalry to Leesburg and attack a party of Federal cavalry and Loudoun Rangers under Henry A. Cole and Samuel C. Means that had "infested that country and harassed the inhabitants." Reaching the town late in the morning on September 2, Munford routed the Federals and drove them from the region in a clash that came to be known as the Battle of Mile Hill. Munford's new command remained disorganized as the Army of Northern Virginia descended on Leesburg, so Stuart detailed Munford to stay in Virginia and collect his regiments while Jackson, Longstreet, and the unattached divisions of McLaws, Anderson, and Walker advanced into Maryland.[55]

Munford probably also requested time to bring up Chew's battery for repairs, further delaying his advance.[56] As George Neese of that battery wrote after the war,

> We arrived at Leesburg in the middle of the afternoon [September 5] and fed our horses, then moved about a mile from town to a large spring, remained there till sunset, when we returned to town and camped. This evening we passed a great many infantry marching toward the Potomac. There are thousands of soldiers camped around Leesburg . . . and all seem to be in joyous gayety, caused, I suppose, by the eager desires and bright anticipations of crossing the Potomac and entering Maryland. As I am writing I hear soldiers shouting, huzzahing all around us. Just now a brass band has struck up, which helps to swell the cheer of the merry throng.[57]

54 Lee confirmed Robertson's relief from duty in Special Orders No. 188. See *OR* 19, 2:595 *OR* 19, 1:828.

55 *OR* 19, 1:814, 825; *OR* 19, 2:595.

56 Neese's description sounds like the traffic jam that blocked White's Ford, suggesting Munford's brigade used that ford to cross into Maryland. See Neese, *Three Years*, 111-112.

57 Ibid.

Neese and his comrades "remained in camp at Leesburg until we had our guns repaired; then we moved to the Potomac [on September 6], where we arrived a little before sunset; but it was impossible for us to ford the river immediately after our arrival in consequence of the vast number of wagons and artillery there waiting for an opportunity to ford. . . . It was midnight when we left the Southern Confederacy last night, forded the Potomac, and landed in the United States, in Montgomery County, Maryland."[58]

The balance of Stuart's command moved out on September 5 at "About two o'clock in the afternoon," crossing the Potomac "at Leesburg," according to Capt. Henry B. McClellan of the 3rd Virginia Cavalry. Fitzhugh Lee led his roughly 2,000 men to Edwards' Ferry by skirting east of the town. They forded the river without incident and rode on to Poolesville, Maryland, where the advance guard from the 5th Virginia Cavalry engaged a portion of the 1st Massachusetts Cavalry, which Brig. Gen. Alfred Pleasonton had detailed to picket the area.[59]

Driving the Federals from the village at a cost of three killed and four wounded, Fitz Lee and his men suddenly found themselves in the midst of a joyous and sympathetic crowd. "The farmers are bringing in hay and provisions of all kinds, and giving them away," observed a report in a Northern newspaper with disgust several days later. "There is not a loyal man, with one or two exceptions, there. The women received them with flags, and other tokens of joy."[60]

Stuart, for his part, rode through Leesburg ahead of Wade Hampton's brigade on September 5, traveling first to Big Spring before turning east toward the crossing at Conrad's Ferry. Reaching the ferry required "a dusty and very much impeded march of two hours, winding through infantry columns," recalled Heros von Borcke. "Compelled frequently to halt, we reached the Potomac at White's Ford."[61]

---

58 Ibid., 112-113.

59 Beale, *History of the Ninth Virginia Cavalry*, 37. For details on the clash at Poolesville see Hartwig, *To Antietam Creek*, 104.

60 *Hudson North Star*, Wednesday, Sept. 10, 1862.

61 Von Borcke, *Memoirs*, 184. William Blackford, another member of Stuart's staff, made a similar mistake in his recollection of the crossing point, writing, "General Stuart with his cavalry, forming the advance guard of the army, crossed the Potomac at White's Ford near Leesburg." William W. Blackford, *War Years with Jeb Stuart* (New York, NY, 1946), 139. White's Ford is not located near Leesburg, whereas Conrad's Ferry, later renamed White's Ferry after Elijah Viers White purchased it in 1865, is only 2.5 miles away from the town center, explaining why Blackford, like von Borcke, confused both the name and location of the crossing.

Garbling important details, von Borcke's account has caused confusion ever since its publication in 1866. His use of the term "White's Ford" jumbled both the location and the place name where Stuart, and eventually Hampton's command, crossed the Potomac. In addition, his description of the place does not match White's Ford. Writing that "The banks of [the] noble river, which is of great width at this point, *rise to the height of about sixty feet above the bed of the stream* [emphasis added]," von Borcke's details better match the higher ground around Ball's Bluff south of Conrad's Ferry than the flatter shoreline at White's Ford. Von Borcke also wrote that "The passage of the Potomac by the cavalry column occupied about two hours, and was attended with some difficulty to our artillery, as the water in many places rose quite up to the middle of the horses bodies." The water level did not run that high at White's Ford, but it did at Conrad's Ferry, where the depth made crossing by boat more of a necessity for local traffic.[62]

There is also an account of Hampton's march that differs from von Borcke's on several critical points. Von Borcke claimed, for instance, that the march to the Potomac took roughly two hours, which would have put Hampton's brigade at Conrad's Ferry well before sundown if it departed from Leesburg at around 2:00 p.m. According to a trooper with Hampton's brigade, however, they crossed the Potomac long after sunset, meaning it probably took them longer than the two hours it took Stuart to reach the river, and several hours thereafter to cross it:

> The long line of our cavalry moved on through the streets of [Leesburg]; debouching to the right, filed down the last crest of hills that overlooks the Potomac, and rested on its banks, just above the bloody scenes where nearly eleven months before the Ball's Bluff tragedy was enacted. . . . The Potomac was to be crossed; splendid bands of music both from the Virginia and Maryland side struck up, and continued discoursing their most inspiriting martial airs. The wearied and worn soldier momentarily forgot his fatigue as the Rubicon of his long cherished hopes lay out before him. The moon and stars never shone more brightly on the placid rolling waters of this classic stream—though many a heart silently beat with indefinite longings and sad forebodings, as one would reflect that that same bright moon would shine on strangely contrasted scenes to this. Her gentle rays were soon to play into many a cold pale face, the gurgling waters alone to hum the requiem.[63]

62 Von Borcke, *Memoirs*, 184.

63 "Sketches of Hampton's Cavalry," in Ulysses R. Brooks, ed., *Stories of the Confederacy* (Columbia, SC, 1912), 78.

R. Channing Price, Stuart's Adjutant General who trailed the general by one day, also confirmed Stuart and Hampton passing into Maryland via Conrad's Ferry. On "Friday afternoon . . . I . . . started to Leesburg," wrote Price on September 10. Reaching "there about 9 o'clock [I found] the town blocked up with wagons and artillery moving towards the river." The following day (September 6) "[I] made a start for Maryland and reached White's Ford, where Longstreet's Corps was crossing about the middle of the day. It was a beautiful sight to see our ragged & toil-worn veterans leaving the Old Dominion which has suffered so heavily from this horrid war, and crossing to free a sister state from the Federal yoke. Getting across I heard that *the Cavalry had crossed the evening before at Conrad's Ford* [emphasis added] & gone up to Poolsville." Price's account confirms that a body of cavalry crossed at Conrad's Ferry on the evening before, a fact echoed by James Longstreet, who wrote that "Stuart's cavalry . . . passed to front and right flank of the army," offering an accurate, if general, description of Hampton's and Fitzhugh Lee's movements. Lastly, in his compilation of short histories and anecdotes, Ulysses S. Brooks noted that Capt. James Hart's South Carolina battery with Hampton's brigade "carried the first piece of artillery that crossed the Potomac, crossing at Crousod's Ferry," a muddled reference to Conrad's Ferry.[64]

Upon gaining the Maryland shore ahead of Hampton, Stuart and his staff rode to Poolesville, which they reached about nightfall. "The inhabitants of Maryland whom we met along the road, with some exceptions, did not greet us quite so cordially as we had expected," wrote Heros von Borcke, "this portion of the state being less devoted than others to the Confederate cause." Poolesville proved to be altogether different, illustrating to von Borcke and his comrades the fragmented nature of Maryland's political landscape:

> The enthusiasm of the citizens [in Poolesville] rose to fever heat. The wildest and absurdest questions were eagerly asked by the honest burghers concerning the strength of our armies,

---

64 See R. Channing Price, Sept. 10, 1862 in Robert J. Trout, *With Pen and Saber: The Letters and Diaries of J.E.B. Stuart's Staff Officers* (Mechanicsburg, PA, 1995), 95-96; Longstreet, *From Manassas to Appomattox*, 201. Jeb Stuart also noted in his report that "The cavalry followed the rear of the army to Leesburg, and, crossing the Potomac on the afternoon of the 5th, Lee's brigade in advance, moved to Poolesville." Lee's brigade was in the advance because it crossed the Potomac farther to the east earlier in the day. See Stuart's Report, *OR* 19, 1:814; Hampton reported on Oct. 25, 1862, "we were ordered to Leesburg, where, after halting a few hours, we proceeded to the Potomac, which we crossed on the afternoon of September 5, and marched to Poolesville, where we halted for the night." *OR* 19, 1:822. The author clearly meant Conrad's Ferry. See "Record of Hart's Battery from Its Organization to the End of the War" in Brooks, ed., *Stories of the Confederacy*, 251.

Alfred Waud's depiction of Wade Hampton's cavalry crossing the Potomac River at Conrad's Ferry. See Appendix A for more details. LOC

our intended movements, &c. &c. A number of young men became so much excited that they immediately mounted their horses and insisted upon joining our ranks. Two young merchants of the village, suddenly resolving to enlist in the cavalry, announced the peremptory sale of their extensive stock of groceries upon the spot for Confederate money. Our soldiers cleared out both establishments during the hour, to the last pin.[65]

Camping two miles from the village, Stuart and his staff waited for Hampton's column to arrive, and on the following day they pushed to Urbana and New Market, leaving picket posts along the way to watch enemy movements. Stuart himself rode to Best's Grove, near Frederick, arriving there in the afternoon on September 6 to pause for a day and enjoy some of the local hospitality before rejoining his headquarters staff in Urbana.[66]

65 Von Borcke, *Memoirs*, 185-187.

66 Ibid., 187.

James Longstreet got his column moving "early in the morning" on September 6, most likely with General Lee, still confined to the plain black ambulance that had been his conveyance since the end of August, traveling in advance of it. That Lee forded the river early in the day is confirmed by Capt. Henry Lord Page King, Lafayette McLaws's aide-de-camp, who recorded in his diary before 10:00 a.m. on September 6, 1862, "General Lee has gone over."[67]

Arriving at White's Ford with his headquarters staff and Company A of the 6th Virginia Cavalry acting as his security detachment, Lee's wagon rocked unevenly through the waist-deep river in advance of Longstreet's artillery. Upon reaching the Maryland bank, Lee "concluded to abandon his bodyguard and leave it at the river" in order to turn back stragglers once the army's main body had passed. Those men who fell behind, recalled Luther Hopkins of Company A, received instructions "to move toward Winchester, beyond the Shenandoah."[68]

There is some evidence that Lee then lingered at the riverside watching his men before he proceeded down the C&O towpath to the makeshift bridge at Lock No. 26 built by Jackson's engineers one day earlier. Straggling continued to irritate the general as he moved across the countryside, and so at some point before he reached Best's Grove near Fredrick City he paused to issue General Orders No. 103, naming Brig. Gen. Lewis A. Armistead the army's provost marshal with the authority to detain those who left their commands without authorization and punish those guilty of stealing from civilians. Lee also took the occasion to announce Kirby Smith's victory at Richmond, Kentucky, to the army, an event that had occurred "simultaneous" with his own army's defeat of John Pope's Federal Army of Virginia at Manassas at the end of August. "Soldiers, press onward!" he exhorted his men, assuring the ranks that "our brethren of our sister States will soon be released from tyranny, and our independence be established upon a sure and abiding basis."[69]

---

67 The time of day comes from Owen, *In Camp and Battle*, 129-130; Helen Trimpi, ed., "Lafayette McLaws' Aide-de-Camp: The Maryland Campaign Diary of Captain Henry Lord Page King" in *Civil War Regiments: A Journal of the American Civil War*, Vol. 6, No. 2 (1998), 30, hereafter King Diary. Harsh, *Taken*, 104, and Hartwig, *To Antietam Creek*, 110, concluded that Lee crossed the river early in the morning. Neither scholar cited King's diary.

68 "My company was detached from the Sixth Regiment and made a bodyguard to Gen. Lee." Luther W. Hopkins, *From Bull Run to Appomattox: A Boy's View* (Baltimore, MD, 1908), 49, 51. Company A of the Sixth Regiment remained at White's Ford for almost a week turning back stragglers trying to reach the army.

69 See Trimpi, ed., "Lafayette McLaws' Aide-de-Camp," 30, where King notes that Lee sent orders for McLaws to cross his division north of White's Ford after a prodigious traffic jam had

Returning to Longstreet's command, the Washington Artillery of New Orleans likely accompanied Lee's ambulance in the advance to Maryland ahead of the infantry.[70] "As full of hope as the soldiers of Hannibal going over the Alps . . . the men splashed through the water, too happy to be moving forward to trouble themselves about wet clothing," recalled Napier Bartlett of the 1st Battalion's 3rd Company. "The careful artillerists . . . by the side of their pieces, mounted the caissons—the laggards behind shouted frantically for a little delay . . . It was with a deep heaving of the chest and expansion of the lungs . . . that we stood at last upon the Maryland shore, and thought of the battle fields behind and before." After "all the batteries were safely across the Potomac," wrote Lieutenant Owen, also of the Washington Artillery's 1st Battalion, "I immediately straggled" from the column to look for something to eat.[71]

The first infantry division of Longstreet's column under Brig. Gen. David R. "Neighbor" Jones collected at the water's edge behind the artillerists at 8:00 a.m. Jones's men, led by Richard Garnett's brigade, then followed the guns across the Potomac, the eager ranks wading into the current. "The men were triumphantly rejoicing and confident," remembered G. Moxley Sorrel of Longstreet's staff. "They believed [we] were moving into the friendly fields of a sister State, whose men would surely rise and join us."[72]

---

backed up for miles in Virginia. Presumably Lee knew about the jam because he had witnessed it. *OR* 19, 2:596.

70 The assumption made here that Longstreet's artillery crossed ahead of his infantry rests upon the following. Napier Bartlett, *Military Record of Louisiana* (New Orleans, LA, 1875), 129, states, "On the 5th we marched through Leesburg and bivouacked in a half a mile of the Potomac, which stream was next morning crossed." Owen, *In Camp and Battle*, 129-130, notes similarly, "On the 6th the army began early in the morning to ford the river into Maryland. After all the batteries were safely across the Potomac this morning ..." The close proximity of the artillery to the river, as well as the fact that D. R. Jones's division took several hours to cross, followed closely by the division of Richard H. Anderson, which began crossing around 10:00 a.m., and that of John B. Hood, which entered the river around noon, suggests that in order for the guns to have made it into Maryland before noon they must have led Longstreet's column. The possibility also exists that the artillery may have crossed between the infantry divisions, but this seems unlikely given that Jones, McLaws, Anderson, and Hood approached the river in that order on Sept. 6 and no source from any of these commands mentions artillery crossing in a column mixed with the infantry.

71 Owen, *In Camp and Battle*, 130.

72 G. Moxley Sorrel, *Recollections of a Confederate Staff Officer* (New York, NY, 1905), 104. Diary of J. Evans Edings, Sept. 5, 1862. Edward Willis Papers, Collection ID MSS45898, Manuscript Division, Library of Congress, Washington, D.C. Captain Edings served as Brig. Gen. Thomas Drayton's assistant adjutant general. My thanks to Scott Hartwig for the source.

The enthusiasm among the men carried over from the previous day when, while passing through Leesburg, they encountered "a reception committee consisting of the entire community, white and black, old and young, male and female," before spending the night at the Big Spring encampment. Upon coming to the Potomac, recalled Frank Mixson of the 1st South Carolina Volunteers, the troops received orders "to leave all their baggage" behind. "On this trip," noted Mixson, "we had nothing but a haversack, canteen, and a blanket or oil cloth besides the accoutrements gun, cartridge box, and scabbard."[73] Jones's men disrobed at the river's edge and then waded into the water "amid the singing of 'Maryland, My Maryland,' and the shouts and cheering of the men [crying] 'Back to Washington'."[74] The air temperature rose steadily into the 70s under a cloudless sky as Jones's command filed out of the water on the far side to pull on their shoes and trousers before marching up the C&O Canal.[75]

Onward tramped the butternut column, bringing up the divisions of Lafayette McLaws and Richard Heron Anderson while Jones's men were still crossing. McLaws, however, soon found his command, which was not formally attached to Longstreet's wing of the army, redirected. Henry King, a captain on the staff of Maj. Gen. McLaws, noted in his diary that they had learned of the planned crossing only one day earlier. "Hurrah!" rejoiced the Georgia officer. "We go indeed at last into Maryland!"[76]

As it approached White's Ford at 10:00 a.m., the column backed up so far that Gen. Lee diverted them north. With Jackson's command already in Maryland, and pushing hard for Frederick City, there was no longer a need for the army's other columns to maintain the secrecy that had motivated the use of little-known White's

---

73 Frank M. Mixson, *Reminiscences of a Private* (Columbia, SC, 1910), 26. Robert K. Charles, "Brief Sketch of the First Maryland Campaign," in *Confederate Veteran*, Vol. 14, No. 2 (February 1906), 65, echoed Mixson's memory: "We lost no time after the battle of Second Manassas, but marched direct to Leesburg, where we divested ourselves of all superfluous baggage and "impedimenta." General Lee had all of these personal items gathered up and shipped to Winchester.

74 "All the men first reduced themselves to that scantiness of apparel which seems to have constituted the distinguishing feature of Adam's and Eve's costume prior to the apple-stealing scrape into which they were tempted by that bad boy, Old Nick." See Hamilton, ed., *The Papers of Randolph Abbott Shotwell*, 1:310, and Johnston, *The Story of a Confederate Boy*, 132. See Harsh, *Sounding the Shallows*, 8, for meteorological data.

75 "After crossing the Potomac the Army marched northwestwardly along the river and canal to the line of Monocacy river." Hamilton, ed., *The Papers of Randolph Abbott Shotwell*, 1:310.

76 Trimpi, ed., "Lafayette McLaws' Aide-de-Camp," 30. "Reached the river at White's Ford with the Gen. about 10 oclk some 7 miles from Leesburg. Jones' Division crossing the river."

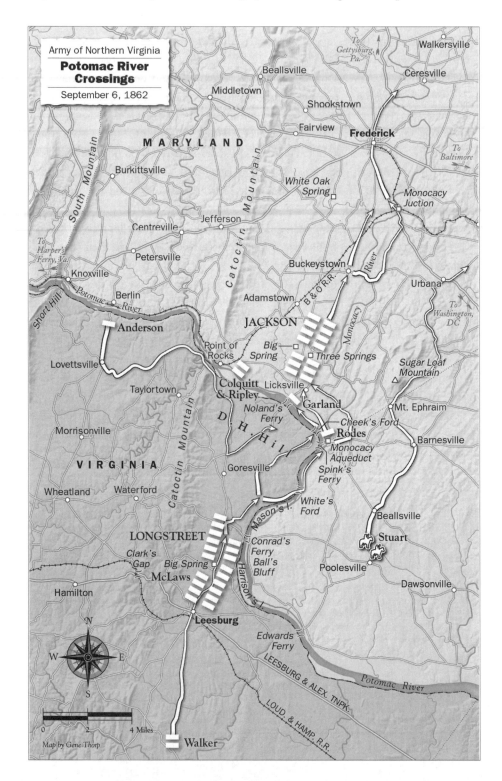

Army of Northern Virginia
Potomac River Crossings
September 6, 1862

Map by Gene Thorp

Ford. Any crossing point within a reasonable distance would do. Lee therefore sent McLaws northward through Virginia heedless of the fact that any Federal observers still left on Sugarloaf Mountain would easily spot the column. According to Capt. King, "We marched across the country to another road and reached the river again at Cheek's ford some three miles above [White's Ford]."[77]

Once there, "the Division crossed before dark" with King himself tumbling into the water around 4:30 p.m. after his horse stumbled over a rock. The South Carolinians of Joseph Brevard Kershaw's brigade also "waded the Potomac River," in the late afternoon, according to the brief account written by J. J. McDaniel. "Some soldiers stripped naked, but the great mass stripped only their pants and drawers," observed McDaniel. "Others 'rolled up their breeches' . . . [and] got them wet, as the water came up higher than they could roll them. The river here was about 400 yards wide, having two small islands."[78]

A comrade in Kershaw's brigade recalled the wave of emotion surrounding the event:

> Bands played 'Maryland, My Maryland,' men sang and cheered, hats filled the air, flags waved, and shouts from fifty thousand throats reverberated up and down the banks of the river, to be echoed back from the mountains and die away among the hills and highlands of Maryland. Men stopped midway in the stream and sang loudly . . . Never before had an occurrence so excited and enlivened the spirits of the troops as the crossing of the Potomac into the land of our sister, Maryland. . . . If ever Lee's troops could have wept for joy, it was at the crossing of the Potomac.[79]

As for White's Ford, although R. H. Anderson's division came up behind McLaws, practically no accounts of it traversing the river have been located. All that can be assumed from the sources is that once Lee ordered McLaws to take his division north, Anderson's men, belonging formally to Longstreet's wing of the army, probably forded the Potomac next, followed by the division under John Bell Hood. The impressions of S. F. Tenney of the 3rd Georgia, a part of Brig. Gen. Ambrose Ransom Wright's brigade, provide the only color for the experience of

77 Hartwig, *To Antietam Creek*, 111, got the location slightly wrong, writing that McLaws crossed at Noland's Ferry. Cheek's Ford is close to Noland's Ferry, being located some 1,000 yards to the southeast.

78 J. J. McDaniel, *Diary of Battles, Marches, and Incidents of the Seventh S.C. Regiment* (1862), 10. Emphasis in the original.

79 D. Augustus Dickert, *History of Kershaw's Brigade* (Newberry, SC, 1899), 144-145.

Anderson's men. "We crossed the Potomac and for the first time, as soldiers, stood on Maryland soil," recalled Tenney many years after the war, he and his fellows hailing "the event . . . with cheers and 'My Maryland' from the brass bands."[80]

William Wofford's brigade of Hood's division reached the river next, the impatient ranks in an increasingly joyful mood as the much-heralded Maryland shoreline came into view. "It was about noon before our brigade started across," recalled John Stevens, a member of the 5th Texas, describing the setting:

> Imagine a river (as I remember it) about 500 yards wide, from two to three feet deep, the water very swift. Now it is just as full of men as it can be for 600 or 700 yards, up and down, yelling and singing all sorts of war and jolly songs, and in this connection you must find room for eight or twelve regimental bands in the river all the time, the drums beating, the horns a tootin' and the fifes a screaming, possibly every one of them on a different air, some 'Dixie,' some 'My Maryland, My Maryland,' some 'The Girl I Left Behind Me,' some 'Yankee Doodle.' All the men are apparently jolly. . . . In we bulged, our bands playing, and the dust is so dense you can't see a hundred yards ahead of you. We also have some kind of head cover, either an old piece of a hat or an old cap and if we have not worn them out, we have some sort of footwear, in the shape of old army shoes, but many of us are bare-footed, the boys yellin', as jolly as any who had gone before or any who came after us.[81]

Despite the temperature approaching 80 degrees that afternoon, several of Stevens's comrades recalled the Potomac's waters being icy cold. Captain James Roberdeau of the 5th Texas found it a rather pleasant experience to "plunge into a cold stream . . . after having marched [just] long enough to warm the blood." On the way across, some of Roberdeau's comrades took time to stop on a small island and hold a brief prayer service, concluding with a rousing chorus of 'Jordan is a hard road to travel!' before they waded back into the chilly stream. Bob Murray of the 1st Texas did not share their enthusiasm. Finding the water too cold for his liking, he stumbled over a rock in the midst of crossing and sank completely underwater, crying "ach-ai!" as he plunged in. "Darned if I don't believe all the ice

---

80 S. F. Tenney, "The Battle of Sharpsburg: A Letter Written Fifty Years Ago Just After the Famous Engagement," reprinted in Joe Owen, Philip McBride, and Joe Allport, eds., *Texans at Antietam: A Terrible Clash of Arms, September 16–17, 1862* (Fonthill Media, 2017), 251.

81 John W. Stevens, *Reminiscences of the Civil War* (Hillsboro, TX, 1902), 65.

houses in western Maryland were emptied into this river last night," commented Joe Polley, a comrade of Murray's who watched the man disappear.[82]

Despite the temporary discomfort, even cold water could not cool the excitement of Polley's comrades "wading the Potomac bent on effacing the print of the despot's heel from Maryland's shore." As John Stevens colorfully described the sentiment in his regiment, "we understand Maryland is ready to link her fortunes on to the fortunes of the Red Cross, and take 'pot luck' with Jeff Davis and his army. And we are going over there, not to make war on her, but to 'make love' to her. Ahem!"[83]

With the passage of Longstreet's command, the two brigades under John Walker remained the only large infantry formations on the Virginia side of the Potomac not filled with convalescents or barefooted men bound for Winchester. Walker's turn to cross came when his division marched north from Leesburg on September 7 to wade the Potomac at Cheek's Ford.[84]

Like Robert E. Lee, there is no record of when James Longstreet forded the river. Presumably, Longstreet crossed at White's Ford with his divisions, but lacking sources there is no way to pinpoint the time when he first set foot on Maryland's soil. Longstreet's memoirs do confirm that he entered Maryland on September 6, because at some point during the day he caught up to Lee on the road to Buckeystown.[85]

The two men completed the journey to Best's Grove that same day, arriving at some point in the afternoon to begin a period of rest, planning, and anticipation of Maryland's response to the Confederate call to arms. Unfortunately, there is no evidence for when or where Nathaniel George 'Shanks' Evans crossed his brigade,

---

82 Letter of Capt. James D. Roberdeau, 5th Texas Infantry, Sept. 17, 1899, reprinted in Owen, McBride, and Allport, eds., *Texans at Antietam*, 127; Letter of Oct. 8, 1862, in Joseph B. Polley, *A Soldier's Letters to Charming Nellie* (New York, NY, 1908). Available online at www.loyalbooks. com/book/a-soldiers-letters-to-charming-nellie-by-joseph-benjamin-polley.

83 Stevens, *Reminiscences*, 65.

84 "On the night of the 6th of September my division reached the vicinity of Leesburg, and the next morning crossed the Potomac at Cheek's Ford, at the mouth of the Monocacy . . . At Cheek's Ford I overtook G. B. Anderson's brigade of D. H. Hill's division and crossed into Maryland with it." Walker, "Jackson's Capture of Harper's Ferry," 604. "Marched at 6:00 a.m. this morning (Sept. 7) and pushed on to cross the Potomac as near as possible to join the main army under Jackson" Herbert M. Schiller, ed., *A Captain War: The Letters and Diaries of William H. S. Burgwyn, 1861-1865* (Shippensburg, PA, 1994), 16.

85 Longstreet, *From Manassas to Appomattox*, 201.

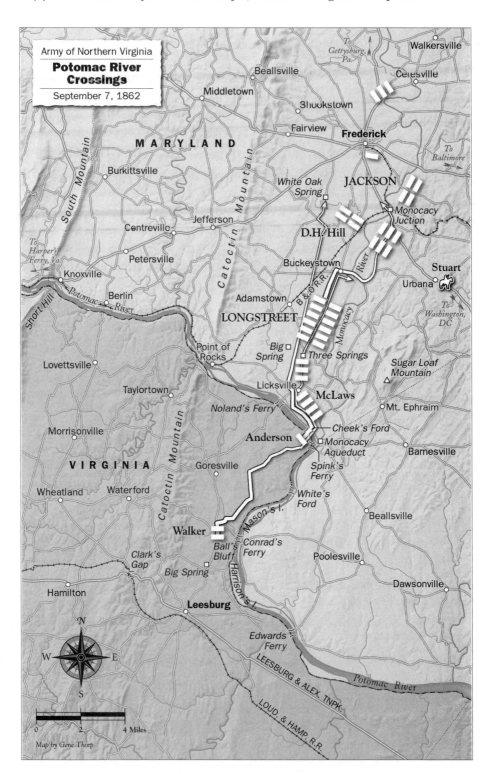

Army of Northern Virginia
**Potomac River
Crossings**
September 7, 1862

Map by Gene Thorp

either. It is assumed here for the sake of continuity that Lee had the South Carolinian cross the Potomac at White's Ford.

The various batteries of William Nelson Pendleton's Reserve Artillery brought up the rear of Lee's long column. Captain John J. Ancell's 2nd Fluvanna Artillery reached Leesburg ahead of Pendleton's other batteries on September 4. After being told to proceed to the old battlefield at Ball's Bluff, Ancell received orders "to fire upon anything or body we saw on the other side of the river." The artillerists took up a position on the heights, unlimbered their pieces, and opened on three boats plying the C&O Canal. "A half dozen [Federal] cavalrymen . . . seen riding along the towpath" also drew the gunners' attention before nightfall brought the action to an end.[86]

The balance of Pendleton's command, meanwhile, rumbled through Leesburg two days later on September 6 before camping at Big Spring in the wake of General Longstreet's command. Many of the batteries were broken down or in otherwise poor condition, so Pendleton undertook a rapid reorganization of them to weed out those that could not stand additional front line service. "The more depleted batteries, including Leake's Goochland, Stribling's Fauquier, Rogers' Loudoun, Fleet's Middlesex, Latham's Branch North Carolina, and Anderson's Thomas batteries, with all the animals of the artillery and train unfit for service," observed Jennings Wise in his classic study of the Army of Northern Virginia's artillery, "were ordered to be detained at Leesburg in command of Maj. Richardson, who was directed to proceed with them as soon as possible to the neighborhood of Winchester and establish there a remount depot and recruiting station for the Artillery."[87]

Pendleton also began the process of assigning artillery battalions to each of the infantry divisions in addition to providing a reserve battalion for each of the army's wings under Jackson and Longstreet. A general reserve remained in place for the entire army. "Each battalion, whether with the divisions or in the reserve, was to have its own field officer," noted Wise, with the battalions assigned to the divisions "under the command of the Division Chief of Artillery." Ultimately, much of this reorganization remained incomplete when Pendleton's command, with the

---

86 David G. Martin, *The Fluvanna Artillery* (Lynchburg, VA, 1992), 47.

87 Jennings C. Wise, *The Long Arm of Lee or The History of the Artillery of the Army of Northern Virginia* (Lynchburg, VA, 1915), 279. Also see Pendleton's report in OR 19, 1:829.

exception of the battalion under Maj. William Nelson, crosssed at White's Ford on the 7th.[88]

For most of the men in the Army of Northern Virginia, the crossing of the Potomac River into Maryland proved to be an exhilarating success. Not only had they made the journey unopposed; thus far many of the communities close to the river had received the arriving Rebels with kindness, generosity, and, in some cases, open arms. Hope in the ranks rose accordingly as the army moved northward with expectations of successfully recruiting thousands of fellow Southerners, and perhaps even sparking a popular uprising, in the Old Line State. "To us 'tis a day of deep and solemn feeling," commented a Maryland man serving in the Army of Northern Virginia:

> To the noble exiled Marylander tears alone can express the sentiment of the heart. We take our lives in our hands, sons of Virginia, and go into our sister State to lift the yoke from her neck. If her exiled children truly represent those left at home, let them be of good cheer, for their redemption and the redemption of Maryland draweth nigh. If not, your glory hath truly departed, and we can but leave you to hug the chains that bind thy once beautiful limbs. But we will not indulge such sad and unworthy suspicions. Already is thy great heart swelling and sending its hot currents to thy flashing eyes and unfettered limbs. Blessed be God, she comes! She comes! How auspicious the hour! All things are now ready. Go to the high altar of Liberty with your most precious offerings.[89]

Others shared the sentiment, being "considerably exercised" as to their destination. "We thought surely we were headed for Washington," recalled Mercer Otey of the Rockbridge Artillery, "and naturally were eager to make a dash for the capital." Along the way, the marching troops gorged themselves on the bounty of Maryland's farmland, collecting cattle and sheep, and plucking "young ears of corn" and green apples, which they fried in a pan with hardtack whenever possible to make "a delectable dish that all [of them] relished greatly."[90]

The rich territory of west-central Maryland and the route to Pennsylvania lay open before them, beckoning Lee's men to take revenge upon the hated Yankee

---

88 Wise, *The Long Arm*, 279; "On Sept. 7, Nelson's battalion received orders to cross the Potomac twelve miles above Leesburg." Martin, *The Fluvanna Artillery*, 48. Nelson's guns forded the river at Point of Rocks.

89 Anonymous letter dated Sept. 6, 1862, from a member of Parker's Richmond Battery, 2nd Battalion Longstreet's Reserve Artillery printed in the *Richmond Dispatch*, Sept. 17, 1862.

90 Otey, "The Story of Our Great War," 366.

enemy who had wreaked so much havoc in Virginia. Never before, and perhaps never again, would those in Lee's army believe themselves so close to winning the war and achieving the Confederacy's cherished dream of independence. Poised on the cusp of realizing John Ryder Randall's vision, the butternut legions surged "Forward . . . upon the soil of Maryland, wondering if she is now going to 'breathe and burn', 'Maryland, my Maryland!'"[91]

91 Owen, *In Camp and Battle*, 131.

THREE

FOUR DAYS ON THE MONOCACY

~~*~~

Confederate Encampments Near Frederick City and the Implications for the Lost Orders Debate

ONE of the Maryland Campaign's most enduring stories holds that once Robert E. Lee's Army of Northern Virginia reached the vicinity of Frederick City on September 6, 1862, it camped for four days on the grounds of John T. Best's rented farm along the Monocacy River. This axiom, passed down from scholar to scholar for more than 100 years, appears to have originated after the war from inexact descriptions penned by Confederate officers. Further research demonstrates that it is only partially true.

According to Jubal Early's January 1863 report, for example, "on the morning of the 6th [of September we] marched to the railroad bridge over the Monocacy, at the junction of the railroad to Frederick City with the Baltimore and Ohio Railroad, and took up a position so as to command the approaches on and adjacent to the railroad from the direction of Washington City."[1] He followed this up half-century later in his autobiography: "On the 6th we resumed the march and in the afternoon occupied Frederick City and the Monocacy Junction on the Baltimore & Ohio

1 OR 19, 1:966.

Railroad. Jackson's division took position near the city, and Hill's and Ewell's near the Junction, which is about three miles from the city in the direction of Washington. Ewell's division covered the railroad and the approaches from the direction of Baltimore, and Hill's those from the direction of Washington."[2]

Neither version mentioned Best's farm by name, but its proximity to Monocacy Junction has led scholars to conclude it must have been the place where Lee's troops camped. Artillerist William Owen seemed to confirm this in the 1880s when he described in his memoirs how his battery "encamped . . . in a beautiful grove of oaks" near the headquarters tents of Robert E. Lee, James Longstreet, and Thomas Jackson. The mention of oak trees pinpointed the location as Best's Grove, which stood on Best's farm. This was something first observed in the 1880s by Ezra Carman, whose massive (and at that time unpublished) history of the campaign appears to have been the first to mention the farm by name.[3]

Researchers since Carman have not deviated from this interpretation. Writing in the 1930s, Lee biographer Douglas Southall Freeman concluded, "Once in Maryland, Lee rode with the infantry straight for Frederick . . . His tents were pitched near those of Longstreet, in a beautiful grove of oaks." In the 1950s and '60s, Jackson biographer Lenoir Chambers and modern Maryland Campaign pioneer James V. Murfin offered similar descriptions.[4]

It is only in recent decades that nuances in our understanding of the Rebel army's positions began to appear in the work of Joseph Harsh and D. Scott Hartwig. Harsh clarified, among other things, that the division Jackson had previously commanded actually camped north of Frederick City and not on the

---

2 Early, *Autobiographical Sketch*, 135.

3 Owen, *In Camp and Battle*, 131-132; "Jackson's old division went into camp on Best's farm." Carman, *The Maryland Campaign*, 1:93. Histories of the campaign before Carman rarely stated with any detail where Lee's army camped. For example, see Edward A. Pollard, *The Lost Cause: A New Southern History of the War of the Confederates* (New York, NY, 1866), 311, John Esten Cooke, *Stonewall Jackson: A Military Biography* (New York, NY, 1866), 309, and Comte de Paris, *History of the Civil War in America*, 2:311. Of all the early researchers, the Comte de Paris offered the most accurate account, explaining that "Jackson occupied the right bank of this river (i.e., the Monocacy) with his three divisions, so as to cover the march of the army against any attack which might come from Washington or Baltimore." He erred, however, when he claimed, "On the 8th the whole army was drawn up on the left bank of the Potomac."

4 Freeman, *Robert E. Lee*, 2:355. Freeman added more precision to his description some years later, writing that Lee, Longstreet, and Jackson "pitched their tents . . . in Best's Grove." Douglas Southall Freeman, *Lee's Lieutenants: A Study in Command*, 3 vols. (New York, NY, 1943), 2:154; Chambers, *Stonewall Jackson,* 183-184, and Murfin, *Gleam*, 101-102.

farm itself, while Hartwig added that Lafayette McLaws's division approached Monocacy Junction from the southeast via the road to Georgetown and not due south on the road from Buckeystown. Their valuable contributions notwithstanding, even these esteemed students of the campaign retained Best's farm as the spot where most of Lee's army rested during its time near Frederick.[5]

This ongoing focus on the farm has shaped the debate about the loss of Lee's Special Orders No. 191. Why, for example, would an errant copy of the orders have been found southeast of Frederick if the bulk of the Confederate army had not camped between the city and Lee's headquarters at Best's Grove? The case for Best's farm seemed closed, but to date no researcher has delved into the sources to identify more precisely where Lee's various brigades and divisions actually camped. Research demonstrates that for the four days it lay sprawled near Frederick City, the Army of Northern Virginia occupied a much wider geographic area than has been recognized. Best's farm was at the center of this area, but it did not run northwest toward Frederick itself. Rather, most of Lee's troops camped in an elongated crescent stretching from the Baltimore Pike east of the Monocacy River to Buckeystown in the south and, finally, to the large farm in the southwest at White Oak Springs near Ballenger Creek.[6]

After crossing the Potomac River on September 4-5, the commands of Stonewall Jackson and Daniel Harvey Hill approached Frederick City from two directions on September 6. Both commands had formed a single column after camping near Three Springs, Maryland, on the night of September 5. Then Jackson's men, consisting of three infantry divisions, split off from Hill's division at Buckeystown to cross to the eastern side of the Monocacy River. Correspondents with the *Philadelphia Inquirer* quickly caught wind of this movement and reported two days later that "Part of the Rebel force turned off at Buckeystown, as if going either toward the Washington road or the Baltimore pike."[7]

Jackson's men traversed the Monocacy on an obscure road south of what is today known as Fingerboard Road and either turned his column north along present day Baker Valley Road to the Georgetown Pike, or veered farther east to Urbana before turning back up the pike toward Frederick. The evidence is not clear

---

5 Harsh, *Taken*, 102; Hartwig, *To Antietam Creek*, 112.

6 Locals referred to the waterway as "Ballenger's Creek" in 1862. I have chosen to use the modern form of the name.

7 *Philadelphia Inquirer*, Sept. 8, 1862.

which route he took. Jackson's topographer, Jedediah Hotchkiss, explained in his diary why the general chose a circuitous path to Monocacy Junction: "We marched on towards Frederick City by the way of Monocacy Bridge to cut off the enemy's retreat." This shift to the east did not escape the watchful eyes of local informants, one of whom promptly reported to Union Maj. Gen. John E. Wool, commander of the Eighth Corps in Baltimore, that "the enemy were advancing to Frederick in large force, by the Georgetown road, and that 5,000 [men] had then passed, and still more following, as far as they could see."[8]

The first elements of Jackson's command, mounted troops with Capt. Lige White's border cavalry, arrived at the Monocacy Junction telegraph station about 4:00 a.m. on September 6. These outriders, according to the *Baltimore American*, "cut the telegraph wires and removed the instruments, seized the operator and took him off" with them. Six hours later, William Starke's division (also known as Jackson's old division), led by the Second Brigade under Col. Bradley Johnson, halted south of Frederick City while Lt. Henry Kyd Douglas rode ahead on Jackson's orders to locate a "suitable camp beyond the city." According to the report of U.S. Sanitary Service officer Lewis Steiner, a Frederick resident and hostile witness to these events, "at ten o'clock Jackson's advance force, consisting of some five thousand men, marched up Market street."[9]

8 McDonald, ed., *Make Me a Map of the Valley*, 79. Few Federal troops occupied Frederick and its environs at the time. These included the 14th New Jersey, which guarded the B&O bridge over the Monocacy, and several companies from the 1st Potomac Home Brigade, commanded by Capt. William T. Faithful. The Marylanders departed from Frederick one day before the arrival of Jackson's troops, while Col. William S. Truex evacuated his New Jersey regiment from Monocacy Junction at 3:00 a.m. on Sept. 6. *The Cecil Whig*, Sept. 13, 1862, and J. Newton Terrill, *Campaign of the Fourteenth Regiment New Jersey Volunteers* (New Brunswick, NJ, 1884), 8; OR 19, 2:198.

9 Jackson wrote in his campaign report that he did not have "any cavalry with me except the Black Horse, under Captain Randolph." This is not entirely true. See, for example, OR 19, 1:951. D. H. Hill confirmed after the war that a company of horse under Capt. Lige White rode in the vanguard. "I rode forward and joined Captain White's scouts, and together, we crossed the bridge over the Monocacy, and went first to the telegraph office." Hill, "The Lost Dispatch," 274. Hill's mention of crossing the Monocacy suggests he traveled back and forth between Jackson's command and his own. *Baltimore American* report reprinted in the *Alexandria Gazette*, Sept. 8, 1862; Otey, "The Story of Our Great War," 366. "A few days after fording the Potomac our column reached Frederick City. About half a mile from that place the column was halted and 'Old Jack' sent forward his inspector general, Col. Kidd Douglass, to select suitable camp beyond the city." As a brigadier, Starke was the ranking officer in the division until John R. Jones returned to command on Sept. 7; *Steiner Report*, 8.

Reports from Starke's men place their bivouac around Worman's Woods, about two miles north of Frederick City.[10] Colonel Johnson's brigade served as the lone exception, occupying Frederick proper as the army's provost guard.[11] Johnson quartered his men at the old Hessian Barracks and former Agricultural Society of Frederick County fairgrounds on the south end of Market Street, a logical place given the space available there and the fact that the posting enabled provost troops to control a major access route into town. Starke's remaining three brigades and divisional artillery straddled the Liberty Turnpike north of town in what appears to have been a strategic placement on Jackson's part, given that they covered the northeastern approach to Frederick from behind a large bend in the Monocacy River.[12]

The balance of Jackson's command—Richard S. Ewell's division under Brig. Gen. Alexander R. Lawton after Ewell's wounding at Second Manassas, and Ambrose Powell Hill's division, commanded by Brig. Gen. Lawrence O'Bryan Branch due to Hill's arrest by Jackson on September 4—camped several miles southeast of Frederick on the east side of the Monocacy. Neither division entered Frederick itself until the army began its march toward Hagerstown on September 10. As Jackson noted in his campaign report the following spring, "Ewell's and

10 Major Hazael Joseph Williams of the 5th Virginia Infantry with Winder's brigade, then under the command of Col. Arnold Grigsby, noted in his official report on the campaign "entered Frederick September 7, and encamped about two miles from the city, on the Emmittsburg road." The actual date of entry into Frederick was Sept. 6. Robert J. Driver, Jr., & Kevin C. Ruffner, *1st Battalion Virginia Infantry, 39th Battalion Virginia Cavalry, and 24th Battalion Virginia Partisan Rangers* (Lynchburg, VA, 1996), 28, recalled something similar: "The command passed through Frederick and camped in the woods north of town." See also, John D. Chapla, *42nd Virginia Infantry* (Lynchburg, VA, 1983), 25: "Col. Johnson led the brigade to Worman's Woods, just north of Frederick, Maryland."

11 *OR* 19, 1:1006-07. Johnson named Lt. Lewis Randolph as town provost marshal during the occupation. Driver & Ruffner, *1st Battalion Virginia Infantry*, 28, and Chapla, *42nd Virginia Infantry*, 25.

12 Worsham, *One of Jackson's Foot Cavalry*, 138. "Soon afterwards we entered Frederick City, many of the men having watermelons in their arms. We marched to the Fair Grounds, which had been fitted up as a large hospital for the enemy. Our brigade stacked arms, and were told to make themselves comfortable for the night." The *Baltimore American* reported, "At 10 o'clock at night the men were all ordered to their camps on the outskirts of the city." *Baltimore American* reprinted in the *Alexandria Gazette*, Sept. 8, 1862. The only fairgrounds in Frederick at the time were those of the Agricultural Club of Frederick County near the Hessian Barracks. The Frederick Agricultural Society established new fairgrounds on East Patrick Street in June 1866. Terry Reimer, *One Vast Hospital: The Civil War Hospital Sites in Frederick, Maryland, after Antietam* (Frederick, MD, 2001), 36.

Hill's divisions occupied positions near the railroad bridge over the Monocacy, guarding the approaches from Washington City."[13]

An entry in the diary of Samuel Hoey Walkup, a colonel with the 48th North Carolina, put these troops at a location "4 miles East of Frederick," which generally agreed with an article in the *Washington Republican* newspaper containing information received from a civilian witness who had recently passed by the Confederate encampment. Although this source claimed erroneously that "Longstreet's division . . . consists of thirty to fifty thousand" men, the informant did note that the Confederates camped "at Ijamsville," east of the Monocacy. Lewis Steiner also learned from local sources that "The main body of rebel troops is said to be encamped about Urbana," indicating how rumors spread through Frederick of Confederates positioned east of the Monocacy River.[14]

Those men of Lawton's (Ewell's) division who wrote about it recalled camping within sight of the Monocacy rail bridge. Captain Samuel Buck, serving with the 13th Virginia, a regiment of Early's Brigade, recorded in his memoir that "September 6th found us near Frederick City, and camped at Monocacy Bridge where we were in line waiting for the enemy who were expected from the direction of Washington."[15]

Buck's memory echoed that of Henry Thomas, a soldier with the 12th Georgia, also of Lawton's division, who noted, "On the morning of the 6th [we] marched to the railroad bridge over the Monocacy at the junction of the railroad to Frederick City with the Baltimore and Ohio Railroad. We remained in this position until the morning of the 10th."[16]

These accounts clarify the campaign report of Jubal Early mentioned earlier: "On the morning of the 6th [the division] marched to the railroad bridge over the Monocacy, at the junction of the railroad to Frederick City with the Baltimore and Ohio Railroad, and took up a position so as to command the approaches on and

---

13 McDonald, ed., *Make Me a Map of the Valley*, 79. Colonel George Dennis in Gettysburg communicated to Maj. Gen. Wool in Baltimore on Sept. 7 that, "Brig. Gen. B. [T.] Johnson, with 5,000 infantry, came into Frederick about 12m. yesterday. General Jackson followed with 25,000 at 2.30 p.m. Three batteries of artillery only were seen. Johnson's brigade encamped a mile north of the city; his troops much jaded. He said he would be there only one day . . . Johnson came into Frederick over Georgetown Bridge, 3 miles south of Frederick." OR 19, 2:205; OR 19, 1:952.

14 *Steiner Report*, 11.

15 Buck, *With the Old Confeds*, 60.

16 Henry W. Thomas, *History of the Doles-Cook Brigade* (Atlanta, GA, 1903), 221.

adjacent to the railroad from the direction of Washington City." Lastly, William McClendon, a man with the 15th Alabama, pinpointed the location of Lawton's brigade "on the east side, or the Washington side, of the river opposite the town. Our camp was near the railroad and wagon bridges that spanned the Monocacy at this place."[17]

These sources make it clear that Lawton's men camped north of the Georgetown Pike to keep an eye on the Baltimore Pike, five miles down which a brigade of Jeb Stuart's cavalry under Fitzhugh Lee operated at New Market. The testimony of the civilian informant in the *Washington Republican* also reveals that thousands of Confederate troops camped west of Ijamsville. Additionally, Lt. Col. Sam Walkup confided to his diary that on September 8 his regiment marched to the encampment of Jackson's men east of the Monocacy river, but "in sight of Frederick, Md."[18]

Taken together, this evidence suggests that statements long read to indicate Jackson's command camped on the west side of the river have been incorrectly interpreted. Indeed, to an experienced military man like Jackson, defending the approaches to Frederick from ground west of the Monocacy would have made little sense because the terrain there is lower in elevation and would have been subject to plunging artillery fire if Federal troops occupied the heights to the east. Jackson recognized this vulnerability and accordingly posted Lawton's division to mitigate it.

General Branch's division also camped east of the Monocacy, although none of the accounts found to date provide details about the location. The reminiscence of Rev. Wayland Dunaway, a captain in the 40th Virginia, for example, mentions only that "From the Potomac the march was continued to the Monocacy river, near Frederick City." The lack of detail is puzzling given how many men from Lawton's division and Longstreet's command commented on the large B&O rail bridge at Monocacy Junction. It may be that Branch's men could not see the bridge, which is a possibility if they camped behind the hillside that rises west of the road they took to the Georgetown Pike. Stonewall Jackson noted in his April 1863 report that

17 McClendon, *Recollections of War Times*, 129.

18 Walkup Diary, Sept. 9, 1862.

Branch's men guarded the approach from Washington, something echoed by Jubal Early.[19]

There is also the location of Maj. Gen. Ambrose Powell Hill's headquarters to consider. Hill had been traveling at the rear of his column during its trek to Frederick since his arrest in northern Virginia after clashing with Jackson about the pace of his division's march. Once his men reached the Monocacy Bridge and went into camp, Hill found quarters along the Georgetown Pike in the house of a man named James Montgomery, Sr., about halfway between the river and Urbana, Maryland. If Hill had been in command of his division, he likely would have established his headquarters closer to the bulk of his men. Instead, he remained at the back of the column well down the road to the southeast. The evidence shows that none of Jackson's men camped on Best's farm where the general made his headquarters. Lawton's and Branch's divisions bivouacked four or five miles from Frederick City, compared to the two-mile distance of Starke's men. All of them remained in place until departing on the morning of Wednesday, September 10, in accordance with General Lee's Special Orders No. 191.[20]

Unlike Jackson's advance from the southeast, the elements of Maj. Gen. D. H. Hill's division traveled due north toward Frederick via the road from Buckeystown, a route topographer Jed Hotchkiss referred to in his diary as marching "on the left" of the Monocacy. The vanguard of D. H. Hill's march seems to have had a supply-gathering aspect to it. Reports of these activities first reached Frederick on the evening of September 5 when "a party of Confederate cavalry and artillery were [seen] at White Oak Springs . . . collecting cattle and sheep from the farmers of the surrounding country." They paid for the animals with "Virginia and South Carolina money and United States Treasury notes at a fair valuation, [and told] people that they came as friends, and not as enemies." Their identity is not difficult to establish. In an 1868 article published by D. H. Hill in *The Land We Love*, the general wrote

19 Folsom, *Heroes and Martyrs of Georgia*, 151, comes the closest by mentioning how the column "marched to Monocacy bridge, near Frederick City, Maryland." Dunaway, *Reminiscences*, 48-49. Readers will note that Dunaway did not write his regiment crossed over the Monocacy; *OR* 19, 1:966: "Ewell's division covered the railroad and the approaches from the direction of Baltimore . . . Hill's those from the direction of Washington." See also, Early, *Autobiographical Sketch*, 135; "A. P. Hill is again under arrest. . . . He marches at the rear of his Division." Graham T. Dozier, ed., *A Gunner in Lee's Army: The Civil War Letters of Thomas Henry Carter* (Chapel Hill, NC, 2014), 137.

20 Distances have been calculated from the intersection of Patrick and Market streets in Frederick to the vicinities of Worman's Mill, the Monocacy River crossing on the Old National Pike, and the Monocacy National Battlefield.

that Jackson summoned him on September 5, and Hill "found [the general] at the head of his division examining a map held by Captain E. V. White."[21]

A Maryland man whose family owned the land in Virginia along the Potomac where White's Ford is located, Tige White led a unit that entered Maryland with Jackson. Federal eyewitnesses described the first rider to arrive in Frederick on the morning of September 6 as a "horseman clad in butternut." This man told the Officer of the Day at U.S. General Hospital #1 that "he belonged to White's company of border cavalry, and was the advance of Lee's army that would soon be up." Upon reaching the vicinity of Frederick, this trooper and his comrades fanned out in all directions, spending the next few days securing "droves of sheep, hogs, beeves, cow, and horses" for the army, which they herded back toward the Potomac on the same road that D. H. Hill's men had used for their advance.[22]

General Hill's command, which consisted of five infantry brigades, approached the city behind White's cavalry. Hill noted in his post-campaign report that he "marched into Frederick," but the evidence does not support this unless he was referring only to himself and his command staff or to some unnamed portion of his division. The sources instead point to Hill's command spreading out from White Oak Springs, southwest of Frederick, to the eastern end of Ballenger Creek where it empties into the Monocacy—and perhaps even as far south as Buckeystown. John Tucker, an officer with the 5th Alabama, part of Robert Rodes's brigade, attested to these arrangements. Tucker recalled that on September 6, his regiment stopped within "4 ms (miles) of the Town," which puts it in the vicinity of Ballenger Creek. Tucker rode into town soon thereafter, where he got "dinner on the way side at 2$ and a very good one at that." According to Jim Folsom of the 28th Georgia, the mixed Alabama and Georgia brigade of Col. Alfred Holt Colquitt followed Rodes's troops into place along the creek. After stopping "within four miles of Frederick City" once they had marched from the vicinity of "Buckeyetown, Maryland," Folsom explained that "the regiment pitched camp and remained until the 12th."[23]

---

21 McDonald, ed., *Make Me a Map of the Valley*, 79; *Baltimore American*, quoted in the *Alexandria Gazette*, Sept. 8, 1862; Hill, "The Lost Dispatch," 274.

22 *Baltimore American*, quoted in the *Alexandria Gazette*, Sept. 8, 1862.

23 *OR* 19, 1:1019; Wilson, ed. "The Diary of John S. Tucker," 19; Folsom, *Heroes and Martyrs of Georgia*, 55. Folsom remembered the departure date incorrectly. Hill's entire command, except for Anderson's brigade, left the Frederick area by late in the day on Sept. 10.

Brigadier General George B. Anderson's North Carolina brigade took a more circuitous route to its bivouac. "We crossed the Balt & O rail and camped in a fine grove for the night, near a very large spring of good water," recalled James Shinn in his diary, describing a location that sounded very much like the farm at White Oak Springs. That the grove of trees referred to by Shinn was likely White Oak Springs and not the grove on Best's farm can be deduced by several points. The first is a report that appeared in the *New Albany Weekly Ledger* on September 10 that "The rebels . . . crossed between the ferries, above the Point of Rocks, and marched to White Oak Springs," which describes the line of march taken by Anderson's brigade.[24]

Second, Confederate artillery and outriders were reported camping at the springs as early as September 5. If Lige White's troopers knew about the place, it is more than likely that they informed General Hill so that a portion of his division could take advantage of the plentiful fresh water there. Shinn also left a description of the place that matched details provided years later in the local newspaper. "One of the best-known farms in Frederick county," boasted the *Frederick News Post*, was White Oak Springs, which consisted of 142 acres covered by white oak trees and thirteen springs of fresh water. Shinn wrote about camping for the night "in a fine grove . . . near a very large spring of good water." No record has been found of a spring of equal size at Best's Grove, and more than enough Confederate officers and men sojourned at Best's Grove for one of them to have noted the presence of a large spring had one existed. Even today there is no sign of a fresh water spring where Best's Grove once stood.[25]

Finally, there is Shinn's diary entry from September 8. "We lay in camp after being aroused very early, until nearly 10 a.m. expecting to march every minute," wrote the private. "At the above . . . hour the drums rolled and soon the shouts of mules sounded through the grove. The line of march was soon formed and we learned that we would only march about 3 miles to camp with the division, who had been resting there a day or two." Shinn's statement confirms that Anderson's brigade camped in isolation from the rest of D. H. Hill's division, which Shinn took to have bivouacked several miles away. He noted that once they got underway, he and his comrades "crossed the [B&O] railway and also the Big Monocrisy on the

24 Shinn Diary, Sept. 6, 1862; *New Albany Weekly Ledger*, Sept. 10, 1862.

25 *Frederick News Post*, Jul. 7, 1923; Shinn Diary, Sept. 6, 1862; Williams and McKinsey, *History of Frederick County*, 2:175.

turn pike bridge about where the railway crossed. By 2 ½ o'clock we camped in a beautiful grove of chestnuts on a high ridge."[26]

The distance from Best's Grove to the high ground east of the Monocacy River is less than two miles, but George Anderson's brigade marched three miles to reach its new bivouac, a strong indication that the men of his command had stayed at a fine grove and large spring farther away than the Best farm. Only White Oak Springs fits both the description of the grove, the spring, and the distance away from the heights east of the Monocacy River. James Shinn assumed that he and his comrades would remain in place east of the Monocacy for several days, and orders they received on September 9 to "wash their clothes and bathe" in the river seemed to confirm this. On September 10, however, "revile at day light . . . [brought] with it an order to be ready to march by seven. By the appointed hour we had formed line of march but soon found that everybody and thing had been ordered to move at the same time. The road was cramed and jamed and by 12 we had marched 2 ½ miles and halted." Shinn and his comrades had encountered the columns of Jackson's and Longstreet's commands taking to the road in accordance with Special Orders No. 191.[27]

The three divisions under Longstreet moved out behind Jackson's 20,000 men, guns, and wagons up the Georgetown Pike through Frederick City, along with the unattached commands of Lafayette McLaws and Nathan 'Shanks' Evans. McLaws's division entered the long procession after Longstreet's troops. They made little progress. According to Capt. Henry King's diary entry on September 10, he was "up early, [and] found the way as far as I could see blocked with troops, artillery & wagons."[28]

McLaws's division "moved out but had to halt" when it met "[D. H.] Hill's waggon train &c" coming up from the road to Buckeystown. We "went up to the [toll] gate and back," observed King, indicating that the column had made it as far as the intersection of the Georgetown Pike and Buckeystown Road south of Frederick. Then, "at last [the] column moved," with Paul J. Semmes's brigade bringing up the rear of McLaws's command as it finally passed through Frederick City around 4:30 p.m. George Anderson's brigade brought up the rear of the Confederate army as it departed the vicinity of Frederick, but in the enormous

26 Shinn Diary, Sept. 8, 1862.

27 Ibid., Sept. 10, 1862; *OR* 19, 2:604.

28 Trimpi, ed., "Lafayette McLaws' Aide-de-Camp," 31.

traffic jam that ensued Anderson's men marched only a short distance before stopping "in a field of wood" on the Georgetown Pike (possibly Best's Grove) until they could proceed early the next day.[29]

The Reserve Artillery, as specified by Special Orders No. 191, marched ahead of D. H. Hill and also made slow progress. "Were all day in traveling one mile owing to bad Generalship," James Blackshear of the Sumter Artillery complained to his diary, " . . . & in my opinion that somebody was Gen. Lee." Blackshear and his comrades "Encamped one mile from Frederick City."[30]

To those versed in the minutiae of the campaign, the September 8 date of Anderson's move might appear curious. Special Orders No. 191 was issued on September 9 and designated D. H. Hill's division as "the rearguard of the army" for its march from Frederick to Boonsboro. A close examination of the copy found by men of the 27th Indiana, however, indicates its original date may have been September 8. The writer of those orders, presumably Col. Robert H. Chilton, crossed out the "8" and replaced it with a "9." Anderson's brigade was shifted east of the Monocacy on the 8th, where it could take position at the army's rear, suggesting D. H. Hill knew about the impending operation against Harpers Ferry one day before the official date of the written orders Lee addressed to him.[31]

There were two remaining two brigades in Hill's division, one under Samuel Garland and the other under Roswell Ripley. The location of Garland's encampment remains a mystery because of a lack of sources pinpointing the location. Even the duration of Garland's stay near Frederick is open to question. Adjutant N. S. Smith of the 13th North Carolina recalled only that the brigade "crossed the Potomac at Point of Rocks . . . [and] marched to Frederick City, Md., where we camped for a day or two. After battering down a stone bridge across the Monocacy River we marched through Frederick City." Mention of the rail bridge suggests Garland's men may have stayed near the Best farm or, instead, that they

---

29 Shinn Diary, Sept. 11, 1862. The names noted are found on the 1858 Isaac Bond Map of Frederick County approximately two miles from Monocacy Junction. Shinn recorded a number of residences near him: "[we] halted in a field of wood near and thickly settled but the dwellings all shut up and the folks all invisible."

30 Diary of James Appleton Blackshear, Sept. 10, 1862. Manuscript Collection No. 302, Stuart A. Rose Manuscript, Archives, and Rare Book Library, Emory University.

31 Stotelmyer, *Too Useful to Sacrifice*, 28, also discusses McClellan's copy of Special Orders No. 191.

may have moved east of the Monocacy along with Anderson's men. Unfortunately, there is at present no way of confirming either scenario.[32]

The little evidence for Ripley's line of march and bivouac must be untangled from the murky entries of a diary written by Pvt. Calvin Leach. A member of the 1st North Carolina, Leach recorded catching up with his regiment in the dark on September 6 after it had crossed into Maryland. We do not know where Leach found his comrades. If we assume Ripley's brigade traveled with the others of Hill's division, it had probably at least reached the vicinity of Buckeystown six miles from Frederick. Leach and the others rested in place for the next two days before receiving orders on September 9 to march an additional three miles to a new but as yet unidentified location.[33]

The following scenario is speculative, but if Ripley's brigade halted near Buckeystown for two days, it could have been because Hill had assigned it to guard the local bridge over the Monocacy. After all, this position fit well with Jackson's defensive posture covering the Liberty Turnpike north of Frederick and the Baltimore Pike and Georgetown Pike east-southeast of Frederick.[34]

Once the brigade received its September 9 orders to come up and join the rest of the division, the three-mile march from Buckeystown would have put Ripley near Ballenger Creek—precisely where Colquitt's and Rodes's brigades camped. This course of events also makes sense in light of the orders Anderson received on September 9 because it suggests Hill called on Ripley to abandon his position guarding the Buckeystown crossing once he knew General Lee had ordered the army to march the following day. The one thing that seems certain from Private Leach's diary is that Ripley's brigade did not enter Frederick City before Hill's command, with the exception of G. B. Anderson's brigade, which marched through early in the day on September 11.

---

32 N. S. Smith, "Additional Sketch Thirteenth Regiment," Clark, ed., *Histories of the Several Regiments and Battalions from North Carolina*, 1:694.

33 "We left and marched some 3 miles and lay down to rest." Leach Diary, Sept. 9, 1862.

34 Even Randolph Shotwell of Richard Garnett's brigade thought it Lee's intention to defend the line of the Monocacy: "After crossing the Potomac the Army marched northwestwardly along the river and canal to the line of Monocacy river, which General Lee proposed using as a line of defence if promptly followed and attacked by the Federals." Hamilton, ed., *The Papers of Randolph Abbott Shotwell*, 1:310. See also, Blackford, *War Years with Jeb Stuart*, 140: "Our infantry occupied Frederick, eight miles to the west, with a line extending north and south so as to serve as a cushion against any sudden attack from Washington and thus allow the infantry time to prepare for action."

(Confidential)

Hd Qrs Army of Northern Va
Sept 9th 1862

Special Orders }
No. 191   }

III. The army will resume its march to-morrow taking the Hagerstown road. Gen Jackson's Command will form the advance and after passing Middleton with such portion as he may select take the route towards Sharpsburg. Cross the Potomac at the most convenient point & by Friday morning take possession of the Baltimore & Ohio R.R.; capture such of the enemy as may be at Martinsburg and intercept such as may attempt to escape from Harpers Ferry

IV. Gen Longstreet's command will pursue the main road as far as Boonsboro where it will halt, with reserve supply and baggage trains of the army

V. Gen McLaws with his own division and that of Gen R.H. Anderson will follow Gen Longstreet. on reaching Middleton will take the route to Harpers Ferry and by Friday morning possess himself of the Maryland Heights and Endeavor to capture the enemy at Harpers Ferry and vicinity

VI. Gen Walker with his division

Special Orders No. 191 with crossed-out date.

The final piece of the puzzle swirls around D. H. Hill and is the most vexing: where was his headquarters? Some reports place him in town, while others suggest he camped outside Frederick. It is possible both are correct.

Contemporary newspapers reported that after entering Frederick and establishing a provost marshal's office, Col. Bradley Johnson ordered the Council Street mansion of Union Brig. Gen. James Cooper "taken for his head Quarters." Rebel troops seized the house and placed it under guard, "but for reasons that have not transpired, [Johnson] did not occupy it." A local diarist also noted the confiscation of the house, but clarified that while "General James Cooper's house has been taken," it was "as headquarters" for the Confederate army in town.[35]

If Cooper's house was the army's city headquarters, who occupied it? According to the *Baltimore American*, "Most of the [Rebel] officers were quartered at the hotels and at the houses of prominent men. It is said, though we cannot vouch for the fact, that the house of General Cooper was taken possession of on Saturday night for the headquarters of General Jackson." This claim is demonstrably false because reliable sources put Jackson's headquarters near Best's Grove. It does, however, suggest that a senior officer took up residence for a time in Cooper's house. According to the statement of a man who had been in Frederick until Saturday, September 6, reported *The Cecil Whig*, the occupant was none other than Daniel Harvey Hill. "General Jackson was not in the city," clarified the *Whig*, dispelling the earlier rumors about Old Jack. "All the troops there [were instead] under command of General Hill, who occupied the house of General Cooper as his headquarters." This claim echoed an account printed on September 10 by the *New Albany Weekly Ledger*: "Fugitives who left Frederick City . . . report the city occupied by about 5,000 rebels under Gen. Hill."[36]

35 *Frederick Examiner*, Sept. 24, 1862, diary entry printed in the newspaper. Johnson probably did not stay in the Cooper house because his own family home stood only a short distance away on the southeast corner of Public (Court) and Second streets. N. Mahony Williams, *Frederick Directory, City Guide, and Business Mirror*, Vol. 1 (Frederick, MD, 1859), 1:67; William R. Quynn, ed., *The Diary of Jacob Engelbrecht, 1840-1882*, 3 Vols. (Frederick, MD, 2001), 3:179.

36 *Baltimore American*, reprinted in the *Alexandria Gazette*, Sept. 8, 1862. The *New York Herald* reported the same rumor, as quoted in the *Richmond Enquirer* on Sept. 16, 1862; *The Cecil Whig*, Sept. 13, 1862; *New Albany Weekly Ledger*, Wednesday, Sept. 10, 1862. The *Ledger* was published in New Albany, Indiana. See also, Hill, "The Lost Dispatch," 274: "I [Hill] rode forward and joined Captain White's scouts, and together, we crossed the bridge over the Monocacy, and went first to the telegraph office [at Monocacy Junction]. For the next two or three days, we drew all our supplies and received all our orders through General Jackson." Hill may have spent a night or two at the mansion of Gen. Cooper, but statements naming him as commander of Confederate forces in Frederick City were erroneous.

Hill taking temporary quarters in a Frederick townhouse is not that far-fetched. His 1862 Maryland Campaign report implies the possibility: "The night of the 5th, my division followed General Jackson to within a few miles of Frederick. The general being disabled by the fall of his horse, the next morning I was placed in charge of all the forces, and marched into Frederick." So according to Hill, he marched his division "to within a few miles of Frederick" and personally entered Frederick. Before he filed his official report, Jed Hotchkiss wrote a letter to his wife that on September 6, Hill "went on to Frederick City, which he found evacuated."[37]

Hill reiterated this point in 1868 when he wrote that he rode into town ahead of Starke's (Jackson's) division. Just a few days earlier the division had numbered about 5,500 men, which reasonably matches the size ("about 5,000 rebels") reported by the *New Albany Weekly Ledger*. Bradley Johnson was more familiar with Frederick than was Hill, and he either knew in advance or learned from local sympathizers that Cooper's mansion was vacant and ordered it seized for the army's use. Hill was the senior officer in Frederick, so it would have made sense for Rebel soldiers and local gossips to assume he commanded both the column that had just passed through town and the provost troops posted in Frederick proper. There is also the curious claim made by the Comte de Paris in the mid-1870s to consider. According to the French officer and former Union general, "On [McClellan's] arrival at Frederick on the morning of the 13th, a scrap of paper picked up from the corner of a table *in the house which had served as headquarters to the Confederate D. H. Hill* [emphasis added] was placed in his hands." This story is clearly incorrect in terms of where Federal troops found the errant copy of Special Orders No. 191, but it does repeat the claim that Hill had used a house in Frederick City as his headquarters.[38]

Unfortunately, this is not the only scenario concerning D. H. Hill's bivouac. There is also evidence that Hill maintained a field headquarters close to his command. Decades after the war Hill wrote to Rev. J. William Jones, the secretary of the Southern Historical Society, in an effort to defend himself against accusations that he was the man who lost Lee's orders: "There are many still living

---

37 OR 19, 1:1019. Jackson's topographer, Jed Hotchkiss, explained Stonewall's injury by noting the general "was thrown from his new horse, in the morning, and considerably hurt; so much so that he gave up the command, for awhile." McDonald, ed., *Make Me a Map of the Valley*, 79; Hotchkiss Letters, Sept. 8, 1862.

38 Sept. 2, 1862, roll call returns for William Starke's division totaled 5,578 men. Hartwig, *To Antietam Creek*, 679; Comte de Paris, *History of the Civil War in America*, 2:318.

who know that I occupied a tent, not a house, outside of Frederick." Hill's claim, written nearly three decades after the event, agrees with a comment made in 1893 by Alphonso Calhoun Avery, D. H. Hill's brother-in-law and a Supreme Court Justice of North Carolina, claiming that "Lee and Hill were encamped in sight of each other near Frederick-town."[39]

If this was the case, where might Hill have camped? There is no record that he camped at or near Best's Grove, where Lee had his headquarters. If Hill had camped there someone would have known about it and noted the fact in either an official document or some other source. As it is, no one did. In his essay on Special Orders No. 191, Wilbur D. Jones mentions a theory held by the staff of the Frederick Historical Society that D. H. Hill located his field headquarters on the farm of George Markell along the Buckeystown Road. Markell's house was close to the confirmed Ballenger Creek positions of Rodes's and Colquitt's brigades, so this is a plausible location.[40] We also know from the September 7, 1862, letter of Capt. Thomas H. Carter, commander of the King William Artillery, that his battery camped "3 ¾ miles from Fredericktown." That was almost exactly the distance of Markell's farm from the town's center, which suggests that Hill's divisional artillery also rested near Ballenger Creek.[41]

In addition, Capt. Henry King of McLaws's staff recorded in his diary that he met Generals Hill and D. R. Jones at Hill's headquarters after King arrived there from Buckeystown.[42] Finally, it is worth noting that in September 1862, the Best farm and Markell house both stood less than one mile apart on the flood plain west of the Monocacy River. This ground, flat and cleared for agricultural cultivation, may have offered the clear line of sight from Hill's to Lee's headquarters described by Judge Avery.

39 "The Lost Dispatch—Letter from General D. H. Hill, Jan. 22, 1885," *SHSP* (1885), 13:421; A. C. Avery, "On the Life and Character of Lieut.-General D. H. Hill," *SHSP* (1893), 21:136. Avery was serving as a captain in the 6th North Carolina in September 1862, part of Evander Law's brigade in John Bell Hood's division, which was attached to James Longstreet's command. Avery was promoted to major and transferred to D. H. Hill's staff in December of 1862.

40 Wilbur D. Jones, Jr., "Who Lost the Lost Orders? Stonewall Jackson, His Courier, and Special Orders No. 191," in *Civil War Regiments: A Journal of the American Civil War*, Vol. 5, No. 3 (1997), 10.

41 Dozier, *A Gunner in Lee's Army*, 138.

42 Trimpi, ed., "Lafayette McLaws' Aide-de-Camp," 30.

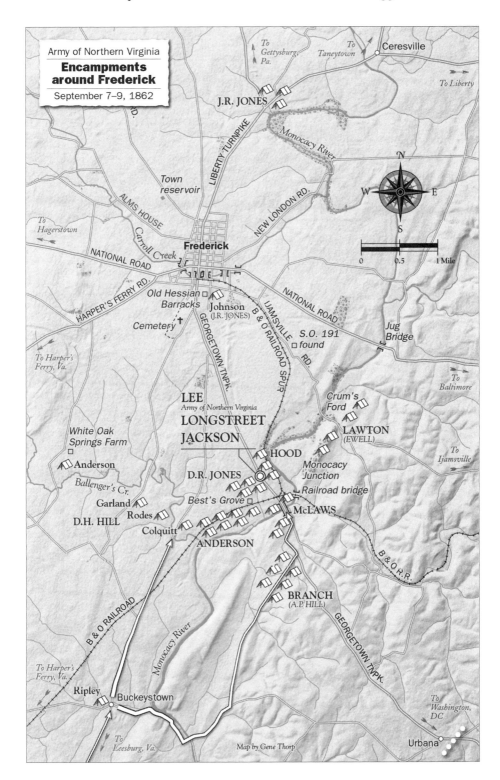

Army of Northern Virginia
Encampments around Frederick
September 7–9, 1862

Map by Gene Thorp

Given this evidence, there is no way of telling which headquarters location is the most plausible, but it is possible that both were correct. Hill may have occupied General Cooper's house for a night until he established a field headquarters near his command. Such an arrangement would have allowed Hill to act as the senior commander in Frederick City for 24 hours and spend a short time in more comfortable circumstances than a field tent. Hill's command had been on the march for weeks, covering long distances on foot when it came up from Richmond to support Lee's Maryland operation. No one could blame Hill for taking the occasion to sleep into a real bed and dine at a table instead of resting on an army cot and eating roasted ears of corn. There is, however, a much larger point to this discussion: regardless of which location is accurate, D. H. Hill's headquarters was far away from where Indiana troops found the copy of Special Orders No. 191 addressed to him.

At least three, and perhaps four, of Hill's five brigades camped for a time along Ballenger Creek, west-southwest of Best's Grove, until Anderson's brigade moved from that location to bring up the army's rear on the Georgetown Pike. This opens the possibility that Anderson may have been in possession of the copy of Lee's orders that ended up being lost close to Frederick City, but there is no evidence to support that theory. More important is the fact that Hill ordered Anderson into his new position one day *before* Special Orders No. 191 were officially distributed. In other words, Hill had to have known about his assignment before Lee's headquarters sent him a paper copy. None of this fully absolves D. H. Hill of being the man who lost the copy of Lee's dispatch, but it makes it much less likely that he was the culprit.[43]

Of all the major Confederate commands thought to have bivouacked on or near Best's farm, only men under James Longstreet and Lafayette McLaws actually did so, and they probably remained as close to the riverbank as possible.[44]

---

43 Longstreet recalled Jackson and Lee discussing the Harpers Ferry operation on September 8, making it possible that Hill received his assignment as the army's rearguard that day. It is generally assumed that Lee did not have Special Orders No. 191 put in writing until Sept. 9, although the crossed out date on the copy that fell into McClellan's hands suggests that is not necessarily the case. James Longstreet, "The Invasion of Maryland," Johnson and Buel, eds., *Battles and Leaders*, 2:663.

44 "The army has been resting to-day along the shady banks of the Monocacy river, cooking, washing and bathing." Peter W. Alexander, "Our Army in Maryland," in *Savannah Republican*, Sept. 8, 1862.

Longstreet's divisions under John Bell Hood, Richard H. Anderson, and David Rumph Jones, as well as the independent brigade of Shanks Evans, appear to have marched with the unattached division of McLaws, jumbling the order of their arrival at the Monocacy Junction bridge. Longstreet's column brought up the rear of the Army of Northern Virginia on September 6, with the general himself reaching Best's Grove at the same time as General Lee.[45]

Hood's division, specifically the brigade of Col. William Tatum Wofford, appears to have been the first unit in Longstreet's column to arrive. Nicholas Davis of the 1st Texas, Wofford's brigade, recalled "Passing through Buckeystown" on September 6 and arriving afterward "at the Monoccacy river, at the crossing of the Baltimore & Ohio Railroad. Here also is the junction of the Frederick road." His comrade in the 1st Texas, Joe Polley, confirmed September 6 as the date when their regiment caught up with the rest of the army at "Monocrasy" Junction.[46]

Hood probably halted his men on the junction's north side. Several accounts refer to the proximity of the rail bridge. John Stevens, for example, remembered camping "on the Monococy river . . . near the railroad bridge, a very large and costly bridge built on stone piers from one high bank to another." Within one or two days of their arrival, recalled Stevens, Hood gave orders for the men to "go into the river with our clothes on and wash the dirt out of them . . . We then came out and stood

---

45 The "unattached" designation used here refers to the organizational order of the Army of Northern Virginia when it embarked upon the Maryland Campaign, as detailed in Harsh, *Sounding the Shallows*, 33-36. "On the 7th our infantry and artillery commands came together near Frederick City," recalled Longstreet. "Riding together before we reached Frederick, the sound of artillery fire came from the direction of Point of Rocks and Harper's Ferry, from which General Lee inferred that the enemy was concentrating his forces from the Valley." Longstreet, *From Manassas to Appomattox*, 201. Douglas, *I Rode with Stonewall*, 148, confirmed Longstreet's arrival with Lee, but got the time of day incorrect: "On the morning of the 6th of September . . . Generals Lee, Longstreet, Jackson, and for a time Jeb Stuart established their several Headquarters in Best's Grove, near one another." Owen, *In Camp and Battle*, 130, also confirmed Lee's presence in Maryland with Longstreet's troops, but placed it in the afternoon: "On the 6th the army began early in the morning to ford the river into Maryland. . . . The young ladies are wild to see Gen. Lee, and we agree to find him for them; so in the afternoon a caravan is made up of all the old family carriages in the country, and filled with pretty girls, and we escort them to where 'Uncle Robert' is resting. He is immediately surrounded, and kissed, and hugged, until the old gentleman gets very red in the face, and cries for mercy." See also, Bartlett, *Military Record*, 129: "Adjutant Owen brought back a string of ladies, who overwhelmed the old man (Lee) with kisses and welcomes."

46 No record could be found for the arrival of Col. Law's brigade; Nicholas A. Davis, *Campaign from Texas to Maryland* (Richmond, VA, 1863), 88; "Next morning (Sept. 6), on our way to rejoin the command on the Monocrasy near Frederick city, we ran across three Georgians butchering a beef." Polley, *A Soldier's Letters*. Available online at www.loyalbooks. Com/book/a-soldiers-letters-to-charming-nellie-by- joseph-benjamin-polley.

in the sun and dried off," which suggests the division camped directly on the riverbank. Neill Ray of the 6th North Carolina, part of Col. Evander Law's brigade, also noted that marching "to Monocacy Bridge, near Frederick, in Maryland," stood out in his memory.[47]

The balance of Hood's division came up over the next two days. The final elements of his artillery did not reach the junction until September 8. These late arrivals—North Carolinians with the Rowan Artillery pulling a mixed battery of rifles and howitzers—got less than two days of rest compared to the longer recuperation time enjoyed by their comrades.[48]

According to a source unearthed by Scott Hartwig, the six brigades under Maj. Gen. Richard H. Anderson arrived "shortly after noon" on the next day. In a September 6 letter published by the *Houston Post*, Pvt. S. F. Tenney recorded that his regiment, the 3rd Georgia (part of Ambrose Wright's brigade) "crossed the Potomac and for the first time, as soldiers, stood on Maryland soil." The Georgians marched "directly on . . . towards Frederick city," continued Tenney. They arrived at the Monocacy on September 7 and camped "near the city [for] three days." Captain William H. Hardy of the 16th Mississippi, a regiment with Col. Carnot Posey's brigade, echoed Tenney in a letter to his wife Sallie dated September 8: "On the 7th, yesterday, we marched to this place and are now bivouacked on the banks of the Manoxie River, two miles of Frederick City." George S. Bernard of the 12th Virginia provided a bit more detail about the division's encampment. Straggling after the Potomac River crossing due to a lack of shoes, Bernard only reached Best's farm late on September 7. He found his comrades there camped "in a wheatfield—two or three hundred yards from the road." Another man named Bailey G. McClellan of the 10th Alabama, Col. Orlando B. Wilcox's brigade, provided an important feature identifying where Anderson's division camped. McClellan joined his Company D comrades "in the vicinity of Frederick City, Maryland. They were bivowacking on the bank of a big creek . . . close to the iron

---

47 Stevens, *Reminiscences*, 66-67; Neill W. Ray, "Sixth Regiment," Clark, ed., *Histories of the Several Regiments and Battalions from North Carolina in the Great War, 1861-'65,* 1:306. See also the Diary of M. M. Cottingim, 18: "We have stoped on the Baltamore and ohio RR to coock up rashuns." Available online at www.civilwardigital.com/CWDiaries/M.M.%20Cottingim.pdf.

48 Captain John Ramsay of Light Battery D, Rowan's North Carolina Artillery recalled, "On 8th encamped at Frederick Junction, on the Baltimore and Ohio Railroad" after spending the previous night near Buckeystown. John A. Ramsay, "Additional Sketch Tenth Regiment. Light Batteries A, D, F and I," Clark, ed., *Histories of the Several Regiments and Battalions from North Carolina,* 1:573.

bridge [and] the well-known double track Baltimore and Ohio." Captain George C. Whatley, also of the 10th Alabama, made a similar observation in a letter written on September 8 that eventually found its way into the pages of the *Jacksonville Republican*. "To-day we are blowing up a RR bridge across the river here," he recalled. "It is an iron one, and the railroad here is double track." It is safe to conclude that Anderson's division camped near the rail junction southwest of Hood's men.[49]

Brigadier General David Rumph Jones's division appeared next at Monocacy Junction late on the afternoon on September 7 after spending the night "at a little village . . . called Buckeystown." Jones's men approached Monocacy Junction from the Georgetown Pike, confirmed George Wise, a soldier with the 17th Virginia. Wise recalled in 1870 that he and his comrades had "crossed the [Potomac] river at Noland's Ferry" on September 6. The Virginians, he continued, "marched as far as [the] Monocacy river, crossing that stream and bivouacing beyond." Wise could have meant that they camped on the eastern bank near Buckeystown, but other men from the brigade make it clear that this was not the case.[50]

John Dooley of the 1st Virginia, also of Kemper's brigade, added a critical detail that placed his regiment, and by extension Jones's division, at Monocacy

49 Hartwig, *To Antietam Creek*, 112; S. F. Tenney, "The Battle of Sharpsburg," Owen, McBride, and Allport, eds., *Texans at Antietam*, 251; William Harris Hardy to Sallie J. Hardy, Monday, Sept. 8, 1862, in Robert G. Evans, ed., *The 16th Mississippi Infantry: Civil War Letters and Reminiscences* (Jackson, MS, 2002), 112; George S. Bernard, ed., *War Talks of Confederate Veterans* (Petersburg, VA, 1892), 23. There is some evidence that Wilcox may have been too ill to command his brigade in Maryland and that Col. Alfred Cumming led it instead. See Harsh, *Sounding the Shallows*, 71-72; Vaughn M. Stewart, *Bailey G. McClellan and His Civil War* (1977) Copy in Alabama Vertical File, ANBL. McClellan's mention of a double-track railway is significant because at the time a double-track portion of the B&O railroad split west from Monocacy Junction while the spur north to Frederick consisted of only a single rail line; Letter of Capt. George Croghan Whatley to J. F. Grant, Sept. 8, 1862, in the *Jacksonville* (AL) *Republican*, Sept. 25, 1862. Another source for D. R. Jones's division cited in Hartwig, *To Antietam Creek*, 112, mentioned "early in the evening [of Sept. 7] arrived in the vicinity of Frederick City" after crossing over the Monocacy River twice.

50 Johnston, *The Story of a Confederate Boy*, 132. Johnston served with the 7th Virginia, part of Brig. Gen. James L. Kemper's brigade; Wise, *History of the Seventeenth Virginia Infantry*, 109-110. The 17th Virginia crossing at Noland's Ferry is unusual because most of David R. Jones's division is believed to have division crossed at White's Ford. The only other unit from Jones's division for which there is a record of having crossed at Noland's Ferry is the 11th Georgia Volunteers of George T. Anderson's brigade. See, for example, Kittrell J. Warren, *History of the Eleventh Georgia Vols.* (Richmond, VA, 1863), 49: "After going by Drainsville and through Leesburg, we waded the Potomac ten miles above the latter place, and entered Maryland on the sixth. From thence we wound through Buckeytown, across the Monocacy river, and on towards Frederick."

Junction itself: "About noon today, Sunday 7th we moved towards Frederick near which we arrived about 4 p.m. We bivouacked just at Monocacy Station on the bank of the river and close by the bridge." The 19th Virginia from Richard Garnett's brigade did the same, proceeding "to the bridge of the Baltimore and Ohio railway over the Monocacy, and [going] into camp." From September 7 on Jones's division remained beside the river between Anderson and Hood's divisions, where the men enjoyed "a good bath" and some rest. They participated in the demolition of the B&O rail bridge at 1:00 p.m. on September 9 before departing for Hagerstown on September 10.[51]

As for Shanks Evans's brigade, it also bivouacked "on the banks of the Monocacy River," but no information has been found identifying either the date of its arrival or the location of its encampment. Presumably, it occupied ground close to Hood and Jones, but this cannot be confirmed given the lack of evidence. The one part of the story that remains missing is the route Hood's, Anderson's, and Evans's commands took to their encampments. Coming up third in the column, Jones's division used the Georgetown Pike to approach Frederick from the southeast. It makes sense to assume therefore that the other divisions did the same.[52]

Longstreet's artillery joined the rest of the command on September 7, the same day D. R. Jones's men arrived. Lieutenant William M. Owen, an adjutant to Col. James B. Walton, commander of the 1st Battalion of the Washington Artillery of Louisiana, noted in his memoir after the war that he and the guns "crossed the Monocacy river, and encamped near Frederick" on September 7. His statement adds weight to the idea that all of Longstreet's command took the road east of the river to Monocacy Junction after passing through Buckeystown. Private Napier Bartlett of the 1st Battalion's 3rd Company similarly recalled that they "crossed the Monocosy and camped near Frederick City" after marching up from the Potomac River. Once they attained the west side of the Monocacy, the two reserve batteries of Colonel Walton's artillery "encamped . . . in a beautiful grove of oaks" beside

---

51 Robert E. Curran, ed., *John Dooley's Civil War: An Irish American's Journey in the First Virginia Infantry Regiment* (Knoxville, TN, 2012), 36. Garnett commanded George Pickett's brigade during the Maryland Campaign. Wood, *Reminiscences of Big I*, 34; Wise, *History of the Seventeenth Virginia Infantry*, 110, and Curran, ed., *John Dooley's Civil War*, 36: "Tuesday 9th [September] about 1 o'clock p.m. the Monocacy Station bridge was blown up."

52 Welburn J. Andrews, *Sketch of Company K., 23rd South Carolina Volunteers, in the Civil War, from 1862-1865* (Richmond, VA, 1909), 13-14. Available online at https://digital.tcl.sc.edu/digital/collection/access/id/334.

Longstreet's headquarters. General Lee, noted Lieutenant Owen, camped near Longstreet on one side of Best's Grove, while Stonewall Jackson "pitched his tents" on the other. "The latter passes our camp and our tent several times a day," remembered artillerist, who complimented the general for telling Longstreet, "he was the only commanding officer he ever knew who had a body guard of artillery. He thought it a good joke, [and] it was for 'old Jack'."[53]

General McLaws's unattached division came up next and finally reached the Monocacy on September 8. Diarist William H. Hill noted that he and his comrades in the 13th Mississippi, William Barksdale's brigade, marched 18 miles on September 6 to camp one mile north of the Potomac. The next day, September 7, they "marched 9 miles" before stopping just past Buckeystown for the night. During this trek "The citizens of Maryland did not receive us with much enthusiasm," recalled Hill, as only "A few manifested their pleasure at our presence by waving of handkerchiefs hallooing &c."

It was at this point that McLaws found himself unsure about the route he was to take to Frederick. The Georgian sent his aide-de-camp, Capt. Henry King, to get instructions from General Lee while his division remained halted near Buckeystown. According to King, he met Brig. Gen. Robert Toombs before traveling on to D. H. Hill's headquarters. Once there, he found Hill in the company of General Jones. These officers sent King on to Lee's headquarters, which King found after he "passed the junction" at Monocacy.[54] Encountering the rail junction before army headquarters implies that King crossed the Monocacy River from the east using the bridge on the Georgetown Pike. The more likely scenario, however,

---

53 Owen, *In Camp and Battle*, 131, and Bartlett, *Military Record*, 129. The proximity of Lee's, Longstreet's, and Jackson's headquarters to each other has long been unclear. "The general's tents," recalled one of Jackson's aides, "were found on a hillside in a grassy field" near Frederick. Capt. James Power Smith, "With Stonewall Jackson in the Army of Northern Virginia," 17. The terrain across the Georgetown Pike from where Best's Grove stood slopes gently to the southeast, amounting to the only "hillside" near where Lee and Longstreet camped. Federal Gen. Columbus O'Donnell provided an important additional clue when he reported to the *Baltimore American* in early September that, while seeking a pass from Gen. Lee to travel through Confederate lines, he went "to the General's headquarters, four miles from Frederick on the Georgetown road. . . . [H]e found General Lee's headquarters on one side of the road and General Jackson's on the other side." *Baltimore American*, Sept. 10, 1862. Jackson's aide's mention of a sloping hillside, together with O'Donnell's statement, leads to the conclusion that Jackson did not camp in Best's Grove proper, but in the field east of the Georgetown Pike.

54 Hartwig, *To Antietam Creek*, 112, argues for the arrival of McLaws ahead of D. R. Jones on Sept. 7; Hill Diary, Sept. 7, 1862.

is that King met Toombs near Buckeystown where his command, which was part of D. R. Jones's division, had also camped on the night of September 6.[55]

King next traveled directly north from near Buckeystown to D. H. Hill's headquarters in the vicinity of Ballenger Creek. Hill sent King east along the B&O rail line, an easily identifiable landmark, telling him to look for Lee's headquarters in the vicinity of Monocacy Junction. Doing so eventually brought King to Best's Grove, where Lee forwarded the captain to James Longstreet for instructions on McLaws's route of march. Instead of ordering King to return to McLaws, Longstreet "sent back a courier" with the general's marching orders. King ended the day visiting Frederick, where he "bought gloves & engaged coffee &c."[56]

The next day, a clear and warm September 8, McLaws's command "crossed the Monocacy River" near Buckeystown on route to Frederick. William Hill recorded in his diary that the 13th Mississippi, along with the rest of Barksdale's brigade, proceeded to "a narrow vally between high hills" where it remained until September 10. Hill's description of the valley matches almost exactly the terrain along the Georgetown Pike running from Urbana to Monocacy Junction. This description, and the fact that Hill never mentioned crossing the Monocacy a second time, make it likely that Barksdale's brigade camped east of the river close to Brig. Gen. Branch's (A. P. Hill's) division of Stonewall Jackson's command. In the meantime, at least one of McLaws's brigades camped near the Best farm itself. J. J. McDaniel, a soldier with Company M of the 7th South Carolina Infantry, Brig. Gen. Joseph Kershaw's brigade, reported crossing to the west bank of the Monocacy, which indicates that portions of McLaws's division may have straddled the river for the two days they rested near Frederick City.[57]

Where McLaws's other three brigades camped remains unknown, but Capt. William Burgwyn of Robert Ransom's brigade, part of John G. Walker's division coming up behind McLaws, recorded "passing McLaws division" while on the march east of the Monocacy River. The part of the division Ransom encountered

55 See Curran, ed., *John Dooley's Civil War*, 36. Dooley recorded in his diary that his regiment (part of D. R. Jones's division) did not march from Buckeystown until noon, which would have given King plenty of time in the morning to encounter Toombs.

56 Trimpi, ed., "Lafayette McLaws' Aide-de-Camp," 30.

57 Hartwig, *To Antietam Creek*, 112. "On the 8th, we crossed the Monocacy River and camped near Frederick City." McDaniel, *Diary of Battles*, 10.

could have been Barksdale's brigade, or it might have been other units with McLaws. Lacking additional sources, there is no way to confirm this.[58]

Brigadier General John Walker's unattached division of two infantry brigades brought up the rear of the army's long column. Walker followed McLaws by crossing the Potomac at Cheek's Ford on September 7. He halted at Buckeystown later that day before getting his soldiers underway again early the following morning. Robert Ransom's brigade took the lead, followed by the brigade commanded by Col. Vannoy H. Manning. The column crossed the Monocacy on the route to Frederick east of the Monocacy River. After a march of four miles, recalled the 48th North Carolina's Lt. Col. Sam Walkup, they encountered the camps of Jackson's men on the heights east of Monocacy Junction "in sight of Frederick, Md." Here, Ransom's men also met the elements of McLaws's division mentioned above.[59]

General Walker rode ahead before noon to meet up with General Lee, probably hoping to receive instructions as to where his men should camp. He found the army commander at Best's Grove contemplating the next phase of his operation. Walker would later claim to have learned that as he "had a division which would often, perhaps, be ordered on detached service, an intelligent performance of [his] duty might require a knowledge of the ulterior purposes and objects of the campaign."[60]

In the meeting with Walker, the commanding general directed him "to return to the mouth of the Monocacy and effectually destroy the aqueduct of the Chesapeake and Ohio canal." Once that important task was done, continued Lee, Walker was to rejoin the army "by way of Jefferson and Middletown." Walker dutifully returned to his command and ordered his foot soldiers to retrace their

---

58 Schiller, ed., *A Captain's War*, 17.

59 Walkup Diary, 23; Schiller, ed., *A Captain's War*, 17.

60 Walker depicted these events incorrectly after the war by claiming that Lee had informed him of the operation against Harpers Ferry during their meeting at Monocacy Junction. See Walker, "Jackson's Capture of Harper's Ferry," 604. In his official report, however, Walker noted that he did not have foreknowledge of the operation, writing that Lee had ordered him to rejoin the army in Middletown after the aqueduct had been destroyed. Walker received his copy of Special Orders No. 191 telling him of his role in the Harpers Ferry operation on Sept. 10. *OR* 19, 1:913; Harsh, *Sounding the Shallows*, 159-160.

steps to Buckeystown and, following a long march that did not end until close to midnight, to the C&O Canal.[61]

Histories of the Maryland Campaign have long held that from September 6 to September 10, the Army of Northern Virginia camped on the west side of the Monocacy River stretching from the city limits southeast of Frederick to the grounds of John T. Best's rented farm. This exercise tracking the movements of Lee's troops demonstrates that this interpretation is only partially accurate. Instead of camping on the west bank of the river, at least 20,000 of Lee's men bivouacked east of the Monocacy, perhaps as far as two miles in the direction of Ijamsville and Urbana. In addition, a portion of Jackson's command comprising three infantry brigades and artillery camped two miles north of Frederick at Worman's Woods along the turnpike to Liberty, Maryland, with a fourth infantry brigade stationed in Frederick proper; their number totaled more than 5,200 men. The 10,600 men of D. H. Hill's command camped from Ballenger Creek to Buckeystown to protect the river crossing there.

The Army of Northern Virginia occupied a long bulging crescent stretching some ten miles guarding the important roads from Liberty, Baltimore, Washington, and Buckeystown. Best's farm lay at the center of this extended position, with more than 31,000 men under Longstreet and McLaws camped along the river around it or on a portion of its grounds. Apart from Bradley Johnson's brigade in Frederick City, there is no evidence that any of Lee's men occupied ground close to the city itself.[62]

---

61 Walker, "Jackson's Capture of Harper's Ferry," 604-605. Walker's men bitterly recalled the hardship of this long march. See John A. Sloan, *Reminiscences of the Guilford Grays* (Washington, DC, 1883), 41, and Schiller, ed., *A Captain's War*, 17.

62 These estimates of numerical strength for the Army of Northern Virginia, totaling 63,800, come from Gene Thorp, "In Defense of McClellan at Antietam: A Contrarian View," in *The Washington Post* (September 2012). Available online at www.washingtonpost.com/lifestyle/style/in-defense-of-mcclellan-at-antietam-a-contrarian-view/2012/09/06/79a0e5cc-f131-11e 1-892d-bc92fee603a7_story.html. Thorp's deeply sourced and reasonably argued analysis provides a sound statistically-based estimate of Lee's strength. In his own analysis of the subject Harsh, *Taken*, 39, concluded that the Rebel army's strength at the beginning of the campaign hovered around 75,500. Hartwig, meanwhile, in *To Antietam Creek*, 679-680, places the ANV's strength on Sept. 2 at 75,305. The question is how many of these troops were in the ranks to fight at Sharpsburg. According to one anecdotal estimate recorded by a lieutenant colonel with the 23rd Virginia of Taliaferro's brigade, during the campaign the "men had been marched so much and were so broken down, that we had 60,000 stragglers . . . [including] 6000 wounded here" at Winchester. See Clayton Coleman to Lucy Coleman, Sept. 27, 1862 in Clayton G. Coleman Civil War Letters, 1862-1863, Collection #MS-0021, Virginia Military Institute Archives, Lexington, Virginia. Available online at http://digitalcollections. Vmi.edu/digital/

The units posted at Best's farm approached their encampments from east of the Monocacy River. Jackson's wing of the army blazed the trail before Longstreet's wing, and the unattached divisions of McLaws and Walker followed. Only D. H. Hill's division took the road directly north from Buckeystown. The distance that Jackson and Lee kept their men away from Frederick suggests both generals might have been concerned about the potentially detrimental impact of dropping their soldiery into the laps of Frederick's people. The location of the army's camps, at least in this sense, was consistent with an attempt to retain the good graces of the civilians Lee and Jackson hoped would support the Southern cause.

Given the army's position straddling the Monocacy River, it also seems clear that Lee intentionally kept his troops close to the road bridge at B&O rail junction in case a sudden advance by the Army of the Potomac required them to cross back over the river and take position on the eastern heights. Best's farm offered a good jump-off point for half of the army should Jackson's command require rapid reinforcement. Lee assumed that the Federal forces were too demoralized and too disorganized to take the field quickly, but he was hedging his bet just in case. Even with his opponent in disarray, the potential for an enemy advance and attack was always a possibility.

The positioning of the individual components of Lee's army is important when it comes to the discovery of Special Orders No. 191. Debate about the issue has long revolved around where the document was found, and the person to whom the orders were addressed. D. H. Hill's name appeared on the dispatch, so scholars and general students alike have simply assumed that the orders were discovered at General Hill's division's encampment, or where Hill's headquarters was located at that time. This hypothesis appears to have originated with Col. Silas Colgrove of the 27th Indiana, who wrote about it in 1886 in an article in *The Century Magazine*: "We stacked arms on the same ground that had been occupied by General D. H. Hill's division the evening before. Within a very few minutes after halting, the order

---

collection/p15821coll11/id/995. Referred to hereafter as Coleman Letter. Lieutenant Alexander S. Erwin of Company C, Philips Legion, Thomas Drayton's brigade in D. R. Jones's division of Longstreet's command provided another estimate: "General Longstreet issued an order here (Leesburg, Va) that all the barefooted, weak and inefficient troops of each regiment be left with the baggage in charge of an officer. . . . They then ordered all that were left, about five thousand (5,000) in all, to Winchester where we now are." Letter of Alex Erwin, Sept. 15, 1862, printed in the *Athens Watchman*, Oct. 1, 1862. Available online at www.angelfire.com/ga2/PhillipsLegion/erwin.html.

was brought to me by First Sergeant John M. Bloss and Private B. W. Mitchell, of Company F, 27th Indiana Volunteers."[63]

Colgrove did not possess any evidence for making such a claim other than the fact that Hill's name was on the paper. Descriptions of the location near Frederick offer no indication that the spot where Mitchell and Bloss discovered the orders had been used as a Confederate campground. Edmund Brown, a member of Company C and the author of the official regimental history of the 27th Indiana, wrote that as the Hoosiers approached the city "with skirmishers still deployed in our front, we moved on and finally halted in a clover field, adjoining the city on the south. . . . As we lay down upon the *clean grass* [emphasis added], we did so with a sense of relaxation and enjoyment."[64]

Captain David B. Vance of the 27th, discharged after a wound he received at Antietam, swore in an affidavit long after the war, "We advanced across a field to where there had been a fence, but at that time only a row of weeds, grass and some small shrubs or bushes . . . Just after we lay down I saw a large envelope just to my left, lying in the grass and weeds."[65]

George W. Welch of Company F, the same company whose men found the orders, also swore in an affidavit that they stopped to rest "in an old meadow" before the orders were discovered.[66]

---

63 Silas Colgrove, "The Finding of Lee's Lost Orders," Johnson and Buel, eds., *Battles and Leaders*, 2:603. A letter written by Colgrove in 1879 indicates that he thought the location was a Confederate encampment well before his piece appeared in *The Century Magazine*. "The facts are these. On the 13th of Sept. 1862, our army marched to Frederick City and took up its position on the same ground that had been occupied by the Confederate Army and had been left as I believe on that same day." Robert W. Menuet, "Corporal Barton W. Mitchell and the Lost Orders," *America's Civil War* (Sept. 2007), www.historynet.com/corporal-barton-w-mitchell-and-the-lost-orders.htm. General George B. McClellan also took from what he had been told that "[Lee's] order was said to have been found on one of the abandoned camp-grounds of the Confederate troops by a private soldier, and, as I think, of an Indiana regiment." Ibid. Lastly, Cpl. George W. Welch of Company F, 27th Indiana, swore an affidavit in 1906: "we stopped to rest and it was here where D. H. Hill of the Confederate Command had occupied the day before." He had nothing upon which to make that claim except that the document bore Hill's name. Copy in Richard C. Datzman, "Who Found Lee's Lost Dispatch?" (Feb. 1973), MNBP.

64 Edmund R. Brown, *The Twenty-Seventh Indiana Volunteer Infantry in the War of the Rebellion 1861 to 1865* (Monticello, IN, 1899), 228.

65 Affidavit of David B. Vance, Sept. 15, 1905, in Datzman, "Who Found Lee's Lost Dispatch?" MNBP. Vance's mention of an envelope was incorrect, as the orders themselves formed the "envelope," wrapped around the cigars.

66 Affidavit of George W. Welch, Jul. 24, 1906 in Datzman, "Who Found Lee's Lost Dispatch?" MNBP.

Sergeant John M. Bloss, one of those who personally witnessed the incident, wrote two weeks later after he had been wounded at Antietam: "We found the dispatch out in a wheat field under a Locas tree with two cigars with it."[67]

Tall grass, weeds, shrubs, clover, or wheat field—none of these accounts mentions the refuse commonly found after a large number of men had camped on the same spot for several days. Compare, for example, the image of "clean grass" with the description of a nearby Confederate camp seen by men with the 14th New Jersey when they returned to the area on September 16: "Everything looked desolate," and the Federals found "The [B&O rail] bridge destroyed, remnants of wagons, dead horses and mules lying around."[68]

Local Frederick resident Jacob Engelbrecht visited the fields a few days later. "Yesterday afternoon (September 21)," he confided to his journal, "I went down to the Junction to see the destruction at the old camps where the Rebels had encamped. The stench was very offensive from the offal of their butchering. Several dead horses & actually one Secessionist Black man was laying in the field dead & uncovered (of earth); but his clothes & boots were on. Had been laying there nearly two weeks already."[69]

No account of the spot where D. H. Hill's roughly 10,000-man division, which Colgrove claimed had camped for several days, mentions anything like this. There is no description of discarded clothing, broken equipment, lost personal items, the remains of rotting food, cold campfire remnants, crumpled newspapers, empty bottles, or anything else related to what one would expect to find. For all intents and purposes, the men of the 27th Indiana took their rest in a fresh field unsullied by previous occupation.

Exactly where the Hoosiers finally settled down remains undetermined, and therefore controversial, to this day. The official position of the Monocacy National Battlefield Park (MNBP) is based on research initially carried out by Ezra Carman, which claims the 27th Indiana soldiers discovered the errant copy of Lee's orders in a field alongside the Georgetown Pike, probably between the homes of J. C. Motter and Simon Cronise. Researcher Timothy J. Reese has argued that Bloss, Mitchell,

67 John McKnight Bloss, "Letter written from the barn hospital at Antietam," in Bloss Family Papers, Sept. 25, 1862. Copy of letter provided by Monocacy National Battlefield Park.

68 Terrill, *Campaign of the Fourteenth Regiment New Jersey Volunteers*, 9.

69 Quynn, ed., *Diary of Jacob Engelbrecht*, 3:952.

and the others found Lee's orders "in a clover field, adjoining the city on the south," probably on the farm of a man named J. G. Miller.[70]

Both of these conclusions clash with the analysis offered by Joseph Harsh. According to Harsh, the orders were probably found on the farm of F. Myers, which was east of the B&O railroad a little more than one mile north of the discovery spot currently accepted by the MNBP. "[T]he newly discovered fact that clogged roads prevented Hill's division from marching through Frederick on the 10th and that he spent the night near the Myers farm," argues Harsh, "would seem to bear out the conclusion that the orders were lost from his headquarters."[71]

There are multiple problems with this interpretation, beginning with the claim that Hill's entire division followed Longstreet's command north through Frederick on the Georgetown Pike. Hill's men did indeed eventually join the long column through Frederick. However, as this study has shown, there is no evidence that any of Hill's men other than George B. Anderson's moved to cover the Army of Northern Virginia's rear as it initially moved out. The only evidence that exists puts Hill's command along Ballenger Creek. In other words, when the army marched on September 10, four of Hill's brigades used the road north from Buckeystown, and not the Georgetown Pike, to pass through Frederick. The lone exception was Anderson's brigade, which used the Georgetown Pike. His men encountered a significant delay that forced them to camp for the night in the wooded area they had found south of Frederick.[72] Beyond this, however, nothing more precise can be determined. There is no evidence that Hill's division, or any other Confederate command, camped close to Frederick east of the Georgetown Pike.

In addition, no one has produced evidence indicating that Hill located his headquarters on Frederick's southeastern city limits. The only available sources place Hill's headquarters at either the farm of George Markell, situated several

---

70 See Monocacy National Battlefield Park, "Invitation to Battle: Special Orders 191" (Frederick, MD, n. d.). The names of the families who owned the farmsteads in the vicinity has been confused over the years because scholars have used two different historical maps of Frederick County. My identification of the farm of Simon Cronise and J. C. Motter refers to properties labeled on Isaac Bond, *Map of Frederick County, MD* (Baltimore, MD, 1858); Timothy J. Reese, *High-Water Mark: The 1862 Maryland Campaign in Strategic Perspective* (Baltimore, MD, 2004), 17. This offers an example of the map-generated confusion. Reese clearly used D. J. Lake, *Atlas of Frederick County, Maryland* (Philadelphia, PA, 1873) to identify the homestead of J. G. Miller; Miller's name does not appear on the Bond map from 1858.

71 Harsh, *Taken*, 153. See Datzman, "Who Found Lee's Lost Dispatch?" MNBP, upon which Harsh based his judgment.

72 Shinn Diary, Sept. 10, 1862.

miles southwest of the spot where Lee's orders were found, or at General Cooper's occupied mansion in the city itself. Anderson's brigade did halt several miles south of the city, but there is no reason to think that Anderson possessed a copy of Special Orders No. 191, and no reason for him to have been given one. D. H. Hill maintained until his death in 1889 that he never saw the copy of the orders addressed to him later found by men of the 27th Indiana. The evidence showing where his division camped and where his headquarters might have been located appears to support Hill's claim. Who lost Special Orders No. 191 remains one of the Maryland Campaign's most enduring mysteries, but to it must be added the question of why the Indiana men found the orders where they did. If the location was not an identifiable Confederate encampment, there was no reason for the orders to have been there in the first place.

There is one final intriguing detail about the location where the orders were found: the 27th Indiana may have camped on the Elias Luckett Delashmutt, Jr. farm. When writing up his analysis of the location, Joseph Harsh concluded that the meadow where the Hoosiers came to a halt belonged to F. Myers. Harsh found the name in the unpublished 1973 manuscript of Richard C. Datzman, a radiologist and amateur historian who, in turn, probably got Myers's name from D. J. Lake's 1873 *Atlas of Frederick County*. Lake's atlas places the Myers farm east of the road leading from Crum's Ford to Frederick City (known today as the Reich's Farm Road). This location also fits descriptions of the position marched to by other regiments with the Federal Twelfth Corps on September 13. Lieutenant Colonel Newton T. Colby of the 107th New York Infantry, for example, recorded that his men "encamped about a mile east of the city."[73] Similarly, Miles Huyette of the 124th Pennsylvania noted that, "The afternoon of September 13th, we—of First Division, 12th Corps—crossed the Monocasy River and bivouacked in a stubble-field south of the Baltimore Pike, about half [the] distance from the river and Frederick City."[74]

One of the homesteads located one mile southeast of Frederick City was directly in the path of the 27th Indiana, 107th New York, and 124th Pennsylvania.

73 William E. Hughes, ed., *The Civil War Papers of Lt. Colonel Newton T. Colby, New York Infantry* (Jefferson, NC, 2003), 139.

74 Miles C. Huyette, *The Maryland Campaign and The Battle of Antietam* (Buffalo, NY, 1915), 17. Also see the Diary of Sgt. C.D.M. Broomhall, 124th Pennsylvania Infantry, Sept. 13, 1862. Transcribed by Carolyn Ivanoff (Janes family papers): "We halted about a mile from Frederick City at 1 p.m."

The location of Elias L. Delashmutt, Jr. Farm
Isaac Bond, Map of Frederick County, MD, 1858

According to Isaac Bond's Map of Frederick County, MD, it belonged to Delashmutt, who owned the farm in 1858. By 1873, when D. J. Lake produced his Atlas, the farm had been either sold or rented to F. Myers, which is why it was later identified as the Myers farm.

The name of the owner is potentially important in this case because Delashmutt belonged to a family of known Confederate sympathizers and his farm was exactly where one could reasonably expect the 27th Indiana to have stopped if statements from men with other regiments about halting one mile from Frederick are accurate. In other words, while there may not be evidence that any part of

Daniel Harvey Hill's command camped near or marched past Elias Delashmutt's farm, there is a reasonable possibility that the Hoosiers of the 27th Indiana discovered the lost copy of Special Orders No. 191 on the farm of a potential Rebel supporter who may have hosted a Confederate officer during the Army of Northern Virginia's stay near Frederick.[75] After all, as the *Alexandria Gazette* reported on September 8, it was well known that "Most of the [Rebel] officers were quartered at the hotels and *at the houses of prominent men* [emphasis added]."[76]

It could have been this man, then, or the courier sent to deliver the order to him, who lost the dispatch, which in turn set off the chain of events that led to Lee's reverse at South Mountain on September 14 and the shattering of his plan to awaken "Confederate" Maryland with an advance into Pennsylvania.[77]

---

75 According to the 1860 Census Delashmutt owned one slave (a 24-year-old woman). National Archives and Records Administration, Washington DC, Eighth Census of the United States 1860, Series Number M653, Records of the Bureau of the Census, Record Group 29. Referred to hereafter as NA.

76 *Baltimore American*, reprinted in the *Alexandria Gazette*, Sept. 8, 1862.

77 See Appendix B for more information.

FOUR

DREAMS DASHED ON THE ROCKS OF REALITY

∽

The Army of Northern Virginia's
Mixed Reception in Maryland

FOR more than a year after the outbreak of war, claims that Maryland belonged in the new Confederacy circulated through the Army of Northern Virginia. The literate in the ranks read newspapers editorializing about it, politicians in Richmond waxed eloquently on the subject, Marylanders in the army supported the idea, and John Ryder Randall's lyrics sang of it. By the time Robert E. Lee turned his columns north from the blood-drenched fields of Virginia, the men in the ranks were in favor of proving that Maryland's white star belonged on the spangled bars of their army's scarlet battle flag. A few men may have grumbled about preferring to defend the South in favor of invading the North, but their voices represented a small minority when compared to the more widespread approval of their fellow soldiers.[1]

To most of these men, and especially to the most fervent believers in the cause, the argument for entering Maryland made good sense. The slaveholding state's location below the Mason-Dixon line supported the idea of it being rightfully

---

1 See Appendix C for more details on this topic.

Southern. How could an army of Southern men "invade" a sister state that had not shown hostility to the Confederacy? Neutral Maryland had not openly declared for the South, but many in Lee's army felt the martial law regime imposed by Washington kept it from doing so. Thus it stood to reason that, if given the chance to do so, the people would rise up. Everything Lee's troops learned during the months leading up to September 1862 indicated that Old Line Staters would welcome the army with open arms, that recruits would flock to its standards, and that the urban centers, especially Baltimore, would erupt in revolt. For better or worse, rightly or wrongly, the soldiers in the Army of Northern Virginia believed all of these things as they crossed the Potomac River, hoping their march into a friendly state would bring the war to swift and decisive end.

Histories have emphasized the coolness with which Marylanders received the Army of Northern Virginia and cite this as evidence that Lee and his men never realistically had a chance of wooing the state into seceding. This image of Maryland as firmly pro-Union is, however, a post-campaign contrivance generated by unionist Marylanders eager to stress their state's loyalty to the national government, and the disgust of Southern soldiers writing about the reception they had received.[2]

The situation on the ground during the campaign itself was much less clear-cut. Relations between Confederate troops and Maryland civilians varied as the Army of Northern Virginia moved through the state. A fair but unmeasurable number of Maryland's people received Confederate troops with warmth and friendship and provided them with food, clothing, and moral support. Many others remained aloof, shut their doors to begging soldiers, or openly disparaged them as the butternut columns passed by.

Lee's men recognized these variations in behavior and recorded their thoughts on the subject in their letters, diaries, and postwar histories. While expressing these sentiments, Southern soldiers revealed three types of experience that ultimately shaped their impression of Maryland's people: their treatment by the populace, the willingness of Marylanders to take Confederate currency as payment for goods; and, especially, the inclination of Maryland's men to take up arms for the Rebel cause. Each type of experience built upon the next, enabling Lee's men to judge the

---

2 For a thoughtful consideration of how memory of the Maryland experience evolved over time, see Gary W. Gallagher, "The Net Result of the Campaign Was in Our Favor: Confederate Reaction to the Maryland Campaign," and William A. Blair, "Maryland, Our Maryland: Or How Lincoln and His Army Helped to Define the Confederacy," in Gallagher, ed., *The Antietam Campaign*, 3-43 and 74-100, respectively.

success of their campaign and weigh the validity of claims that Marylanders were sympathetic fellow travelers waiting to join the new Confederate States of America.

Writing years after the conflict, Capt. D. Augustus Dickert, a son of South Carolina and veteran who would pen one of the most important histories of any command to serve in Lee's army, complained about the Maryland experience in his study of Joseph Kershaw's brigade. "The people of the South had been led to believe that Maryland was anxious to cast her destinies with those of her sister States," he argued, and "that all her sympathies were with the people of the South, and that her young men were anxious and only awaiting the opportunity to join the ranks as soldiers under Lee." Dickert blasted "these ideas and promises . . . [as] delusions, for the people we saw along the route remained passive spectators and disinterested witnesses to the great evolutions now taking place."[3]

Many in Lee's army shared Dickert's experience, which embittered them all the more because of the high expectations of support and assistance they had entertained upon entering the state. By the time he crossed the Potomac on September 5, for example, Edward Moore of the Rockbridge Artillery (known affectionately to his family and friends as "Ned") had been hearing for months the grandiose claims of John Ryder Randall's *Maryland! My Maryland*. Descended from ancestors who had distinguished themselves in the Revolutionary War, Moore served in a battery with members who had "brothers or other relatives" in the Confederate 1st Maryland Regiment. Talk from these men, remembered Moore, put the battery in fevered anticipation of the welcome they would receive north of the Potomac. "We were . . . eager [to see] the whole population rise to receive us with open arms, and our depleted ranks swelled by the younger men, impatient for the opportunity to help to achieve Southern independence," he recalled. "The prospect of what was in store for us when we reached Baltimore, as pictured by our boys from that city, filled our minds with such eager yearnings that our impatience to rush in could scarcely be restrained. On the evening of our arrival within the borders of the State, with several companions, I took supper at the house of a Southern sympathizer, who said much to encourage our faith."[4]

---

3 Dickert, *History of Kershaw's Brigade*, 145.

4 Edward A. Moore, *The Story of a Cannoneer Under Stonewall Jackson* (New York, NY, 1907), 53. William Mercer Otey of the same battery confirmed this excitement by noting that he and his fellow artillerists entertained "visions of the beautiful and bountiful things we were told awaited our entry in Frederick City . . . prepared by the patriotic sympathizers of 'Maryland, My Maryland'." Otey, "The Story of Our Great War," 366; Dickert, *History of Kershaw's Brigade*, 130.

John Robson of the 52nd Virginia shared Moore's outlook and identified Randall's *Maryland! My Maryland* as a key source of the army's eagerness. "Up to this time we had sung [it] with a good deal of hope and vim," Robson recalled, "for this song asserted positively . . . 'She Breathes, She Burns, She'll Come, She'll Come,' etc." Captain Wayland Dunaway of the 40th Virginia echoed this sentiment: "There was some expectation that when we came into Maryland many of her sons would rally to our banners, according to the prediction of a well-known song: 'She breathes, she burns, she'll come, she'll come, Maryland, my Maryland'." This matched expectations generally, according to Maj. G. Moxley Sorrel, James Longstreet's assistant adjutant general: "The men were triumphantly rejoicing and confident [when crossing the Potomac] . . . as they believed we were moving into the friendly fields of a sister State, whose men would surely rise and join us." Col. Benjamin G. Humphreys of the 21st Mississippi agreed: "It was confidently asserted and believed that the down trodden people of Maryland were panting for 'the recovery of their lost liberties,' and were only waiting for the armed occupation of the state by the Confederate army to induce an immediate uprising of the people in armed insurrection to throw off the 'tyrant's foot'."[5]

Numerous incidents, from the orchestrated greeting of Stonewall Jackson's troops at White's Ford to the more spontaneously enthusiastic reception of Fitzhugh Lee's cavalry brigade in Poolesville, seemed to confirm the most optimistic claims about Maryland's loyalty to the South. Ned Bayol, a volunteer with the 5th Alabama and part of Robert Rodes's brigade, crossed the river on September 4 with the first elements of Maj. Gen. D. H. Hill's command. Writing to his parents and sister one day later, Bayol reported that the local populace had proved welcoming. "So far we have been met by the people with glad hearts and open hands," he gushed. "They seem perfectly delighted to see us."[6]

Lieutenant William Owen of the Washington Artillery's 1st Battalion, part of Longstreet's command, likewise encountered friendly faces after he forded the river on September 6. "Every one we meet says he is a 'rebel'," he recalled of the march north, and "we are most hospitably received wherever we go [and] we get plenty to eat and to drink." One of Owen's comrades in the 1st Battalion named

5 Robson, *Reminiscences of the Civil War*, 118; Dunaway, *Reminiscences*, 48; Sorrel, *Recollections*, 104; Benjamin Grubb Humphreys, Unpublished Autobiography. MDAH, Jackson, Mississippi. My thanks to Douglas J. Ashton for the source.

6 Bayol Family Papers MSS2 B3455b2 (Entry #50). Alabama Vertical File, ANBL.

Napier Bartlett also saw promising signs of sympathetic Marylanders: "At all of the farm houses near the river the people appeared hospitable and reb down to their boots." George Bernard of the 12th Virginia echoed this impression when he confided to his diary on September 7, "people along the road [are] almost unanimously in favor of the South." The war correspondent PERSONNE recorded a curious encounter while standing on the Maryland shoreline with an older gentleman watching Longstreet's command ford the river. The unnamed man, who had given the reporter a place to sleep after he had crossed the river with Jackson's command the night before, exclaimed, "Goodness gracious, look at the secesses! I never seen such a sight n all my life. Why, you've got enough soldiers to whip all creation; but look yere, won't these fellers hurt us Marylanders? I'm a little afeard that when they get to ranging around the country, they'll interfere with my family and do something wrong." PERSONNE assured the man that he had nothing to fear, and "later saw the reassurance verified by the good behavior of the Confederate soldiery at the home of his erstwhile host."[7]

Given his reputation, General Lee attracted the most attention in Maryland, particularly among the local women. "The young ladies are wild to see Gen. Lee," reported Lieutenant Owen, "and we agree to find him for them; so in the afternoon a caravan is made up of all the old family carriages in the country, and filled with pretty girls, and we escort them to where 'Uncle Robert' is resting. He is immediately surrounded, and kissed, and hugged, until the old gentleman gets very red in the face, and cries for mercy." Stonewall Jackson proved popular as well, reported a correspondent from the *Rockingham Register* traveling with the general. "Greeted by . . . the people [during the] grand triumphal march," Jackson was even presented by one enthusiastic Marylander with a "gigantic gray mare."[8]

Jed Hotchkiss of Jackson's headquarters group witnessed much the same as their column advanced. He reported it in a letter to his wife, noting that "the news

7 Owen, *In Camp and Battle*, 130; Bartlett, *Military Record*, 129; Bernard, ed., *War Talks*, 23; Andrews, *The South Reports the Civil War*, 205.

8 Hotchkiss noted that the civilian who presented this horse to Old Jack did so at Three Springs on Sept. 5. Hotchkiss Letters, Sept. 8, 1862. Jackson would soon regret mounting this horse. After climbing into the saddle the following morning, "she seemed stupid about starting. He touched her with a spur, and then with distended nostrils and flashing eyes she rose on her hind feet into the air and went backward, horse and rider, to the ground. The General was stunned, bruised, and injured in the back." Douglas, *I Rode with Stonewall*, 147. Jackson traveled the rest of the way to Best's farm stretched out in an ambulance. Owen, *In Camp and Battle*, 130 and Bartlett, *Military Record*, 129.

of our coming spread rapidly, and young men & old flocked to see Gen. Jackson, whom they look upon as their deliverer—we passed on through a corner of Montgomery Co, and crossed the Monocacy river and encamped near Three Springs in Frederick Co—six miles from Frederick City, where the people came from every direction as the news spread and offered us anything they had for the use of our army."[9]

Sympathetic civilians did not reserve their affection for Lee and Jackson alone, noted William McClendon of the 15th Alabama, believing the "Cheers and smiles, and the waving of hats and handkerchiefs by the women, girls and boys . . . [were] a token of our welcome." Similarly, Draughton Haynes of the 49th Georgia, part of A. P. Hill's division, wrote on September 6 that, after "a hard day's march," his regiment passed "a small town called Buckettown" in the vicinity of which "Many of the Marylanders appeared glad to see us. I hope our cause is favorable with them."[10]

This was also PERSONNE's experience, the aforementioned reporter to the *Richmond Dispatch*. "Thus far we have everywhere met with hearty hospitality," he informed his readers back in the Confederate capital in a missive dated September 7. "Along the road," he continued,

> the farmers have welcomed the presence of our men with a sincerity that cannot be misunderstood, opened their houses and spread their boards with the fat of the land. One Marylander, with whom I met, has fed in twenty-four hours six hundred hungry men, free of charge. Others have been proportionately liberal. Our reception up to this point has been all that we could desire. With a few, the enthusiasm has been highly demonstrative, but the majority content themselves with quiet manifestations of the warm sympathy they feel. Nearly all the houses along the route of march were open, and invitations were freely extended to the officers to spend the day and night.[11]

In their enthusiasm, some of these witnesses may have minimized the troubling number of blank stares that other men in the army noticed during their march to Frederick. The cool reception did not escape James Sheeran, a Catholic priest serving with the 14th Louisiana of Brig. Gen. Harry Hays's brigade: "During

---

9 Hotchkiss Letters, Sept. 8, 1862.

10 McClendon, *Recollections of War Times*, 128; Haynes, *Field Diary*, 16.

11 Letter quoted in John Esten Cooke, *The Life of Stonewall Jackson: From Official Papers, Contemporary Narratives, and Personal Acquaintance* (New York, NY, 1863), 197.

our march this morning the people flocked to the roads to see us. Among the crowds we saw some friendly countenances, but the greater number looked upon us with seeming indifference."[12] Lieutenant Ham Chamberlayne of the Purcell Artillery of A. P. Hill's division echoed Sheeran's dismay in a letter to his mother written outside Frederick: "Reached this town by 1 p.m. . . . This part of Md. does not welcome us warmly. I have long thought the State was a humbug."[13]

James Shinn of the 4th North Carolina, part of George B. Anderson's Brigade of D. H. Hill's division, committed the following to his diary on September 6: "Our forces were near Frederick city and we marched in that direction through a fine and thickly settled country. Splendid farms and houses were plenty but we saw little symptoms of 'secesh'. We . . . marched through a very small town on the map of Md. called Buckeystown. No signs of secesh there—in fact the houses were all shut up and nearly all the people we saw looked as if they had lost a dear friend. All the signs we saw of secesh were two ladies that hurrahed for 'Jeff Davis'."[14]

A gunner serving with Parker's Virginia battery noticed the absence of enthusiasm and wrote about it. "We have come about fifteen miles into Maryland," he informed the *Richmond Dispatch*, and "have seen no enthusiasm for Southern Rights—not a white handkerchief from a window, though from the stateliness of some of the mansions there must be white handkerchiefs in them." Another man from the 12th Virginia of William Parham's brigade, R. H. Anderson's division, witnessed much the same. "We passed the village of Birchtown, on our route to Frederick. We encountered many talkative old ladies, and some young ladies. But few men were to be seen," he wrote the *Petersburg Express*. "All are Union. But one girl with a secession flag could be seen in our entire route to which we reached on Sunday, the 7th."[15]

William Hill of the 13th Mississippi, William Barksdale's brigade, thought the reception in Buckeystown was a mixed bag: "Clear and warm. Started at daylight. The citizens of Maryland did not receive us with much enthusiasm . . . [although] a

---

12 James B. Sheeran, *Confederate Chaplain* (Milwaukee, WI, 1960), 24.

13 Chamberlayne, *Virginian*, 102. I have switched the order of Chamberlayne's comments to support a clear presentation.

14 Shinn Diary, Sept. 6, 1862.

15 Anonymous letter dated Sept. 6, 1862, from a member of Parker's Battery, *Richmond Dispatch*, Sept. 17, 1862; quote in the *Petersburg Express* reprinted by the *Camden Confederate*, Oct. 3, 1862.

few manifested their pleasure at our presence by waving of handkerchiefs hallooing &c."[16]

J. J. McDaniel of the 7th South Carolina found "some friends and some foes" on the dusty road to Frederick. "Sometimes an old man with all his daughters would come out to the road, smile upon us, and wave handkerchiefs," he recalled. "Others would close their doors, and we could see them making wry faces from the windows up stairs." The sour glances only seemed to encourage McDaniel's more vocal comrades, who cried out when passing "a house of this kind . . . 'You been wanting us in the Union a long time, you got us now'." Private Alexander Hunter also remarked on the ambivalence of the people he and his comrades in the 17th Virginia encountered. "In an hour after the passage of the Potomac the command continued the march through the rich fields of Maryland. The country people lined the roads, gazing in open-eyed wonder upon the long lines of infantry, that filled the road for miles, and as far as the eye could reach, was the glitter of the swaying points of the bayonets. It was the first ragged Rebels they had ever seen," Hunter continued, "and though they did not act either as friends or foes, still they gave liberally and every haversack was full that day at least."[17]

Given the way the history of the campaign has been written over the years, it is perhaps surprising that Lee's men also received a warm welcome on the day they occupied Frederick City.[18] Colonel Bradley Johnson arrived early on the morning of Saturday, September 6, at the head of an infantry brigade in Brig. Gen. William Starke's (Jackson's) infantry division. A group of "some fifty or a hundred horsemen" preceded Johnson to the intersection of Market and Patrick streets, where the colonel halted to read an announcement that Southern troops had come "as friends and not as enemies, to relieve the people of Maryland from the tyranny

---

16 Hill Diary, Sept. 7, 1862.

17 McDaniel, *Diary of Battles*, 10; Hunter, "A High Private's Account," 507-508. A sergeant named Petit of the Fluvanna Artillery noted similarly, "Some of the people here take Confederate notes, and some, I am told, do not. ... I have seen and conferred with only one man, an old one, and he seemed alright, though not enthusiastic, in our behalf." Martin, *The Fluvanna Artillery*, 48.

18 The extent of pro-Southern sentiment in Frederick has been lost over the years because of the Confederate tendency to complain about Marylanders after the campaign ended, and an overweighted focus on the perspectives provided by unionist witnesses. For example, see *Steiner Report*; Quynn, ed., *The Diary of Jacob Engelbrecht*; and *Records of the Past: Ann R. L. Schaeffer Civil War Diary, September 4–23, 1862*, transcribed by Kira Vaughan (Frederick, MD, no date). Engelbrecht and Schaeffer are available at the Frederick Historical Society, Heritage Frederick; *Steiner Report*, 7.

to which they were enchained; that they did not propose to interfere with any non-combatants, to disturb private property, or to inquire into their opinions; and that whatever stores they might require would be paid for either in Confederate notes or United States Treasury notes, as the people might prefer." The response was rather lackluster and "some secession-sympathizers [offered] feeble shouts," recalled U. S. Sanitary Service Inspector Lewis H. Steiner. When the muted affair ended, the Southern horsemen dispersed into the surrounding countryside to collect livestock and other provisions for the army. Some sympathetic local farmers offered some of their animals as gifts, if a letter written by Thomas Yarrington of the 3rd Alabama on September 12 is to be believed. Yarrington claimed "our army was cordially received at Frederick, and presented with a large drove of beeves by the citizens" before closing with news that "the people of Maryland are fully aroused, and their enthusiasm in the cause unbounded."[19]

Steiner's observations have long been cited as support that Frederick was staunchly pro-Union. The supposed weakness of the public response to Johnson's announcement, however, may have had as much to do with the early hour of the day on a weekend as it did with anti-Confederate sentiment. By the time General Starke marched Jackson's division through Frederick at 10:00 a.m., cheering townspeople had gathered on North Market Street to receive them.[20] William Goldsborough of the Baltimore Light Artillery recalled this happy greeting, writing

19 *Baltimore American* reprinted in the *Alexandria Gazette*, Sept. 8, 1862; *Steiner Report*, 7. Concerning the acquisition of livestock, "It is said that an advance guard had preceded them (the Rebels) during the night, who had camped at White Oak Springs, within three miles of Frederick. This latter party had foraged along the road, purchasing cattle and sheep, which they seized and paid for, and had a good stock of provisions collected by the time the main body reached them. They brought with them nothing but ammunition trains. After partaking of food at the Springs they took up their line of march for Frederick, first sending out foraging parties, who seized large numbers of cattle and sheep and drove them back across the river." *Alexandria Gazette*, Sept. 8, 1862. The order of Steiner's comments, but not their sense, has been changed to fit the narrative. *The Columbus* (GA) *Weekly Times*, Sept. 22, 1862.

20 Johnson quartered the 1st Battalion Virginia Infantry, and probably the 42nd Virginia, as provost troops on the grounds of the old Hessian Barracks on the south side of the city. See Driver and Ruffner, *1st Battalion Virginia Infantry, 39th Battalion Virginia Cavalry, and 24th Battalion Virginia Partisan Rangers*, 28, and Chapla, *42nd Virginia Infantry*, 25. There is some evidence that Johnson may have quartered the entire Second Brigade at the same location. John Worsham of the 21st Virginia recalled how the brigade "marched to the Fair Grounds, which had been fitted up as a large hospital for the enemy." Worsham, *One of Jackson's Foot Cavalry*, 138. Worsham's description matches the location of U.S. General Hospital #1, also located near the Hessian Barracks, and was where the old fairgrounds were situated until the establishment of new grounds east of the city. Johnson named Lt. Lewis Randolph provost marshal of Frederick before relinquishing command of the brigade to Capt. John E. Penn. OR 19, 1:1006-07.

how "On the 6th of September the battery passed through Frederick city, and encamped on the suburbs. Many were the congratulations the brave fellows received from the citizens." A second man from Starke's command corresponding with the *Rockingham Register* under the pseudonym INVADER remembered the same: "At Frederick City we were received as we marched through, with waving hats and handkerchiefs, shouts, and all the evidences of joy." John Esten Cooke, a captain in Jeb Stuart's cavalry also recorded these events: "A few of the residences were open . . . and in those ladies and gentlemen were waving their handkerchiefs, and displaying the Confederate flag. From one of these, the residence of a Mr. Ross, a lawyer of high standing, his family were distributing to the soldiers as they passed eatables and clothing to such as seemed most needy."[21]

John Robson saw smiles as well, recalling how the 52nd Virginia "got to Frederick City on the 6th, and . . . the good people of Maryland treated us very kindly." William Heirs of the 3rd Alabama, part of Rodes's brigade, also remarked on how he and his comrades "met with a warmer welcome than we expected, especially from the ladies." Clayton Coleman, a lieutenant in the 23rd Virginia, wrote home that "we were rec'd with a good deal of kind feeling" in Frederick. Even Anne Schaeffer, a member of a unionist family, observed how when the Confederate column appeared, the men "were received with open arms by those who favored their cause."[22]

William Mercer Otey and a few of his comrades straggled from their artillery unit to explore the town and see the hospitality that Maryland comrades in their battery had promised would be forthcoming. "What a time we had!" recalled the artillerist. "Everything was free, and the citizens told us to help ourselves. How refreshing [was] the cool lager beer in the Dutch cellars and the ice cream and iced drinks of every description!" A man sitting on his front porch "with half a dozen beautiful ladies surrounding him" hailed Otey as he walked the city streets and invited him to come into their home. The ragged soldier "found half a dozen 'Johnny Rebs' [in the dining room] trying to strike a general average for the many meals missed since we commenced the campaign." The ladies of the house waited

---

21 Goldsborough, *The Maryland Line*, 305; *Rockingham Register and Virginia Advertiser*, Harrisonburg, Virginia, Sept. 19, 1862; Cooke, *The Life of Stonewall Jackson*, 198. Federal forces imprisoned William J. Ross, Esq. at Fort McHenry for a time in 1861.

22 Robson, *Reminiscences of the Civil War*, 118; Letter of William Andy Heirs, 3rd Alabama Infantry Regiment, Near Frederick, Sept. 7, 1862. Copy in Alabama Vertical File, ANBL. Coleman Letter, Sept. 27, 1862; Schaeffer, *Records of the Past*, Sept. 6, 1862.

on Otey and the others until they had eaten their fill and accompanied him through the back garden, one on each arm "listening intently to the blood-curdling tales of battle." Otey returned to his battery hoping the evening's pleasures would be compensation enough to "brave the anger and punishment that I knew was sure to be meted to me when I reported . . . for duty."[23]

Not all of the men in Jackson's old division had as enjoyable a lark as William Otey. A number of the general's troops got into trouble passing through Frederick, so much so that Jackson received a complaint about soldiers identified as "foreigners" insulting women on the street. Old Jack took the description of the perpetrators to mean Starke's heavily-accented Louisianans and "ordered the 2d Louisiana Brigade to be marched to town for identification" by the offended women. A proud man, Starke took issue with his men being singled out and refused to comply unless every other regiment in town received the same orders. Jackson responded as he usually did when a subordinate failed to obey and placed Starke under arrest while an investigation of the incident could be carried out. This inquiry eventually revealed "that the malefactors came from Jackson's old Stonewall brigade," recorded Louisianian Napier Bartlett. Starke returned to command his own brigade once John R. Jones arrived to resume command of the division. The offending Virginians never received punishment.[24]

During these early hours of the Confederate occupation, local secessionists who had long awaited the arrival of Lee's army took advantage of the situation by seizing the post office, the telegraph office, and city hall. Johnson's men joined them in tearing down U. S. flags on the public buildings and unfurling the Stars and Bars. By the afternoon of September 6, Rebel officers had occupied all of Frederick's hotels and "the streets were swarming with ragged, filthy, worn out men," granted leave from Jackson's command and John Bell Hood's division.[25]

Visiting Frederick proved to be an extraordinary experience for many in the ranks, for up to that point the army had subsisted entirely off the countryside. Frederick was the first city outside of the Confederacy that any of Lee's men had encountered. Given Maryland's assumed status as a friendly state, expectations ran

23 Otey, "The Story of Our Great War," 366.

24 Bartlett, *Military Record*, 31.

25 *The Cecil Whig*, Sept. 13, 1862; Schaeffer, *Records of the Past*, Sept. 6, 1862. "Most of the officers were quartered at the hotels and at the houses of prominent rebels." *Baltimore American* quoted in *Richmond Dispatch*, Sept. 16, 1862. Also see Gordon, *Never the Like Again*, 144.

high that the shopkeepers would accept Confederate notes for payment as readily as they would paper currency from the United States. Initially, this assumption appeared correct, with storekeepers selling destitute Southerners all the goods they required. "Confederate money," wrote John Esten Cooke of their first day in Frederick,

> was taken without a murmur by all who opened their stores, and for the first time during the campaign we enjoyed the privilege of purchasing at peace prices the articles we most required. Coffee could be had in abundance at twenty-five cents per pound, sugar at eleven and twelve cents, salt fifty cents a sack, boots five and seven dollars a pair, shoes three dollars, flannel forty cents a yard, and every thing else in proportion. Lager beer, ice cream, dates, confections, preserves, all found ready sale, and were liberally dispensed and disposed of.[26]

Some men in Bradley Johnson's command were lucky enough to procure watermelons, which they plucked from freight cars parked at the Baltimore & Ohio rail yard. According to a letter written to the *Richmond Dispatch* by a soldier identified only as A. T., other men purchased their melons "at cheap rates" in Frederick's shops. "At every corner, and, in fact, at almost every door," he continued, "you might see a party eagerly devouring them. By evening the pavement was so covered with the seed and rinds that one could scarcely walk without falling."[27]

Lewis Steiner also witnessed how the "stores were soon thronged with crowds, the shoe stores [being] most patronized, as many of their men were shoeless and stockingless." The only money most of them had "was Confederate scrip, or shinplasters issued by banks, corporations, individuals, etc.—all of equal value," he explained:

> To use the expression of an old citizen, 'the notes depreciated the paper on which they were printed.' The crowded condition of the stores enabled some of the chivalry to take what they wanted, (confiscate is the technical expression,) without going through the formality of even handing over Confederate rags in exchange. But guards were placed at the stores whenever requested, and only a few men allowed to enter at a time. Even this arrangement proved inadequate, and the stores were soon necessarily closed.[28]

26 Cooke, *Life of Stonewall Jackson,* 198.

27 *Richmond Dispatch,* Sept. 20, 1862.

28 *Steiner Report,* 9.

Unionist Marylanders commonly referred to Southern soldiers as "the chivalry," so seeing it used in Steiner's writing reveals his political inclination. In addition, while many of Frederick's shopkeepers complained about receiving Confederate notes, Steiner's definition of payment in the currency as "confiscation" is a red flag cautioning that his testimony may not have represented opinion across the entire community.[29]

"We find a good many friends [when we] went into the city," wrote Jackson's map-maker Jed Hotchkiss on September 6 . "[S]ome of the merchants sold freely and took Confederate money; others would not take it, but no one was constrained." Adding in a letter to his wife on September 8 that "our men were in a paradise to them," Hotchkiss elaborated on the situation, writing "those that would take Confederate money could not hand out goods fast enough—especially such things as boots, shoes &c—and especially eatables. Some refused to take Confederate money because they said they had to pay notes in bank and our money was not bankable here, though it soon might be—but many sold freely, especially of the needed articles & many things were bought."[30]

Napier Bartlett observed how "grocers were found with sufficient sympathy to take Confederate money in return for a variety of eatables and drinkables. Our supplies were replenished and that night there was a Sardanapalan feast, on a limited scale, which effectually banished the memory of hard marches." William Goldsborough remembered the experience in Frederick fondly, writing only a few years after the war that "during the three days [his battery] remained [near Frederick] their wants were abundantly supplied." Even Jacob Engelbrecht, a pro-Union diarist in Frederick, noted how "The first 8 or 10 thousand [Rebels] got a tolerable good supply of clothing & shoes & boots but the stores & shops were soon sold out."[31]

S. F. Tenney of the 3rd Georgia heard confirmation of this as well: "Many of our troops purchased articles at very low prices," even though "a number of the merchants refused to take Confederate money and closed their stores." Reverend Sheeran with the 14th Louisiana had a similarly positive experience, entering "a

---

29 Pro-Union Fredericktonians consistently described transactions in Confederate currency as theft or confiscation. See *Frederick Examiner*, Sept. 24, 1862, and *The Cecil Whig*, Sept. 13, 1862.

30 McDonald, ed., *Make Me a Map of the Valley*, 79; Hotchkiss Letters, Sept. 8, 1862.

31 Bartlett, *Military Record*, 129. Sardanapalan refers to being self-indulgent in the fashion of Sardanapalus, the legendary last king of Assyria in the 7th century B.C.; Goldsborough, *The Maryland Line*, 305; Quynn, ed., *The Diary of Jacob Engelbrecht*, 948.

Jew's clothing store in company with some of the boys who soon supplied me with a white shirt, handkerchief, and many other useful articles. The storekeeper being appraised of who I was, invited me to a room and furnished me with water, soap, and a towel. Oh! that happy moment! A good wash and a clean shirt were luxuries I had not enjoyed for over three weeks." Some Confederate quartermasters also fared well, buying "supplies of shoes and clothing" in bulk that they later distributed to the men in their brigades.[32]

Not everyone had the best of times. Ned Bayol, for example, complained about not being able to buy food because unionist shopkeepers would not accept Confederate money. The rejection of Southern currency could have signaled an individual's political leaning, but it might also have been a sober response to an extraordinary situation, as a letter penned by an unidentified Southern soldier killed at Sharpsburg suggests: "the mild and conciliatory policy we have adopted [toward Maryland's people] is already beginning to have a good effect, [but] the great difficulty with us is our money, the folks here, even those who sympathize with us are reluctant to receive it for their goods and as most of us have no other sort, we have not a little trouble to get what we want." The experience of Arthur J. Delashmutt illustrates Bayol's point. A fervent secessionist, Delashmutt rode out with other prominent citizens to greet Confederate troops as they approached Frederick. In an effort to help them, he returned to his dry goods store and threw open its doors. Lee's delighted men quickly overran the place, buying out "a large stock of boots and shoes" with Rebel scrip, which prompted Delashmutt to "grit his teeth in silence when some of his Union friends congratulated him on the fine business he was doing."[33]

Lee's men did the best they could with what they had, for their only means of payment was with Confederate currency; none of them could be blamed for not having U.S. dollars. The Rebs did not demonstrate a widespread tendency to

---

32 Tenney, "The Battle of Sharpsburg," in Owen, McBride, and Allport, eds., *Texans at Antietam*, 251-252; Sheeran, *Confederate Chaplain*, 26. Sheeran's reference to "who I was" presumably meant a member of the clergy with ties to the Jesuit community in Frederick. "[Winder's] brigade marched through Frederick and camped two miles from the town on the Emmittsburg road. Here they were assigned supplies of shoes and clothing." Lee A. Wallace, Jr., *5th Virginia Infantry* (Lynchburg, VA, 1988), 41. Captain Samuel Stevens, the quartermaster of the 12th Virginia, also secured "a lot [of shoes] he had that day (Sept. 7) purchased in Frederick city." Bernard, ed., *War Talks*, 23.

33 Bayol Family Papers MSS2 B3455b2 (Entry #50). Alabama Vertical File, ANBL; letter, *Frederick Examiner*, Oct. 8, 1862; *Cumberland Civilian and Telegraph*, Sept. 18, 1862.

"confiscate" whatever they wanted, as claimed by Lewis Steiner. As a civilian witness traveling through Frederick at that time later reported to the *Washington Republican*, "The soldiers are not allowed, under a penalty of death, to touch a thing or take articles without the consent of the owner, and then pay liberally for it (in Confederate scrip). The orders are strictly enforced, and as a consequence, not an ear of corn or a fence rail is disturbed." Most of Frederick's shops closed about 4:00 p.m. on September 6, as much for having sold out their stock as for anti-Confederate animus.[34]

The fact that it was a Saturday may have contributed to the closures. Even so, it did nothing to dim the celebratory atmosphere in town. Many sympathetic local citizens hosted parties and open houses to fete Rebel soldiers. John Worsham and a comrade from the 21st Virginia attended a number of these feasts after they managed to slip past the guard set up around their regiment's encampment. As the Virginian noted, they were "invited into several houses and entertained handsomely at supper, eating enough for half a dozen men." Robert Charles of the 7th South Carolina Cavalry, which served as Longstreet's bodyguard in Maryland, experienced the generosity of Frederick's people, recalling "the huzzas of an enthusiastic crowd of sympathizers in beautiful Frederick City, where we supplied ourselves with many good things."[35]

The offer of good food and conversation naturally attracted the likes of Jeb Stuart and even General Lee, with the latter responding to a dinner invitation in Frederick that night. Stuart's Prussian chief of staff, Heros von Borcke, found Frederick "in a tremendous state of excitement" on September 6. "The Unionists living there had their houses closely shut up and barred," he recalled,

> but the far greater number of the citizens, being favourably disposed to the Confederate cause, had thrown wide open their doors and windows, and welcomed our troops with the liveliest enthusiasm. Flags were floating from the houses, and garlands of flowers were hung across the streets. Everywhere a dense multitude was moving up and down, singing and shouting in a paroxysm of joy and patriotic emotion, in many cases partly superinduced by an abundant flow of strong liquors.[36]

34 *Washington Republican*, reprinted in the *Rockingham Register and Advertiser*, Sept. 19, 1862; Schaeffer, *Records of the Past*, Sept. 6, 1862.

35 Worsham, *One of Jackson's Foot Cavalry*, 138; Charles, "Brief Sketch," 65.

36 Von Borcke, *Memoirs*, 189.

That same evening, Bradley Johnson arranged for a public meeting. The Marylander, reported a newspaper, "used the most conciliatory language and made great predictions as to the power of the Confederate army not only to hold Western Maryland but to capture Baltimore and Washington, and dictate terms of peace in Independence Square at Philadelphia." The townspeople who attended Johnson's meeting then broke up and joined the evening's festivities until the official curfew of 10:00 p.m. when Rebel troops returned to their encampments along the Monocacy River fed, freshly-clothed or shod, and plied liberally with alcohol.[37]

Plenty of shopkeepers appear to have remained open until their stocks were exhausted on September 6 or until they decided that they had done enough business for the day. Most stores remained closed for the Sunday Sabbath. By Monday, September 8, word began to spread of food shortages brought about by the descent of tens of thousands of ravenous men into the area. William Owen remembered arriving in Frederick on Sunday after "Jackson's 'foot cavalry' . . . [had already] gobbled all the plunder." He and his comrades got lucky when they located "a grocer, a good, sensible fellow, with 'rebel sympathies,' and we invested a few hundred dollars, 'Confederate scrip,' in coffee, sugar, whiskey, Scotch ale, champagne, and a few other 'necessaries of life'." The shopkeeper's unionist partner objected "when the last of his stock of groceries was exchanged for Confederate notes," to which the Rebels in his store responded, "when Maryland began to 'burn' they would be good in New York for gold."[38]

Another civilian witness recalled that by the time he departed Frederick on September 9, Lee's troops had "perfectly cleared every thing out of the city in the way of clothing and provisions, so much so that if they remain a week longer both soldiers and people will be in a starving condition." Barren shelves notwithstanding, some Rebels still wandered "around the town . . . begging something to eat." One disappointed Southerner noted in his diary that his companions were "anxious to purchase at the stores in town . . . [but] not many [were] open after Saturday."[39]

---

37 *Baltimore American* reprinted in the *Alexandria Gazette*, Sept. 8, 1862. "At 10 o'clock at night the men were all ordered to their camps on the outskirts of the city, and the first day of Confederate rule in Frederick passed off quietly and peacefully." Ibid.

38 Owen, *In Camp and Battle*, 131.

39 *Cumberland Civilian and Telegraph*, Sept. 18, 1862; Michael Schuler Diary, Sept. 6, 1862. Library of Congress, Manuscript Division, Miscellaneous Manuscript Collection, Washington, D.C.

Even Lewis Steiner had to admit that as of Monday, September 8, shortages did as much as political leanings to dictate the behavior of many vendors. "The supplies in our stores having nearly given out, some of the Union merchants resolutely closed their stores to the soldiers," he admitted, "and sending for their customers asked them to take what they required at the usual rates." Fellow townsman Jacob Engelbrecht agreed. "[T]he men had leave of absence [on Monday] to visit the town & make purchases. I think I am within bounds when I say there were at least ten thousand in town. A complete jam," he explained. "All the stores & shops were sold out & not the one half supplied . . . Today (Tuesday, September 9) there is nothing to sell." According to Steiner, some merchants took advantage of the situation to increase their profits. "The wealthiest grocer in the town raised the price of coffee to seventy-five cents, and brown sugar to forty cents per pound, to be paid in gold or in our own currency," he complained. "This outrageous attempt to take advantage of the troublous condition of the community has excited considerable indignation . . . all around."[40]

Complaints about the closed storefronts in Frederick eventually reached Robert E. Lee, whose comment about them at the top of Special Orders No. 191 has long been understood as an expression of thinly veiled disgust. "The citizens of Fredericktown, [were] unwilling while overrun by members of this army, to open their stores," wrote the general, who ordered his subordinates to prohibit "all officers and men of this army . . . from visiting Fredericktown except on business, in which cases they will bear evidence of this in writing from division commanders. The provost-marshal in Fredericktown will see that his guard rigidly enforces this order."[41]

Lee's order could have reflected disappointment with the response of Frederick's shopkeepers to his men, but given the shortages noted by Confederate troops and unionist witnesses alike, it may also have been a simple statement of the situation as it existed at the time and an effort by Lee to maintain good relations with the local populace. Correspondent Peter Wellington Alexander, for example, summed up the situation in a missive to the *Savannah Republican* on September 8: "All the hats, clothing and shoes in the town have been bought up by the quartermasters or the troops themselves," he wrote. "We have found less trouble about our currency than was expected. The farmers and merchants prefer

---

40 Quynn, ed., *The Diary of Jacob Engelbrecht*, 946; *Steiner Report*, 17-18.

41 Dowdey and Manarin, eds., *The Wartime Papers of Robert E. Lee*, 301.

Maryland or Virginia money in exchange for their produce and wares, but still they are not indisposed to receive Confederate notes at some discount. Those who are unwilling to take them are generally unionists, who close their stores and barns against us."[42]

Political leanings notwithstanding, the shortages may have created a turning point in relations between Frederick's people and Lee's army; thereafter, Confederate troops made increasingly resentful comments about anyone who refused their currency for payment. Under strict orders to refrain from plundering while in a "friendly" state, the rank and file remained on good behavior even though men who arrived toward the end of the army's stay near Frederick got the worst of it. Hoping to purchase both clothing and food, Pvt. Michael Hubbert of the 13th Mississippi confided to his diary on Wednesday, September 10 (the day the army marched toward Hagerstown), that Frederick's shops "were all closed and people, on no terms, would accept our money for anything."[43]

Sympathetic Fredericktonians tried their best to show support when Lee's men moved out. Multiple Confederate accounts mention spectators waving, cheering, and flying Rebel flags, just as they had when Starke's column marched through four days earlier. Jed Hotchkiss estimated that "about half the population is strongly with us." David Johnston, a young man in the 7th Virginia, witnessed "unmistakable signs of friendship and sympathy [including] a bevy of pretty girls, singing 'Maryland, My Maryland,' [who] on seeing our battle flag inscribed 'Seven Pines,' proposed 'three cheers for the battle flag of Seven Pines,' which were heartily and lustily given by us."[44]

Local children also enjoyed watching the procession, something Cpl. Orlando Hanks of the 1st Texas took the time to recall. Our regiment, he explained,

took up our line of march and pressed forward, passing through Frederick, a beautiful southern city. The people appeared awe stricken. The women and children, of course, were gathered to the front to see the soldiers pass. One little fellow was perched on the fence and asked if these were Texicans. On being told, 'Yes,' he remarked 'Oh, Mama, they look

42 *Savannah Republican*, Sept. 22, 1862.

43 Diary of Michael M. Hubbert, Pvt., Co. I, 13th Mississippi, Sept. 10, 1862. Center for American History, University of Texas at Austin. My thanks to Douglas J. Ashton for the source.

44 Hotchkiss Letters, Sept. 8, 1862. Johnston, *The Story of a Confederate Boy*, 138.

just like our folks.' Another one was heard to say: 'Here comes the Bonny Blue Flag now, come and see it.' It was a large Lone Star flag carried by the first Texas Regiment.[45]

"Over 300 soldiers took meals and lunch at our house," wrote Susannah Thomas Markell in her diary that day. Markell was a member of one of the more prominent secessionist families in town. Among those Rebels, she added, were "a number of officers and hundreds of soldiers [who] . . . nearly all took meals . . . many had in ordering meals mistaking the house, from its size, for a hotel." Markell continued:

> Captain J. W. Bondurant, Jeff Davis' Artillery, Alabama, Major James M. Goggin, of General McLaw's staff (Lynchburg, Virginia) here part of the day, also Captain Henry Fontaine of Mississippi, Fanny Ebert and other girls here all day. Mrs. Douglas displayed a pretty little rebel flag (which Alice McLanahan gave Henry) at the window. Fanny Evert had my southern cross which caused great cheering. I pinned, at his earnest request, a tiny Confederate flag to the hat of a South Carolina soldier as the army passed.[46]

John Dooley of the 1st Virginia remarked on the "good deal of noise and cheering among our particular friends on this occasion," while William Hill of the 13th Mississippi observed simply, "We found many friends" lining the streets. According to William Owen, "The citizens crowded the streets and windows to see the troops pass. Ladies were demonstrative, and waved their handkerchiefs." William White of the 3rd Richmond Howitzers took note that when his battery "commenced moving slowly along the road to Frederick city . . . a goodly number of Southern ladies appeared upon the balconies and at the windows, waving their handkerchiefs and wishing success to our brave troops."[47]

The cheering of Frederick's women attracted the attention of an anonymous letter writer in the 12th Virginia. "There are many ladies here who are strongly Secesh," he wrote home. "They have no hesitancy in expressing their sentiments." A comrade in the 12th Virginia shared the experience, writing in his diary:

45 Owen, McBride, and Allport, eds., *Texans at Antietam*, 65-66.

46 Diary of Catherine Susannah Thomas Markell, *Frederick Maryland in Peace and War, 1856-1864* (Frederick, MD, n.d.), 107.

47 Curran, ed., *John Dooley's Civil War*, 36; Hill Diary, Sept. 10, 1862; Owen, *In Camp and Battle*, 133; McCarthy, ed., *Contributions*, 130.

"Sentiment of the people strongly Southern, to judge from the demonstrations made to us."[48]

When George B. Anderson's brigade faced delays at the rear of the army's column, the always enterprising Rev. Alexander Betts of the 30th North Carolina took the opportunity to "Dine at Mr. Fitzhugh's in Frederick City." Betts declared Fitzhugh's to be a "lovely family." The reverend also met "Mr. Jones, next door. . . . Rev. Auguste, Chaplain 15th Virginia Regiment, Joseph Shawen, a good Southern Methodist, Col. Henson, President of the County Bank, aged and venerable (but had been arrested by the Federals), and Rev. Mr. Ross, a Presbyterian. Spend the night with Colonel Carmack in Frederick City. Strong Southern feeling among these good people." A soldier with the 13th North Carolina, part of General Garland's brigade, found Frederick "ornamented with Confederate flags" when his regiment passed through late in the day on September 10.[49]

A few well-wishers stepped out on the following day, recalled Capt. James Appleton Blackshear of the Sumter Artillery in his diary. Passing through Frederick in the army's wake, the Georgian spotted "The prettiest and only secession lady that I saw whilst in Maryland standing on the balcony of the third story in one of the principal buildings. Dressed in virgin white [she] dared to cheer for Jeff Davis and to raise her lovely arms in favor of the Rebels."[50]

Despite welcome demonstrations of support, the coldness of unionist Fredericktonians, including many displays of outright contempt, struck a jarring note with Lee's troops. Instead of recalling the warmth of their welcome, they would forever after remember the city as symbolic of Maryland's scorn for the Confederate cause. "The sentiment of this place is deep Union," complained a man from the 12th Virginia in a letter home. J. J. McDaniel of the 7th South Carolina, agreed: "As we passed through Frederick City, great demonstrations were made by friends and foes—some ladies were bringing pails of water to quench the thirst of the soldiers—some milk—some bread—some waved handkerchiefs and Confederate flags." Others, he continued, "waved Union flags from windows and held their noses as we passed—some crying, while our bands were playing and the

48 Quote from *Petersburg Express* reprinted by the *Camden Confederate*, Oct. 3, 1862; Bernard, ed., *War Talks*, 24.

49 Smith, "Additional Sketch Thirteenth Regiment," in Clark, ed., *Histories of the Several Regiments and Battalions from North Carolina*, 1:694.

50 Blackshear Diary, Sept. 11, 1862.

troops cheering." McDaniel and a man named Ledford from the 14th North Carolina both told the tale of "A crowd of pretty, well dressed ladies . . . conspicuously standing on the sidewalk, indulging in cutting remarks, using such expressions as rebel and traitor very freely" while the butternut column tramped past. One of the women arrogantly singled out a particularly seedy looking soldier. "Look at that ragged, dirty rebel," she exclaimed. Unfazed by the insult, the man coolly retorted, "Our mammas always taught us to put on our worst clothes when we go to kill hogs." Another of the women inquired why so many of the men went without shoes, inspiring a second man to respond, "We wore out our shoes running after the Yankees." Cullen Battle, an ardent secessionist from Alabama who led regiment in Rodes's brigade, was outraged when he witnessed "Our brave, but poorly clad men . . . jeered and ridiculed" by the citizens as they marched through town, including insults about their appearance shouted by "Women with Yankee effrontery [draped] from their windows."[51]

Alexander Hunter of the 17th Virginia remarked how he and his comrades "were rather disappointed [with the] . . . decidedly cool" reception, finding "the streets . . . generally well filled with citizens, and the balconies and porches too, but there was positively no enthusiasm, no cheers, no waving handkerchiefs and flags—instead a death-like silence—some houses were closed tight, as if some public calamity had taken place; there were many friendly people in the windows and doors, but they seemed afraid to make any manifestation of their feelings—only smiling covertly."[52]

Georgian James Nisbet observed outward expressions of unionist support when he and the 21st Georgia filed through Frederick. The bands played *Maryland! My Maryland*, but unionist sympathies ruled the day. "Some Confederate flags" flew in the town, recalled Nisbet, but there were "many more Union flags, expressive of the prevailing sentiment of that part of Maryland!" Frank Mixson of the 1st South Carolina studied the inhabitants as best he could to discern the political divisions: "As we passed through the town everybody was out to see us; streets crammed, doors and windows full; some cheering and waving Confederate flags; others jeering us and waving United States flags. We went through the town in a 'hurrah'

51 *Petersburg Express*, reprinted by the *Camden Confederate*, Oct. 3, 1862; McDaniel, *Diary of Battles*, 10-11; P. L. Ledford, *Reminiscences of the Civil War, 1861-1865* (Thomasville, NC, 1909), 54; Beck, ed., *Third Alabama*, 43.

52 Hunter, "A High Private's Account," 508.

and let them know that we knew we had just given the Yankee army a good licking at Manassas and were ready for them again."[53]

Some of the sharp banter between Rebel troops and unionist citizens resulted in humorous exchanges. Artillerist William Owen noticed "a buxom young lady, with laughing black eyes, watching the scene before her; on her breast she had pinned a small flag, the 'stars and stripes'." According to Owen, an observant soldier saw this patriotic demonstration and sang out as he strode past, "'Look h'yar, miss, better take that flag down; we're awful fond of charging breast-works!' This was carried down the line amid shouts of laughter. The little lady laughed herself, but stood by her colors."[54]

Thus the Army of Northern Virginia, cheered by some and disparaged by others, moved out to fulfill the objectives set out in General Lee's Special Orders No. 191. Along the way, Southern troops encountered divisions in public opinion similar to those found in Frederick City. The reception in Middletown, Maryland, for example, proved more hostile than anything Lee's men had yet encountered— so much so that Sgt. George Wise of the 17th Virginia described it as "very pronounced."[55]

The story of Stonewall Jackson meeting two young ladies with red, white, and blue ribbons in their hair, standing on the street waving American flags at him, is well known. Jackson politely lifted his cap in their direction before turning to his staff with a quiet smile. "We evidently have no friends in this town." Sergeant Wise encountered ladies in Middletown "on the street with cockades of ribbon, red, white and blue upon their breasts." A man with Company E stepped up and politely warned them to "return into the house and take off those colors [or] some damned fool may come along and insult you." The advice "had its effect," recalled Wise, "for they at once withdrew."[56]

The cold treatment continued. William Hill's diary relates that he and his fellow Mississippians "were treated very poor" in Middletown, where the townspeople "refused to sell us anything or take our money." Virginian John Dooley agreed:

53 Nisbet, *Four Years on the Firing Line*, 150; Mixson, *Reminiscences*, 25.

54 Owen, *In Camp and Battle*, 133-134.

55 George Wise, *Campaigns and Battles of the Army of Northern Virginia* (New York, NY, 1916), 172.

56 Henry Kyd Douglas, "Stonewall Jackson in Maryland," in Johnson and Buel, eds., *Battles and Leaders*, 2:622; Wise, *History of the Seventeenth Virginia Infantry*, 110.

"We find the villagers of Middletown quite a contrast to the kind prodigality and rich profusion of their fields and orchards. They are as sour as vinegar and it is generally the case in this part of Maryland . . . that where the soil was richest and the produce most liberal, the cultivators were dried up, cross groined and mean." Draughton Haynes reported meeting "some secessionists & some unionists" on the road through Frederick and Middletown. He likely met the former closer to Frederick than in the next valley over.[57]

James Shinn was marching in D. H. Hill's division bringing up the column's rear. "In the evening we passed through Middletown and found it a considerable little town," he recalled, "but . . . the people were peeping at us from the upper windows of the houses and a few ladies we saw looked as if they had just buried their 'Mammas'." David Johnston "met no smiles" in Middletown, where "a decided Union sentiment . . . [was] in evidence." George Bernard declared the same in his diary: "passing through the small village of Fair View and the town of Middletown, at which last place the people told us the last district vote was sixty Union and forty State Rights. The people here did not hesitate to declare themselves Union."[58]

The mixed experience continued, and only served to further reduce their confidence that Marylanders would rally to the secessionist cause. "On the 11th the march . . . continued towards Boonesboro and Hagerstown," wrote William Owen of his battery in Longstreet's column. "We find that our welcome along the road is not cordial, and the 'general rising' of 'down-trodden Maryland' will not be on hand." Jed Hotchkiss and Clayton Coleman agreed, the former sensing unionist sentiment becoming "stronger as we go northwest," while the latter noted in a letter home after the campaign "not so much [kind feeling] in . . . Washington Co."[59]

---

57 Hill Diary, Sept. 10, 1862; Curran, ed., *John Dooley's Civil War*, 37; Haynes, *Field Diary*, 17.

58 Shinn Diary, Sept. 10, 1862; Johnston, *The Story of a Confederate Boy*, 138; Bernard, ed., *War Talks*, 24.

59 Owen, *In Camp and Battle*, 135; McDonald, ed., *Make Me a Map of the Valley*, 80. Coleman Letter, Sept. 27, 1862. "I was in Frederick City & Hagerstown. In the former county we were rec'd with a good deal of kind feeling, but with not so much in the latter (Washington Co.), as that county had already furnished 14 companies to the Federal Army, 11 of wh[ich] surrendered at Harper's Ferry."

Artillerist William White observed much the same thing when he and his battery "Passed through the villages of Middletown and Boonsboro . . . [to] within six miles of Hagerstown." White continued:

> a great many ladies wear the Secession badge, but most of the people seem afraid of us, and seem to look upon our troops as invaders. . . . So far, our march into Maryland has resulted in but little good to our cause, and has lasted but a single week. There is no doubt of this fact (and 'tis useless to attempt to conceal it) the people, or at least the larger portion of them, are against the South, and that, too, most bitterly.[60]

Whether it was their foreign-sounding accents or personal conduct, several Louisiana boys met with the scorn they often seemed to arouse in Maryland. They arrived in the vicinity of Boonsboro with one wearing light blue trousers stripped from the body of a Yankee scout shot dead that morning. The small party ended up at "a neat little farm house, where milk jars, peace and plenty seemed to reign." There, the men "called for some milk," which brought an elderly woman (later described by one of the men as "repugnant") to the door. Spitting insults at the group, the defiant farm woman growled that "she had no milk for rebels . . . that she would give it to the neighbors' pigs first; and that it would be her heart's desire to give every rebel that crossed the Potomac a good drink of poison."

One of the leading Pelican State soldiers took umbrage at this verbal abuse and retorted with equal malice, triggering a heated shouting match that finally ended when he leaned in close to exclaim, "Madame, you fight so well with your tongue, it is a great pity you ain't a man, to fight for your 'glorious Union'." The matron gave as good as she got, thanking him for the compliment before replying that she had a "son there fighting for it, and I only wish I had twenty."

Flummoxed by the "repugnant" Marylander's refusal to back down, the soldier admitted she was "the worst Union case I've met in Maryland, and I want to take your name, as a contrast to some kind people I've met . . . let me have it as a remembrancer." The woman promptly provided it and the name of her son serving in the Union Army. It was then, continued the story, that the soldier recalled reading her son's name stitched into the waistband of his stolen trousers. "Madam," he observed coldly, "he'll kill no more rebels, for I killed him this morning, and these are his pants I now have on." When he showed the disbelieving

---

60 White, "A Diary of the War," 131.

woman the letters she herself had sewn, the grief- stricken mother cried in despair before fainting to the floor. She was still there when the Louisiana men left her.[61]

This exchange, quite remarkable for its nose-to-nose malice, proved exceptional during the campaign. A hardened mountain widow with children huddled around her skirt would angrily confront 6th Alabama troops under Col. John Gordon on her property amidst the fight on top of South Mountain on September 14, calling them "low down thieving rebels" and denying them water, but for the most part the negative reactions to Lee's columns tended to manifest themselves as sour facial expressions, the waving of Union flags, and offensive hand gestures.[62]

The experiences of these marching men reflected the complexity of life in a border state. As William McClendon of the 15th Alabama recalled: "The people along our route [through Washington County] did not seem to realize what was going on . . . At many of these houses, women, girls and boys had assembled to see 'Stonewall' Jackson's Corps pass. At nearly every place we were greeted with cheers and hoozas for Jeff Davis and the Southern Confederacy. Of course, we acknowledged by giving the 'Rebel Yell'." Reverend Betts also passed through Boonsboro on September 11, taking the occasion to visit with a Dr. Josiah Smith, where he found quiet, but "Strong intelligent Southern feeling." Similarly, John Tucker, a soldier with the 5th Alabama, "Passed through Boonsborough early [on September 12] & found many warm Sympathizers in the place." Fortunately for some of the men, "at every cross road we would find a lot of ladies with tables set with something to eat and coffee and buckets of water," recalled Frank Mixson of the march to Hagerstown. "It was impossible for them to feed us all but what they did do helped out considerably and was highly appreciated."[63]

According to J. J. McDaniel, the men under Lafayette McLaws met some local support in Pleasant Valley while on their mission to capture Harpers Ferry. After camping "for the night near the village of Brownsville," they discovered "the people generally sympathized with our cause, giving us liberally of whatever they could spare, for in our rapid marches and scanty means of transportation, our

61 "Sketches of Hampton's Cavalry," in Brooks, ed., *Stories of the Confederacy*, 94-95.

62 John Michael Priest, *Before Antietam: The Battle for South Mountain* (Shippensburg, PA, 1992), 232-233.

63 McClendon, *Recollections of War Times*, 133; Betts, *Experience of a Confederate Chaplain*, 16; Wilson, ed., "The Diary of John S. Tucker," 19; Mixson, *Reminiscences*, 27.

commissaries could not furnish us sufficient subsistence." Of the experience as a whole, McDaniel offered, "I must say in justice to Maryland, we have some warm friends, even in these Union Counties through which we passed. An old man was [even] seen to pull off his shoes and give them to one of our barefooted soldiers, and ride off in his socks." Lee's men met with at least some acts of kindness.[64]

On September 11, Longstreet's command, accompanied by General Lee, continued northwest from Boonsboro. One man recalled a column of "Two wagon trains [moving] side by side in the center of [the] road. Then on either side [marched] a line of infantry in four ranks . . . to protect our trains." Approaching armies naturally attracted teenaged boys, one of whom was David Clough of Hagerstown. The lad "rushed away to the square to see the first of the army ride into town." Clough found them "not at all like the knights in shining armor [he] had imagined they would be." Instead, he described the men of Lt. Col. Luke Brien's 1st Virginia Cavalry as "dirty and ragged, though full of good spirits [while] they laughed and called out to the girls, that they were a 'sight for sore eyes;' . . . the girls all giggled, and there was a general air of good fellowship and gaiety."[65]

According to a correspondent from the *Mobile Advertiser and Register* traveling with Longstreet's men, the Rebels found "strong southern feeling" in this part of the state. Perhaps so, but Frank Mixson and his comrades encountered a 16-year-old girl standing in the door of 'Hager's Store' in Hagerstown boldly waving the Stars and Stripes. When she asked the passing South Carolinians "'why don't you fight under this flag?' . . . Some fellow in [the] ranks remarked 'Hagerstown, Hager's store, Hager's daughter, hurrah for Hager,' and as was the custom we gave them the yell."[66]

Alexander Hunter of the 17th Virginia remembered the "actions of the citizens of Hagerstown [stood] . . . in vivid contrast to Frederick City, for not only were the men and women outspoken in their sympathy for the Southern cause . . . they threw wide open their hospitable doors and filled their houses with the soldiers, feeding the hungry, and clothing the naked, as well as their limited means allowed. I saw a

---

64 McDaniel, *Diary of Battles*, 11.

65 Stevens, *Reminiscences*, 67; Parks, *Turnpikes and Dirt Roads*, 256-257. On Sept. 11, the 1st Virginia Cavalry "charged into Hagerstown and captured [Federal] Lieutenant A. Nesbitt and a small number of enlisted men." *Valley News Echo*, Vol. III, 3 cited in Daniel C. Toomey, *The Civil War in Maryland* (Baltimore, MD, 1983), 50.

66 *Mobile Advertiser and Register*, Vol. XXX, No. 152. Friday, Sept. 26, 1862; Mixson, *Reminiscences*, 27.

Rebel troops camped near Hagerstown, Maryland. *Harper's Weekly, Sept. 27, 1862*

citizen in that place absolutely take the shoes off of his feet, in the streets, and give them to a limping bare-footed soldier." For the next two days, the always-ravenous troops collected "butter, honey, bacon, &c., [which they] brought into camp for both individual and social enjoyment."[67]

William Owen's gun crews also experienced a welcoming atmosphere in Hagerstown, which they reached on September 12 to find,

> the people . . . more demonstrative, and [bestowing] much polite attention. Many young girls approached us as we marched through the streets, and presented us with beautiful flowers. We remember gratefully the kind attention of Dr. Maguire and his charming family. . . . We did some 'shopping' . . . devoting ourselves chiefly to the 'dry-goods line,' and bought water-proof cloth and some dress patterns to present to our lady friends in Richmond, where they were in great need of such things. I should have liked to carry a wagon-load back.[68]

67 Hunter, "*A High Private's Account*," 511; Wise, *History of the Seventeenth Virginia Infantry*, 111.

68 Owen, *In Camp and Battle*, 135.

Owen also witnessed another of the more amusing episodes of the campaign involving Rebel troops and fanciful headgear. "One merchant had upon his top shelves, where they had lain for many years, about one hundred old-fashioned, bell-crowned beaver hats, with long nap upon them, just the style our fathers wore, and caricaturists are wont to place upon the head of Brother Jonathan," recalled the lieutenant, who continued:

> These were discovered by some funny fellow who appeared upon the street with one upon his head. The new 'mode' took like wildfire— as new fashions always do—and the store was soon relieved of the stock of beavers, and the streets were thronged with men with the new 'Brother Jonathan' hat. They wore them upon the march, and went into the battle of Antietam with this most peculiar head-gear for warriors. On the 13th it was reported that a cavalry skirmish had occurred at Frederick, and that McClellan with a large army, was following in our wake. . . . We found excellent lager beer and cigars in Hagerstown, and the 'Secessionists' entertained us hospitably.[69]

Even though the populace in and around Hagerstown seemed more inclined to welcome Southern troops than the people of Frederick or Middletown, some of the men encountered unionist sentiment. As artillerist John Ramsay discovered, these "Marylanders were so patriotic they would not sell us wood" when he and his men tried to buy kindling with Confederate currency. An Alabama correspondent with Longstreet's command thought the people of the region even more hard-headed than Fredericktonians when it came to accepting Rebel scrip. "[I]n this part of the State, where we must procure our supplies," he reported, "it is with great trouble we can pass it at all."[70]

The pro-Union sentiment would have been stronger had most of the area's unionists not fled to Pennsylvania. "Those who remained have given us a very cordial reception," admitted correspondent Peter Alexander, who continued:

> They have thrown open their houses to us, and exerted themselves to render us as comfortable as possible. Several Confederate flags were displayed, and the ladies met us at

---

69 Ibid., 136. An early predecessor to Uncle Sam, complete with beaver top hat and striped trousers, Brother Jonathan was a folk-tale character who appeared in pre-Civil War era newspapers and periodicals.

70 Ramsay, "Additional Sketch Tenth Regiment," Clark, ed., *Histories of the Several Regiments and Battalions from North Carolina*, 1:573; *Mobile Advertiser and Register*, Vol. XXX, No. 152. Friday, Sept. 26, 1862.

every corner with smiles, boquets and waving handkerchiefs. The boys hurrahed for Jeff Davis as lustily as they do in Richmond, and one can almost imagine he is in the far South. Intelligent citizens tell me there is not a county, even along the Pennsylvania border, that would not, if left to a free choice, cast its lot with the South.[71]

The most vexing experience for Lee's men and the source of their greatest disappointment remained the failure of Marylanders to flock to their cause. Several examples from a wide variety of sources make this abundantly clear. David Johnston of the 7th Virginia complained outside Hagerstown that he had "observed indications and heard some expressions of Southern sentiment [but none of it] satisfied us . . . [Maryland's people] were ready and willing to shed their blood for the Southern cause."[72]

John Ryder Randall's lyrics had promised social and political upheaval in the state and those expectations, reinforced by Marylanders in the ranks, fired the imaginations of weary Rebels far from home who were desperate to win the war. The prospect of adding large numbers of fresh men to the army appealed to soldiers who consistently faced Northern armies larger than their own. Despite a summer filled with victories, Lee's men knew they needed help if their cause was to succeed. The dream of receiving Maryland's support fueled high expectations that became divorced from reality.

"Sergeant Green," an unidentified Confederate who penned a letter found on his body at Sharpsburg, gave voice to this sentiment when he noted, "We were told that Md was ripe for revolution, and that as soon as we entered her borders 40 or 50 thousand would rush to our standard." Writing with obvious resentment on the field near Sharpsburg, Green complained that he and his fellows "had been fooled the damndest for the people here all appear to be very well satisfied with their condition." Like so many others around him, Green gave up his life for this fantasy.[73]

The reluctance of Maryland's people to actively join the Southern cause also confounded John Stevens. The state "had already sent many regiments in to our army, among them the commands of Generals Elzey and Bushrod Johnson . . . choosing such commanders as suited their fancy," wrote Stevens, "it seemed to be

---

71 *Savannah Republican*, Sept. 24, 1862.

72 Johnston, *The Story of a Confederate Boy*, 138.

73 *Frederick Examiner*, Oct. 8, 1862.

well understood that Maryland was as strong in her Southern sentiment as Virginia and all she needed was a chance to show her hand." The indefatigable Brig. Gen. James Jay Archer, "who at one time was colonel of the Fifth Texas," had been born in Stafford, Maryland, near the port town of Havre de Grace, explained Stevens. With men like this among them, "we confidently expected that when we marched into the state it would rise up en masse and fill our depleted ranks."[74]

Perhaps Maj. Robert Stiles of the Richmond Howitzers put it best when he observed after the war, "it is by no means admitted among intelligent Confederate soldiers that the only or the main design of the first Maryland campaign was to stir up revolt in Maryland or to recruit our army by enlistments there. It is not disputed that these may have been among the objects sought to be accomplished, nor that, so far as this is true, the campaign was a failure."[75]

William Blackford of Jeb Stuart's was also disappointed that their expectations did not bear fruit. The cavalryman explained to readers of his postwar memoir that

> Lee's force had been seriously diminished by the casualties of the vigorous campaign he had made and the reinforcements that our government should have had in readiness had not been called out to any adequate amount and those we had were not prepared and came in but slowly. . . . To cross over from war-wasted Virginia to the fresh rich fields of Maryland, where the people were represented as only awaiting our coming to flock to the Southern standard, was a source of delight to the whole army.[76]

Colonel John Gordon of the 6th Alabama also remembered how at the time "there was still a prevalent belief among Southern leaders that Southern sentiment was strong in Maryland, and that an important victory within her borders might convert the Confederate camps into recruiting-stations, and add materially to the strength of Lee's army."[77]

Even some newspapers in the North carried stories of the hope common throughout the Army of Northern Virginia that Maryland's men would rise to the occasion and take up arms for the South. The *Philadelphia Inquirer* ran a short piece on September 15 based on information received from "A Virginia captain, of much

74 Stevens, *Reminiscences*, 67, 68. I have slightly rearranged the order of Stevens's comments to enhance readability.

75 Robert Stiles, *Four Years Under Marse Robert* (New York, NY, 1904), 125.

76 Blackford, *War Years with Jeb Stuart*, 139-140.

77 Gordon, *Reminiscences*, 138.

intelligence, [who] told a relative in Leesburg, during the recent passage of Lee's army through it, that the Rebel force was eighty-four thousand, though Lee expected it would be increased thirty or forty thousand by [the] Secessionists of Maryland." Hundreds of miles west in Iowa, the *Davenport Daily Gazette* published a similar report on September 9, 1862. "Assistant Surgeon Dr. Greene of the 19th Indiana," noted the paper, claimed Rebels he had met "express confidence in being able to get into Maryland, where they expect to get 50,000 recruits." Chaplain James Sheeran of the 14th Louisiana agreed, effusing at the campaign's start: "The long cherished dream . . . was about to be realized. Maryland was to be invaded. The greater number of our men were enthusiastic, expecting that the Marylanders would flock to our standard by thousands, and that thus recruited we would carry the war into the enemy's country, [and] that we would soon unfurl our flag on the banks of the Susquehanna." These few statements represent but a handful of comparable declarations found in the letters, diaries, newspapers, and memoirs. None of this cherished dream would come to pass.[78]

Bradley Johnson quickly set up a recruiting office in Frederick City, and for a time reports came in of the army doing a brisk business. As INVADER informed the *Rockingham Register* in Harrisonburg, Virginia, "Recruits are flocking to the Confederate Standard, and even from Pennsylvania they come in. Where are the hearts of these people? Can Lincoln be such an ass as not to know that even the North are disgusted with his petty tyranny?" And as the anonymous Confederate A. T. wrote to the *Richmond Dispatch*, "we entered Frederick City to the great joy of many good hearts, who had been long looking anxiously for our coming. . . . Whilst there about 1,800 Marylanders enlisted in our army. Many came down from Pennsylvania and joined. I saw a squad of eight Pennsylvanians myself, who reported numbers of others as on their way to join us."[79]

Other witnesses made much of Keystone Staters registering for the cause as well and mentioned them in letters to Richmond that eventually found their way into the local newspapers. Writing from Frederick on September 9, "X" sought to

---

78 Sheeran, *Confederate Chaplain*, 23-24.

79 "Your correspondent visited Frederick yesterday. He found the city filled with Confederate officers. Recruiting for the Confederate army was going on very briskly." Special Dispatch to the *Philadelphia Enquirer* printed in the *Alexandria Gazette*, Sept. 10, 1862; *Rockingham Register and Virginia Advertiser*, Sept. 19, 1862; *Richmond Dispatch*, Sept. 20, 1862. The *Alexandria Gazette*, Sep. 17, 1862, also reported this: "The number of recruits to the Confederate army in Maryland is said to be about a thousand; fifty or sixty joined from the town of Frederick and its neighborhood."

sustain expectations in the Confederate capital that the campaign thus far had been a roaring success. "A large number of persons within twenty-five or thirty miles around us are enlisting," he claimed. "[Just] yesterday, some from York county, Pennsylvania, came to Frederick and enrolled their names. I confess I had my doubts about the people of Maryland in many of the counties, but I believe now the State will furnish forty thousand men." On September 16, the *Richmond Dispatch* printed "the statement of an officer of the Confederate army who arrived in this city yesterday, and who left Frederick a few days ago, [saying] . . . a company of Pennsylvanians, from Adams county, numbering one hundred and fifteen, arrived at Frederick last week, and tendered their services to the Confederate Government. This company was regularly organized, with its own officers, before they left their own State, and declared that they were unwilling to stay at home and be drafted into the abolition service."[80]

Similar rumors of recruiting success rapidly circulated throughout the Virginia army. "Recruiting here [in Frederick] goes on rapidly," declared John Esten Cooke of Jeb Stuart's command, citing PERSONNE's letter in the Richmond press dated September 8, 1862. The numbers reported were remarkably similar. "Within two days five companies have been formed, and it is stated that from the surrounding country over seven hundred entered our ranks while en route." Another of Stuart's staff officers, working out of cavalry headquarters in Urbana, Maryland, shared what he believed was optimistic news in a letter home on September 10 by claiming enlistment efforts thus far obtained in the campaign had been successful. "Col. Bradley Johnson of the 1st Maryland Regt is recruiting for the Maryland line & I understand has gotten about 1,500 in the neighborhood," he wrote. "This is the most Union part of the state, & I augur very well from our success here." Ned Bayol of the 5th Alabama shared this optimism by scribbling in his diary, "[I] understood yesterday [September 8] that 500 Marylanders had joined our Army. I truly hope that they may all do the same." Cavalryman Ulysses Brooks echoed Bayol's tally of recruits, estimating that "five hundred young men of the first families flocked to our standard" when the army sojourned at Frederick, and

80 *Richmond Enquirer*, Sept. 18, 1862; *Richmond Dispatch*, Sept. 16, 1862. A newspaper in Savannah, Georgia, published a similar statement: "A private letter from a respectable officer in Confederate service, dated Frederick, Sept. 9, says that fully eight hundred Pennsylvanians and fourteen hundred Marylanders have joined the Confederates since their occupancy of that city." *Daily Morning News*, Sept. 22, 1862.

Michael Schuler confided to his diary on September 6, "Citizens welcome us in Maryland. Many are flocking in to join us."[81]

Unfortunately for Brooks, Bayol, Schuler, and the rest, these reports were not true. In the end, between 100 and 200 recruits ended up joining the Army of Northern Virginia during its brief time in the Old Line State. Several Confederate and local Maryland sources proved much more reliable and confirm this range of estimates. S. F. Tenney of the 3rd Georgia, for example, reported that while near Frederick "two companies were made up in and around the city, which joined our army." Maryland diarist Jacob Engelbrecht kept a close accounting of secessionist volunteers. "A company of [47] southern rights men was made up in Frederick the past few days," he wrote on September 11, "and today a little after 12 o'clock PM they left town following the army towards Hagerstown." He embellished on this estimate a few days later by adding, "when the Rebels had possession of our city, a company was made up of the young men . . . to join the Rebel army. I recorded the list of the company (which passed our door) on that day (11 September) but have since found a more correct list [of 77 individuals] in the [*Frederick*] *Examiner* of today which I now copy."[82]

The number cited by Engelbrecht agreed with the sense of a report sent from Hagerstown on September 12 by a special correspondent traveling with Longstreet's command. "A company of recruits arrived this evening from Frederick," recorded the writer, and "others are coming in singly or in squads from the surrounding country. A recruiting office has been opened here, and a sufficient number have been enrolled to make up a company." Lastly, the newspaper in Middletown, Maryland, reported on September 19 "that only 50 or so from Frederick and 40 from the entire neighborhood enlisted" in the Southern army when it was in the vicinity, while a September 24 report published in the *Frederick Examiner* put the number at "one hundred and thirty recruits."[83]

Many of the men in Lee's army recognized the feebleness of Maryland's response to Confederate recruiting efforts and vented their anger in letters, diaries,

---

81 Cooke, *The Life of Stonewall Jackson*, 203; Trout, *With Pen and Saber*, 97; Bayol Family Papers MSS2 B3455b2 (Entry #49). Alabama Vertical File, ANBL; Brooks, *Stories of the Confederacy*, 83; Schuler Diary, Sept. 6, 1862.

82 Tenney, "The Battle of Sharpsburg," in Owen, McBride, and Allport, eds., *Texans at Antietam*, 251-252; Quynn, *The Diary of Jacob Engelbrecht*, 949, 953. See Harsh, *Sounding the Shallows*, 158, for a discussion of failed Confederate recruiting efforts.

83 *Middletown Valley Register*, Sept. 19, 1862, and *Frederick Examiner*, Sept. 24, 1862.

and postwar histories. A missive from the anonymous "C" to the *Richmond Dispatch* in September 1862 declared, "One word as to the reception of our army on the Maryland side. Many may be disappointed. Recruits came by the hundreds, when they were expected by some to have joined us by thousands." James Caldwell of the 1st South Carolina Volunteers expressed similar frustration: "We marched to the vicinity of Frederick City, where we rested until the morning of the 10th. . . . An effort was made to procure recruits for the army, but I would not be surprised if two figures could express the whole number obtained. We already realized that 'My Maryland' must be conquered to be brought into the Confederacy." After the war, William Smith of the 14th North Carolina referenced John Ryder Randall's lyrics while lamenting in his regimental history how "The invasion of Maryland was a political move [by Lee] rather than a military movement—hoping the Marylanders would flock to his banner and help to drive 'the despot's heel' from off 'her shore.' Disappointed! Not one enlisted in the Southern army." The weak response pleased unionist Lewis Steiner: "Recruiting goes on slowly in the town. We are told that three companies are to be raised here. It may be so, but one 'can't see it'."[84]

Perhaps the most poignant testimony came from a letter written by a man with the 5th Alabama who fell during the fight for the sunken road near Sharpsburg. The unidentified soldier captured the sense of despair in Lee's army:

> In Camp, Sept. 16, 1862. There is much more Union sentiment here than we expected to find. I think our officers are sadly disappointed with their reception here although they don't say much; I don't think the people of Maryland generally wish to cast their destiny in our hands. There are many here who wish us well, whilst but few will come forward to assist us. I think our leaders have been greatly deceived by misrepresentations as to the true sentiment of the people here. They are not with us.[85]

Lee's men offered multiple explanations for the recruiting debacle. The most common rationale rested on the mixed reception they had received. Blank stares, cutting remarks, and the flying of the Stars and Stripes in the face of passing Rebel columns proved to men that they had entered a part of Maryland more unionist in sentiment than they had thought. As J. B. Polley put it in his history of John Bell

---

84 *Richmond Dispatch*, Sept. 23, 1862. Emphasis in the source; James Fitz James Caldwell, *The History of a Brigade of South Carolinians Known First as "Gregg's" and Subsequently as "McGowan's Brigade"* (Philadelphia, PA, 1866), 41; *Steiner Report*, 12.

85 *Frederick Examiner*, Oct. 8, 1862.

Hood's Texas brigade, "large accessions to our ranks were promised . . . [but] the reception . . . Confederate commands were accorded by the Marylanders was as nearly freezing as the waters they waded—the truth being that they were entering a section of the State the residents of which were, as a rule, pronounced Unionists."[86]

Anonymous letter writer "C" agreed with Polley's assessment by explaining to readers of the *Richmond Dispatch* that, despite the friendly welcome he and his comrades had received from sympathetic Marylanders, "the whole route through which we passed was that part of the State considered most strongly Union."[87]

Lieutenant Ham Chamberlayne made a similar complaint in a letter to his sister dated September 8: "Maryland is foreign . . . People are kind enough generally, but they fear us with a mortal terror; many of them seem to think us Goths and Vandals and Huns, they tremble sometimes when spoken to, and are astonished to see us without the torch and tomahawk." Warming to his topic, Chamberlayne blamed the reluctance of Marylanders to fight for their rights on their low "Yankee" disposition, which differed in quality from more honorable, States' Rights oriented, Southern patriotism:

> The character of the population is not high with the education of the common schools, with dutch instincts dashed with Yankee blood, their minds disregard everything except the Baltimore & Ohio R. R. and the pursuit of gain. A kind of people among whom a republic is impossible, since they cannot guide themselves nor help others to guide them, but can only work, work, work, making money. The vice is incurable too, for they hold that this is the whole duty of man, and that he is worthiest who most unremittingly toils with his hands, or if with his brains, he must dry them up with years of mechanic toil over Day Book & Ledger; any thing else being blank heresy and schism. Of Lower Maryland nothing of this is true but this county, Frederick, it is as Yankee as Hartford or Cape Cod.[88]

Most observers paid little attention to character differences between Northerners and Southerners. Maryland's people, noted William Smith, "were Union sympathizers to the core," and could not be relied upon for help.[89]

---

86 J. B. Polley, *Hood's Texas Brigade: Its Marches, Its Battles, Its Achievements* (New York, NY, 1910), 112.

87 *Richmond Dispatch*, Sept. 23, 1862.

88 Chamberlayne, *Virginian*, 105.

89 Smith, *The Anson Guards*, 150-151. Tom Garber of the 12th Virginia Cavalry agreed, writing to his sister, "I don't think Maryland will go with the south. I think more than two thirds of the

The second most commonly offered reason why Marylanders did not rally to the Stars and Bars was the hardship of life in the field and the wretched state of the army. George W. Booth, a Marylander serving under Stonewall Jackson, explained as much in his memoir. "The appearance of our men was not conducive to the inspiring of confidence. Instead of the well-equipped bodies of soldiery to which they had been accustomed," he continued,

> they now beheld the ragged, barefooted confederates, who appeared at their very worst. The losses of the summer campaign had depleted the ranks of our regiments, the hard marches had caused a fearful amount of straggling, and in every way the outward appearance was most unpromising. For weeks the men had subsisted on the most irregular issue of rations, and the corn fields had been resorted to for food. Green roasting ears are not to be despised, but for a constancy, without meat, salt or other condiment, their continued use is not altogether wholesome. The fierce rays of the mid-summer sun and the consequent heat, with this poverty in supplies, had caused considerable sickness, and the poor feeble soldier, in his effort to keep up with his comrades in a strange land, presented a spectacle which, however much it appealed to the sympathy of the Marylander, did not inspire his confidence.[90]

Randolph Shotwell of Richard Garnett's Virginia brigade agreed with Booth's assessment, and left a lengthy explanation that is worth reproducing in full. "Most of the young recruits—especially those of the gentry class," he explained,

> no sooner 'came and saw' than they were 'conquered' of all desire to join such a Falstaffian crew, as presented itself to their fastidious wonder! One single look answered in some cases to turn back to peace and comfort the most ardent sympathizer. After all, there is a wide interval between 'sympathizing with' and 'serving with,' the half-clad, half-shod, half-fed, half-armed, unshaven, unshorn, unkempt, uncouth-looking, sunbrowned, battle-scarred, 'Rebel rag-tag.' Human nature, however patriotic, revolts from the idea of this sort of life, with daily peril added!

---

people are Union, anyhow they were in the part I was in; it is true as we passed along we would meet a Secesh family here and there but they were scarce." Thomas M. Garber to Addie Garber, Sept. 17, 1862, Garber Family Letters, Augusta County, Virginia Collection, Center for Digital History, University of Virginia, Charlottesville, VA. Available online at https://valley. lib. Virginia.edu/VoS/personalpapers/collections/augusta/garber html.

90 George W. Booth, *Personal Reminiscences of a Maryland Soldier in the War Between the States* (Baltimore, MD, 1898), 70-71.

Just think of a well-bred young gentleman giving up his comfortable home; his wine, cigars, morning paper, and afternoon canter with the ladies—giving it up to go away into strange places, and get wet, and sleep in the mud, and march in everlasting dust, carrying an old musket, and having to wear a dirty shirt, and cut off his hair and beard for lack of comb and brush to keep them clean, and go without food for days on days, and wear out his teeth on hard crackers, and turn his stomach on rancid bacon, or ill smelling beef (picking out the maggots first), and herd in daily, hourly, nightly association with a lot of ill-bred, illiterate, vulgar, sweaty, cursing, disorderly fellows—that speak such dreadful bad English! And then, you know, to go and have fleas and lice, and bugs and things crawling all over you, and have to plaster your-self all over with sulphur and stuff to cure the itch you took from the fellow who washed your solitary shirt—AWFUL!!!![91]

Very few of Maryland's eligible men could be expected to voluntarily enlist with the Army of Northern Virginia under such circumstances—regardless of the victories it had scored in Virginia. As William Smith learned while on the march, "citizens would stand, look, [and] engage in remarks—'They look hard; clothes in rags.' 'Half of them are barefoot; have not even dirty uniforms.' 'No uniforms at all'." Precisely these negative impressions," Smith continued, "are alleged to have discouraged a number of volunteers from Calvert County who initially rushed to join General Lee's army upon hearing it had entered the state, but returned to their homes . . . when they saw the sorry condition of the men." The voicing of such opinions by Marylanders led Lt. Thomas Carter of the King William Artillery to conclude, "I do not think [this state's men] are prepared to undergo the privation we are now enduring." Napier Bartlett believed Maryland's "refined population could only see [in us] the result of long soldiering, rags and filth, and barefooted soldiers . . . and so the sentiment of 'My Maryland' evaporated in poetry and paper."[92]

Some participants in the campaign offered additional reasons why Marylanders failed to heed the secessionist call. These explanations ranged from the legitimate fear that Southern troops would not remain north of the Potomac River long enough to protect open sympathizers, and a belief that the Virginia army had not been in Maryland long enough to attract a large number of men. Also, by the

---

91 Hamilton, ed., *The Papers of Randolph Abbott Shotwell*, 1:312-313.

92 Smith, *Anson Guards*, 151; Gordon, *Frederick County*, 145. The *Frederick Examiner*, Sept. 24, 1862 also reported: "Tuesday, 9th inst. Recruiting goes on slowly; many, who came to town to join the rebels, thought better of their folly and returned quietly to their homes." Dozier, ed., *A Gunner in Lee's Army*, 138; Bartlett, *Military Record*, 130.

second autumn of the conflict, the romantic novelty of war had been replaced by the visceral experience of intensifying bloodshed and the fear among the people that their state would become soon become a battleground. According to George Booth, "the continuous presence of large bodies of federal troops had the effect of making the people overcautious and doubtful of the ability of the confederates in maintaining themselves and of affording adequate protection."[93]

Anonymous letter-writer "C" agreed with Booth's assessment, arguing "even the Southern men of that section, before joining our army and risking their all, wished to know whether the movement was to be a more temporary raid, or an effort for permanent relief." Even Lee's own soldiers had a hard time answering the straightforward question, which led "C" to conclude, "When we consider these things we can well understand why it was idle to expect any more from Maryland than we actually received."[94]

War correspondent Peter Alexander wrote something along the same lines in his report to the *Savannah Republican* dated September 10. "While passing through Frederick, we were welcomed with many demonstrations of sympathy by the citizens, the women and children taking the lead," he observed. "The people in this part of the State have felt the heel of the oppressor, and hence even in the presence of a Confederate army they find it necessary to be as cautious as possible. They say if they only knew we would not abandon the State," he continued, "they would, throw off every disguise and array themselves on our side at once, with arms in their hands."[95]

Captain Sam Buck of the 13th Virginia admitted that he had fully "expected . . . Maryland men would rush into our army," before having his hopes dashed by their palpable lack of enthusiasm. By September 1862, argued the discouraged officer, "War had become a reality, men were being killed by hundreds and thousands and the novelty had worn off. Had such an opportunity been presented the first year of the war we would have had the state of Maryland with us and many most excellent soldiers. I did not hear anyone express delight at our presence."[96]

---

93 Booth, *Personal Reminiscences*, 70.

94 *Richmond Dispatch*, Sept. 23, 1862.

95 *Savannah Republican*, Sept. 24, 1862.

96 Buck, *With the Old Confeds*, 60.

John Stevens from Texas arrived at the same conclusion, writing plainly that "the romance . . . about it all [had] vanished from . . . patriotic sentiments. War was now a reality; they had learned that war meant fight and fight meant kill and kill meant to be dead."[97]

Armistead Long of General Lee's staff did not entirely share this general disillusionment with Marylanders. According to his way of thinking, "as a people [they] sympathized with the Confederates," but, he maintained, they "stood aloof because they did not wish to see their State become the theatre of war." His was a rational assumption that anyone who had witnessed the devastation in Virginia could well understand.[98]

Ultimately, however, the same unidentified "Sergeant Green" whose letter appeared after his death in the *Frederick Examiner* had no doubt where the responsibility rested. As far as he was concerned, the blame for failing to draw recruits was because they had been "fooled by a set of god damned office seeking villains." The march into Maryland proved to be an epiphany for the ill-fated-soldier. The frustrated Confederate launched into a remarkably vitriolic tirade against the cause for which he had enlisted to fight, and for which he would soon die. According to Green, he had

> talked with a good many yankee or Union men, as they call themselves here, and they generally talk pretty sensible talk. They seem to be down on the nigger as much as anyone in the South, and say they only want to preserve the Union under government, and I almost begin to think it would be a damned shame to divide it for the sake of a few office seekers. I have found a great deal of kindness among the people here, and find they don't differ with us upon many points: they only say preserve the Union and let the damned nigger go to hell. . . . To speak candid, I can't fairly see myself what rights we have lost, to make such a hell of a fuss about. I find things here quite different from what I expected.[99]

When considered with the other sources cited above, Green's letter suggests a good number of the Maryland's residents greeted Lee's troops with kindness and voiced a common outlook on the issue of slavery. Only the idea of preserving the Union seemed to separate them from Confederate soldiers, who had taken up arms

97 Stevens, *Reminiscences*, 68.

98 Long, *Memoirs*, 209.

99 *Frederick Examiner*, Oct. 8, 1862.

"A Pictorial Commentary upon Gen. Lee's Proclamation to the People of Maryland."
Harper's Weekly, Sept. 27, 1862

to establish a republic they believed would be more consistent with the precepts of the Constitution as it existed at the time. Marylanders, by contrast, did not feel threatened enough by Lincoln's administration to think secession necessary. In the end, the overwhelming majority of Marylanders elected not to carry a musket for the cause of States' Rights. Many in Frederick and Washington counties (even some unionists) offered whatever support they could, but providing food, water, and other provisions to keep Lee's men from feeling terrible disappointment. Propagandized to for more than a year, the Rebels had entered Maryland carrying naive expectations that deeply misjudged public sentiment.

* * *

John Ryder Randall's lyrics "shook our hearts like a trumpet!" admitted James Nisbet of the 21st Georgia, and that led Nisbet and his comrades to believe that nothing short of total revolution would demonstrate Maryland's pro-Confederate proclivities. When Marylanders did not rise *en masse*, Southern troops responded with the resentment of men jilted by the object of their affection. Referencing *Maryland! My Maryland*, Nisbet lamented that while the Old Line State was "'not dead, nor deaf, nor dumb!'" she remained "mute [and] inglorious" all the same, a condition that weary men desperate for help with their struggle for independence found unacceptable almost beyond the ability of written words to convey.[100]

100 Nisbet, *Four Years on the Firing Line*, 150.

Five

Rebels Photographed in Frederick, Maryland

❧

The Case for September 1862

IN April 2018, *Battlefield Photographer: The Journal of the Center for Civil War Photography* published an article claiming to offer fresh insight into the famous photo of a Confederate infantry column halted in the streets of Frederick, Maryland. Historians have long thought the subjects in the photo are troops with Maj. Gen. Thomas J. "Stonewall" Jackson's command, a portion of which passed through Frederick twice during the September 1862 Maryland Campaign. The press quickly latched onto the piece. Following "three years of painstaking research," exclaimed the *Washington Post*, the authors conclude the picture was "actually taken" during the passage of Jubal Early's Army of the Valley through Frederick on July 9, 1864.[1]

In fact, that is not what the authors concluded. Instead, Paul Bolcik, Erik Davis, and Craig Heberton IV wrote: "It may never be known for sure whether the Confederate photo was taken in September 1862 or July 1864." In other words, they suggested there may be reasons to question the September 1862 date.[2]

---

1 John Kelly, "Two history buffs sleuth the truth in a rare photo of Confederates in Maryland," *The Washington Post*, June 6, 2018. Available online at www.washingtonpost.com/local/on-this-spot-two-history-buffs-debunk-the-story-of-a-famous-civil-war-photo/2018/06/05/6ccb6ba0-6850-11e8-bea7-c8eb28bc52b1_story.html.

2 Paul Bolcik, Erik Davis, and Craig Heberton IV, "Confederates in Frederick: New Insights on a Famous Photo," in *Battlefield Photographer: The Journal of the Center for Civil War Photography*, Vol. 16, No. 1 (Apr. 2018), 3-20.

Rebel Troops on N. Market Street in Frederick, Maryland, on September 10, 1862.
Heritage Frederick

The authors of the article offered a scenario of events in 1864 that could account for the photo being taken that July, but admitted there is no definitive proof one way or the other. More importantly from a historical standpoint, Bolcik, et. al., identified exactly where the picture was taken, which is a valuable addition to our overall knowledge of the artifact.

The lack of conclusive evidence leaves unanswered the questions of the date and time of the image, and the identity of the men. No source has surfaced confirming when or by whom the photo was taken, so we are left with attempting to place the image in the historical context that makes the most sense. The strongest argument is that the long-accepted earlier date of September 1862, rather than the speculative new date of July 1864, is correct.

The *Battlefield Photographer* article provided evidence that proved beyond a doubt the picture was taken in Frederick from the upper floor photographic studio of Jacob Byerly at what was then 27 North Market Street. The authors also demonstrated that the image shows Confederate troops facing south about one-half block north of the intersection of Market and Patrick Streets, precisely where Byerly's studio was located. Market Street ran from the Georgetown Turnpike south of town to the Liberty Turnpike north of Frederick in the 1860s, intersecting the road to Emmitsburg at Worman's Mill some two miles beyond the city limits. Patrick Street served as the city's major east-west axis, its western end leading to the Hagerstown Turnpike and Harpers Ferry Road, while its eastern extremity became the Baltimore Pike. Bolcik, Davis, and Heberton IV provided an invaluable service by identifying precisely where the Confederates in the picture were standing, i.e., at the strategic intersection in the heart of Frederick through which every army that entered the city during the Civil War would pass. This discovery corrected many years of mislabeled public signage placing the Rebel column on Patrick Street.

General Jackson's command, spearheaded by Jackson's old division under the temporary command of Brig. Gen. William Starke, entered Frederick City late on the morning on Saturday, September 6, 1862. The First, Third, and Fourth Brigades of Starke's command halted briefly in the center of town before marching on to their encampment at Worman's Woods.[3] Colonel Bradley T. Johnson, commander of the Second Brigade, quartered his troops at the old Hessian Barracks and agricultural fairground on the south end of Market Street before turning over command to Capt. John Edmund Penn. The Second Brigade occupied Frederick proper as the army's provost guard.[4]

---

3 "A large portion of the army had marched through the city and went into camp a few miles to the north, at Worman's Mill, the main body encamping at Frederick Junction, on the Baltimore side of the Monocacy Bridge." Williams and McKinsey, *History of Frederick County*, 2: 377. "The command passed through Frederick and camped in the woods north of town." Driver & Ruffner, *1st Battalion Virginia Infantry, 39th Battalion Virginia Cavalry, and 24th Battalion Virginia Partisan Rangers*, 28. "Col. Johnson led the brigade to Worman's Woods, just north of Frederick, Maryland." Chapla, *42nd Virginia Infantry*, 25.

4 "Soon afterwards we entered Frederick City, many of the men having watermelons in their arms. We marched to the Fair Grounds, which had been fitted up as a large hospital for the enemy. Our brigade stacked arms, and were told to make themselves comfortable for the night." Worsham, *One of Jackson's Foot Cavalry*, 138. "At 10 o'clock at night the men were all ordered to their camps on the outskirts of the city." *Baltimore American* reprinted in the *Alexandria Gazette*, Sept. 8, 1862. See also, OR 19, 1:1010-1012, 1014-1015, and Douglas, *I Rode with Stonewall*, 148. "On the morning of the 6th of September, General Jackson's command— with the exception of his old division—which went through Frederick City and encamped on the Emmittsburg Road—went into camp about Monocacy Junction." OR 19, 1:1006-07. Johnson named Lt. Lewis Randolph as town provost parshal during the occupation. Driver & Ruffner, *1st Battalion Virginia Infantry*, 28, and Chapla, *42nd Virginia*, 25.

Jackson's remaining two divisions under Richard S. Ewell and Ambrose Powell Hill (under the temporary command of, respectively, Brig. Gens. Alexander R. Lawton and Lawrence O'Bryan Branch), camped east-southeast of Frederick on the eastern bank of the Monocacy River. Their bivouac was about four miles from Frederick (Starke's men north of town were about two miles distant). Neither division entered Frederick until the morning of September 10, when the Army of Northern Virginia began its operation to capture the Federal garrison at Harpers Ferry. By that time Brig. Gen. John R. Jones, fully recuperated from a wound he had received on July 1 at Malvern Hill, had returned to assume command of the brigades north of town, leaving Starke to resume command of his brigade.[5]

Once they had settled in on September 6, Jackson's troops spent the next few days visiting Frederick hunting for food, clothing, liquor, and any other supplies they needed or wanted. The inhabitants of Frederick recorded the Southerners in their midst as "dirty . . . repulsive" and "unkempt;" Jackson's men described themselves as "ragged" and "shoeless," or in a "sad plight."[6]

The long summer of marching and fighting had taken its toll, but their general state of decrepitude, confessed South Carolina Pvt. Frank Mixson, was because "the entire army [was] ordered to leave all their baggage, and on this trip we had nothing but a haversack, canteen and a blanket or oil cloth, besides the accoutrements—gun, cartridge box and scabbard. You will see from this that we were prepared for *quick marching*." Gunner Edward "Ned" Moore of the Rockbridge Artillery, a unit with Jackson's division, echoed Mixson's sentiment in his postwar memoir, writing "our extra baggage—and extra meant all save that

---

5 Williams and McKinsey, *History of Frederick County*, 2:377. "On the morning of the 6th [the division of Brig. Gen. Lawton] marched to the railroad bridge over the Monocacy, at the junction of the railroad to Frederick City with the Baltimore and Ohio Railroad, and took up a position so as to command the approaches on and adjacent to the railroad from the direction of Washington City. In this position it remained until the morning of September 10." OR 19, 1:966. "Jackson's division took position near the city, and Hill's and Ewell's near the Junction, which is about three miles from the city in the direction of Washington. Ewell's division covered the railroad and the approaches from the direction of Baltimore, and Hill's those from the direction of Washington." Early, *Autobiographical Sketch*, 135.

6 *Steiner Report*, 8-9, and OR 19, 1:1011. "Our short sojourn in the land of promise wrought a salutary change in the general appearance and condition of the troops. The ragged were clad, the shoeless shod, and the inner man rejoiced by a number and variety of delicacies to which it had been a stranger for long, long weary months before." Moore, *The Story of a Cannoneer*, 131: "Our apparel was now in sad plight."

worn on our backs—had been left weeks before near the banks of the Rapidan," meaning Confederate troops carried very little with them into Maryland.[7]

Many of the men replenished their worn-out clothing while in Frederick, an important detail to keep in mind when analyzing the photo of Rebel troops in the street. The First Brigade in particular received "supplies of shoes and clothing," in addition to whatever the men could purchase on their own. The handful of troops who can be seen in detail appear to be clean-shaven, well-clothed, and shod. Some, of course, sported beards. Not every man would take the time to shave knowing he was about to return to the road. Still, the few who are clearly visible look to be in better condition than one might expect based upon eyewitness testimony.[8]

The equipment carried by the troops in the picture seems to closely match Frank Mixson's description. Most carry little more than their musket, cartridge box, and haversack (single-strap bags typically used to carry rations). A larger number can be seen with bedrolls slung over their shoulders, but fewer than a half-dozen are wearing knapsacks. This distinction is important because knapsacks held personal items including photos, writing implements, Bibles, shaving kits, etc. Few are not carrying these or even bayonets, which illustrates that they had indeed stripped down for Mixson's "quick marching."

After four days of rest and refitting, the First, Third, and Fourth Brigades of Jackson's division marched through Frederick on the morning of September 10. Establishing the hour of their departure is important because the photographer needed sunlight to capture his image. Had Jackson's men marched at "early dawn," as was the general's habit, it would have been too dark for the photograph to be taken, meaning the men in the image definitely could not be Jackson's in 1862.[9]

7 Mixson, *Reminiscences of a Private*, 26. The emphasis is Mixson's. Moore, *The Story of a Cannoneer*, 131. The *Atlanta Southern Confederacy*, Sept. 28 1862, printed a letter penned by a Capt. Redding of the 2nd Battalion Georgia Volunteers in which Redding claimed, "I do not think Gen. Lee contemplates a long stay in Maryland, as all of the baggage of his army has been sent back to this place (i.e., Rapidan Station)."

8 "The first 8 or 10 thousand [rebels] got a tolerable good supply of clothing & shoes & boots but the stores & shops were soon sold out." Quynn, ed., *The Diary of Jacob Engelbrecht*, 948. "[Winder's] brigade marched through Frederick and camped two miles from the town on the Emmitsburg road. Here they were assigned supplies of shoes and clothing." Lee A. Wallace, Jr., *5th Virginia Infantry* (Lynchburg, VA, 1988), 41.

9 Early dawn is approximately one to two hours before sunrise.

Despite some inconsistency in the sources, it is clear that Jackson's men did not leave at early dawn. The generally accepted sequence of events follows Robert E. Lee's instructions in Special Orders No. 191. Jackson distributed orders on the evening of September 9 for his command to march early the next morning. Several sources estimate that Jackson's men got on the road at 3:00 a.m., although U.S. Sanitary Service officer Lewis Steiner recorded it was "at four o'clock this morning the rebel army began to move from our town, Jackson's force taking the advance." Some of Jackson's men (particularly teamsters) may have gotten underway that early, but there is convincing evidence that the general himself did not expect his troops to move until sunrise.[10]

In the early hours of September 10, Jackson had one of his staff officer, Maj. Elisha Paxton, send the following instructions to Brig. Gen. Lawrence Branch: "the major general commanding directs me to say that, *instead of moving at dawn, as hitherto ordered* [emphasis added], you will follow General Lawton when he comes up, he being ordered to move at dawn." Jackson may have ordered his troops roused at 3:00 a.m., and some may have even begun moving. However, Jackson did not expect his entire command to be on the road until at least dawn, which, if defined as the first gray light before sunrise, arrived between 5:20 and 5:30 a.m. on September 10.[11]

Whatever Jackson's expectations may have been, his advance rapidly bogged down in the streets of Frederick. The general got an early start in an ambulance rather than on his horse because of a back injury he had suffered on September 6. Leaving his bivouac near Best's Grove "about sunrise," he finally mounted his horse on the outskirts of the city. According to staff officer Henry Kyd Douglas, the general entered Frederick about sunrise to visit a family friend, the Rev. Doctor John Ross on Second Street. At that early hour the good doctor was still asleep, so

---

10 See also, *Steiner Report*, 19. Haynes, *Field Diary*, 16-17: "Wednesday, September 10th, 1862. This morning we left our camping ground about three o'clock." Also see Charles W. Turner, ed., *Captain Greenlee Davidson, C.S.A. Diary & Letters, 1851-1863* (Verona, VA, 1975), 47-48, and Schuler Diary, cited in Hartwig, *To Antietam Creek*, 702, Note 88. McDonald, ed., *Make Me a Map of the Valley*, 80: "We started before day 3 A.M. and cross the South Mountain (Blue Ridge) at Braddock's Gap and encamped, on the western slope, near Boonsboro." Schaeffer, *Records of the Past*, Sept. 10, 1862: "At 12 M. last night the Rebel army . . . began moving and are passing through our streets and the Hagerstown pike as fast as they can travel."

11 OR 19, 2:604. See also Harsh, *Sounding the Shallows*, 12 for the exact times of sunrise and sunset.

Jackson left a note before taking Mill Alley south to Patrick Street and riding out of Frederick at the head of his entourage.[12]

All of this timing is important. According to Jubal Early, "the General went through Frederick, with a cavalry escort, *in advance of his troops, who did not pass through the town until he was some distance beyond* [emphasis added]." A second source corroborated Jackson's departure ahead of his column. "It is a perfectly well-known fact that Stonewall Jackson did not pass through Frederick along with his corps," wrote Valerius Ebert to the *Baltimore Sun*, "but rode rapidly through the town with a small cavalry escort *about an hour before his troops marched through the streets* [emphasis added]."[13]

If we account for the time it would have taken Jackson to reach Frederick from his bivouac some three miles away, and add a few minutes for his short visit at the Ross house, it is reasonable to conclude that Jackson moved out of Frederick between 5:30 and 5:45 a.m. The bulk of his command followed him roughly an hour later, or between 6:30 and 6:45 a.m. This means Jackson's troops passed through Frederick after the sun had come up, giving Jacob Byerly or one of his studio associates ample light to take the now famous photo.[14]

Once in town, Old Jack's three divisions quickly snarled Frederick's streets. Despite Jackson's orders for Ewell's division (under Lawton) to take the lead, Hill's division (under Branch) got underway first, with its wagons in the front of the column.[15] It marched north up the Georgetown Road and into town on South

12 Bradley T. Johnson, "Address," 515. Also see Douglas, *I Rode with Stonewall*, 151. "On the morning of the 10th Jackson's corps was put in motion and the General went to Frederick in an ambulance and then mounted his horse." Williams and McKinsey, *History of Frederick County Maryland*, 378-379; Harsh, *Sounding the Shallows*, 12. Mill Alley is called Bentz Street today.

13 "Letter from Jubal A. Early" in *SHSP*, Vol. 7, No. 9 (1879), 436. McCabe with Valerius Ebert. i.e., Valerius Ebert, "The Real Barbara Frietchie," in *SHSP* (1899), 27:288.

14 The average walking speed for a horse is four miles per hour. The average trotting speed is between eight and 12 mph. Some combination of both would have taken him between 15 and 30 minutes to travel from Best's Grove to downtown Frederick. Evidence exists that Jackson may have been on the move even earlier than Douglas's estimate of "about sunrise." According to the note Jackson is alleged to have left for Dr. Ross, he arrived at the doctor's house at 5:15 a.m. See Priest, *Before Antietam*, 60. I did not use this because there is some argument about the note's authenticity. See Joe Ryan, The Thomas Stonewall Jackson & Reverend Dr. John B. Ross Connection Revisited online at http:// joeryancivilwar.com/Special-Order-191/ Jackson-Ross-Connection/Stonewall-Jackson-Connection-Reverend-Ross.html. The point remains that Jackson's troops moved through Frederick after the sun had already come up.

15 "Early on the morning of the 10th we were ordered to be ready to move at a moment's notice, and at about 9 A. M., A. P. Hill, with his division, begun to pass and cross the river on

Market Street, where it encountered Jones's division moving down from its encampment two miles north of Frederick.[16]

Once the First, Third, and Fourth brigades filed onto the road about dawn The march from Worman's Woods took about an hour to reach town, which puts the head of Jones's column in Frederick between 6:45 and 7:30 a.m. According to James Parsons, a soldier with Taliaferro's Third Brigade (under the command of Col. Edward T. H. Warren), "upon reaching Frederick a lighter division (Branch's) was ordered to precede the main army. In order to do this they marched by way of the Mill Alley to West Patrick street, while Tolliver's Brigade *marched down Market street and out West Patrick* [emphasis added], halting before Mill Alley a sufficient time to allow A. P. Hill's division to come through." Put another way, Hill's infantry tramped up Market Street from the south and found themselves stuck behind the division's wagons in the streets of Frederick as Jones's men approached from the north.[17]

Jacob Engelbrecht, a local diarist who lived across West Patrick Street from the famed Barbara Frietchie of John Greenleaf Whittier's poem, corroborated portions

---

the wagon bridge, entering the streets of Frederick City. Our division (i.e., Ewell's under Lawton) came next following Hill on the Hagerstown turnpike, Jackson's old division, following us." McClendon, *Recollections of War Times*, 131. Hartwig, *To Antietam Creek*, 712-713, notes 41, 44, and 48, cites three diaries referring to Hill's division leading the way. D. F. Carraway, "Lieutenant-General A. P. Hill: Some Reminiscences of the Famous Virginia Commander," in *SHSP* (1891), 19:180. "We were breaking camp at early dawn—in fact, before dawn. Our wagons, with the headquarter wagon driver by a noble son of the Emerald Isle, were to take the lead on the road."

16 "At sunrise . . . [Winder's] brigade marched to Boonsborough." Wallace, *5th Virginia Infantry*, 41. A source for Jones's division notes, "they broke camp early on the morning of September 10, and marched into Frederick with Tolliver's brigade in the lead." James L. Parsons, cited in Eleanor D. Abbott, *A Sketch of Barbara Fritchie, Whittier's Heroine* (Frederick, MD, 1921), 15. According to a man who marched with Jackson, the troops in Taliaferro's brigade pronounced his name 'Tolliver'." James H. Wood, *The War: "Stonewall" Jackson: His Campaigns and Battles, the Regiment as I Saw Them* (Cumberland, MD, 1910), 39.

17 The presence of Jones's command (Jackson's division) in Frederick at dawn is confirmed in Thomas M. Rankin, *23rd Virginia Infantry* (Lynchburg, VA, 1985), 47: "On September 10, the Rebel columns moved. The 23rd Virginia, with Jackson's Division, marched through Frederick at dawn." Parson's recollection is in Abbott, *A Sketch*, 15. His account of this marching order is cited twice by Abbott—once in a letter to the *Baltimore Sun* on Nov. 12, 1913, and once in a letter to a Mrs. Samuel Grafton Duvall. There is no record of a James Parsons on the roster of any regiment in Taliaferro's brigade, but this is not unusual given the sketchy nature of Confederate record-keeping and the destruction of records over time. Abbott may have also mistakenly identified him as belonging to that unit. The roster of Crenshaw's Battery, A. P. Hill's division, lists a "J. L. Parsons" in Ellett's Company. If this is the same person, it would put him in the right location for the information on Hill's movement through Frederick. How this Parsons would have known about Taliaferro's movements remains an open question.

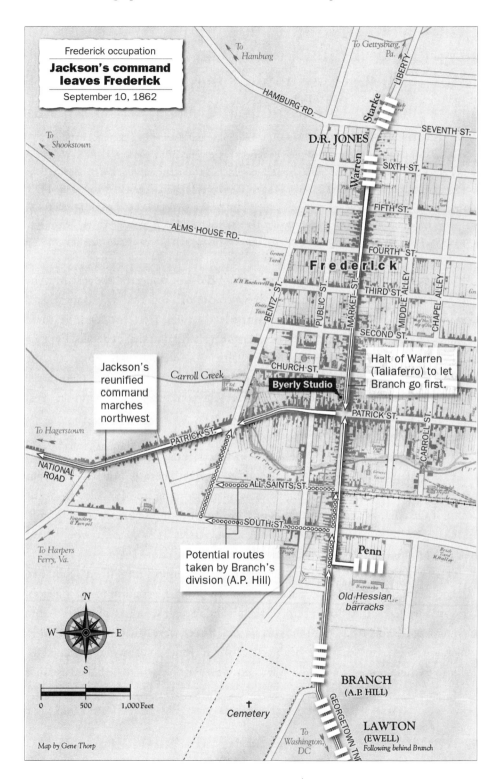

Frederick occupation
Jackson's command leaves Frederick
September 10, 1862

To Hamburg

To Gettysburg, Pa.

LIBERTY

HAMBURG RD.

Starke

SEVENTH ST.

To Shookstown

D.R. JONES

Warren

SIXTH ST.

FIFTH ST.

ALMS HOUSE RD.

Grove Yard

FOURTH ST.

Frederick

BENTZ ST.

PUBLIC ST.

MARKET ST.

THIRD ST.

MIDDLE ALLEY

CHAPEL ALLEY

SECOND ST.

Jackson's reunified command marches northwest

Carroll Creek

CHURCH ST.

Byerly Studio

Halt of Warren (Taliaferro) to let Branch go first.

PATRICK ST.

CARROLL ST.

To Hagerstown

PATRICK ST.

NATIONAL ROAD

ALL SAINTS ST.

SOUTH ST.

To Harpers Ferry, Va.

Penn

Potential routes taken by Branch's division (A.P. Hill)

Old Hessian barracks

N

W   E

S

BRANCH
(A.P. HILL)

GEORGETOWN TNPK.

Cemetery

LAWTON
(EWELL)
Following behind Branch

To Washington, DC

0   500   1,000 Feet

Map by Gene Thorp

of Parsons's account in a June 1874 letter published in the *Baltimore Sun*. "When General Lee passed through our city with his army I was very anxious to see all I could," he wrote. Posting himself at one of the upstairs windows of his house, Engelbrecht "had a full view of all that passed below in the street." He continued:

> When General Lee got in front of Mrs. Fritchie's house and also in front of mine, he and *his whole army halted* [emphasis added], and I afterward ascertained (this, you know, was in West Patrick Street,) that General Stonewall Jackson (who had been encamped north of our city) with his army, was coming up Mill Alley or Bentz street. So, General Lee waited until General Jackson and his army had passed. All the time that General Lee stopped in front of Mrs. Fritchie's house I saw no flag waving. If there had been I certainly would have seen it; and as for General Jackson, he did not pass over the bridge, but passed up another street.[18]

Although a keen eyewitness, Engelbrecht did not understand everything he was seeing. General Lee, for example, traveled out of Frederick with Longstreet's command, not Jackson's, and Lee did not lead a separate army. Despite these inconsistencies, Engelbrecht's testimony confirms a few important details. First, he saw a column of Confederate infantry halted on West Patrick Street on the morning Jackson departed. Second, he confirmed that this event took place while Jackson was leaving the city. Finally, Engelbrecht noted that the column on West Patrick Street halted to allow another part of Jackson's force to pass.

Engelbrecht's use of the words "coming up Mill Alley" is too vague to determine the direction from which Jackson approached. "Coming up" is generally used to reference movement from south to north. There is one aspect of his testimony that could indicate Engelbrecht meant coming up Mill Alley from the south: if the column standing in front of Engelbrecht's house belonged to John R. Jones, then the only column that could have passed in front of it would have belonged to Hill's division, per James Parsons's recollection.

The congestion caused by infantry columns coming into town from two directions appears to have compelled Jackson to order the column marching from the south to take either South Street or All Saint's Street west to Mill Alley before turning north. This route put them on Patrick Street west of Carroll Creek, from which it was an easy march out of the city. John R. Jones, meanwhile, marched his column to the intersection of Mill Alley and West Patrick, where he halted as Hill's

18 *Baltimore Sun*, Apr. 24, 1875.

division filed onto the road ahead. Ewell's division (under Lawton) came up last, forming the column's rear after Jones had resumed the march. Before this, Jones's halted column stretched north up Market Street for a lengthy period of time—directly in front of the Byerly photographic studio.[19]

The Byerly photographer had an excellent opportunity to take the picture on North Market Street that morning because Jones's column loitered on the street outside, in daylight, waiting for Hill's men to come up and take the vanguard in accordance with Jackson's orders. In their *History of Frederick County, Maryland,* Thomas Williams and Folger McKinsey confirmed Jackson's use of Mill Alley. Unfortunately, they claimed the general's entire command used the route to leave Frederick. Their take on the issue reflects a broader problem with much of the local testimony concerning Jackson. As demonstrated, the general rode through Frederick earlier that morning ahead of his command. Locals appear to have conflated these moves into a single incident by stating that Jackson's men marched through Frederick along the route that in the event only the general and his staff and escort utilized.

Williams and McKinsey claimed Jackson's "command left Frederick on its westward march [and] . . . when . . . moving through the city it passed south to Patrick street through a little side street known as Mill Alley, turning from it sharp to the west of the spot where the home of Mrs. Frietchie stood, Carroll creek and the bridge intervening between it." Describing the event surrounding Barbara Frietchie—a reference to the aged widow who allegedly shook a U.S. flag at Jackson as he passed her house—was their primary concern, not the route of march taken by Jackson.[20]

The source for Williams's and McKinsey's account was a letter written in the late 1870s by Valerius Ebert, Frietchie's nephew and a local Confederate sympathizer. "[A]s to the waving of the Federal flag in the face of the rebels by Dame Barbara on the occasion of Stonewall Jackson's march through Frederick," confessed Ebert, the "truth requires me to say that Stonewall Jackson, with his troops, did not pass Barbara Frietchie's residence at all; *but passed through what in this*

---

19 Carraway, "Lieutenant-General A. P. Hill," 130 makes it clear that Starke's division came second in the marching order after Branch's. Jones may have also collected Bradley Johnson's detached brigade here from its bivouac at the fairgrounds, but there is no evidence to determine this one way or another.

20 Williams and McKinsey, *History of Frederick County*, 2:378. See Harsh, *Taken*, 532 for a brief discussion of the Barbara Frietchie incident.

A depiction of J. R. Jones's Division marching through Frederick on Sept. 10, 1862.

Harper's Weekly, Sept. 27, 1862

---

city is called 'The Mill Alley,' about three hundred yards from her residence, then passed due west [emphasis added] towards Antietam, and thus out of the city."[21]

James Parsons's letters clarify that Hill's men used Mill Alley to move north while Jones's division took North Market south to Patrick Street. Ewell's men under Lawton may have also used the Mill Alley route to get out of town ahead of Hill's wagons, but no evidence has surfaced to confirm this. In a twist of irony, the Byerly studio photograph could confirm Parsons's and Engelbrecht's recollections because the *Battlefield Photographer* authors established that the image shows the Rebel column halted one-half block north of the Market Street-Patrick Street intersection.[22]

As for the men in the photograph, their identity may never be known for certain. Based on the letters of Parsons, a reasonable case can be made that they are troops with Taliaferro's Third Brigade (under Colonel Warren). This brigade led

21 Valerius Ebert, "Letter from Mrs. Frietchie's Nephew," in *SHSP* (1879), 7:439.

22 Several sources support the position of Ewell's (Lawton's) command at the rear of the column after it had crossed the Catoctin range. "On the night of the 10th, Ewell's division bivouacked between Middletown and South Mountain." Early, *Autobiographical Sketch*, 135. Also see Hartwig, *To Antietam Creek*, 712, Note 44.

the march to Frederick from Worman's Woods that morning with slightly more than 1,500 men in its ranks. If we assume they are with the Third Brigade, these troops would be toward the rear of the column, with its head halted at the intersection of Mill Alley and West Patrick Street. The image depicts about 90 to 100 men occupying a space of roughly 125 feet, i.e., the distance from Byerly's studio to the corner of North Market and West Patrick streets on the right side of the image.[23]

Using this distance as a clue, we can estimate the length of the column ahead of the location pictured. The distance from the corner of North Market and West Patrick to the intersection of West Patrick and Mill Alley is about 1,125 feet, which suggests between 800 and 1,000 men had already passed the spot where the photo was taken. That means 500 to 700 men were still behind them. According to Parsons, his 23rd Virginia marched at the head of the column, so the men in the image cannot be his comrades. This means the men belonged to one of the remaining regiments (47th or 48th Alabama, or the 10th and 37th Virginia). Unfortunately, this is as much as can be deduced about the identity of the men unless further details come to light. What we do know with certainty is that 168 of the men in the brigade were killed or wounded at Sharpsburg only one week after the Byerly photograph was taken, so the odds are high that some of the men pictured here never made it back to Virginia.[24]

To recapitulate, Jackson issued orders for his three divisions to rise at 3:00 a.m. and march at dawn on September 10. The general's columns began passing through Frederick after sunrise, which provided sufficient daylight for Jacob Byerly or one of his associates to capture their image. The evidence indicates some confusion as to which division was supposed to lead the column, stalling the progress of Jones's division coming in from the north. After an extended delay waiting for Hill's command to clear Mill Alley from the south, Jones, whose divisional column extended east along Patrick Street and north up Market Street, slipped in behind Hill and ahead of Ewell (Lawton). The photographer had plenty of time in the midst of all this to take a picture of Jones's men on the street outside of the studio. Their equipment and general state of dress also fit the descriptions provided by Confederate witnesses. The Byerly photograph is therefore a valuable piece of

---

23 The Third Brigade's strength estimate is from Hartwig, *To Antietam Creek*, 679. The brigade was composed of the 10th, 23rd, and 37th Virginia, and the 47th and 48th Alabama.

24 Total losses included 41 killed and 127 wounded. Carman, *The Maryland Campaign*, 2:609.

primary evidence that likely proves the presence of Jones's men on North Market Street in Frederick exactly where James Parsons says they were on the march out of town. In effect, the picture validates the events discussed in the documentary sources, not the other way around.

An evaluation of whether the soldiers pictured could be from Jubal Early's Valley Army in Frederick on July 9, 1864, only strengthens the case that the image depicts Jackson's troops in September 1862. Indications of an impending clash between Early's command and a hastily organized defensive force under Union Maj. Gen. Lew Wallace developed on July 7, when Bradley Johnson's cavalry brigade engaged in a running fight with Illinois horsemen and a handful of Federal infantry west of Frederick. Once it became apparent that the Rebel army was too formidable for the resources he had on hand, Wallace ordered his command to evacuate Frederick on the afternoon of July 8 and retire to the high ground east of the Monocacy River. After a night of intermittent downpours, Early's army descended on the city the next day, with Robert D. Lilley's brigade of Virginians, part of Stephen D. Ramseur's division, leading the way. The North Carolinians of Robert D. Johnston's brigade came up behind Lilley's men. Both formations entered Frederick via West Patrick Street around 6:00 a.m.[25]

Lilley's brigade proceeded east on Patrick Street and out of the city toward the Jug Bridge, where the Baltimore Pike crossed the Monocacy River. Johnston's brigade turned south onto Market Street to march along the Georgetown Pike toward the road bridge and rail crossing at Monocacy Junction. According to one civilian eyewitness, the march of Ramseur's two brigades through Frederick consumed two hours before the army's wagon train, led by the artillery, entered town at 8:00 a.m.[26]

---

25 "At 4 p.m. on the 8th instant received orders from the general commanding to withdraw my men [from Frederick] and fall back on the Baltimore Pike toward Monocacy bridge." OR 37, 1:216. The last Federal cavalry evacuated the city at 2:00 a.m. on Saturday, July 9. OR 37, 1:220. The 6:00 a.m. arrival time for Early's column is found in Quynn, ed., *The Diary of Jacob Engelbrecht*, 998. We know from Douglas, *I Rode with Stonewall*, 293, that Ramseur's division led Early's advance: "Ramseur's division . . . reached Frederick first . . . on the 9th. I took command of the skirmishers and was the first horseman in town." The marching order of Lilley first followed by Johnston can be found in Brett W. Spaulding, *Last Chance for Victory: Jubal Early's 1864 Maryland Invasion* (Author, 2010), 78. Spaulding mistakenly includes William Lewis's brigade with Ramseur's advance.

26 Quynn, ed., *The Diary of Jacob Engelbrecht*, 998. "About 8 AM on Saturday [July 9] their wagon train commenced passing through town & it lasted 4 or 5 hours. 4 or 500 wagons must have passed." See also Jubal A. Early, *A Memoir of the Last Year of the War for Independence in the*

This train followed Johnston's brigade south down Market Street toward Monocacy Junction. According to local diarist Jacob Engelbrecht, the passage through town took between four and five hours. Engelbrecht's estimate puts the wagon train through Frederick around noon at the earliest. Major General John C. Breckinridge's corps, comprised of two divisions commanded by John B. Gordon and John Echols, followed the train. Reliable reports place Gordon on the field at 2:00 p.m., which makes sense given the time-frame offered by Engelbrecht if Gordon's troops marched on the quick for at least part of the route. Assuming the reports of Gordon's division entering the fight south of Frederick between 2:30 and 3:00 p.m. are accurate, Breckinridge's advance through town took about two hours.[27]

Echols's division, consisting of three brigades under Col. George S. Patton, Brig. Gen. Gabriel C. Wharton, and Col. Thomas Smith, remained on the southern outskirts of Frederick guarding the army's trains until it was called into action later in the day. Those three brigades deployed along the eastern bank of Ballenger Creek between Buckeystown Pike and Monocacy Junction, but never entered the fight.[28]

Robert E. Rodes's four-brigade division brought up the rear of Early's column. Rodes followed Gordon and Echols after taking the southwest road from Jefferson. His men marched due east on Patrick Street to the Baltimore Pike and

---

Confederate States of America (Toronto, ON, 1866), 58. "Breckenridge's command, with the trains, was in . . . between Frederick and the [Monocacy] Junction."

27 There exists the slim possibility that a portion of Gordon's command skirted around Frederick before entering the city. I. G. Bradwell, a veteran of Gordon's division, recalled almost sixty years later: "before we reached the city [of Frederick], the head of our column turned to the right and took a road that led off in a southerly direction. This we followed some distance and then turned toward the east, crossing a creek before we reached the [Monocacy] river." See Confederate Accounts in Glenn H. Worthington, *Fighting for Time: The Battle of Monocacy* (Shippensburg, PA, 1985). OR 37, 1:350. "About 2:30 p.m. July 9 I was ordered by Major-General Breckenridge, commanding corps, to move my division to the right and cross the Monocacy."

28 Early, *Memoir,* 58-59. "Echol's division which had been left to guard the trains, was ordered up during the engagement, but was not needed." Echols left the 22nd Virginia to guard the train. Terry D. Lowry, *22nd Virginia Infantry* (Lynchburg, VA, 1988), 67. "Echols' Division, which had been guarding the wagon trains, marched rapidly to the front." James A. Davis, *51st Virginia Infantry* (Lynchburg, VA, 1984), 30. "Arriving at the imminent battleground Breckenridge's Division was posted east of Ballenger Creek, to the rear of the Baltimore & Ohio Railroad . . . the division was primarily held in reserve, with Patton's Brigade on the left, Smith in the center, and Wharton on the right." Terry D. Lowry, *26th Battalion Virginia Infantry* (Lynchburg, VA, 1991), 53.

the Monocacy River beyond, arriving on the field sometime after 2:00 p.m. to relieve Lilley's brigade. Rodes deployed in three lines and attacked the Jug Bridge east of Frederick around 3:30 p.m., soon after Gordon's successful assault on the Federal left flank near Monocacy Junction.[29]

This detailed exercise demonstrates that nearly all of Jubal Early's infantry marched through Frederick from west to east toward the escalating fight against Lew Wallace's stubborn Union defensive line. The lone Confederate exception was Brig. Gen. William G. Lewis's brigade (under the command of Col. Archibald C. Godwin). According to Early's memoirs, Godwin brought up General Lewis's command in the rear of the army after starting "from Harper's Ferry the night before . . . burning the trestle-work on the railroad, and the stores which had not been brought off."[30]

Lewis's brigade entered Frederick at some point in the mid-afternoon behind Rodes, whose division had marched ahead of Lewis on the road from Jefferson— the most direct route from Harpers Ferry. According to historian Walter Clark, "Colonel Godwin, soon after made Brig.-General, was in command of [Lewis's] brigade, which was left at Frederick, Md., during the battle of Monocacy to protect the rear of General Early's march." In other words, the only rebel infantry behind the lines in Frederick on July 9 were the four regiments of North Carolinians in Lewis's brigade, and they did not enter the city until mid-afternoon. Clark's history also explains that Lewis's men were enlisted to transport the wounded from the battlefield back to Frederick. No other source has surfaced recording what his brigade may have done while in town that day or where it was posted.[31]

The documented identification of Lewis's brigade as the only infantry posted in Frederick on July 9 is important, as is the time and direction of its arrival, because of the details surrounding Jubal Early's infamous financial levy on the city. General Early and several members of his staff entered Frederick around 8:00 a.m. with the

---

29 OR 37, 1:224. "Finally, about 3 p.m. our troops made a charge and drove [the rebels] back, and they then uncovered their forces and came on, in three lines, and forced our troops to retreat." Also see OR 37, 1:205 "At about 3:30 p.m., under cover of their artillery, the enemy came down upon us with a heavy skirmish line, and two lines of battle."

30 Early, *Memoir*, 57.

31 Clark, ed., *Histories of the Several Regiments and Battalions from North Carolina*, 1:419. The four regiments in question are the 6th, 21st, 54th, and 57th North Carolina. No source has been found for the number of men in the brigade. "It fell to the lot of the brigade to care for the wounded of that battle and to have them removed to Frederick." Early reported leaving "about 400" wounded behind in Frederick. OR 37, 1:349.

trains of Ramseur's division. Early rode to the house of Dr. Richard T. Hammond, a reputed Confederate sympathizer, on the northwest corner of Second and North Market streets. There, the general allegedly requested the use of the home to dictate a demand to the mayor and the town for $200,000 "*payable in cash or goods* [emphasis added] at current prices," or he would order his men to burn the city to the ground.[32]

Early's staff officers delivered the demand to Frederick's mayor William G. Cole in the city court house and then haggled with him and as many of the city Aldermen and Common Council members as Cole could gather deep into the afternoon. Colonel William Allan, one of the staffers, finally concluded that the city's leaders were stalling until they could determine who was winning the battle being fought along the Monocacy. General Early did not take part in any of these talks. He rode off soon after dictating his demands and arrived on the field near the Monocacy in time to witness John McCausland's cavalry locate a ford beyond the Federal left flank about 10:30 a.m.[33]

The only other evidence of Early's involvement in the levy negotiations concerns the late-afternoon dispatch of his adjutant, Alexander 'Sandie' Pendleton, to determine the state of the talks.[34] Pendleton, the son of artillery general William Nelson Pendleton, either delivered news of the impending Confederate victory to Frederick's town fathers or he arrived at roughly the same time the news broke

32 Edward S. Delaplane, "General Early's Levy on Frederick," *The 100th Anniversary of the Battle of Monocacy* (Frederick, MD, 1964), 49. David J. Lewis, *Frederick War Claim: Evidence and Argument in Support of Bill to Refund Ransom Paid by the Town of Frederick, During the Civil War, to Save Said Town and Union Military Supplies from Destruction* (Frederick, MD), 5, referred to hereafter as *Frederick War Claim*.

33 The staff officers with Early included Col. William Allan, Chief of Ordnance; Maj. Wells J. Hawks, Chief Commissary Officer; Dr. Hunter McGuire, Surgeon and Medical Director; and Maj. John A. Harman, Chief Quartermaster. William Allan's journal is cited in B. Franklin Cooling, *Monocacy: The Battle that Saved Washington* (Shippensburg, PA, 1997), 97. "From 9 o'clock to 10:30 the action was little more than a warm skirmish and experimental cannonading . . . about 10.30 o'clock the enemy's first line of battle (i.e., McCausland's dismounted cavalry) made its appearance and moved against Ricketts." *OR* 37, 1:196. "The enemy's position was too strong, and the difficulties of crossing the Monocacy under fire too great, to attack in front without greater loss than I was willing to incur. I therefore made an examination in person to find a point at which the river could be crossed, so as to take the enemy in flank. While I was engaged in making this examination to my right, I discovered McCausland in the act of crossing the river with his brigade." Early, *Memoir*, 58.

34 The Pendleton story originates in Delaplane, "General Early's Levy," 53, who did not offer a firsthand source to support his claim. Although the story has been repeated over the years, it should be considered hearsay until otherwise confirmed.

from another source. In either case, Mayor Cole and Frederick's other civil leaders finally paid the levy by borrowing $200,000 from five of the city's banks, two of which stood on North Market Street near the location where the Byerly studio photograph was taken.[35]

The levy from each bank is said to have been given to Early's staff in a wicker basket at city hall (i.e., the city court house). Once paid, Sandie Pendleton and his associates dined on champagne and ice cream at a hotel restaurant before leaving town. All of this is relevant because of the hour at which the levy was paid: around 4:00 p.m. As recounted above, once Rodes's division had cleared the way Lewis's four North Carolina regiments under Colonel Godwin entered the city from the west between 2:30 and 4:00 p.m. In other words, there is no evidence of any organized or sizeable force of Confederate infantry stopped in Frederick proper until at least 2:30 p.m.[36]

There is some evidence that small groups of Confederate soldiers moved through the streets of Frederick, entering buildings and taking what they wished, but were they organized Confederate infantry or stragglers? According to Jacob Engelbrecht, while "some of the Secessionist stores sold out all of their Stock of goods, N. D. Hauer's hat store was entered and robbed of all he had amounting to about 300$." Another local, Elihu Rockwell, recalled something similar in a letter to Eliza Coleman on July 25, 1864. "[T]he rebels nearly ruined Jno. Osborn, your old neighbor," he explained in some detail. "They took from his store everything that they fancied and broke things that they did not take. Their track was marked with destruction wherever they went, particularly to Union men." Neither

---

35 The five financial institutions included the Frederick Town Savings Institution, which paid $64,000, and the Franklin Savings Bank, which paid $31,000. The other banks contributing to the levy included the Central Bank ($44,000), the Frederick County Bank ($33,000), and the Farmers and Mechanics Bank ($28,000); See Isaac Bond, Map of Frederick County ca. 1858, online at http://hdl.loc. gov/loc.gmd/g3843f.la000292; Delaplane, "General Early's Levy," 53.

36 Delaplane, "General Early's Levy," 54. Delaplane quotes from his source that Sandi Pendleton and the others "celebrated the success of their levy in Frederick by 'gorging themselves on ice cream, the rarest of delicacies'," but Delaplane does not cite the identity of the source he relied upon. Jed Hotchkiss, in McDonald, ed., *Make Me a Map of the Valley*, 215, wrote: "I dined, with several, in the city." George Buckey of Frederick witnessed the levy's hand-off to Gen. Jubal Early's staff. "He was sitting on the City Hall steps when they (i.e., the Confederates) got the money and saw them come down with it." Lewis, *Frederick War Claim*, 37.

Engelbrecht nor Rockwell mentioned the time during the day when these things occurred.[37]

Another witness, Theodore Brookey, signed an affidavit after the war stating that "several Confederate soldiers came along, each having a new 'marked' Government United States blanket . . . a Confederate officer . . . asked them where them got them; they stated over in the warehouse, meaning the Baltimore and Ohio freight building. He told them to take them back, that all property was to be respected." This event probably took place in the morning, as attested to under oath by Fritchie Hanshew on January 16, 1902: "Some time during the morning, I think, some Confederate soldiers came to the depot and took away some goods, but they were soon stopped. I don't know by whom, but they did not disturb anything more during the day."[38]

Finally, there is the oft-quoted statement of G. S. Groshon that "between 8 and 9 o'clock at night a party of Confederates came to the depot to burn the bridge across the creek and the warehouse containing Government property." Groshon protested that they could not burn the bridge and building since the $200,000 levy had been paid. The officer in command sent a request for confirmation of Groshon statement to General Early. Once Early verified the claim, the torching party left the scene.[39]

The handful of statements offered above run contrary to the claim made the *Battlefield Photographer* authors that "By 7 a.m., infantrymen were fanning out in multiple directions throughout the town, searching for the banks, depots, and warehouses." The statements are all the evidence currently known about the presence of Confederate soldiers in Frederick doing something other than marching through town en route to the fighting.[40]

It is also important to note that none of these statements describe or identify the Rebels spotted in town ransacking buildings or stores as infantrymen, which

37 Quynn, ed., *The Diary of Jacob Engelbrecht*, 998; Letter of Elihu H. Rockwell of Frederick to Mrs. Eliza Graham Coleman, July 25, 1864, in "Civil War Letters of E. H. Rockwell," Frederick Historical Society, Frederick, Maryland.

38 Lewis, *Frederick War Claim*, 36 and 38.

39 Ibid., 6.

40 Bolcik, *et al.*, "Confederates in Frederick," 11. Curiously, the source they cite for this claim is the report filed by Col. Allison L. Brown, 149th Ohio, July 14, 1864, in *OR* 37, 1:217. Brown's report, however, is concerned only with the fighting on his front near Monocacy Junction, and makes no mention of Rebels in Frederick.

Byerly's studio image clearly depicts. Confederate infantry other than those under Godwin's command could have entered town, or could have been posted at various locations, but there is no proof for either scenario.[41] It is possible that Confederate cavalry remained in Frederick during the day on July 9 until Lewis's brigade arrived, but the Rebel troops in the Byerly studio photograph are clearly infantry, not cavalry.[42]

Another curious detail suggests that Jubal Early left few men in town on July 9, 1864. Seven government warehouses filled with food, clothing, blankets, and medical supplies, materials desperately needed by the Valley Army, remained untouched. David Lewis's *Frederick War Claim*, compiled after the war by the city in an attempt to recoup payment of the levy from the U.S. government, lists dozens of pages of testimony concerning the vast quantity of military supplies in warehouses scattered across the southern part of the city. Major Hawks, Jubal Early's chief commissary officer, listed many items needed by the army in a second July 9 requisition to Frederick's mayor and governing council, including "500 barrels of flour, 6,000 pounds of sugar, 3,000 pounds of coffee, 20,000 pounds of bacon, [and] 3,000 pounds of salt." All of these stores plus "a large amount of property,

---

41 The authors of the *Battlefield Photographer* article make this definitive claim: "At least 300 soldiers were detached to remain in town to collect the ransom and guard against any possible trouble caused by local residents." The source for this claim—Joseph V. Collins, *Battle of West Frederick, July 7, 1864: Prelude to the Battle of Monocacy* (2011), 275, which, in turn, cites Paul and Rita Gordon, *Frederick County, Maryland: A Playground of the Civil War* (Frederick, MD, 1994), 193, and the *Frederick War Claim* document discussed above—does not reference a specific number of men or any orders for a detachment of soldiers to specifically cow the civilian population. Gordon, *A Playground of the Civil War*, 172, claims (without citing a source) that "While in the town, Rebel cavalrymen visited the stores, took what they wanted, and paid in Confederate script—or not at all."

42 Even the presence of a sizeable cavalry force in Frederick is highly questionable. With John McCausland's cavalry brigade engaged on the Monocacy River and Bradley Johnson's brigade riding east on a mission to liberate Confederate prisoners at Point Lookout, Maryland, Jubal Early's remaining two brigades under Col. George H. Smith and Col. William L. Jackson were engaged elsewhere. Smith, for example, only "reached Early's advance on July 9, just after he had defeated Federal Maj. Gen. Lew Wallace at the battle of Monocacy (i.e., 4 o'clock)." Richard B. Kleese, *23rd Virginia Cavalry* (Lynchburg, VA, 1996), 32. William Jackson, meanwhile, spilt his command into detachments before Early's army arrived in Frederick on July 9. These detachments collected in Frederick throughout the course of the day. See, for example, Richard L. Armstrong, *19th and 20th Virginia Cavalry* (Lynchburg, VA, 1994), 57. Early suggests Jackson's detachments were used that day to guard the western approaches to Frederick against "a force of federal cavalry which had followed [the army] from Maryland Heights." Early, *Memoir*, 58.

rice, sugar, sanitary stores, wine, etc." sat in the government warehouses that remained undisturbed.[43]

If Jubal Early had posted hundreds of Confederate infantry in the city to intimidate Frederick's leaders into paying a levy that he stipulated could be settled in cash or goods, why were these men not employed to discover the supplies that the army so sorely required? An eyewitness who watched the depleted Stonewall Brigade (part of Gordon's division) march through Winchester a few days earlier noted, for example, that the men looked "emaciated" and "half-naked." Much like Jackson's men in 1862, the Valley Army's troops in 1864 needed clothing and shoes in addition to food, and yet Early and his senior staff left vast quantities of these vital supplies untouched.[44]

In summary, and as related to the Byerly studio photograph, Jubal Early's Army of the Valley entered Frederick from the west at 6:00 a.m. on July 9, 1864, with Stephen Ramseur's two brigades in the fore. Early's infantry, guns, wagons, and some cavalry moved through Frederick toward a clash with Union troops on the Monocacy River until sometime in the mid-afternoon, when the final brigade (Lewis's under Colonel Godwin) entered the town. This brigade of four North Carolina regiments moved into and out of Frederick for the rest of the day. No evidence exists showing where Godwin posted his men, or whether they did anything other than perform the duties to which they were assigned, i.e., guarding the army's rear and helping transport wounded comrades from the battlefield. Witnesses in Frederick reported Confederate "soldiers" entering shops and/or one warehouse throughout the day, but no time-frame for those activities can be confirmed and the perpetrators cannot be identified as infantry.

The logical conclusion concerning the men who entered the shops and warehouses is that they were stragglers from Early's army. Confederate units on the march shed stragglers like a dog shakes off fleas. This would have especially been the case for men entering a city like Frederick, where the barefooted and the hatless could buy, or in some cases, take, the accessories they needed. According to Frederick resident Jacob Engelbrecht, they took liberally and often threatened "to shoot people if they would not give up their money, Horses &c." The intimidation of Frederick's people by Rebel troops is undeniable, but there is no evidence that it

43 Lewis, *Frederick War Claim*, 15 and 35.

44 James I. Robertson, Jr., *4th Virginia Infantry* (Lynchburg, VA, 1982), 32.

Are the Confederate soldiers pictured in the famous Byerly studio image troops from Lt. Gen. Jubal Early's Army of the Valley taken on July 9, 1864? Not according to the available evidence.

LOC

was either systematic or involved the stationing of soldiers in town specifically to frighten the civilian populace into submission.[45]

A few details in the Byerly studio photograph suggest it could have been taken on July 9. For example, a few dark spots on the street could denote damp areas left behind after the rain that fell the night before on July 8. No rain fell before Jackson's troops marched out of Frederick in September 1862. The image, however, is blurry and the dark spots could just as easily be horse manure or some other detritus waiting to be cleaned-up, particularly since outriders with Capt. Lige White's Loudoun County border cavalry drove herds of livestock through town during the September 1862 occupation.[46]

Put simply, there is no reliable source that proves the presence of Confederate infantry on the march outside of Jacob Byerly's studio on July 9, 1864. There is, however, extensive documentation of infantry tramping past the Byerly studio on September 10, 1862, at a time when Byerly or one of his assistants could have captured the image we have today.

---

45 Quynn, ed., The *Diary of Jacob Engelbrecht*, 1000.

46 Bolcik, *et al.*, "Confederates in Frederick," 11. "They have driven a great deal of cattle through the town, some of them out in the direction of their camps, and some toward the fords." "Four Days Experience with the Rebels in Frederick," in the *Cumberland Civilian and Telegraph*, Sept. 18, 1862. Also see an article from the *Baltimore American* reprinted in the *Alexandria Gazette* on September 8, 1862: "The foraging parties sent out in various directions to secure cattle returned during the evening with droves of sheep, hogs, beeves, cows. and horses."

There is one final fact to consider. When James V. Murfin first published the photo of these troops in his 1965 book *The Gleam of Bayonets*, he recounted hearing from the Rosenstock family, which owned the image, the lore passed down through the years that claimed it depicted Rebels on the street in September 1862. Thus, even the provenance of the photograph points to the men pictured being part of Jackson's command as it departed Frederick on the morning of September 10, 1862, and not Early's soldiers holding the city ransom in July 1864.[47]

47 Murfin, *Gleam*, 14. "The Confederate photograph has never been published and is considered by experts as a rarity . . . although there is no documentation to identify the date or military unit, the Rosenstock family memories substantiate that it was taken during the Confederate occupation, September 1862."

Six

The Army of Northern Virginia Makes a Stand

⌐*ℳ*⌐

A Critical Assessment of Robert E. Lee's Defensive Strategy at Sharpsburg on September 15-16, 1862

INTERPRETATIONS of historical events evolve over time, driven by the discovery of new evidence and the introduction of fresh ideas. Thus it benefits us every so often to reexamine subjects that may be considered settled in the historical literature. Robert E. Lee's preparations for the Battle of Sharpsburg/Antietam offer a case in point. Lee's reasons for fighting in Maryland remain poorly understood, a fact that has influenced the analysis of the decisions he made in the lead-up to the Army of the Potomac's attack late in the day on September 16. One of the results is that, until the last twenty years or so, the story Antietam was sharply focused on the pre-battle planning of George McClellan rather than on the "passive" defense pursued by the Confederate commander.

It has long been said that McClellan telegraphed his September 16 attack on the left flank of Lee's waiting army. When he learned of the movement, Lee shifted troops to meet it, and the long and bloody battle that followed the next day ended in a tactical draw instead of a potentially war-ending Federal victory. William

Swinton appears to have spearheaded this elegantly simple interpretation in his 1866 book *Campaigns of the Army of the Potomac*, with Francis W. Palfrey carrying the torch after him in the 1890s. These early works significantly informed twentieth century writers like James V. Murfin, Stephen W. Sears, and others critical of the Union army commander.[1]

To their credit, recent works by Joseph L. Harsh, Ethan S. Rafuse, and D. Scott Hartwig offer more balanced perspectives. Harsh focused primarily, though not exclusively, on Robert E. Lee's planning. He agreed that McClellan may indeed have telegraphed his September 16 attack. However, argued Harsh, Lee was seeking a way out of Sharpsburg with a northward march up the Hagerstown Pike after Stonewall Jackson's command had rejoined him in Maryland. Joseph Hooker's First Corps advance down the pike against Lee's left flank prevented the Rebel general from moving his army anywhere. Giving McClellan credit for this maneuver, Harsh recognized some efficiency on the Federal commander's part while adding the unique notion that Lee explored the possibility of not giving battle by withdrawing his army from the field.[2]

Ethan Rafuse's detailed 2005 tactical analysis centered more on McClellan's pre-battle decision-making than on Lee's thought process. Rather than focus on the question of Little Mac telegraphing Federal moves or on the possibility of Lee's army escaping to Hagerstown, Rafuse examined the reasons why McClellan believed an assault on Lee's left was his most desirable option. Rafuse concluded it was his best choice and that McClellan launched his attack to eliminate the possibility of a Rebel advance against his right north of Sharpsburg. The argument

---

1 Lee did not escape criticism during the war, but even those commentators who argued that he had no business fighting at Sharpsburg paid less attention to how Lee prepared for the contest than the critique they heaped upon McClellan. See, for example, Gary W. Gallagher, ed., *Fighting for the Confederacy: The Personal Recollections of General Edward Porter Alexander* (Chapel Hill, NC, 1989), 145, and Longstreet, *From Manassas to Appomattox*, 228; William Swinton, *Campaigns of the Army of the Potomac* (New York, NY, 1866), 210, and Palfrey, *The Antietam and Fredericksburg*, 46-47. Also see Carman, *The Maryland Campaign*, 2:Ch. 2. Until recently Carman's manuscript remained unpublished, but scholars used the papers he collected for the Antietam Battlefield Board and the manuscript he produced from them. See editor Thomas G. Clemens's Introduction in Carman, *The Maryland Campaign*, 1:ix-xviii. Writing from across the ocean and thus less subject to the political rancor in the United States, the Comte de Paris offered little critical judgment against McClellan in his history of the Civil War; Murfin, *Gleam*, 208; Sears, *Landscape Turned Red*, 186; Edward H. Bonekemper III, *McClellan and Failure: A Study of Civil War Fear, Incompetence, and Worse* (Jefferson, NC, 2007); and James M. McPherson, *Crossroads of Freedom: Antietam* (New York, NY, 2002).

2 Harsh, *Taken at the Flood*, 344-345.

is a variation on the Harsh thesis of McClellan slamming the door shut on Lee's opportunity for maneuver. Its primary difference is that he argued Little Mac seized the initiative by launching his offensive with a deliberate tactical objective in mind. Throughout this treatment, General Lee remained a passive player waiting to receive the Federal attack.[3]

Scott Hartwig addressed the subject in his 2012 book *To Antietam Creek: The Maryland Campaign of September 1862*, the first volume of a full campaign history. Hartwig offered a nuanced view of events. Instead of judging either commander, he weighed each man's actions over the course of a flowing narrative with only a brief accompanying analysis. The result is by far the most detailed recounting of those critical events to date. Hartwig made an exception in his discussion of Lee's thinking as battle loomed on September 16. Although he refused to speculate on Lee's motives for fighting at Antietam, the influence of Harsh's work forced him to address the notion of Lee seeking to remove his army from Sharpsburg in the direction of Hagerstown. "If Lee pondered these possibilities on the night of September 16," Hartwig concluded, "it was with the knowledge that, for the moment, his campaign of maneuver was finished. The battle now pending must be won, or the entire Maryland Campaign would be over."[4]

The lack of uniformity among interpretations of the events leading up to the clash at Sharpsburg prompts one to wonder if it is possible to develop a clear understanding of Lee's defensive strategy prior to the engagement. The fact that a variety of historical interpretations has emerged is understandable, but it also invites questions. For example, is there hard evidence that Lee sought to escape from Sharpsburg toward Hagerstown before McClellan could get at him, or was the Confederate commander aiming to achieve something different by remaining in Maryland? Moreover, did McClellan's pre-battle maneuvers help shape the

---

3 Ethan S. Rafuse, *McClellan's War: The Failure of Moderation in the Struggle for the Union* (Bloomington, IN, 2005), 309.

4 "Whatever reasons Lee had in making his decision to stand and fight, he was building sand castles." Hartwig, *To Antietam Creek*, 519, 632. Steven W. Knott, "Lee at Antietam: Strategic Imperatives, The Tyranny of Arithmetic, and a Trap Not Sprung," in *Army History*, No. 95 (Spring 2015) speculates Lee remained at Sharpsburg to draw McClellan into moving against the Confederate left flank so that he could attack the Federal right (i.e., in a fashion similar to the assault executed by Jackson at Chancellorsville). Knott was not referring to the counterattack Lee eventually ordered Jackson to attempt on September 17. He meant that Lee planned an attack against the Federal right from the moment his army took up position at Sharpsburg, but found his army was too small to accomplish this objective.

decisions made by Lee, and if so, how? Conversely, did Lee's decisions and moves influence McClellan's plans? Finally, do the measures taken by Lee on September 15 and 16 tell us anything about the kind of engagement he intended to fight? Each of these questions, as well as several others, bears examination because only a reevaluation of the underlying sources can help us develop a clearer understanding of why Lee fought at Sharpsburg, and how he prepared for the battle that erupted there late in the day on September 16.

Strangely enough, there is no consensus on the moment when, or—in the case of Joseph Harsh—*if*, Robert E. Lee actually decided to stand and fight in Maryland. In Harsh's judgment, Lee's 1868 claim that McClellan "forced" battle on him is evidence the Confederate general had intended to withdraw his army from the box at Sharpsburg before Joseph Hooker's First Corps moved down the Hagerstown Turnpike and closed off the route. Harsh claimed repeatedly in *Taken at the Flood* that Lee never intended to fight at Sharpsburg, and called the position assumed by Lee a "stopgap" until circumstances forced him to give battle. This opinion differs categorically from that held by Ezra Carman, who wrote in the decades following the war that Lee consciously made a decision to fight there around noon on September 15 after word arrived from Stonewall Jackson that Harpers Ferry had fallen. Scott Hartwig agrees with Carman, although Hartwig offered a different time-frame for Lee's decision when he wrote that it was "by sunset [that] Lee had made up his mind to stand and offer battle."[5]

Given these diverse perspectives one could be forgiven for being confused. Did Lee decide to fight in Maryland after the reverse at South Mountain or did he not? The premise set forth in this chapter is that Lee intended from early on September 15 to give battle at Sharpsburg. The evidence strongly suggests that after he decided to retreat to Virginia on the evening of September 14, Lee began

---

5 Harsh, *Taken*, 360. Harsh turns his own speculative argument into a statement of historical fact. Compare the conditional language used on page 332, when he first suggests Lee's thought process—"In his thinking, Lee *probably* [emphasis added] inclined, as he usually did, to a turning movement that would carry him around the enemy's right flank . . . It must have made the most sense to Lee to march north to Hagerstown"—with the definitive language used twelve pages later: "The evening before Lee had predicted that 'there would not be much fighting' on the 16th. Implicitly, he believed McClellan would give him another twenty-four hours to escape from the box at Sharpsburg." Consider also the unambiguous title of the chapter sub-section immediately following the aforementioned quote: "McClellan Shuts the Window." See Harsh, *Taken*, 344; Carman, *The Maryland Campaign*, 1:428. Murfin *Gleam of Bayonets*, 196-197, adheres largely to this interpretation while Sears, *Landscape Turned Red*, 161, is decidedly vague on the matter. See also, Hartwig, *To Antietam Creek*, 518.

rethinking his decision within a few hours. The temporary construction of a defensive position at Sharpsburg grew out of Lee's concern about the fate of Lafayette McLaws's and Richard Anderson's divisions in Pleasant Valley and his desire to safely extract those commands from their predicament. By 8.00 a.m. on September 15, however, Lee came around fully to the idea of fighting in Maryland and latched firmly onto that course of action after a note from Jackson reached him announcing the anticipated fall of Harpers Ferry. The evidence also shows that once Lee made a decision to fight on September 15, he never modified, second-guessed, or otherwise strayed from it.[6]

The Rebel general's choice of Sharpsburg as the place where he would give battle intentionally forfeited any opportunity to conduct a campaign of maneuver in favor of a straightforward clash with the reconstituted Army of the Potomac. Why did Lee take such a grave risk at a time when his army was flagging after months of hard campaigning? His objective for being in Maryland in the first place, as he would write to President Davis in August of 1863, was to draw McClellan's army away from fortified Washington and attack it in the hope that a "military success might afford us an opportunity to aid the citizens of Maryland in any efforts they might be disposed to make to recover their liberties." This suggests the general devised a military operation intended to achieve a larger political objective, i.e., to spark a secessionist rebellion in Maryland that would take the state out of the Union, isolate the District of Columbia, and force the Lincoln administration to sue for peace.[7]

According to a long-overlooked column in the *Philadelphia Inquirer,* Lee also stated this objective *during* the campaign. "We have now come to redeem our pledge to the people of this State," the general informed a man from Baltimore while the Army of Northern Virginia was resting around Frederick. "We extend the olive branch to them," he continued,

---

6 OR 19, 1:951. Jackson sent his note to Lee at 8:15 p.m. on Sept. 14. Somehow, what should have been a four-hour ride by courier from Harpers Ferry to Keedysville turned into a 12-hour odyssey and thus delayed Lee's decision until early the next day. (For example, a note sent by Jackson from Harpers Ferry "near 8:00 A.M." on Sept. 15 reached Lee on Cemetery Hill east of Sharpsburg around noon.) The delay was likely brought about by the presence of Federal cavalry under Col. Grimes Davis who crossed the courier's path on their way north. Once in Sharpsburg, the Federals stopped to water their horses at the Big Spring in the center of town, a process that would have taken some hours given that Davis's command consisted of some 1,300 mounted men. Also see Hartwig, *To Antietam Creek,* 546.

7 OR 19, 1:144.

and, should they accept it, we shall welcome and protect them, with the assurance that the next battle ground will be in Pennsylvania. But, should they not come forward, after having been amply assured that their property would be unmolested, and every guarantee given that the Southern army should remain on Maryland soil, for the maintenance of their sacred rights, then the battle-ground must hereafter be in Maryland.[8]

The *Inquirer* published this statement in a column titled "Our Baltimore Letter," calling the information it contained "Special Correspondence of the *Inquirer*" obtained "Near Baltimore, Sept. 11, 1862." The column also added, "it appears to be a fixed fact that the Rebels are intent upon carrying out the plan proposed to be adopted by General Lee, or at least what he told a gentleman of this city (i.e., Baltimore) it was, in an earnest conversation with him one day last week. Each day's movements go to prove the earnestness of the Rebel General's intentions."

The first chapter of this study argues that Lee appears to have changed his thinking on the evening of September 6 concerning the support from his army required by Maryland's secessionists. It is likely that he made the statement that appeared in the *Inquirer* during the dinner he attended in Frederick (at which the informant may have been present), or during a separate visit by the informant to army headquarters between September 7 and September 9. In either case the content of the statement is consistent with Lee's 1863 letter to Jefferson Davis concerning the actions he took during the campaign, and with other comments he made after the war. William Allan, who knew Lee personally, explained, for example, "It was not General Lee's original intention to dispute the passage of South Mountain with McClellan. His design, on the other hand, was to induce the Federal army, if possible, to cross that range into the Hagerstown Valley, and when this army had thus gotten fairly out of the reach of Washington the Confederate commander expected to give it battle upon his own terms." This summary of Lee's thinking closely matches the content of the general's comment printed in the *Philadelphia Inquirer*.[9]

Lee told Allan in April 1868 that "he would have fought McC after [Harpers Ferry] if he had had all his troops in hand, and McC out [in the open] so that he could get at him." Lee also stated to Edward Clifford Gordon that, "if McClellan

---

8 *Philadelphia Inquirer*, Sept. 12, 1862.

9 William W. Allan, "First Maryland Campaign," in *SHSP* (Jan.-Dec. 1886), 14:106.

could have been kept in ignorance but two or three days longer, he did not doubt then (nor has he changed his opinion since) that he could have crushed the army of McClellan." It was the discovery of Special Orders No. 191 by Federal troops outside Frederick on September 13, and McClellan's quick response to the information contained in them, that changed Lee's calculations for the worse; in other words, the loss of the orders forced battle on him earlier than Lee had intended. As the general would later complain to Allan, "had the Lost Dispatch not been lost, and had McClellan continued his cautious policy for two or three days longer, I would have had all my troops reconcentrated on [the] Md. side [of the Potomac], stragglers up, [and] men rested . . . I intended then to attack McClellan."[10]

Lee's own statements make it clear that he planned from the beginning of the campaign to give battle north of the Potomac River. What is more, he intended that battle to take place in "the Hagerstown Valley" if Maryland's people did not rise up in revolt against the Federal forces occupying the state. Reviewing the content of Special Orders No. 191 brings the elements of this plan into sharp relief. Lee sent Jackson to capture Harpers Ferry in order to keep its men from attacking his supply line in the Shenandoah Valley and from reinforcing McClellan's army. Lee, meanwhile, moved the rest of his force into position at Boonsboro and Hagerstown in order to lure the Federals after him. Lee assumed that once Jackson captured Harpers Ferry he could march up the Virginia side of the Potomac with the divisions of Walker, McLaws, and Anderson, recross the river at Williamsport, and join Longstreet and D. H. Hill for the intended clash with McClellan in Washington County. In other words, while Lee may have found accepting a fight with McClellan at Sharpsburg less than ideal, he thought it consistent with his objectives and believed the location favorable enough given the circumstances in which he found himself at the time.

The importance of the morning of September 15 begins with the retreat of Longstreet's and D. H. Hill's commands from South Mountain the night before. Once Federal troops were in position to turn both flanks of the Confederate force at Turner's and Fox's gaps on the evening of September 14, and a report arrived

---

10 Allan, "Memoranda," Gallagher, ed., *Lee the Soldier*, 8, 13. For more information on this issue, see Thorp/Rossino, *The Tale Untwisted*, and Stotelmyer, *Too Useful to Sacrifice*, both of which include detailed treatments of McClellan's handling of Lee's lost orders on Sept. 13, 1862; E. C. Gordon, "Memorandum of a Conversation with General R. E. Lee, Feb. 15, 1868," Gallagher, ed., *Lee the Soldier*, 26.

confirming the fall of Crampton's Gap, General Lee ordered the portion of the army under his direct command to withdraw to Virginia. McClellan's rapid advance from Frederick had shattered his plans. "The day has gone against us and this army will go by Sharpsburg and cross the river," wrote Lee to Lafayette McLaws at 8:00 p.m. Lee ordered the Georgian to abandon his position on Maryland Heights and "unite with this command" before instructing him to "Send forward officers to explore the way, ascertain the best crossing of the Potomac, and if you can find any [river ford] between you and Shepherdstown leave Shepherdstown Ford for this command." This message to McLaws confirms that Lee thought his campaign in Maryland had come to an end. Stonewall Jackson thought so as well. According to Henry Kyd Douglas, Jackson received a letter from Lee on September 14 ordering him to "march to Shepherdstown and cover the crossing of Longstreet and [the] others." General Lee, recorded Douglas, "was withdrawing toward the Potomac with a view to crossing into Virginia."[11]

Safely extracting McLaws and Anderson from Pleasant Valley while reuniting the army occupied the Confederate commander's mind. Did Lee think he could bring the Army of Northern Virginia's separated parts back together in Virginia or in Maryland? His 8:00 p.m. orders to McLaws and message to Jackson suggested the former. Only two hours later, however, Lee sent a dispatch to Col. Thomas Munford, the commander of a cavalry brigade in Pleasant Valley, suggesting that he had already rethought his decision. This dispatch (time-stamped 10:15 p.m.) instructed Munford to hold his "position at Rohrersville" and determine if he could "discover . . . a practicable road below Crampton's Gap by which McLaws, at Weverton at present, *can pass over the mountains to Sharpsburg* [emphasis added]." If he could do this, instructed Lee, Munford was to send McLaws "a messenger to guide him over immediately."[12]

Lee supplemented this message at 11:15 p.m. with a note to McLaws that the Georgian might take his command back into Virginia to escape the danger posed by McClellan's advance. Lee suggested McLaws explore using the ford at Point of Rocks, Maryland, some 14 miles east of his position. Lee also presented McLaws with the second option of moving his command farther north in Maryland to join

11 OR 51, 1:618-619. Douglas, *I Rode with Stonewall*, 164. Jackson referred to this order from Lee in OR 19, 1:951.

12 OR 19, 2:609. Lee's Sept. 14 mention of Sharpsburg as a rallying point echoed a note sent to McLaws at 10:00 p.m. on Sept. 13 ordering him to "move your force as rapidly as possible to Sharpsburg." OR 19, 2:607.

the rest of the army near Keedysville. Lee informed McLaws that his own portion of the army would "take position at Centreville, commonly called Keedysville," and that he was doing so "with a view of preventing the enemy . . . from cutting you off, and *enabling you to make a junction with it* [emphasis added]." Lee confirmed this motive eleven months later in his official campaign report by writing that the position at Keedysville provided a place "where we could more readily unite with the rest of the army" due to the availability of a road over Elk Ridge from Rohrersville. Lee added a second reason for moving in the direction of Keedysville that he did not mention in September 1862: he wanted to place his command "upon the flank and rear of the enemy should he move against McLaws."[13]

Shortly after sending this dispatch, "General Lee started from his headquarters at the foot of South Mountain . . . [and] arrived at Keedysville about an hour before daybreak" on September 15. There, Lee dictated a third message to McLaws, repeating the idea expressed in the 11:15 note that he wished the Georgian to rejoin him in Maryland. "We have fallen back to this place to enable you more readily to join us," he explained, despite not having received a reply to his earlier messages. "You are desired to withdraw immediately from your position on Maryland Heights, and join us here. If you can't get off any other way, you must cross the mountain. The utmost dispatch is required." To this the general added, "Should you be able to cross over to Harper's Ferry, do so and report immediately," a clear indication that it would also be acceptable if McLaws combined his force with Jackson's in Virginia.[14]

Lee's thinking at this point is difficult to discern, which has led historians to speculate about his plans. According to Ezra Carman, a reply from Colonel Munford reached Lee soon after he sent his third message to McLaws: "McLaws could not come up the valley and that the difficulties in getting over Elk Ridge and Maryland Heights were very great." With McLaws unable to join Lee near Keedysville, Carman concluded that the Confederate commander decided to move his army to the heights near Sharpsburg, where it could assume "a better defensive [position] against McClellan's larger army" and wait there for the Georgian to come to him.[15]

---

13 OR 19, 2:608, and OR 19, 1:147.

14 Carman, *The Maryland Campaign*, 1:390. Sunrise came at 5:50 a.m. according to Harsh, *Sounding the Shallows*, 17; OR 19, 2:609-610.

15 Carman, *The Maryland Campaign*, 1:391.

Joseph Harsh expressed agreement with Carman's conclusion, while observing there was no evidence Munford's note reached Lee after he had already sent his third message to McLaws. Harsh added that engineers reporting to Lee must have told him the ground around Keedysville provided a poor defensive position compared to the higher terrain west of Antietam Creek. As a result, Lee "decided to cross Antietam Creek and fall back about three miles to Sharpsburg. There, he could anchor each flank on the serpentine bends of the river. Moreover, Boteler's Ford would be but five miles distant and safely within the perimeter of his defense, safeguarding either a retreat or the arrival of reenforcements from Jackson." Scott Hartwig's treatment followed the same reasoning: the choice of standing at Sharpsburg "was not a reversal of Lee's decision to withdraw from Maryland. That option remained on the table and might well need to be used, but Lee had shaken off his moment of doubt, which was when he sent word to McLaws that Longstreet and D. H. Hill would retire to Virginia."[16]

Perhaps so, but there is no source confirming that Lee still entertained the idea of retiring to Virginia. In fact, there are several clues indicating that he did not. The first was Lee's messages to Munford and McLaws ordering that the latter rejoin the main body of the army in Maryland. The Confederate commander's tone grew more insistent with each message until Lee finally demanded, in unusually strong language for him, that McLaws attempt the extremely difficult march over Elk Ridge "with the utmost dispatch." If Lee still intended to concentrate his army in Virginia, he would not have issued such instructions. Admittedly, his messages to McLaws also contained exhortations to escape into Virginia if he could, but these read like pragmatic suggestions compared to the more forceful language Lee used when calling McLaws to join him.

Lee took position at Sharpsburg *after* Munford reported that McLaws could not make it over Elk Ridge. Standing at Sharpsburg made little sense as a "stopgap" at this point because geographic barriers ensured that neither Lee nor McLaws could come to the assistance of the other. Not only did a mountain range and Maj. Gen. William Franklin's Federal Sixth Corps separate the two commands, but Lee had not received any word from McLaws and did he know whether McLaws had received the orders sent to him. This silence suggested that that enemy had cut communications with Pleasant Valley, rendering the coordination of any defensive action by the two commands impossible under the circumstances. Lee also did not

16 Harsh, *Taken*, 301 and Hartwig, *To Antietam Creek*, 481.

know whether Jackson had successfully reduced Harpers Ferry, which would allow him to rejoin the army in Maryland. In addition, it soon became clear that a strong Federal column had pushed through Turner's Gap, engaged Fitzhugh Lee's rear guard near Boonsboro, and initiated its pursuit of the Confederate army toward Sharpsburg.[17]

The prudent act under these circumstances would have been for Lee to withdraw to Virginia and defend the Potomac line against McClellan's army until Harpers Ferry fell, but the Confederate commander chose not to do this. With the Federals bearing down on him, McLaws unable to join the army in Maryland, Lee unable to assist McLaws if the Georgian needed help, and the outcome of Jackson's operation uncertain, who was Lee trying to buy time for by remaining in place at Sharpsburg? The most satisfactory and logical answer is that Lee had made *two* decisions by early on September 15: he hoped that standing in Maryland would buy enough time for Jackson to complete his mission and rejoin the army, and more importantly, Lee had already decided not to leave Maryland without a fight if it was at all possible.

A stubborn adherence to his campaign plan and the terrain he observed west of Antietam Creek certainly helped inform Lee's choice. Only a dozen hours earlier after reports suggested the fight for South Mountain had been lost, he had ordered General Pendleton, his commander of the army's reserve artillery, to establish a defensive fallback position on the heights behind Beaver Creek. These orders have not received the attention they deserve. They repeat Lee's written message to McLaws at 10:00 p.m. on the 13th that "General Longstreet will move down to-morrow and take a position on Beaver Creek, this side of Boonsborough," and they demonstrate that Lee was on the lookout for good defensive terrain while moving through Washington County. Both orders also support William Allan's later claim that Lee intended to fight in "the Hagerstown Valley."[18]

The hills west of Beaver Creek halfway between Boonsboro and Hagerstown rival, and in some places exceed, the elevation of the heights in front of Sharpsburg.

---

17 OR 19, 1:147. General Lee: "This movement was efficiently and skillfully covered by the cavalry brigade of General Fitzhugh Lee, and was accomplished without interruption by the enemy, who did not appear on the west side of the pass at Boonsborough until about 8 a.m. on the following morning."

18 Ibid., 1:830. William Nelson Pendleton: "I arrived and reported to you a short distance from the battlefield, you directed me to place in position on the heights of Beaver Creek the several batteries of my command. This was accordingly done, just before nightfall."

Before learning that the fight at South Mountain had been lost, Lee weighed the option of withdrawing to a location in Washington County that offered an advantageous defensive position atop a high ridge line. It was only after his "moment of doubt" on the evening of September 14 that Lee elected to retreat in the direction of Sharpsburg with an eye toward crossing the Potomac. Two or three hours later he had already begun to change his mind.

The orders to Pendleton demonstrate that Lee intended to continue the fight in Maryland after he lost South Mountain—if he could. When reaching Beaver Creek proved impractical because it took him too far from the other parts of the army, he moved toward Keedysville instead. There, Lee found terrain along Antietam Creek similar to the position he had wanted to take up earlier—an array of hills that offered a strong defensive location several miles closer to the detached commands of Jackson, McLaws, and Walker in Virginia. Perhaps his plan to confront defeat McClellan in western Maryland could be carried out after all.

It was at this point early on September 15 that Jackson's message from the evening of September 14 finally reached Lee. "While resting . . . in a meadow by the roadside, on the high ground nearly a mile west of [Keedysville]," wrote Ezra Carman, "a farmer's kindly wife sent him (Lee) a pot of hot coffee and, but a few minutes later, a courier rode up with the belated dispatch from Jackson, dated 8.15 p.m. of the 14th." It is "Through God's blessing, the advance, which commenced this evening, has been successful thus far," wrote Jackson. "I look to Him for complete success to-morrow. The advance has been directed to be resumed at dawn to-morrow morning. I am thankful that our loss has been small."[19]

Jackson sent this message on September 14, meaning Lee could reasonably expect word of the Federal garrison's surrender to reach him at some point on September 15. Thus, he continued positioning his fragment of the army on the heights near Sharpsburg. As Carman noted, Lee set this process in motion *before* receiving Jackson's note: "To the west, beyond the Antietam, he saw D. H. Hill's Division going into position and the wagon train moving over Cemetery Hill and down into Sharpsburg. Then, when the long trains had nearly passed, Lee, leaving Longstreet to bring up his command, was assisted into his ambulance and driven across the Antietam to where D. H. Hill was forming his command." Lee confirmed this course of events in a letter to Jefferson Davis on September 16, although he reversed the order of their occurrence. "Believing from a report from

19 Carman, *The Maryland Campaign*, 1:392 and OR 19, 1:951.

General Jackson that Harper's Ferry would fall next morning," wrote the general to the president, "I determined to withdraw Longstreet and D. H. Hill from their positions [on South Mountain] and retire to the vicinity of Sharpsburg, where the army could be more easily united."[20]

Lee personally verified on September 16 that Jackson's message on the morning of September 15 solidified his decision to remain in Maryland. D. H. Hill's division led the Confederate column forming on the high ground beyond Antietam Creek before Jackson's missive arrived, which suggests that Lee had already selected the position his army would assume for its concentration. Doing so was consistent with his search for formidable defensive terrain similar to what he had seen along Beaver Creek. Jackson's note confirmed what Lee had hoped—that the Federal garrison at Harpers Ferry would capitulate in short order and that Jackson's renowned "foot cavalry" could make the journey to Sharpsburg in time for the clash with McClellan's army north of the Potomac River. With the temporary goal of awaiting McLaws no longer attainable thanks to the enemy's advance, and coordinating his own movement to protect McLaws's flank was impossible because communications had been cut, Lee shifted his focus to reuniting his army as rapidly as he could.[21]

As Lee's staff officer Maj. Walter H. Taylor explained after the war, the general "would be guided by circumstances; he would accept battle on the north side [of the Potomac] if he could reunite his army in time [or] . . . failing in that, he would re-cross into Virginia."[22] The hills west of Antietam Creek offered a defensive position that would enable Lee's portion of the Army of Northern Virginia to stand in place until the army's other parts could come up. Concentrating in Maryland ensured that Lee would give battle north of the Potomac, an outcome he intended. This interpretation of his actions is supported by the fact that no dispatch he sent after 8:00 a.m. on September 15, no comment he is known to have uttered, and no report he wrote or order he gave, mentioned withdrawing toward Hagerstown from the position he assumed at Sharpsburg. Circumstances may have forced Lee

---

20 Carman, *The Maryland Campaign*, 1:392. Carman received these details in a letter from Col. Charles Marshall, a member of Lee's headquarters staff, and a direct witness to the events. *OR* 19, 1:140.

21 Jackson asked in his September 14 reply, "Can you not connect the headquarters of the army, by signal, with General McLaws?" which indicated that Lee had informed him he could not communicate with Pleasant Valley. *OR* 19, 1:951.

22 Hartwig, *To Antietam Creek*, 488.

to abandon his original plan for a fight with McClellan somewhere between Hagerstown and Boonsboro, but he clearly found the position at Sharpsburg (still in Washington County) good enough to fulfill his objectives. Lee chose to stand at Sharpsburg even though retiring to Virginia was advisable and easily accomplished. He made that choice around 8:00 a.m. on September 15.

Once he decided to stand his ground, Lee worked on presenting as strong a defensive front to the enemy as possible. While D. H. Hill deployed north of the road to Boonsboro and Longstreet's command filed onto the hills to the south of it, including above the Rohrbach Bridge on Antietam Creek, Lee began posting artillery. Batteries sprinkled along the line covered the approach from the Middle Bridge over the creek, and included some 20 pieces under Col. Stephen Dill Lee, commander of the 2nd Battalion of Longstreet's artillery, and another 16 guns with Col. James B. Walton's 1st Battalion. Acting on Lee's orders, Longstreet instructed Walton to "put them all in, every gun you have, long range and short range." It was a show of force to buy time until Jackson could come up.[23]

This is about the time when men with Company C of the 11th Virginia Infantry, James Kemper's brigade, allegedly heard Lee say, "we will make our stand on these hills." Lee's comment, while generally consistent with the circumstances as they existed at the time, came from a secondhand source many decades later and must be treated with care. There are some inconsistencies around its timing, which make the hour when Lee supposedly uttered his statement problematic. "I have heard some of Company C relate that *on the evening* [emphasis added] of September 15th, when near Sharpsburg, they saw General Lee by the roadside," wrote a Virginia soldier named W. H. Morgan. "When the head of the column, which was falling back before the Yankee army from the direction of South Mountain, reached a certain point, General Lee remarked, as the troops by his order filed off the road to form line of battle, 'We will make our stand on these hills'." In nineteenth century parlance, "evening" could mean any time after noon. Lee, or even Longstreet, however, posted Kemper's brigade early in the morning, which makes it unlikely that the general would have spoken those words later in the day.[24]

---

23 This includes Robert Toombs's brigade of Georgians, which Lee summoned from Hagerstown where it had been guarding a portion of the army's supply train. Harsh, *Taken*, 289. Also see Longstreet, *From Manassas to Appomattox*, 228. "General Toombs's brigade joined us early on the 15th, and was posted over the Burnside Bridge." Owen, *In Camp and Battle*, 138.

24 W. H. Morgan, *Personal Reminiscences of the War of 1861-5* (Lynchburg, VA, 1911), 140.

A more plausible account comes from John Dooley of the 1st Virginia, also of Kemper's command. In his 1871 memoir, Dooley recalled that his regiment had fallen behind the main body of the army during the retreat from South Mountain to get some sleep. The men rose early and immediately set out to join the rest of Longstreet's command. "The sun was just beginning to spread his roseate hues upon the dull grey sky," recalled Dooley, "[when] we overtook our Brigade which was leisurely resting around some tall hay stack off the road and enjoying a meagre but well seasoned breakfast. Just before overtaking the Brigade," he continued, "we passed the ambulance of our Great General Lee who was in the act of descending from his ambulance remarking that the present spot would be a good position for a stand against the pursuing enemy." It was then, according to Dooley, that Lee made the comment shortly after sunrise on the morning of September 15, which corroborates that he had already decided to fight at Sharpsburg well before the second message from Jackson arrived at noon to report the fate of Harpers Ferry.[25]

When the anxiously awaited news from Jackson finally appeared, it confirmed that "Harpers Ferry and its garrison are to be surrendered." Old Jack informed Lee, "As Hill's troops have borne the heaviest part in the engagement, he will be left in command until the prisoners and public property shall be disposed of, unless you direct otherwise. The other forces," Jackson added, "can move off this evening so soon as they get their rations. To what point shall they move?" Lee directed Jackson to return to Maryland immediately, which prompted him to reply, "I will join you at Sharpsburg." With that, Jackson ordered his men to cook rations and prepare to march.[26]

Carman concluded from Jackson's message that it "determined Lee [would] accept battle north of the Potomac and on the banks of the Antietam. He was now

---

25 Curran, ed., *John Dooley's Civil War*, 43. A third version of Lee's statement exists, allegedly made by the commander late on Sept. 14, 1862, after D. H. Hill and James Longstreet reported that they could not hold their position on South Mountain another day. When he heard the report, Lee purported to have replied, "Well, then, gentlemen, proceed to bring off your men —as quietly as possible. We will retire to Sharpsburg, and make a stand there. We shall thereby gain one more day for Jackson." The stylized nature of the quote and the fact that it contradicts Lee's own written statement that night claiming the army would return to Virginia makes this version suspect. Hamilton, ed., *The Papers of Randolph Abbott Shotwell*, 1:340.

26 OR 19, 1:951, 1007. Also see Carman, *The Maryland Campaign*, 1:423-424, and Douglas, *I Rode with Stonewall*, 164. Jackson wrote in his campaign report that he left "General Hill to receive the surrender of the Federal troops and take the requisite steps for securing the captured stores." He "moved, in obedience to orders from the commanding general, to rejoin him in Maryland with the remaining divisions of my command."

certain that Jackson, closely followed by Walker, would be with him in the morning of the next day and had the best of reasons for the belief that McLaws would not be far behind." This is a fair reading, but it is equally valid to think of Lee's order as verification of his earlier decision to stand in Maryland. All we know about the order is that Lee called Jackson to join him. We do not know what more Lee may have thought about his situation at the time. The available evidence shows only that Lee decided to make a stand at Sharpsburg early on the morning of September 15, and that all his actions thereafter flowed from that decision. Whatever else Lee might have intended *after* 8:00 a.m. on September 15 was known only to the general himself because the documentary evidence and subsequent events demonstrate only that Lee had decided to stand and fight.[27]

Having established that he would give battle at Sharpsburg, Lee did not have long to wait for the enemy to appear. As the blue masses covered the hills east of Antietam Creek, the positions they assumed influenced the shape of the Confederate defensive line. Around noon on September 15, about when Lee learned of Harpers Ferry's surrender, the two infantry brigades under John Bell Hood finally crossed Antietam Creek after having served as the army's rear-guard, as did Col. Thomas Rosser's 5th Virginia Cavalry. These men filed into position with the rest of Longstreet's command on the right side of the Boonsboro Pike and waited as the enemy came up.[28]

Elements of Alfred Pleasonton's Federal cavalry and Israel Richardson's First Division of the Federal Second Corps appeared shortly after noon on the heights east of the Antietam. Sporadic shelling continued in fits and starts as the day wore on. In the interim, Union signalmen atop a spur of South Mountain near Boonsboro alerted McClellan to Lee's defensive position at 12:40 p.m.: "[A] line of battle—or an arrangement of troops which looks very much like it—is formed on the other side of Antietam Creek and this side of Sharpsburg." A message from Capt. George Armstrong Custer arrived shortly thereafter confirming the news. "They are in full view," wrote Custer, then a member of McClellan's staff on detached reconnaissance duty. "Their line is a perfect one about a mile and a half long . . . Longstreet is in command and has forty cannon that we know of."[29]

27 Carman, *The Maryland Campaign*, 1:424.

28 *OR* 19, 1:922-923.

29 See Stotelmyer, *Too Useful to Sacrifice*, 113, for a recounting of sources that confirm the roughly noontime arrival of Richardson's division. Signal Station at Washington Monument to

General Joseph Hooker's First Corps, now comprised of fewer than 9,500 men after the losses suffered at South Mountain on September 14, arrived behind Richardson.[30] Hooker's troops "reached a position in front of us about 2 p.m.," recorded Lee in his August 1863 report. James Longstreet confirmed the time in a report printed in the *Richmond Daily Dispatch* at the end of September.[31]

While Hooker's men spread out north of Keedysville and the Boonsboro Pike, Brig. Gen. George Gordon Meade, commander of the Third Division in Hooker's corps, reported his men marching "beyond Keedysville [and] bivouacking on the forks of the Big and Little Antietam." The riders of Tom Rosser's cavalry regiment keeping the area under observation had a good view of this position near Pry's Ford and the Upper Bridge spanning the Antietam. According to Carman, "Rosser's cavalry skirmishers were . . . gradually forced back from one position after another, and at 2 p.m., had all fallen back beyond the Antietam. . . . As his was the only cavalry command on the field [Rosser] threw out detachments on both flanks of the army, south beyond Burnside Bridge and north on the Hagerstown pike, beyond the Dunkard Church and down the Smoketown road in the direction of the upper crossings of the Antietam."[32]

Rosser reported this activity to Lee, who ordered John Bell Hood's division to shift from its position on the right side of the Boonsboro Pike to a new location concealed in the West Woods near the Dunker Church. Lee later noted that he

---

George B. McClellan, 12:40 p.m., Sept. 15, 1862, Library of Congress, Papers of George B. McClellan, Washington, D.C., Box A79, Reel 31, cited hereafter as McClellan Papers; George Custer to George B. McClellan, Sept. 15, 1862, in McClellan Papers, LOC Microfilm, Box A79, Reel 31.

30 OR 19, 1:217. Hooker's battle report claimed, "I said to the general (McClellan) that he had ordered my small corps, now numbering between 12,000 and 13,000 (as I had just lost nearly 1,000 men in the battle of South Mountain), across the river to attack the whole rebel army, and that if re-enforcements were not forwarded promptly, or if another attack was not made on the enemy's right, the rebels would eat me up." Hooker also mentions losing 878 men killed and wounded at South Mountain. Carman, *The Maryland Campaign*, 2:571-573, arrived at the conclusion that Hooker entered the fight on Sept. 17 with only 9,438 in the ranks.

31 OR 19, 1:140. See Longstreet, *From Manassas to Appomattox*, 233-234: "About two o'clock in the afternoon the advance of the Union army came in sight." *Richmond Daily Dispatch*, Sept. 30, 1862: "About 2 P. M. Monday, clouds of dust indicated the approach of the enemy."

32 OR 19, 1:268; Carman, *The Maryland Campaign*, 1:394-395, 401-402. The balance of Fitz Lee's cavalry brigade, including the 3rd, 4th, and 9th Virginia, also "crossed the Antietam north of Keedysville and reached the left of General Lee's line, near the Dunkard Church, that evening." Also see Beale, *History of the Ninth Virginia Cavalry*, 41. "The regiment . . . fell leisurely back without further annoyance, and bivouacked late in the night in the neighborhood of Sharpsburg."

moved Hood "in anticipation of [a] movement [against our left]." The word "anticipation" is loaded, suggesting prescience on Lee's part. It is more likely that he relied on the intelligence delivered by Rosser's men. The vulnerability of the Army of Northern Virginia's defensive line to an attack from the north was almost certainly obvious to Lee. After all, with his troops covering the Middle and Lower bridges, the only Antietam crossing not closely guarded was the Upper bridge on the Keedysville to Williamsport Road. Lee nevertheless appears to have taken measures to shore up his left flank only after Federal numbers began building north of his position late on September 15.[33]

The enemy threat to the Rebel left became even more apparent after nightfall as Hooker adjusted his approach in response to Lee's repositioning of Hood. Hooker noticed that "at 5 o'clock p.m. about one-half of the enemy's infantry force . . . passed to the rear . . . behind a forest, on which appeared to be the Williamsport road." Thinking perhaps that the Confederates were retreating behind an artillery screen, Hooker dispatched "Major D[avid] C. Houston, of the Engineers . . . up the [creek] to find practicable fords, by the means of which my troops might be thrown across the Antietam River to attack the enemy, and perhaps cut off his artillery, as soon as his numbers were sufficiently reduced to justify the movement. A bridge was found, and also two fords, which *with [a] little labor on the banks* [emphasis added] were rendered practicable for the passage of infantry and artillery."[34]

33 *OR* 19, 1:937. "When the army arrived at the height on the south side of Antietam river on the morning of the 15th, I was ordered to take position about a mile from Sharpsburg, on the Hagerstown turnpike. The right of my brigade rested at Saint Mumma's Church (Dunkers' Chapel), and the line extended along the turnpike in the edge of a wood which bordered it on the southwest. Across the road (on the northeast) was an open field a quarter of a mile in width, extending along the whole front of the line and beyond it about 600 yards. This open space was bounded on the northeast (to my front) and northwest (to my left) by woods, an opening being left at the north corner." For other sources describing Hood's movement see *OR* 19, 1:922-923, 927, and Davis, *The Campaign from Texas to Maryland*, 89.

34 *OR* 19, 1:217. Steep creek sides must be leveled (i.e., "rendered practicable") in order for fords to be made useful. Carman, *The Maryland Campaign*, 1:404, altered the timeline for these events, significantly muddying subsequent understanding of how they developed. Writing that D. C. Houston had carried out his scouting of Antietam Creek *by* 5 o'clock, Carman made it seem as if Hooker decided the Rebel force was too strong to attack. Hooker wrote nothing of the sort, reporting instead that the hour was too late "to come up with the enemy, without a night march through a country of which we were profoundly ignorant." The possibility exists that Carman relied on, but forgot to cite, Hooker's Mar. 11, 1863, testimony before the Joint Committee on the Conduct of the War, where he said, "About *two o'clock* [emphasis added] I saw the rear of the enemy's line was breaking into column and marching to the rear, in the direction of Williamsport, where there was another ford across the Potomac." See U.S. House of Representatives, *Report of the Joint Committee on the Conduct of the War*, Part 1 (Washington, DC,

With sunset coming shortly after 6:00 p.m., and the fords across Antietam Creek lying in shaded hollows, at least a portion of this engineering work on the Antietam fords must have been carried out by torchlight, which surely alerted Rosser's cavalrymen. Word of the continued enemy activity north of Keedysville from Rosser prompted Lee to move Col. Stephen Dill Lee's 20-gun artillery battalion to support Hood after darkness had fallen. These guns took position in front of the Dunker Church on low ground that partially shielded them from the long-range Federal artillery on the heights along the Antietam.[35]

Twice on September 15, therefore, General Lee shifted a portion of his force to meet the looming threat on his left flank. All of this took place before George McClellan had settled on a plan of battle. Little Mac did not telegraph the attack on the Rebel left. Joseph Hooker did it by concentrating his corps on the Rebel left and preparing fords across the creek. Lee ordered his redeployments in direct response to information he received on the enemy's actions, which also explains why he took no measures on his right flank that day. Jacob Cox's Ninth Corps came up very slowly on September 15 after getting underway well past noon. Major General Ambrose Burnside, accompanied by Cox, reached the "junction of the Rohrersville and old Sharpsburg roads" late in the day and rode ahead to meet McClellan at Hooker's headquarters at the Philip Pry House.[36]

During that meeting, McClellan ordered Burnside to bring up his command and move it to the left, close to the Rohrbach Bridge. Oliver Bosbyshell of the 48th Pennsylvania Infantry described this advance as follows: "A halt was called at 6 o'clock in the evening, and whilst preparing to bivouac in a large field. General Burnside came along, and directed a further move forward. An hour and a half

---

1863), 581. Why Hooker would change the time of his observation of Hood's command moving to the left to 2:00 p.m. after noting the 5:00 time only four-and-a-half months earlier in his Nov. 7, 1862, campaign report is a mystery. He may have intended to slight McClellan for not ordering an attack earlier than he did.

35 *OR* 19, 1:844-845. "During the night the battalion, excepting Moody's battery, shifted farther to the left of our line, taking a sheltered position on the Sharpsburg and Hagerstown pike, in front of a church." Also see Longstreet, *From Manassas to Appomattox*, 234.

36 Carman, *The Maryland Campaign*, 1:406. McClellan, heeding Franklin's early afternoon message that McLaws's command in Pleasant Valley outnumbered his by 2:1, contributed to Burnside's slow approach by instructing the general at 3:45 p.m. to "move on Rohrersville communicating meantime with Franklin. If with your assistance he can defeat the enemy in front of him, join him at once. If, however, he can hold his own, march direct on Sharpsburg and co-operate with us." *OR* 51, 1:Sec. 2, 837-838.

additional marching was made before the command halted for the night."[37] In other words, Burnside's command remained hidden from Confederate view on September 15 because it approached Antietam Creek from around the lip of Red Hill and moved into position after dark. A heavy fog filled the valley when dawn broke the next morning, further obscuring the presence of Burnside's troops until the mist burned off between 8:00 and 8:30 a.m. Consequently, Lee made no changes to the right side of his line on September 15 because no information had reached him of the threat developing there. Word of this arrived only on the following day.[38]

At daybreak on September 16, a portion of Stonewall Jackson's victorious command finally came up from Harpers Ferry. Jackson had left behind the Light Division of A. P. Hill to parole prisoners, take possession of captured materiel, and deal with more than 1,000 captured contrabands while marching his remaining two divisions under John R. Jones and Alexander Lawton to Sharpsburg late in the day on September 15. The leading elements comprising Lawton's division, recalled James Cooper Nisbet, "marched to Boteller's Ford that night [and] early next morning, [and] while it was yet dark, the Division crossed the Potomac and marched towards Sharpsburg."[39] Jones's division came up after Lawton's, "reaching the Potomac at sunrise [before it] hurried across and on to Sharpsburg." The infantry division under Brig. Gen. John Walker brought up the rear of the

---

37 Oliver C. Bosbyshell, *The 48th PA in the War* (Philadelphia, PA, 1895), 77. Also see Jacob D. Cox, *Military Reminiscences of the Civil War*, 2 vols. (New York, NY, 1900), 2:300. "Orders were then given for the Ninth Corps to move to the left, keeping off the road, which was occupied by other troops. We moved through fields and farm lands, an hour's march in the dusk of evening, going into bivouac about a mile south of the Sharpsburg bridge, and in rear of the hills bordering the Antietam."

38 The lack of an obvious threat on his army's right flank may have been what prompted Lee to "[express] his belief [on Sept. 15] that there would not be much fighting on the morrow." See Owen, *In Camp and Battle*, 139. Lee could probably see from Federal movements that arrangements for an attack were incomplete on Sept. 15 and would take time to develop the following day. It is reasonable to assume, therefore, that Lee was simply expressing an understanding of what McClellan would be required to do before an attack could be launched. Owen did not record when Lee made his comment. Presumably, he said it before nightfall when he could see at least part of what McClellan's army was doing.

39 See Appendix D. Nisbet, *Four Years on the Firing Line*, 151-152. Also see Moore, *The Story of a Cannoneer*, 143-146. "We arrived at Shepherdstown before dawn [on Sept. 16] . . . Half a mile below the town we forded the Potomac for the third time, and by the middle of the afternoon were on the outskirts of Sharpsburg."

column after Walker caught up to Jackson's command on the road to Shepherdstown during the night.[40]

These 10,300 troops commenced crossing the Potomac while Jackson himself rode ahead to meet General Lee and announce the arrival of his command. He found Lee and Longstreet conferring in the fog atop Cemetery Hill, where he spoke with the two men for a time.[41] What passed between them has been lost to history, although based on a postwar comment written by Lee in a letter to Jackson's widow, it appears they discussed the army's situation at that moment, including Lee's reasons for electing to fight in Maryland. As Lee stated in the letter, "when he (Jackson) came upon the field, having preceded his troops, and learned my reasons for offering battle, he emphatically concurred with me." In other words, if Lee's memory of the event can be trusted, he remained as determined to fight on the morning of September 16 as he had been when he settled upon his plan a day earlier.[42]

Lee's resolve remained intact even though the divisions of A. P. Hill, Lafayette McLaws, and Richard Anderson had not yet re-joined the army. Lee had commented before Jackson arrived in Sharpsburg that "all will be right if McLaws gets out of Pleasant Valley." He had expected McLaws would approach the Potomac with Old Jack. When Jackson confirmed that McLaws was not with him, Lee immediately issued an order for the Georgian to march to Sharpsburg. This order to "hasten" his troops reached McLaws on the afternoon of September 16 when he was in Charles Town, Virginia, seven miles southwest of Harpers Ferry, looking after the sick and wounded from his command who had been recently transported there. No courier would have known to look for McLaws in Charles

---

40 OR 19, 1:914. "The division . . . crossed the Blue Ridge, the Shenandoah, and the Potomac, the latter at Shepherdstown, and reached the neighborhood of Sharpsburg, Md., on the 16th ultimo."

41 The numerical estimate for Jackson's command comes from Carman, *The Maryland Campaign*, 2:17. Douglas, *I Rode with Stonewall*, 166. "Leaving General Hill very early on the morning of the 16th and passing my home . . . I joined General Jackson on what is now Cemetery Hill, where he was in conversation with Generals Lee and Longstreet."

42 See Lee's letter dated Jan. 25, 1866, quoted in Harsh, *Taken*, 335. Dabney, *Life and Campaigns of Lieut.-Gen. Thomas J. Jackson*, 570, wrote something very similar: "In the daring policy of delivering this battle, General Jackson had emphatically concurred with [Lee] upon his arrival from Harper's Ferry in advance of his corps. When the Commander-in-Chief determined to withdraw across the Potomac again, he also approved this movement; but added that, in view of all the circumstances, it was better to have fought the battle in Maryland, than to have left it without a struggle."

Town unless he had first asked after the general in Harpers Ferry, which is where McLaws should have been.[43]

McLaws reported receiving Lee's message before 3:00 p.m., after which he returned to his encampment near Halltown to get his command underway. If a courier took the usual four hours to ride from Sharpsburg to Harpers Ferry and required an additional undetermined amount of time to locate McLaws, including a seven-mile ride to Charles Town, it is realistic to assume that Lee sent for McLaws right after he had met with Jackson on Cemetery Hill. This meeting must have taken place before 8:00 a.m., which was when the fog thinned enough for Federal artillery to open on the Confederate line. There is nothing in the sources to suggest that Lee, Longstreet, and Jackson were together on Cemetery Hill when this firing started, so, working from at least the time of 8:00 a.m., a four-hour ride to Harpers Ferry has Lee's dispatch arriving there around 12:30 p.m. Add another two to three hours for the courier to locate McLaws and it becomes clear that Lee must have sent his order early on the morning of September 16. The fact that Lee sent this order demonstrates he intended to maintain his position.[44]

Where the weight of the expected enemy attack would fall remained the major mystery at that moment. With the field obscured by a thick mist, no one could tell how McClellan might have shifted his forces during the night. Lee, therefore, ordered Jackson to bring up his command and allow the men to rest in the fields behind army headquarters, which he had established in a grove of oak trees on the western outskirts of Sharpsburg just beyond the range of Federal artillery fire. He next ordered Jeb Stuart to conduct a reconnaissance "up the Potomac" to determine the enemy's activities. William Blackford, a member of Stuart's staff, later wrote of this operation that "General Stuart was actively engaged during the morning of the 16th in a reconnaissance to discover their (the enemy's) movements" on the Army of Northern Virginia's left flank; an activity prompted

43 Carman, *The Maryland Campaign*, 2:15. OR 19, 1:857. "I had ridden on to Charles-town to look after the sick and wounded from Pleasant Valley, when notice was sent me to hasten the troops to Sharpsburg. I returned to camp and started the command at 3 p.m."

44 *OR* 19, 1:857. "On the morning of September 16 ultimo, my command, consisting of my own division and that of General Anderson, marched through Harper's Ferry from Pleasant Valley, and halted near Halltown and a short distance from the road which turned to the right toward Shepherdstown, which was on the way to Sharpsburg, to which place I had been directed to march by orders direct from General Lee and afterward from General Jackson." The time estimate comes from the period it had taken Jackson's 8:00 a.m. message from Harpers Ferry to reach Lee at noon on Sept. 15.

by the sighting of Federal skirmishers farther west of Antietam Creek than they had previously been seen.[45]

Joseph Harsh argues that Lee ordered Stuart's reconnaissance to explore the possibility of moving the army away from Sharpsburg toward Hagerstown. There is no evidence that Lee intended such a movement. The sources show that Lee intended to fight at Sharpsburg and was concentrating his army as rapidly as possible for the battle to come. Because of his late arrival from Harpers Ferry with but a single courier on September 15, Stuart did not have the manpower to conduct extensive cavalry operations, despite Lee assigning him to watch the army's left.[46]

45 Von Borcke, *Memoirs*, 225-228. "General Stuart started on the morning of the 16th … with a part of his cavalry, on a reconnaissance up the Potomac." Lee probably issued Stuart's orders after he had returned to the Grove House in Sharpsburg. Blackford, *War Years*, 148. "Seeing skirmishers enter a field further to the left than they had yet appeared, General Lee ordered Stuart to discover and unmask their intentions and if necessary for this purpose to attack them with his whole cavalry force."

46 OR 19, 1:819. Stuart: "I reported, in person, to General Jackson at Harper's Ferry, and thence rode, at his request, to the commanding general, at Sharpsburg, to communicate to him General Jackson's news and information. Our army being in line of battle on the heights overlooking the Antietam, I was assigned to the left." The time of Stuart's arrival on Sept. 15 is another Maryland Campaign conundrum. Carman, *The Maryland Campaign*, 1:428, places it at "about noon," shortly after the arrival of Jackson's initial message informing Lee of Harpers Ferry's surrender, while Harsh, *Taken*, 322, suggests "around one o'clock." The argument made here holds that Stuart probably arrived around 2:00 p.m. due to the distance he needed to travel. McClellan, *Life and Campaigns*, 124, notes that as of Harpers Ferry's surrender at 8:00 a.m. "Stuart was on McLaws' line of battle [above Brownsville] in Pleasant Valley." McLaws did not send word of the capitulation to his command until after he received it himself by signal at his Brownsville headquarters at 10:00. This time is confirmed by Capt. Henry King in Trimpi, ed., "Lafayette McLaws' Aide-de-Camp," 36. According to a letter written by R. Channing Price, a member of Stuart's staff, "Gen. Stuart was far in front of our line of battle, examining the position of the enemy [when] news came by a courier of the surrender of Harper's Ferry." Trout, *With Pen and Saber*, 100. Stuart gathered the horsemen he had with him (elements of Wade Hampton's brigade), and rode the 4.5 miles to Harpers Ferry. After crossing the pontoon bridge over the Potomac, Stuart met with Jackson, who requested that he take the inventory of captured items to Lee. To sum up: if Stuart left Brownsville at 10:15 a.m., after word reached him of the surrender, he could not have reached Harpers Ferry until 11:00 a.m. at the earliest. Then, after speaking with Jackson for an undetermined length of time, he rode to Sharpsburg, which puts him at Lee's side by around 2:00 p.m., if he pushed his mount to make the four-hour ride at a quicker pace. There is some evidence Stuart may have done this. Carman, *The Maryland Campaign*, 1:428, mentions Stuart meeting Lee at Sharpsburg on a "horse covered with foam," which suggests Stuart pushed his mount hard to get there. Lee also told an orderly to "keep Stuart's horse moving, not to let him cool off too soon." Incidentally, as a way of confirming the timing of the Federal surrender, on Sept. 15, Union Gen. Howe of Darius Couch's command captured a member of Stuart's staff carrying a message from Jackson to Lee confirming that the Federal garrison at Harpers Ferry formally capitulated at 9:30 a.m. Gen. Franklin passed this information to McClellan late on the same day. See OR 19, 2:296. Franklin also confirmed in congressional testimony on Mar. 30, 1863, that "The firing stopped at half-past nine o'clock that morning, which gave us an intimation that the place (i.e., Harpers

Events discussed by Carman indicate that Stuart must have encountered detachments of Tom Rosser's 5th Virginia Cavalry north of Sharpsburg, but the remainder of Fitzhugh Lee's command—the 3rd, 4th, and 9th Virginia—did not come up until nightfall on September 15. Moreover, most of Wade Hampton's cavalry brigade remained in Virginia until September 17. In other words, Jeb Stuart had no significant cavalry force under his command at Sharpsburg before dark on Monday, September 15.[47]

The cavalry general slept that night at the home of Dr. Jacob Grove in the center of Sharpsburg, where he met Heros von Borcke and the rest of his staff who had come up from Harpers Ferry late in the day.[48] On the morning of September 16, Stuart formally established the Grove House as his headquarters and communications center, leaving von Borcke and ten couriers "to receive and open all reports and despatches addressed to him, and to forward any important information to Generals Lee, Jackson, and Longstreet" while he carried out Lee's reconnaissance order. At that point (early on the morning of September 16) Lee required as much firsthand information about Federal activities as possible because of the fog that obscured portions of the field and because, according to Blackford, Federal troops had been spotted west of Antietam Creek.[49]

Lee may have also suspected that McClellan would move a column across the Antietam farther north than the Upper Bridge because Fitzhugh Lee's three cavalry regiments had crossed the creek above Keedysville late on September 15. By September 16 Stuart also had men available for reconnaissance that he did not have with him on the previous day. In addition, Hooker's First Corps continued

---

Ferry) had surrendered." U.S. House of Representatives, *Report of the Joint Committee on the Conduct of the War*, 626.

47 See Beale, *History of the Ninth Virginia Cavalry*, 41, and Carman, *The Maryland Campaign*, 1:401.

48 Blackford, *War Years*, 147. "At Harper's Ferry most of the staff got separated from our General . . . and it was late at night before we overtook him at Sharpsburg, and spent the remainder of the night at the house of Dr. G., sleeping as usual on the porches or in the passages with our saddles for a pillow." Also see R. Channing Price in Trout, *With Pen and Saber*, 100: "Towards evening I went to the town & going to Mr. Grove's (Gen. Stuart's Hd. Qrs. the night before) got a good dinner. The General came from the field after dark having been engaged in posting batteries all day."

49 Blackford, *War Years*, 148. "Seeing skirmishers enter a field further to the left than they had yet appeared, General Lee ordered Stuart to discover and unmask their intentions and if necessary for this purpose to attack them with his whole cavalry force." Blackford implies Lee personally saw these skirmishers, but it is more likely he received a report about them from Stuart's men watching the upper crossings of the creek.

throughout the night to collect near the Upper Bridge, compounding the danger that Rosser had warned of before sundown on the previous day.[50]

Even Confederate officers far from Antietam Creek knew of the enemy build-up. Stephen D. Lee, commander of the artillery battalion that General Lee sent to support Hood, attested to this in his after-action report when he wrote, "since early in the morning [on September 16] they (the Federals) appeared to be engaged in massing their troops opposite our left." If Col. Lee knew this on the Rebel front line north of Sharpsburg, then it is almost certain that Stuart made General Lee aware of it as well.[51]

While Rebel cavalry watched for a Federal advance across Antietam Creek, Jackson and Walker marched their commands from the Potomac to Sharpsburg. Their weary and footsore infantry reached the western outskirts of town a little before noon, after which Jackson rode with Walker to meet Lee and report the arrival of their men. They found the general at his headquarters in the oak grove west of town looking "calm, dignified, and even cheerful . . . [as] if he had had a well-equipped army of a hundred thousand veterans at his back." According to Walker, after the war Lee "expressed his satisfaction with the result of our operations at Harpers Ferry, and of our timely arrival at Sharpsburg; adding that with our reinforcement he felt confident of being *able to hold his ground* [emphasis added] until the arrival of the divisions of R. H. Anderson, McLaws, and A. P. Hill,

---

50 Using information provided to him in an 1896 letter from Fitzhugh Lee, Carman recounted in *The Maryland Campaign*, 1:401, how Lee's cavalry "crossed the Antietam north of Keedysville and reached the left of General Lee's line, near the Dunkard Church, that evening." Fitz Lee's odyssey north and west toward the Hagerstown Pike occurred after Pleasonton's Federal cavalry separated the Rebel cavalry regiments from the Army of Northern Virginia during a ferocious charge at Boonsboro on the morning of Sept. 15. With his direct route to Keedysville cut off, Lee took "by-roads" across Antietam Creek before striking Hagerstown Pike and riding south to Sharpsburg. Assuming Lee traversed the Antietam via a bridge and not a ford he must have crossed at either Manor Church Road or at Lappans Road, both of which lie north of Keedysville. *OR* 19, 1:261. "September 15, we moved forward, and at night crossed the Antietam near Keedysville, bivouacking on the opposite side." Also see Franklin B. Hough, *History of Duryee's Brigade During the Campaign in Virginia Under Gen. Pope and in Maryland Under Gen. McClellan in the Summer and Autumn of 1862* (Albany, GA, 1864), 115: "At about eleven o'clock in the evening, Duryee's Brigade advanced through the village of Keedysville, and a little beyond turned by a narrow road to the right, crossed a new stone bridge and lay down for the night."

51 *OR* 19, 1:844-845. Skirmishers from Hood's division posted along Antietam Creek also could have been Stephen D. Lee's source of information. See Polley, *Hood's Texas Brigade*, 129-130. "[A]fter the army crossed the Antietam, we were on the skirmish line along the west bank of that stream, until the 16th. In the meantime the brigade had formed a line of battle along the Hagerstown and Sharpsburg Turnpike, near the Dunkard church."

which were still behind." Here again, Lee expressed an intent to remain at Sharpsburg and fight McClellan's army when it attacked, even if McLaws and the others had not yet arrived.[52]

At this point it is worth considering the actions of the Federal commander, who is often condemned for giving Lee more time to prepare on September 16 than he should have. This accusation against McClellan contains a kernel of truth given the fragmented state of the Confederate army, but Lee had unwittingly helped influence McClellan's delay by shifting S. D. Lee's guns after nightfall on September 15. Little Mac began September 16 intent on attacking Lee's army as soon as possible, communicating at 7:45 a.m. to Maj. Gen. Franklin, whose Sixth Corps remained in Pleasant Valley, "if the enemy is in force here, I shall attack him this morning."[53]

Scouting parties and the clearing of fog between 8:00 and 8:30 a.m. revealed not only the continued presence of Lee's troops, but also that "the enemy had changed the position of his batteries." The overwhelming weight of McClellan's artillery also appears to have helped confuse the situation. These guns, including 16 long-range 20-lb. Parrott Rifles on the heights east of Antietam Creek, so dominated the field that Longstreet and Hill pulled their troops behind the hills near Sharpsburg. As of mid-morning on September 16, reported McClellan, "the masses of [the enemy's] troops . . . [lay] concealed behind the opposite heights. Their left and center were upon and in front of the Sharpsburg and Hagerstown turnpike, hidden by woods and irregularities of the ground, their extreme left

---

52 John G. Walker, "Sharpsburg," in Johnson and Buel, eds., *Battles and Leaders*, 2:675. Walker's account is suspect on a number of levels, including the fact that he mentions Lee shaking hands with himself and Jackson even though the general nursed a broken bone in his right hand at the time and it was heavily bandaged. Still, enough of Walker's story agrees with the other sources regarding the timing of his arrival that I have chosen to use it. An even more questionable record of Jackson's meeting with Lee stated the following: "Jackson saluted Lee, and said: 'The Lord has given us another victory.' Lee replied: 'In behalf of the Confederacy, I thank you and your brave troops.' Jackson then said: 'Where do you want my troops on the line?' Lee replied: 'On the left, and I expect you will have to fight for position.' Jackson said: 'Very well,' and touched his hat, rode off and put his troops in rapid motion." W. H. Edwards, *A Condensed History of Seventeenth Regiment S.C.V. From Its Organization to the Close of the War* (Columbia, SC, 1906), 19.

53 *OR* 51, 1:Sec. 2, 839. McClellan wrote similarly to General-in-Chief H. W. Halleck at 7:00 a.m., "This morning a heavy fog has thus far prevented us doing more than to ascertain that some of the enemy are still there. Do not know in what force. Will attack as soon as situation of the enemy is developed." *OR* 19, 2:307-308.

resting upon a wooded eminence near the cross-roads to the north of J. Miller's farm." [54]

Perplexed by his inability to discern the Rebel army's lines, McClellan delayed his attack for several hours. He spent "the morning of the 16th (during which there was considerable artillery firing) . . . obtaining information as to the ground, rectifying the position of the troops, and perfecting the arrangements for the attack." Ten months later, the Union commander admitted in a second report that "it was afternoon [on September 16] before I could move the troops to their positions for attack, *being compelled to spend the morning in reconnoitering the new position taken up by the enemy* [emphasis added]." Ironically, the domination of the field by the Army of the Potomac's artillery forced the Confederates to hide themselves, which in turn confused McClellan about where Lee had established his lines.[55]

This lack of clarity remained in place throughout the run-up to the battle and is reflected in the vagueness of McClellan orders, delivered to Hooker "between 1 and 2 o'clock," to "cross the river with the First Corps, and attack the enemy on his left flank." The lack of detailed instructions prompted Hooker to ride to army headquarters on the north side of Keedysville for clarification. McClellan offered little in the way of additional information except to tell Hooker that he was free to call upon Brig. Gen. Joseph Mansfield's Twelfth Corps for reinforcement, if he required it. Even after hours of intelligence gathering, neither McClellan nor Hooker knew where to find Lee's left flank. Only physical contact by the First Corps would develop its location, so McClellan sent Hooker across Antietam Creek to find out, largely ignorant of the enemy's strength or position.[56]

---

54 OR 19, 1:55. "In front of Generals Sumner's and Hooker's corps, near Keedysville, and on the ridge of the first line of hills overlooking the Antietam, and between the turnpike and Pry's house on the right of the road, were placed Captains Taft's, Langner's, von Kleiser's, and Lieutenant Wever's batteries of 20-pounder Parrott guns." OR 19, 1:29.

55 OR 19, 1:55. *New York Daily Tribune* correspondent George Smalley reported something similar: "the lines and columns that had darkened cornfields and hillcrests, had been withdrawn . . . it was still uncertain whether the Rebels were retreating or re-enforcing . . . as they had withdrawn nearly all of their troops from view." See Smalley, quoted in Hartwig, *To Antietam Creek*, 586. Thanks to a message from the Red Hill signal station reporting "an immense train of the enemy's wagons is moving on the road from Sharpsburg to Shepherdstown" McClellan also may have thought Lee's army had begun retreating the morning of Sept. 16. See OR 19, 1:137.

56 OR 19, 1:217. McClellan clearly meant Antietam Creek and not the Potomac River. There is a possibility that Hooker noted the incorrect time for receiving McClellan's attack order. According to the telegraphed message of one Capt. Palmer to Andrew Curtin, the Governor of Pennsylvania, who took a keen interest in the Army of the Potomac's movements, and who

General Lee, meanwhile, took time around noon to write Confederate President Jefferson Davis. Commenting that "part of General Jackson's corps has reached us and the rest are approaching, except General A. P. Hill's division, left at Harper's Ferry to guard the place and take care of public property," Lee noted that "The enemy have made no attack up to this afternoon, but are in force in our front." He continued to look for the arrival of McLaws's command while bracing for the Union army's assault, although he had yet to deploy Jackson and Walker. Word of the Federal advance finally reached Lee between 2:00 and 3:00 p.m. after Stuart's men spotted a mounted force crossing Antietam Creek.[57]

According to Stuart's after-action report, "On the afternoon of the 16th the enemy was discovered moving a column across the Antietam to the [Hagerstown] pike." Stuart reported the movement and had his men keep the enemy under observation. This report reached the Grove House, Stuart's communications nerve center in Sharpsburg, where General Lee hovered over a map beside Longstreet and Jackson. The news did not immediately prompt him to deploy Jackson's command because the initial Federal foray west of Antietam Creek involved only the 3rd Pennsylvania Cavalry, which had crossed Pry's Ford ahead of the infantry to screen the advance for the First Corps.[58]

Instead, recalled one of Stuart's staff officers, Lee instructed the cavalry commander "to discover and unmask [the enemy's] intentions and if necessary for this purpose to attack them with his whole cavalry force. What General Lee wanted to know was whether at this particular point they were in force or whether it was only cavalry." Stuart dutifully assembled his troopers and sent a detachment of men

---

forwarded Palmer's message to Abraham Lincoln, "Hooker was moving to open the ball at about noon." See OR 19, 2:311. Thanks to expert sleuthing by Tom Clemens, we know that McClellan probably situated his army's headquarters near the intersection of today's Maryland State Route 34 and Coffman Farms Road. See *Civil War Times* (June 2016).

57 OR 19, 1:140, 235. Col. John W. Hofmann of the 56th Pennsylvania Infantry, commanding the Second Brigade in Hooker's First Division, noted in his Sept. 23, 1862, after- action report: "at 2 o'clock p. m. on the 16th the brigade under my command left camp on the left bank of the Antietam Creek, about 2 miles north of Sharpsburg, and, having forded the creek, waited for the rear brigades to cross."

58 OR 19, 1:819; Henry A. White, *Robert E. Lee* (New York, NY, 1897), 211. "The advance of Hooker across the Williamsport bridge, far up the Antietam, was reported by the cavalry to Lee in Sharpsburg. He was in council over a map in an old house with Jackson and Longstreet." Also see William B. Rawle, *History of the Third Pennsylvania Cavalry in the American Civil War, 1861-1865* (Philadelphia, PA, 1905), 120. According to a telegraphed message from Pennsylvania Governor Andrew Curtin, the Keystone State horsemen could have begun moving across the Antietam as early as 1:00 p.m. See OR 19, 2:311.

under the command of his aide-de-camp, Capt. William Blackford, to see what he could make of the enemy's advance. By the time Blackford arrived in a position to scrutinize the Federals, Hooker had already begun moving his infantry across the creek. "My glasses brought them close," wrote Blackford some years later, "and soon revealed the blue trimmings and bayonet scabbards of the infantry soldier and not the yellow of the cavalry. Having obtained this information I hastened back."[59]

Blackford encountered Stuart at the head of a column moving to carry out Lee's attack order, but after learning that the enemy opposite them consisted of infantry—signaling an advance in force—Stuart decided to receive the attack rather than initiate it. He deployed the elements of the 9th Virginia Cavalry and a two-gun section of Capt. John Pelham's Horse Artillery along the Smoketown Road in the East Woods and sent word of his activities back to Lee.

Stuart's message found the commanding general still at the Grove House. The information must not have impressed Lee because he ordered Jackson to march only Jones's division north of Sharpsburg. Lee sent Lawton's division to the right in response to news that Federal troops there were also on the move.[60] Lee could not have known that the advance then being undertaken by Ambrose Burnside represented a repositioning of his men for an attack on the Confederate right the following day, not that afternoon. According to Jacob Cox, commander of the Ninth Corps but still subordinate to Burnside in the army's odd command structure, Gen. McClellan's "aides returned shortly before three o'clock [on September 16], and they immediately proceeded to post the three columns" of the corps. Confederate spotters noted these movements and quickly reported them.[61]

Lee, as he had done since taking position at Sharpsburg, responded by shifting troops to meet the perceived menace. When the Federal movement soon ground to a halt, the general countermanded his orders to Lawton and instructed him to hurry to the left flank to support Jackson's other division.[62] Lee eventually instructed

---

59 Blackford, *War Years with Jeb Stuart*, 148, 149.

60 This is one of McClellan's three "telegraphed" moves referred to in Harsh, *Taken*, 344.

61 Cox, *Military Reminiscences*, 385. McClellan temporarily dissolved the wing structure of the Army of the Potomac on Sept. 15, leaving Burnside without a formal command but still acting as Jacob Cox's superior officer. See OR 51, 1:Sec. 1, 168. "On the evening of the 16th instant, the enemy appearing in force, I sent out a body of skirmishers, who were driven back."

62 OR 51, 1:Sec. 1, 168. "During the progress of the movement of his corps, an aide from General McClellan came to [Burnside] and said that General McClellan was not sure that the proper position had been indicated, and advised him not to hasten the movement until the aide

Walker to move his division to the right flank at three the next morning—a delayed commitment that the Confederate commander appears to have ordered in an effort to see how the Federal movement against his army's left flank played out.[63]

Once Lee committed Jackson's troops to defend the army's left, he allowed the commanders on the spot to dictate where to establish their battle lines. The initial responsibility for this appears to have settled with Stuart, who relied on John Pelham's guns in the East Woods and Tom Rosser's 9th Virginia acting as dismounted support. Hood followed Stuart's lead by advancing Col. Evander Law's brigade some 700 yards north from the vicinity of the Dunker Church to the southern edge of the East Woods. According to Hood's recollection, Lee did not order this advance, having only instructed Hood to "take position near the Hagerstown pike, in an open field in front of [the] Dunkard Church."[64]

Hood appears to have changed Law's position on his own authority in order to support Stuart's thin line of troopers against encroaching Federal skirmishers, although he may have acted in accordance with orders from James Longstreet. "At four o'clock, while Generals Longstreet, D. H. Hill and Hood, were observing the enemy from a point on the left of the town, near where our battalion was in position," recalled a correspondent attached to S. D. Lee's artillery battalion,

---

had communicated with the general commanding." McClellan's aide never re-appeared, prompting Burnside to continue the deployment of his men that already begun.

63 Walker, "Sharpsburg," 675. "At four in the afternoon [on Sept. 16] I received an order from General Lee to move at three o'clock the next morning, and take position with my division on the extreme right of his line of battle, so as to cover a ford of the Antietam, and to lend a hand, in case of necessity, to General Toombs, whose brigade was guarding the bridge over the Antietam." Walter Clark, an adjutant in the 35th North Carolina, part of Walker's division, recalled after the war "About an hour before day, on the 17th, our division began its march for the position assigned us on the extreme right, where we were to oppose the Federals in any attempt to cross either the bridge (since known as Burnside's) or the ford over the Antietam below it, near Shiveley's." Walter Clark, "The Battle of Sharpsburg—Personal Incidents" in *The Wake Forest Student*, Vol. 17, No. 2 (Nov. 1897), 87.

64 Blackford, *War Years with Jeb Stuart*, 149. According to Blackford: "On hearing my report he (Stuart) halted the command and accompanied me back to the place to have a look through the glasses himself, as it was a question of great importance." See Beale, *History of the Ninth Virginia Cavalry*, 41, and George W. Beale, "Maryland Campaign: The Cavalry Fight at Boonsboro Graphically Described" in *SHSP* (1897), 25:278-279; *OR* 19, 1:937. John Bell Hood, *Advance and Retreat: Personal Experiences in the United States and Confederate States Armies* (New Orleans, LA, 1880), 41-42. According to Davis, *Campaign from Texas to Maryland*, 89, "about noon on the 15th, we took position on the right of the road leading to Boonsboro. But, as it was found that the enemy was threatening an immediate attack on the other flank, we were ordered to move to the extreme left, and take position on the Hagerstown road, near St. Mumma Church."

large bodies of artillery and infantry were seen passing to our left through some low ground just in front of us, and beyond a stream which divided the two armies. With our glasses we saw them very distinctly. . . . It was about five o'clock before the whole force passed through this meadow. . . . Just to our left and front was a pine thicket, about five hundred yards distant, and the rear of the column of the enemy had hardly gotten behind it before very sharp picket firing began [65]

Longstreet's personal observation of the advance of Hooker's corps may have prompted him to order Hood's move, particularly since Hood's division was under his command. There is no record of Longstreet giving this order before Jackson came up with his two divisions and deployed them on Hood's left around 5:00 p.m. By this time, Stuart's men had already fallen back to the West Woods and Colonel Law's men had engaged the leading elements of Hooker's corps. Finally, Lee ordered D. H. Hill around 6:00 p.m. to send Roswell Ripley's brigade to support Hood's right, a move that established the basic alignment of the Confederate battle line that Hooker's men would encounter the following morning.[66]

The late arrival of Jackson's command on the field—caused by Lee's tardy deployment of it in response to Hooker's advance—is probably one reason why the Confederates did not dig defensive entrenchments. Although Hood's men had "thrown up a slight breastwork of rails, logs, stones, &c. . . . in readiness for the enemy's advance," Jackson's men arrived after the fighting had already started and Old Jack must have been unsure where the lines would settle on the following day. His men may have also lacked tools for digging into the rocky Maryland soil. They had, after all, completed a "severe" march from Harpers Ferry only several hours earlier. Furthermore, Lee had ordered the army's supply wagons back to Virginia. Some of these may have contained the pick-axes Jackson needed. With the wagon train crossing the Potomac against the flow of his troops, Jackson may have also assumed that his wagons should remain in Virginia with the rest of the vehicles collecting there. Whatever the case, Hood requested the withdrawal of his command several hours after dark to allow his men to cook rations. Jackson filled

65 *Richmond Daily Dispatch*, Sept. 30, 1862.

66 According to Jackson's topographer, "Maj. Robbins, N.C., tells of Jackson's picking out his line on foot on the evening of 16th." See Jedediah Hotchkiss, Field Notes on Sharpsburg Battle Field. Dec. 7, 1894, Library of Congress Geography and Map Division Washington, DC: www.loc.gov/item/2005625261/. Although the date of the document is 1894, it is probably much earlier in origin. Harsh, *Taken*, 359.

Hood's place in the line with Lawton's men, which was they were when Hooker attacked at first light.[67]

Over the years, the revelation of new evidence and disputed interpretations of events have shaped our understanding of the battle that Lee intended to fight at Sharpsburg. This critical assessment of the available sources offers several key observations about Lee's operations that are intended to clarify the general's plans and activities on September 15-16, 1862. Foremost among these is the fact that once Lee made his decision around 8:00 a.m. on September 15 to stand at Sharpsburg, every action he took thereafter sought to concentrate his army for a clash with the Army of the Potomac. Lee called Stonewall Jackson to join him in Maryland as soon as he learned about Harpers Ferry's fall, and when he heard on the morning of September 16 that Lafayette McLaws had not marched with Jackson, he repeated his orders for the Georgian to bring up his command. Lee wrote Jefferson Davis about the situation, making it clear that he planned to give battle where he stood, hopefully with the commands of McLaws, Anderson, and A. P. Hill on the field by the time the engagement began.

Once Lee made up his mind to fight there is no evidence that he ever second-guessed himself or sought to move his army. Concentrating at Hagerstown after the Harpers Ferry operation may have been Lee's goal as of September 13, but the engagements at South Mountain changed all of that because George McClellan forced Lee to fight where he could. Lee found the ground near Sharpsburg to be to his advantage and he chose it without hesitation as the place to give battle. Indeed, moving farther north would have been irrational for the Army of Northern Virginia under the circumstances. Jackson made an exhausting march to reach Sharpsburg on the morning of September 16, and as of the morning of September 17, the divisions of Lafayette McLaws and A. P. Hill had still not rejoined the army. Moving in the direction of Hagerstown would have carried the main portion of the

---

67 *OR* 19, 1:1032. "During the evening I received orders to move my brigade to the left of our division, and take up a position to cover a road leading from our left to the turnpike leading from Sharpsburg to Hagerstown, and in support of certain batteries of artillery in our vicinity." Also see Report of Maj. S. D. Thruston, commander of the 3rd North Carolina Infantry, to Governor Zebulon Vance on the action at Sharpsburg, Sept. 27, 1862, in the William L. DeRossett Collection, North Carolina State Archives, Raleigh, North Carolina, at http://northcarolinastatetroops.blogspot.com/2011/06/third-north-carolina-at-sharpsburg.html.
"[At] about 6 P.M. [on September. 16] we moved by the left flank to an exposed position near the center, and in supporting distance of Genl. Hoods[?] Brigade, then skirmishing with the enemy: here we rested for the night; prepared at a moment to move in that direction where our service might be required."

Rebel army farther from those vital reinforcements at the same time it faced an opponent Lee could assume from experience was stronger than he was. He therefore positioned his cavalry, initially the few men under Tom Rosser and later several regiments under Jeb Stuart, to keep the enemy's activities along Antietam Creek under surveillance, and he used the intelligence they provided to adjust his battle line in a way that slowed McClellan's preparations for an assault on his army's left on September 16.

The hours that Lee earned by unwittingly forcing McClellan to delay his attack generated the time he needed for McLaws and Anderson to come up. If the artillery Lee moved after dark on September 15 had remained in its prior place, and if McClellan's heavy guns had not forced Longstreet's and Hill's infantry to take cover behind the heights east of Sharpsburg and the forest north of it, the Federal commander might have issued orders for Hooker to attack several hours earlier. An additional 2-3 hours of daylight on September 16 could have contributed mightily to a successful assault by Hooker at a time when Lee had very few reinforcements to send Jackson. Imagine the Battle of Sharpsburg/Antietam without the counterpunch of McLaws's and Walker's commands in the West Woods, and we glean some idea of the impact Lee's unplanned delay of McClellan's advance had on the course of events. How long could Jackson have withstood the combined pressure of attacks by Hooker and Mansfield? The battle as we know it would look completely different and not in the Confederate army's favor.

Lee responded promptly to each of McClellan's moves as he learned them, including his orders for Jeb Stuart to attack the cavalry regiment Hooker sent across Antietam Creek before his infantry got underway. Lee also remained aware of the opportunity for enemy offensive action presented by the open northern end of the field—not just because it was obvious, but because his mounted observers told him of the developments occurring there. Tom Rosser first reported the build-up of Federal infantry in the vicinity of the Upper Bridge on September 15. Once he received these initial messages, Lee made sure that Stuart kept him apprised of the enemy's activity. When fog obscured the field on the morning of September 16, Lee ordered Stuart to reconnoiter the approaches to the Upper Bridge and other potential crossing points north of Sharpsburg. He did not seek an escape route up the Hagerstown Pike, as the orders to McLaws make clear. Under no circumstances would Lee have repeated his instructions for McLaws to hasten the march of his command if he did not intend to stand where he was.

The Confederate commander never sought a way out of the box at Sharpsburg. He put his army into it deliberately and with a full understanding of the tactical advantages offered by the position. Lee initially sought these advantages on the heights behind Beaver Creek, where he thought to fall back from the reverse at South Mountain, but circumstances beyond his control forced him to find a comparably strong position at Sharpsburg and fight there instead. The strength of the defensive position at Sharpsburg made facing McClellan less a throw of the dice and more a calculated risk for Lee, especially because he believed the recent defeats in Virginia had "disorganized" and "demoralized" the Federal army, and because he had faith in the fighting capacity of his men.[68]

The defensive strength of the position at Sharpsburg offered Lee a chance for a war-ending victory he might not have otherwise possessed, something the general saw from the very beginning and sought to maximize until his army's withdrawal on the evening of September 18, 1862.

---

68 Gordon, "Memorandum," in Gallagher, ed., *Lee the Soldier*, 26. Lee's post-war opinion of the Army of the Potomac's weakness during the Maryland Campaign mirrored his belief in September 1862. See OR 19, 2:590 in which Lee wrote, "The two grand armies of the United States that have been operating in Virginia, though now united, are much weakened and demoralized."

SEVEN

A VERY PERSONAL FIGHT

⟡

The Role of Robert E. Lee
on the Field at Sharpsburg, September 17, 1862

THE presence of an inspiring general officer can make a critical difference to an army's performance in the field. The personal participation of a beloved commander inspires troops who benefit from his ability to make decisions on the spot. Historians have long recognized the critical role Robert E. Lee played during the Overland Campaign of 1864. Rallying Texas and Arkansas troops during the Battle of the Wilderness, Lee's actions on the Army of Northern Virginia's right flank held the line against powerful enemy assaults until James Longstreet's command could come up and throw back the Federal Second Corps. Several weeks later Lee's absence from the field due to illness had an equally decisive opposite effect when A. P. Hill failed to attack Ulysses S. Grant's divided forces along the North Anna River, losing an opportunity for Lee to strike his opponent a potentially devastating blow.

These events illustrate the more active role in battle that Lee played as the war progressed. This occurred out of necessity as his subordinates were killed or wounded. There was another occasion earlier in the war at Sharpsburg on September 17, 1862, when Lee also took a direct role in the fighting. On that day he rallied troops, directed artillery fire, bypassed the chain of command by sending orders to division commanders, and established a secondary defensive position as his lines crumbled. Lee helped shore up his army's left-center during the fight, ensuring that McClellan's troops did not drive his men from the field on that fateful day and end once and for all the Confederacy's desperate bid for independence.

Any analysis of Lee's role at Sharpsburg must take into account two key historical studies: Ezra Carman's examination of the Maryland Campaign, and Joseph L. Harsh's *Taken at the Flood: Robert E. Lee and Confederate Strategy in the Maryland Campaign of 1862*. Carman's detailed study, edited by Thomas G. Clemens and published in 2012, was the first attempt to locate Lee on the field during the day's fighting. Harsh's work, published in 1999, provided the first systematic modern examination of Lee's movements on September 17. Both studies must be consulted when assessing the role played by Lee during the battle because each brings a different perspective to the table. Carman, for instance, focused on the operations of both combatant armies and fit Lee in where he found him. This contrasts with Harsh, who combined an analysis of the Rebel general's movements with actions on the field and pieced them together on a timeline.

Harsh's research is detailed, but during the process of developing his chronology of events, he proposed several conclusions that are not supported by the evidence. The analysis presented in this chapter reassesses Lee's role in the battle and suggests corrections to the timeline that more accurately represent how his presence shaped the Army of Northern Virginia's operations on that long and bloody day. Critical details lacking in many of the sources render parts of this analysis a speculative exercise, but such is the nature of historical studies. The objective is to ground the analysis in the facts to the extent they can be established.

Writing in the 1880s that "[Gen.] Lee's position during the engagement was on a hill to the east of Sharpsburg, which gave him an oversight of the whole field," Armistead Long conveyed the impression to subsequent generations that Lee spent much of the battle on the summit of Cemetery Hill.[1] The Army of Northern Virginia's commander did indeed observe some of the fighting from that vantage point early in the day, but a series of crises on his army's left and left-center quickly forced Lee down from the hilltop and onto the field itself.

During the opening phase of the battle, while Maj. Gen. Joseph Hooker's First Corps clashed with Stonewall Jackson's command north of the West Woods, Lee can be placed on Cemetery Hill for under sixty minutes, starting roughly at 6:30

---

1 Long, *Memoirs*, 221.

a.m. and ending before 7:30 a.m. Harsh claims in *Taken at the Flood* that Lee first mounted the summit of Cemetery Hill around 6:00 a.m. It seems improbable that Lee could have arrived there earlier than 6:20 - 6:30 a.m. given the arrival of Maj. Gen. Lafayette McLaws with his command just west of Sharpsburg at "about sunrise." McLaws himself is responsible for considerable confusion on this point. He wrote in his battle report and several times after the war that he reached Lee's headquarters at the head of his division, but McLaws actually made two trips to Sharpsburg that morning. He rode ahead of his men during the first trip to locate Lee while his division was crossing the Potomac at Shepherdstown Ford. Unable to find Lee in the pre-dawn fog and darkness, McLaws instead encountered Maj. Gen. James Longstreet, who told him where Lee could be found. Armed with this knowledge, McLaws rode back past Lee's headquarters to the Potomac and returned to Sharpsburg with his command an hour or two later.[2]

It was only at the end of this second trip that McLaws rode into army headquarters to speak with Lee personally. According to Ezra Carman, who provided details he learned in postwar letters from McLaws himself, the Georgian found Lee dressing for the day. Lee greeted McLaws by saying "I am glad to see you," and, after thanking McLaws for his role in the capture of Harpers Ferry, added, "we have I believe a hard day's work before us, and you must rest your men. Do not let them come quite this far as the shells of the enemy fall about here. Halt them about a quarter of a mile back in the road and I will send for you when I want you." McLaws also informed Carman that Jackson had sent him an order to deploy his command on the Confederate right flank (near John Walker's division) when it came up. When he told that to Lee, the general replied, "Never mind that order, but do as I told you and consider yourself as specially under my orders." This provides the first example that day when Lee involved himself personally in positioning his army's troops.[3]

How much time did this exchange consume? The sun rose at 5:53 a.m. on September 17. If his division arrived "about sunrise," as McLaws wrote in his battle report, or "just after day light," as he informed John Bell Hood via letter in May

---

2 See Appendix E. Harsh, *Taken*, 377, imagines Lee mounting Traveller and being led down main street in Sharpsburg at 5:30 a.m. Oeffinger, ed., *A Soldiers General*, 182.

3 See Appendix E and Carman, *The Maryland Campaign*, 2:184-185.

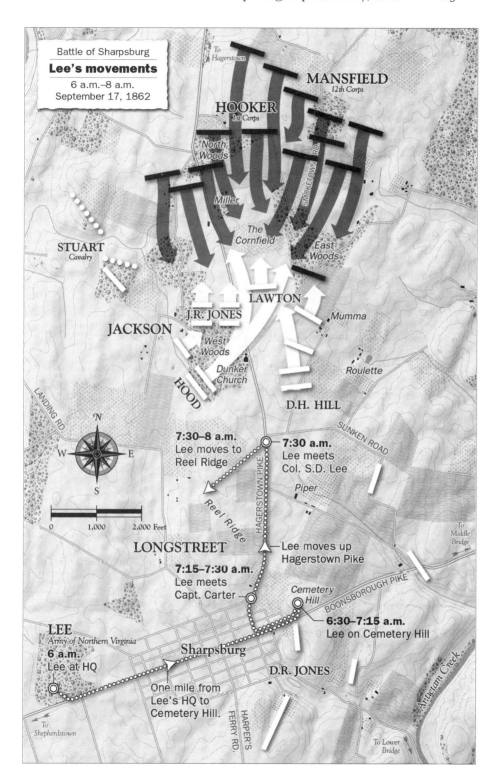

Battle of Sharpsburg
Lee's movements
6 a.m.–8 a.m.
September 17, 1862

MANSFIELD
12th Corps

HOOKER
1st Corps

North
Woods

SMOKETOWN RD.

Miller

The
Cornfield

East
Woods

STUART
Cavalry

LAWTON

J.R. JONES

Mumma

JACKSON

West
Woods

Dunker
Church

Roulette

HOOD

D.H. HILL

N
W   E
S

SUNKEN ROAD

7:30–8 a.m.
Lee moves to
Reel Ridge

7:30 a.m.
Lee meets
Col. S.D. Lee

LANDING RD.

HAGERSTOWN PIKE

Piper

Reel Ridge

0   1,000   2,000 Feet

LONGSTREET

*To
Middle
Bridge*

Lee moves up
Hagerstown Pike

7:15–7:30 a.m.
Lee meets
Capt. Carter

Cemetery
Hill

BOONSBOROUGH PIKE

6:30–7:15 a.m.
Lee on Cemetery Hill

LEE
Army of Northern Virginia
6 a.m.
Lee at HQ

Sharpsburg

One mile from
Lee's HQ to
Cemetery Hill.

D.R. JONES

Antietam Creek

*To
Shepherdstown*

HARPER'S
FERRY
RD.

*To Lower
Bridge*

1863, McLaws was at Lee's tent shortly before 6:00 a.m.[4] After his talk with McLaws, Lee finished dressing and traveled from his headquarters to Cemetery Hill. How he arrived there is a mystery. Harsh surmised that at this early hour that Lee, with both of his hands still bandaged and his right arm in a sling, "decided the time had come to return to the back of Traveller." There is no source that states how Lee got from his headquarters on the western outskirts of Sharpsburg to Cemetery Hill on the eastern side of town.

Whether he walked or was led on horseback, it would have taken Lee around 20 minutes to travel the one mile from his headquarters to the top of Cemetery Hill, particularly if he stopped at the Grove House to read any new intelligence reported by Jeb Stuart about the enemy's movements. As best as can be determined, and assuming that he promptly left his headquarters after meeting with McLaws, Lee probably reached Cemetery Hill about 6:20 - 6:30 a.m. By this time the violent struggle on the Confederate left had been raging for about 45 minutes.[5]

What the general saw around 6:30 a.m. from that position cannot be said with certainty, but it is difficult to believe he could make out much of anything. Powder smoke covered the embattled area between the East Woods and West Woods, and a thick cloud of smoke was blowing southwest across Lee's field of view from Samuel Mumma's burning farmhouse.[6] Lee could only hold his field glasses in his left hand, and a more powerful spyglass was needed to see more than one mile north to Jackson's line. What little he could see appears to have angered him. According to Harsh, "a huge stream of stragglers" could be seen moving to the rear

---

4 See Harsh, *Sounding the Shallows*, 19 for meteorological observations recorded that day. Oeffinger, ed., *A Soldier's General*, 182.

5 Harsh, *Taken*, 331, and *Sounding the Shallows*, 193. Harsh's documentation of this subject is problematic. He cites two sources that claim Lee was seen riding that make no mention of it on the pages he lists. For example, *Sounding the Shallows*, 250, cites Sorrel, *Recollections of a Confederate Staff Officer*, 96, but this concerns events during the Battle of Second Manassas. The correct page in Sorrel's book is 103, where Sorrel wrote: "For some time the saddle had to be given up and the ambulance called into use. General Lee made the campaign on wheels. At Sharpsburg he was far enough cured to allow him to ride a little." Harsh also cites Walter H. Taylor, *Four Years with General Lee* (New York, NY, 1878), 115, but this deals with July 5, 1863, and the Army of Northern Virginia's retreat from Gettysburg. The estimate of 20 minutes is derived from the assumed average human walking speed of 15-20 minutes per mile. There is also a third option: that Lee may have used the ambulance that had carried him through Maryland since Sept. 6. No evidence exists for this.

6 D. H. Hill ordered the farm burned to deny its use to enemy sharpshooters. OR 19, 1:1033, 1043. The light breeze that morning carried the smoke across the field from northeast to southwest at a sluggish two miles per hour. Harsh, *Sounding the Shallows*, 20.

from Jackson's beleaguered command at the southern edge of the Miller Cornfield. The sight of these men irritated Lee, who was standing near Capt. Charles Squires's battery north of the Boonsboro Pike. When Lee complained loudly that the men were "acting badly," the surprised captain, thinking that Lee was commenting on his own command, countered by pointing out that his crews were "working their guns in excellent style." Lee barked quickly in response, "the infantry, sir, are straggling, they are straggling."[7]

After this exchange Lee appears to have loitered by Squires's battery, under enemy artillery fire, until Maj. James Ratchford, a staff officer sent by D. H. Hill, reached him with an urgent request for reinforcements. Lee initially declined the request and responded that he "had no troops to spare"—despite Hill's boast, as conveyed by Ratchford, that Hill could "have the victory won by eleven o'clock" if support was sent his way. Unaware of Jackson's situation, Ratchford suggested to Lee that he send some of Stonewall's men. Lee considered this and finally capitulated to Hill's request, although the men he dispatched were not from Jackson's command. Instead, he ordered Maj. Walter Taylor of his headquarters staff to ride with Ratchford and bring up Lafayette McLaws's division, which was resting behind army headquarters.[8]

7 A staff member could have held a spyglass for Lee, but there is no evidence that this occurred. The issue of what Lee could grasp in his left hand has caused unnecessary debate. Multiple sources indicate he could hold binoculars for at least short periods of time. According to Owen, *In Camp and Battle*, 150, "While standing with Col. Walton in Squires' battery, about noon, Gen. Lee walked over to us. One hand was in a sling, it not having recovered from the accident at the second Manassas; the other held his field-glass." Longstreet, "The Invasion of Maryland," 671, noted, "General Lee and I stood on the top of the crest with our glasses." Nisbet, *Four Years on the Firing Line*, 156, saw "General Lee, whom I found viewing our right-field through his glasses." Harsh, *Taken*, 373. Squires's battery partially occupied the summit north of the Boonsboro Pike where the Mountain View Cemetery is located today. See Charles W. Squires, "The 'Boy Officer' of the Washington Artillery, Part 1," in *Civil War Times Illustrated*, Vol. XIV, No. 2 (May 1975), 19. "My battery was at a point where our line of battle . . . turned sharply to the south . . . most of the time Gen. Lee was near my guns." Squires gave no estimate of the time when Lee spoke these words. The time-frame offered here is my estimate.

8 Evelyn R. Sieburg and James E. Hansen II, eds., *Memoirs of a Confederate Staff Officer: From Bethel to Bentonville* (Shippensburg, PA, 1998), 27. Harsh argues that D. H. Hill appeared personally on Cemetery Hill about this time to request reinforcements, and that he was awaiting Lee's decision when a Federal artillery shell shot off the front legs off his horse. None of the four existing accounts of Hill's horse being injured mention a request for reinforcement by Hill, and Maj. Ratchford's account makes it clear that Hill had sent him back from a position near Roswell Ripley's and Alfred Colquitt's brigades on the north side of the field to Lee. Hill did not personally run the errand.

We can reasonably conclude that Lee's exchange with Ratchford took place after 7:00 a.m. by comparing events taking place on the field with the time it took for McLaws's division to arrive. According to McLaws, his men settled in for "about an hour" of well-deserved rest. The orders to move were carried "by an aide-de-camp of General Lee, Major Taylor." Taking into account the time McLaws would have needed to get himself and his command situated, and the 10- or 15-minute ride from Cemetery Hill that Taylor and Ratchford would have made, the orders reached McLaws between 7:30 and 8:00 a.m. This time-frame is consistent with the battle report filed by Lt. Col. William MacRae, commanding Howell Cobb's brigade: "General McLaws' division . . . was ordered, about 8 a.m., to take position on the left."[9]

McLaws roused his bleary-eyed men and led them cross-country on the double-quick around the north side of Sharpsburg for about one mile and a half until they "came in [the] rear of the position, which was pointed out by Major Ratchford, of General D. H. Hill's staff, as the one the division was to occupy." It is generally accepted that McLaws's three brigades arrived behind the West Woods about 9:00 a.m. For example, Maj Gen. James Longstreet wrote after the war, "McLaws's column came up at nine o'clock." Brigadier General Joseph B. Kershaw of McLaws's command reported: "About 9 o'clock we were ordered forward to the relief of General Jackson's forces, then engaged on the left, in the wood in rear of the church," which indicates the men of his brigade stepped off as soon as they came up.[10]

---

9 Ratchford's depiction of these events is riddled with inconsistencies. According to his account in Sieburg and Hansen, eds., *Memoirs*, 27, "About nine o'clock . . . our division, forming the left of the army, was attacked by the enemy in in heavy force. As before, we soon had them in a bad way," Ratchford continued, "but we could see massive reinforcements coming to their aid. At this point General Hill sent me to General Lee with a message that if he (Hill) could have some help he could have the victory won before eleven o'clock." Because Federal troops had already swept Jackson's and Hill's commands from the north end of the field by 9:00 a.m. there was no force on the field near Hill's original position for Lee to reinforce. In addition, supposing the enemy had "massive reinforcements" coming up, how could Hill reasonably boast that he could have the battle won by 11:00 a.m. if Lee sent him his own reinforcements? Given these problems, I have ignored Ratchford's 9:00 a.m. estimate and timed his trip to Lee at the earlier hour of 7:00 a.m., when it fits the situation and the sources. *OR* 19, 1:858, 871. Harsh, *Sounding the Shallows*, 205, justifiably discounts the report of Brig. Gen. William Barksdale, *OR* 19, 1:883, because it states that his brigade did not even reach Sharpsburg until 9:00 a.m., which is clearly too late.

10 *OR* 19, 1:858; Longstreet, *From Manassas to Appomattox*, 244; *OR* 19, 1:865. Antietam Battlefield Historical Tablet No. 357 says, "At about 9 A.M., it (McLaws's Division) moved across the fields northwest of the town and deployed on the rising ground south and west of

Several other pieces of evidence support the proposition that McLaws's attack commenced around nine in the morning, including the reports of two Federal artillerists. Captain John A. Tompkins of Battery A, 1st Rhode Island Light Artillery, recalled: "At 9.30 the enemy appeared upon my right front with a large column, apparently designing to charge the battery." Tompkins's battery occupied a piece of high ground near the Mumma farm several hundred yards east of the West Woods, which suggests that the appearance of a Confederate column on his side of the woods meant McLaws's attack had already pushed Federal troops from the trees by 9:30. Similarly, Lt. George A. Woodruff, commanding Battery I of the 1st U.S. Artillery, reported that "about 10 a.m. on the 17th instant . . . I moved to the front . . . and took a position in an open field, in front of which, at a distance of about 300 yards, was a piece of woods occupied by the enemy in force. At the time when we came up," he continued, *our line of infantry had been broken* [emphasis added], and was retreating rapidly and in great disorder." Woodruff's account suggests that by 10:00 a.m., the remaining Federal forces in the vicinity of the West Woods had fallen back due to the Rebel advance. Lastly, in a report filed with the *Savannah Republican* on September 18, war correspondent Peter Wellington Alexander estimated that Lee sent McLaws "to the relief of Jackson about nine o'clock [and he] arrived just in the nick of time."[11]

Ezra Carman's observation about the arrival of George 'Tige' Anderson's brigade also helps document more of Lee's actions that morning. Anderson's command, part of D. R. Jones's division, arrived behind the West Woods ahead of McLaws and arranged itself in line of battle. The brigade took fire from the 125th Pennsylvania, which occupied the high ground west of the Dunker Church when McLaws's attack stepped off. The fact that Anderson's brigade came up before McLaws helps document Lee's actions between 7:00 and 7:30 a.m. After sending Ratchford and Taylor to fetch McLaws, Lee must have witnessed Jackson's

---

this point, the right near the Hagerstown Pike, nearly opposite the Bloody Lane, the left extending about 250 yards northwest of the Hauser house." Tablet texts are available online at http://antietam.aotw.org/tablet.php?tablet_id=all. William Barksdale estimated in OR 19, 1:883, that his brigade went into action around 10:00 a.m. The battle report of Capt. Philologus Hawkins Loud, commanding the 10th Georgia in Paul Semmes's brigade, noted that his regiment "went into the action at the battle of Sharpsburg, Md., at 8 a.m." which is too early. OR 19, 1:877.

11 OR 19, 1:308-309. Report reprinted in the *Atlanta Southern Confederacy*, Oct. 4, 1862. Another report from Alexander repeated this statement in the *Savannah Weekly Republican* on Sept. 27, 1862: "the timely appearance of McLaws on the left, about nine o'clock in the morning, saved the day on that part of the field."

shattered command falling back from its position near the Miller Cornfield. He also would have watched John Bell Hood's small division of two brigades exit the West Woods, cross the Hagerstown Pike near the Dunker Church, and press northward into the fight.[12]

The timing of Hood's attack is generally well-established. "Soon after daylight the brigade formed line of battle in regular order," recalled Lt. Col. Benjamin Franklin Carter of the 4th Texas, with the "the Fifth Texas being on my right and First Texas on my left, and, about 7 a.m., [we] were ordered to advance." At some point around this time, Lee also received a request for reinforcements from Stonewall Jackson. This plea arrived in the form of Jackson's aide, Capt. Alexander Swift "Sandie" Pendleton, who had been riding back and forth between Jackson and Hood.[13]

According to a letter Sandie Pendleton wrote to his mother four days later on September 21, on Jackson's orders he rode "out to Hood's front line," where Hood told him, "'Tell General Jackson unless I get reinforcements I must be forced back but I am going on while I can'." Pendleton reported this back to Jackson, who sent Pendleton on to find General Lee "with Hood's message and our appeal for help." Lee, continued Pendleton, replied by saying, "'I'll send McLaws,'" after which Pendleton returned to deliver the news to Hood. The portion of Pendleton's account mentioning McLaws is probably not reliable because, as James Ratchford makes clear, it was D. H. Hill's earlier request for reinforcements, not Stonewall Jackson's subsequent appeal, that prompted General Lee to act. While Pendleton surely carried Jackson's message to Lee, the reinforcements sent in response were most likely Tige Anderson's troops. Anderson's soldiers were huddled on the ground on the west side of Cemetery Hill near Lee, sheltered from the distant enemy cannon fire. With less than half the distance to march compared to McLaws, it is easy to see how Anderson could have received his marching orders after

---

12 Carman, *The Maryland Campaign*, 2:180.

13 *OR* 19, 1:935, 930: "About 7 a. m., the brigade was ordered to move forward in the direction of the firing. Advancing about a quarter of a mile through the timber [behind the Dunker Church]." Longstreet confirmed after the war that Jackson's request for reinforcements arrived at 7:00 a.m. James Longstreet to Ezra Carman, Jan. 28, 1895, Box 2, Folder 3, Item 41 in Ezra Carman Papers, Manuscripts and Archives Division MSS-473, New York Public Library. My thanks to Tom Clemens for an index to Carman's papers that revealed this item.

McLaws got his, but moved and deployed in line of battle before McLaws arrived for his attack.[14]

Evidence that Lee sent instructions to Anderson in response to Jackson's request is confirmed by Anderson's own battle report: "About 7.30 a.m. . . . . I was ordered to the left to support General Hood." The one piece of the puzzle that cannot be clarified is where Pendleton found the general. A circumstantial case can be made that Lee received Hood's request for reinforcements after he had come down from Cemetery Hill and begun moving toward the fighting on the Hagerstown Pike. The proof for this comes from Capt. Thomas Carter, General Lee's cousin and the commander of the five-gun King William Artillery. Carter reported that he found his guns in an unsafe position without infantry support, and decided to lead "the whole battery across the Hagerstown road [to] the eminence to the left (the Reel farm ridge), where it could command any position taken by the division, whether in the direction of the burning [Mumma] house or toward the line of the enemy, then on the open field to the left of the Hagerstown road."[15]

The stone walls enclosing both sides of the Hagerstown Pike forced Carter to move his guns nearly all the way back to Sharpsburg before he could find an opening that allowed him to cross. "On my way," recalled the artillerist, "I met General Lee [who] seemed to fear that the whole left wing, then hard pressed and losing ground, would be turned, and that the enemy would gain possession of the range of hills some three-quarters of a mile to the left of Sharpsburg." By the time Carter encountered Lee, the general had already left Cemetery Hill. Lee also voiced concern that Jackson's front would collapse, implying it had not yet done so, and that he had received no additional word from Jackson or Hood about the situation.

Considering Jackson's command fell back around 7:00 a.m. and Hood's division followed it to the rear between 7:30 and 7:45, it seems plausible that Lee met Carter after he had met Pendleton and after he had sent orders for Tige Anderson to march to Hood's aid, but before Hood had fallen back. His time on Cemetery Hill was now finished. Lee had decided by no later than 7:30 a.m. to personally enter the fight, where he would use his presence to rally his faltering troops and see what he could do to shore up his army's defenses.

---

14 Letter of Alexander 'Sandie' Pendleton to his mother, Sept. 21, 1862, in Lee, *Memoirs of William Nelson Pendleton*, 216-217.

15 *OR* 19, 1:909, 1030.

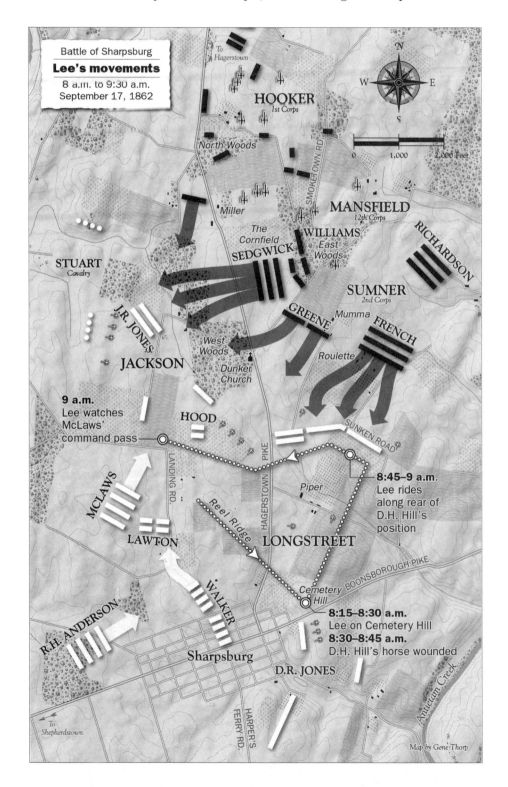

Battle of Sharpsburg
Lee's movements
8 a.m. to 9:30 a.m.
September 17, 1862

HOOKER
1st Corps

North Woods

Miller

MANSFIELD
12th Corps

The
Cornfield   WILLIAMS
                      *East
SEDGWICK   Woods*

RICHARDSON

STUART
Cavalry

SUMNER
2nd Corps

J.R. JONES

GREENE   *Mumma*

FRENCH

West
Woods   *Roulette*

JACKSON

*Dunker
Church*

9 a.m.
Lee watches
McLaws'   HOOD
command pass

SUNKEN ROAD

8:45–9 a.m.
Lee rides
along rear of
D.H. Hill's
position

MCLAWS

Piper

LAWTON

LONGSTREET

WALKER

BOONSBOROUGH PIKE

Cemetery
Hill

8:15–8:30 a.m.
Lee on Cemetery Hill

R.H. ANDERSON

8:30–8:45 a.m.
D.H. Hill's horse wounded

Sharpsburg

D.R. JONES

*To
Shepherdstown*

HARPER'S
FERRY RD.

Map by Gene Thorp

According to a letter that Carter later wrote to Ezra Carman, Lee also apparently set off for the field on foot, lending credence to the idea that he may not have been led to Cemetery Hill on Traveller. It would have taken only a few seconds for a staff officer to boost Lee into the saddle, and yet the general elected to walk instead of ride. In addition, Carter encountered Lee close to Sharpsburg, which indicates that by around 7:30 a.m., the general had not made his way more than a short distance toward the Dunker Church. Lee ordered Carter at this point to take his guns to the high ground on the Reel farm ridge to the left of the Hagerstown Pike and to collect there any other artillery he could find to prevent the enemy from occupying this critical spot behind Confederate lines. Carter's report makes it clear that Lee recognized the importance of the Reel farm ridge as a viable defensive fallback position, and spent the next several hours engaged on that ridge directing artillery fire, collecting guns, and rallying his stragglers.[16]

Lee moved up the pike toward the Dunker Church and encountered another artillerist coming south. The officer, Col. Stephen Dill Lee, bore a second urgent message from General Hood seeking reinforcements, which suggests again that Hood's division had not yet fallen back, and implies Colonel Lee met General Lee no later than 7:30 a.m. When he learned from the colonel that the day was lost "unless reinforcements were sent at once," General Lee responded, "don't be excited about it, Colonel; go tell General Hood to hold his ground; reinforcements are now rapidly approaching between Sharpsburg and the ford. Tell him that I am now coming to his support." A moment later, recalled the colonel, "General Lee pointed to McLaws's division then in sight and approaching at a double-quick."[17]

The last sentence in this exchange is almost certainly a later invention by Colonel Lee. As Tom Clemens notes, the story originated at a dinner conversation between Stephen D. Lee and a number of others that wound up being published in the *Richmond Times Dispatch* in December 1896. Not only is the passage of 34 years between the event and the retelling of it problematic, the content is clearly incorrect when placed within the context of events at the time.[18]

---

16 Carman, *The Maryland Campaign*, 2:182, Note 18. Harsh, *Taken*, 381, insists without supporting evidence that Lee walked up the Hagerstown Pike "trailing Traveller and his staff behind" him. OR 19, 1:1030. Harsh, *Taken*, 381 claims Lee's exchange with Carter occurred around "8:30 or so."

17 Colonel S. D. Lee, quoted in White, *Robert E. Lee*, 218.

18 Carman, *The Maryland Campaign*, 2:183, Note 19.

The sources indicate that Hood's shattered command fell back from the fight between 7:30 and 7:45 a.m. They also show that McLaws's division did not arrive on the field until near 9:00 a.m.. This gap of roughly 90 minutes confirms there is no way that Colonel Lee could have delivered Hood's request for reinforcements and have been alerted by General Lee only seconds later to the appearance of McLaws's approaching command. Tige Anderson's command also could not have come up at that time and been mistaken for McLaws because, as Anderson's after-action report noted, he received orders to advance around 7:30 a.m. In the final analysis, it is likely that Colonel Lee either conflated his delivery of Hood's request to General Lee with the later arrival of McLaws's command, or, as Clemens suggests, he embellished his role in developing the Confederate counterattack.[19]

Assuming for the sake of argument that Colonel Lee presented the message from Hood around 7:30 a.m., it is worth noting that he observed General Lee "on horseback with one orderly, half-way between Sharpsburg and the Dunkard Church." Another version of this story, told by Jed Hotchkiss and published by Clement Evans in 1899, described the encounter a little differently: Colonel Lee met the general "on his led horse," indicating that Lee had once again chosen to remount after he met Captain Carter on foot only a few minutes earlier. Neither of these accounts mention Traveller—an notable omission discussed in more detail later in this chapter.[20]

Piecing together General Lee's movements after his conversation with Stephen D. Lee is complicated, but sources exist that make it possible to paint an informed picture.[21] The first documented event is the well-known story of Lee, Longstreet, and D. H. Hill ascending to the summit of Cemetery Hill, where gunners with Capt. Stephen H. Weed's Battery I, 5th U.S. Artillery, promptly shot the forelegs off Hill's horse. Longstreet recounted the incident in the pages of *The Century Magazine* in 1886. "During the progress of the battle of Sharpsburg General Lee and I were riding along my line and D. H. Hill's," he began,

---

19 OR 19, 1:858. Both Carman, *The Maryland Campaign*, 2:183, and Harsh, *Taken*, 390, accept Stephen D. Lee's tale uncritically. "McLaws's men had reached the Hagerstown Pike just opposite its juncture with the sunken road," wrote Harsh. "They passed some distance in front of Robert E. Lee, who shouted to Col. Stephen D. Lee and pointed out their welcome arrival."

20 Evans, ed., *Confederate Military History*, 3:352.

21 White, *Robert E. Lee*, 218.

when we received a report of movements of the enemy and started up the ridge to make a reconnaissance. General Lee and I dismounted, but Hill declined to do so. I said to Hill, 'If you insist on riding up there and drawing the fire, give us a little interval so that we may not be in the line of the fire when they open upon you.' General Lee and I stood on the top of the crest with our glasses, looking at the movements of the Federals on the rear left. After a moment I turned my glass to the right—the Federal left. As I did so, I noticed a puff of white smoke from the mouth of a cannon. 'There is a shot for you,' I said to General Hill. The gunner was a mile away, and the cannon-shot came whisking through the air for three or four seconds and took off the front legs of the horse that Hill sat on and let the animal down upon his stumps. The horse's head was so low and his croup so high that Hill was in a most ludicrous position. With one foot in the stirrup he made several efforts to get the other leg over the croup, but failed. Finally we prevailed upon him to try the other end of the horse, and he got down.[22]

The evidence suggests that this incident, claimed by Harsh to have taken place "not long after seven o'clock," probably occurred closer to 8:30 a.m. when a break in the morning's fighting had settled over the field. The lull began when the three brigades of D. H. Hill's division under Roswell Ripley, Alfred Colquitt, and Duncan McRae collapsed around 8:15 a.m. after a "short and sharp contest" near the East Woods with the leading elements of Brig. Gen. George S. Greene's Union division. Those who could retreat to Robert Rodes's defensive line in the sunken road did so, while others fled back to the safety of Sharpsburg itself.[23]

In 1896, Longstreet provided proof that the incident with Hill's horse occurred during a break in the fighting when he wrote that it took place "during the lull." He added this detail to his earlier account after receiving a letter from former Union Maj. Alfred A. Woodhull, who wrote in response to the 1886 article that he had witnessed Captain Weed's cannon shot at "about 8 or 9 o'clock" in the morning, which places it within the time-frame of the lull. Longstreet, noted Woodhull in 1886, "kindly writes me that he cannot now recall the hour, but *that there was little*

22 Longstreet, "The Invasion of Maryland," 671. Longstreet's account was apparently the earliest of the four versions published. The version of the incident in Long, *Memoirs*, 22, also emerged in 1886, followed by Longstreet, *From Manassas to Appomattox*, 254, in 1896 and Sorrel, *Recollections of a Confederate Staff Officer*, 111, in 1905.

23 Harsh, *Taken*, 378. Antietam National Battlefield Historical Tablet No. 50. Available online at http://antietam.aotw.org/tablet.php?tablet_id=all. Carman, *The Maryland Campaign*, 2:169 also mentions the temporary cessation of gunfire, although he places it as "nearing 9 o'clock and, with the advance and success of the Twelfth Corps, and the retreat of the Confederates into the West Woods and in the direction of Sharpsburg, there was a grateful lull in the sanguinary contest."

firing at the time [emphasis added], and that the [incident took] place . . . 'about twenty feet from the Boonsboro pike, north'." There was "little firing at the time" because the breakdown of Hill's line had left the northern half of the field entirely in Federal hands.[24]

This tactical reverse, combined with enemy activity near the East Woods, is probably why Lee and Longstreet moved onto Cemetery Hill in the first place. As Longstreet noted, "we received a report of movements of the enemy . . . [and so] General Lee and I stood on the top of the crest with our glasses, looking at the movements of the Federals *on the rear left* [emphasis added]." Enemy actions at the time included the advance of Brig. Gen. Greene's Twelfth Corps division from the East Woods to the edge of the plateau overlooking Robert Rodes's position, and the filing onto the field near the East Woods of Edwin Vose Sumner's Second Corps, led by Maj. Gen. John Sedgwick's division. Both of these movements took place on the Federal rear-left from Lee and Longstreet's perspective.

Returning specifically to Lee, it appears that he either met Longstreet near the Hagerstown Pike around 7:30 a.m., or searched for Longstreet in the vicinity of the Piper farm between the time when Hood's command fell back and D. H. Hill's three brigades retreated (around 8:15 a.m.). The general spent a brief period atop Cemetery Hill before concluding that the Federals intended to attack Hill's position in the sunken road and Jackson's new defensive line in the West Woods. In response to the latter threat, Lee sent orders for Brig. Gen. John G. Walker to hurry his division from the army's right flank northward to support Jackson.[25]

According to Walker's October 1862 battle report, "Soon after 9 a.m., I received orders from General Lee, through Colonel [A. L.] Long, of his staff, to hasten to the extreme left, to the support of Major-General Jackson." Walker's estimate of the time when he received his orders fits what Lee would have known if he saw Sumner's Second Corps assault forming to strike Jackson during the battlefield lull. Walker hastily recalled his skirmishers and "hurried forward, left in front, along the rear of the whole Confederate line of battle" to arrive, deploy, and

24 Longstreet, *From Manassas to Appomattox*, 254. Woodhull quoted in Longstreet, "The Invasion of Maryland," 671. In a letter to the Antietam Battlefield Board, former Col. William J. Colvill, Jr. of the 1st Minnesota also mentioned "a lull in the battle . . . this was near 9 o'clock A.M." See William J. Colvill, Jr. to Antietam Battlefield Board, Dec. 10, 1892. NA, Antietam Battlefield Board Correspondence, Box 1. Available online at https://walkingthe westwoods. blogspot.com/2020/03/the-whole-division-except-our-regiment.html.

25 Longstreet, "The Invasion of Maryland," 671.

go into the fight at around 10:00 a.m. That Walker received his orders around 9:00 a.m. suggests Colonel Long made good time traveling the mile-and-a-half from Cemetery Hill to reach Walker's position, cantering or galloping part of the way. This implies that Lee could have sent his orders as early as 8:30 a.m., which puts the time of his decision during the battlefield lull.[26]

General Hill, meanwhile, secured another horse and rode with Lee toward his line in the sunken road. Colonel John Brown Gordon's 6th Alabama, part of Robert Rodes's brigade, was posted at the elbow of the Confederate position. The Georgia colonel recalled seeing Lee ride "along his lines on the right and centre" soon after "an ominous lull" had fallen on the army's left. "Accompanied by Division Commander General D. H. Hill," continued Gordon, "General Lee had decided that the Union commander's next heavy blow would fall upon our centre, and those of us who held that important position were notified of this conclusion. We were cautioned to be prepared for a determined assault and urged to hold that centre at any sacrifice, as a break at that point would endanger his entire army."[27]

Certain aspects of Gordon's testimony have come under well-deserved scrutiny over the years. Here, he accurately described the events developing on the field, so there is no reason to doubt at least this portion of his account. Indeed, Joseph Harsh accepted Gordon's account without question, claiming plausibly enough that the colonel saw Lee and Hill around 8:45 a.m.

For our purposes, two dimensions of the event must be discussed. The first is Gordon's observation that Lee had decided by this time to personally take control of his horse. This description, published decades after the war, may have been Gordon's way of protecting the hallowed image of an invincible General Lee rallying his men in the face of overwhelming odds, rather than an honest description of a handicapped aging man with one arm in a sling and his other hand barely able to handle his reins. Gordon recounted his story with some consistency after the war, adding a few details during lectures to Confederate veteran groups. He recalled on one occasion how he held the reins of the general's bridle while Lee told him, "I have no support for you." At another reunion in 1894 at Russellville,

---

26 OR 19, 1:914. Clark, "The Battle of Sharpsburg," 87, also recalled: "About 9 a.m. a pressing order came to move to the left; this we did in quick time." Walker, "Sharpsburg," 676-677. Clemens also notes: "Walker's division was engaged shortly before 10:00 a.m. in the West Woods." Carman, *The Maryland Campaign*, 2:228, Note 105. Harsh, *Taken*, 569, Note 24, also arrives at the 8:30 a.m. estimate posited here.

27 Gordon, *Reminiscences*, 84.

Kentucky, Gordon claimed that "Gen. Lee rode up to my command, and said that the fighting to the right and left, then in progress, would continue, but that it would be much worse in my front, and that I must hold my position. He said he could not reenforce me. It was the salient point; and I told him we would stay there."[28]

As previously noted, Gordon's memories have come under criticism for a variety of inaccuracies, so what Lee allegedly told him about the military situation may or may not be embellished. His statements about Lee atop his horse, however, corroborate comments from other witnesses, which suggests that, for at least a brief period, the general fought through the pain in his left hand to direct his own mount and rally Hill's men. It is also worth noting that Gordon's accounts, just like the others examined thus far, make no mention of Traveller—a curious oversight considering how recognizable the general's mount already was by that point in the war.

Determining where Lee moved after traversing Hill's position is simple thanks to Gordon. Lee, he wrote, "had scarcely reached his left before the predicted assault came." The low ridge upon which the Reel and Hauser farms sit is located well to the left of the sunken road. Lee traveled up it to meet the oncoming ranks of McLaws's division, which had just arrived on the field. Before crossing the Hagerstown Pike, Lee paused at the west end of the sunken road to address troops from D. H. Hill's brigades who had broken in front of the East Woods and retreated to the more southerly position held by Robert Rodes. The troops there described Lee as calm and plainly attired, with "his right arm in a sling, his pantaloons tucked inside his boots."[29]

After offering a few reassuring words, Lee moved on, heading up the Reel farm ridge as Joseph Kershaw's and Paul Jones Semmes's brigades came up southwest of the West Woods. Brigadier General William Barksdale's troops arrived next, spotting Lee as they hurried forward. "We moved at [the] double-quick across plowed ground, and formed line behind a high rail fence, just at the edge of a beautiful wood," recalled James Dinkins of the 18th Mississippi. "As our line

28 *Confederate Veteran*, Vol. 2, No. 1 (Jan. 1894), 2, and *Confederate Veteran*, Vol. 2, No. 9 (Sept. 1894), 272. Also see D. Scott Hartwig, "From the Crossroads: White Lies," in *America's Civil War*, Vol. 30, No. 5 (Nov. 2018). Available online at https://www.historynet.com/crossroads-white-lies.htm.

29 Gordon, *Reminiscences*, 84; Robert K. Krick, "It Appeared as Though Mutual Extermination Would Put a Stop to the Awful Carnage: Confederates in Sharpsburg's Bloody Lane," in Gallagher, ed., *The Antietam Campaign*, 228-229.

advanced to [this] position we passed General Robert E. Lee. He sat on his horse near a battery of the Richmond Howitzers, which was actively engaged. We cheered him as we passed." Several years later, in an article on his brigade and its campaigns, Dinkins repeated his description of going into the fight in the West Woods with an additional interesting detail. He and his comrades, he wrote, "passed General Lee . . . He was riding a little black horse, and halted near a battery which was actively engaged. The Mississippians yelled, and General Lee, reining his horse about, watched us go by."[30]

Clemens suggests that Dinkins "may not be a reliable source" because Ezra Carman did not take the man's claims into account when he authored his description of the fight in the West Woods. Carman apparently had doubts about Dinkins's claim that Barksdale's brigade went into action later than Carman concluded it did. Whatever Carman may have thought about Dinkins, his skepticism seems unwarranted given that Carman's own estimates for the timing of McLaws's attack are inconsistent.[31]

For example, the detailed maps prepared by E. B. Cope for the War Department relied on Carman for the placement of the forces engaged. The map for 8:30 a.m. shows McLaws's division still in bivouac along the Shepherdstown Pike, while the map for 9:00 a.m. shows it fighting along the eastern and northern edges of the West Woods after having marched, engaged the Federals, and pushed them nearly out of the woods in the intervening 30 minutes. Even Carman's written treatment of McLaws's arrival and attack offers no estimate of timing, noting only the presence of Sumner and Sedgwick in the East Woods at 9:00 a.m., the advance of Col. Jacob Higgins's 125th Pennsylvania to the eastern edge of the West Woods around the same time, and, curiously, Sumner's orders for Sedgwick to advance from the East Woods at 9:10 a.m. The only hard and fast estimate from

30 See OR 19, 1:865, in which Joseph Kershaw reported: "About 9 o'clock we were ordered forward to the relief of General Jackson's forces, then engaged on the left, in the wood in rear of the church." Also see Harsh, *Taken*, 390, which notes: "Around nine o'clock, after crossing the fields northwest of Sharpsburg, McLaws's men had reached the Hagerstown Pike just opposite its juncture with the sunken road." James Dinkins, *1861 to 1865: Personal Recollections and Experiences in the Confederate Army by an "Old Johnnie"* (Cincinnati, OH, 1897), 59. James Dinkins, "The Griffith-Barksdale-Humphrey Brigade, and Its Campaigns," in *SHSP* (1904), 32:262.

31 See Clemens's annotation in Carman, *The Maryland Campaign*, 2:200, Note 46: "Dinkins also mentioned seeing D. H. Hill's horse killed and argued the timing of McLaws' advance was much later than Carman put it. In short, Dinkins may not be a reliable source, and Carman seemed to ignore his more outlandish claims."

Carman concerning McLaws's attack is Antietam Battlefield Historical Tablet No. 357, which reads: "At about 9 A.M., [McLaws's division] moved across the fields northwest of town and deployed on the rising ground south and west of this point (i.e., the West Woods) . . . The division encountered the left flank and front of Sedgwick's advancing division and forced it back to the fields and woods beyond D. R. Miller's."[32]

Carman's lack of clarity about the timeline suggests there is no substantive reason why he should dismiss James Dinkins as an unreliable witness when it comes to his sighting of General Lee. Harsh also concluded in his summary of the Confederate counterattack that McLaws launched his assault at 9:20 a.m. This means that the evidence he evaluated led him, like Dinkins, to suggest that the attack stepped off later than Carman argued it did.[33]

Dinkins's mention of Lee also contains details that should not be lightly dismissed, including a description of the general sitting atop his horse close to a battery from the Richmond Howitzers. Carman himself acknowledged the battery's presence on the field in the vicinity of Barksdale's advance: "Two guns of the First Company, Richmond Howitzers, under Lieutenant R. M. Anderson, moved on [Brig. Gen.] Semmes' right, but the open, exposed field was no place for artillery, it could not live under the fire which swept it, and, under orders, Anderson withdrew his guns to the high ground in rear, south of Hauser's [farm]."[34]

In a note addressing Carman's source for this information, Clemens explains that the details concerning the howitzers came from Daniel S. McCarthy, an artillerist with Anderson's section of guns. The connection to Dinkins in this respect comes from his claim that the 18th Mississippi moved across a plowed field en route to the West Woods. That topographical feature appears south of the Hauser farm on E. B. Cope's Map No. 8, which Carman helped create. This representation of the terrain, when considered in combination with the

---

32 E. B. Cope, *Maps of the Battlefield of Antietam*, Map No. 7 (8:30 a.m.) and Map No. 8 (9:00 a.m.) (Washington, DC, 1904). Carman, *The Maryland Campaign*, 2:172, 178, and 189. Antietam Battlefield Historical Tablet No. 357. Available online at http://antietam.aotw.org/tablet.php?tablet_id=all.

33 Harsh, *Taken*, 391. "When at last, around 9:20, McLaws was ready to advance ..." The best detailed history of the struggle for the West Woods is Marion V. Armstrong, Jr., *Unfurl Those Colors! McClellan, Sumner, and the Second Army Corps in the Antietam Campaign* (Tuscaloosa, AL, 2008). A condensed version of the events is available in Marion V. Armstrong, Jr., *Disaster in the West Woods: General Edwin V. Sumner and the II Corps at Antietam* (Sharpsburg, MD, 1996).

34 Carman, *The Maryland Campaign*, 2:199.

information provided by McCarthy, suggests that Dinkins could have spotted Robert E. Lee as he watched his army's attack against the West Woods.

As for the intriguing comment about Lee sitting atop a small black horse, Dinkins is the only witness to describe with any precision the mount Lee used at the time. Where Lee got the horse is unknown, but the possibility that he did not ride Traveller during the battle may explain why no other witness mentioned seeing the general atop his famous mount. Lee may have also elected not to ride Traveller while nursing an injured wrist because of the horse's reputation for being difficult to control. As Robert E. Lee, Jr. noted in his postwar reminiscences of the general, his father once lent him Traveller for a ride to Fredericksburg. The stallion, complained the younger Lee, "would not walk a step. He took a short, high trot—a buck-trot . . . some thirty miles. . . . I think I am safe in saying that I could have walked the distance with much less discomfort and fatigue." There is also the matter of Lee holding the reins. Dinkins noted in his 1904 article that Lee reined his horse about when the 18th Mississippi rushed past. Accounting for John Gordon's sighting of Lee behind D. H. Hill's line only a short time earlier, it is possible that from at least 8:45 onward, and despite nursing an injured left wrist, General Lee had personally assumed control of his horse.[35]

Dinkins provides yet another interesting detail that may help shed light on the timing of a well-known incident involving Lee on the morning of September 17 when he collared a straggler fleeing the field with a small pig cradled in his arms. This blatant disregard of his orders against straggling, wrote Armistead Long, coupled with his army fighting for its life at a moment of supreme crisis, prompted Lee to fly "into a hot passion . . . [and he] determined to make an example" of the soldier. He immediately "ordered the man to be arrested and taken back to Jackson with directions to have him shot." Confederate troops "were already scarce" on that part of the field, so Jackson declined to obey the order when the captured straggler appeared before him. Instead, he directed that the man be given a musket and put back into the firing line where the Yankees could shoot him instead of a

---

35 Robert E. Lee, Jr., *Recollections and Letters of General Robert E. Lee* (New York, NY, 1940), 84. On page 373, Lee's son also mentioned Traveller "stepping very proudly," which supports the hypothesis that the horse moved too powerfully for Gen. Lee to have controlled him with an injured wrist. Maj. Thomas L. Broun described Traveller's step as a "rapid, springy walk" in September 1861, also lending credence to the idea that the horse may have been too much for Lee to handle with his hands in an injured state. Letter of Thomas L. Broun to Annie Broun, Sept 16, 1861, in Southern Historical Collection, The Wilson Library, University of North Carolina at Chapel Hill.

Confederate firing squad. The soldier reportedly survived the fight and was thereafter known among his comrades as "the man who had lost his pig but saved his bacon."[36]

The likelihood that this incident with the straggler occurred behind Jackson's line is consistent with Dinkins's observation of Lee in the plowed field south of the Hauser farm, which was located at the rear of Jackson's line on the Confederate left. Dinkins also noted that as his regiment went into battle, "A spotted cow ran through the line, going to our rear" with her tail "high in the air," indicating that men did indeed see livestock at the time.[37]

After McLaws's division and Tige Anderson's brigade went into action in the West Woods, the fighting there raged for roughly an hour, during which Lee appears to have remained on the Reel-Hauser ridge. Evidence for this can be found in the battle report of Capt. Thomas Carter, who recorded seeing the general loitering near his guns during the struggle for the sunken road. That fight broke out around 9:30 a.m., meaning that from his vantage point General Lee witnessed Brig. Gen. William French's division, a part of Edwin Sumner's Second Corps, strike D. H. Hill's line. Carter reported receiving "an order from General Rodes to plant my battery on the left of the Hagerstown road, near the Donaldsonville Artillery," but he immediately requested confirmation of this order from Lee, who, it will be remembered, had posted Carter's guns in the location they occupied at that point. The general gave his consent, but remained where he was when Carter moved.[38]

It might have been during his time on the ridge near Carter that Lee ordered the South Carolina battery (the Macbeth Artillery) under Capt. Robert Boyce to "open fire on a [enemy] battery which had formed on my left almost beyond the range of my pieces." Boyce's report is rather confusing and it is impossible to establish the time Lee issued these instructions. Suffice it to say that Boyce at least

---

36 Long, *Memoirs*, 222. Frederick Tilberg, *Antietam National Battlefield* (Washington, DC, 1960), 25.

37 Dinkins, *Personal Recollections*, 59-60. The cow probably belonged to the Hauser family, on whose farm the incident described by Dinkins took place. William H. Andrews of the 1st Georgia Infantry, George T. Anderson's brigade, also recalled livestock on the field: "while in line of battle in front of Sharpsburg a cow was feeding in front of the line. General Anderson ordered her killed and divided among the men of his brigade." William H. Andrews, "Hardships of Georgia Regulars," in *Confederate Veteran*, Vol. 17, No. 5 (May 1909), 231. In addition, Canton, Mississippi's *The American Citizen*, Nov. 7, 1862, published an eyewitness account from another part of the field, where "we found, mingled with the dead and wounded, a cow, several hogs, a sheep and dog—all on the battlefield, fallen by the same deadly missiles."

38 *OR* 19, 1:1030.

Alexander Gardner's post-battle photo of the Reel farm barn. *National Archives*

provided evidence of Lee himself directing artillery fire during the fight for the sunken road and the West Woods.[39]

Little additional information exists describing Lee's movements during the critical period from 9:30 to 11:00 a.m., but by all indications the general remained in the vicinity of the Reel and Hauser farms. That he would stay in place makes sense given the injuries to his hands and the intensity of the fighting. Although apparently able to direct his own horse for a time, it is unlikely that Lee could keep up the effort long enough to ride out of the area and back again. While in this position, the

39 Boyce recalled: "Early on the morning of the 17th I was ordered by Colonel Walton, chief of artillery, to proceed with my battery beyond the road north of the town of Sharpsburg, to occupy a position to meet the enemy. On reaching the vicinity of the position I supposed I should occupy, I found no person to point it out to me. Colonel Stevens . . . placed me on the slope of the second hill from the road; but, finding my battery could be of no service in this position, I was posted farther down, in front of another battery. Here, discovering that I was still where I could not see the enemy, I moved my battery through a corn-field immediately in front, and, on reaching the farther side of this field, I found the whole line of battle, for at least a mile, extended before me. I placed my guns in battery in easy range of a portion of the line, but had to wait for an opportunity to fire, as our own troops, engaging the enemy, intervened. Shortly after taking this position, General Lee sent me an order to open fire on a battery which had formed on my left almost beyond the range of my pieces." *OR* 19, 1:943.

general probably witnessed Richard Heron Anderson's division coming over the Reel farm ridge to join the fight. There is no evidence of whether it was Lee or Longstreet who sent Anderson his orders to advance.[40]

Captain William T. Poague of Jackson's command offered information for Lee's whereabouts sometime later, recording in his memoir that "about 11 A.M. General Lee with some of his staff rode up to the battery and called for the commanding officer."[41] This observation by Poague begins the tale of the now famous meeting between Lee and his son, Robert, Jr., which took place that day. Lee, wrote Poague,

> wished to know the condition of the battery and its supply of ammunition. I replied that we could . . . use all three guns from our present position, but for any rapid movement only one piece was equipped, as our teams had suffered severely in the morning fights. About this time Private Bob Lee came up and spoke to his father, and said, "You are not going to put us in the fight again in our crippled condition, are you?" "Yes, my son, I may need you" to help to drive those people away" [Lee] replied, as he pointed towards the enemy's lines. After a few pleasant words with his son, General Lee rode away as quietly and composedly as if nothing special was going on.[42]

Joseph Harsh does not accept Poague's claim that it was 11:00 a.m. when all of this happened. Lee, he argued, did not meet his son until between noon and 1:00 p.m. when he rode back behind Jackson's lines to order a counterattack against the Federal right. It is certainly prudent to question the timing of any incident offered

---

40 Presumably, Lee gave the order for Anderson to advance, but there is no evidence to confirm this. Lee's battle report mentions Anderson, but the few details it provides could have easily come from the reports of D. H. Hill, Longstreet, or Col. James Walton rather than from events Lee witnessed himself. *OR* 19, 1:150. Carman, *The Maryland Campaign*, 2:256-260 provides a few additional details about Anderson's deployment.

41 Monroe F. Cockrell, ed., *Gunner with Stonewall: Reminiscences of William T. Poague* (Jackson, TN, 1957), 48. For other accounts of the famous father-son meeting at Sharpsburg, see Moore, *The Story of a Cannoneer*, 153; Lee, Jr., *Recollections*, 77; and Otey, "The Story of Our Great War," 367.

42 Lee, Jr., *Recollections*, 77. Some decades after the war, Jefferson Davis recounted the story of Lee meeting his son as follows: "General Lee told me that at the battle of Sharpsburg this (Poague's) battery suffered so much that it had to be withdrawn for repairs and some fresh horses; but, as he had no troops even to form a reserve, as soon as the battery could be made useful it was ordered forward. He said that as it passed him a boy mounted as a driver of one of the guns, much stained with powder, said, 'Are you going to put us in again, general?' After replying to him in the affirmative, he was struck by the voice of the boy and asked him, 'Whose son are you?' to which he answered, 'I am Robbie,' whereupon his father said, 'God bless you, my son, you must go in'." Jefferson Davis, "Robert E. Lee," in *The North American Review*, Vol. 150, No. 398 (Jan. 1890), 64.

by participants during the heat of battle. In this case, however, Harsh's effort to place the event later in the day required that he devise a complicated argument—including the claim that Lee rode long distances—to make the evidence fit his chronology. This is unfortunate because there is no good reason to reject Poague's recollection of 11:00 a.m. as anything other than generally accurate. No available source contradicts Poague, and it makes sense that Lee would have remained behind the portion of his line that faced the most sustained Federal attack that morning, particularly since he had expressed concern about the stability of his army's left flank to Captain Carter only hours earlier.[43]

After the war, Robert E. Lee, Jr. noted that "our battery had been severely handled, losing many men and horses. Having three guns disabled, we were ordered to withdraw and, while moving back, we passed General Lee and several of his staff grouped on a little knoll near the road." The mention of a road is significant. Ordinarily, it might be assumed that the younger Lee meant the Hagerstown Pike, but there is another road that ran behind the Reel farm known today as Mondel Road. Poague's battery had been active on the left of Jackson's line that morning, a location to which Mondel Road and a cross-country farm lane provided direct access. The road runs straight behind Jackson's position past the Reel and Hauser farms and, as it approaches Sharpsburg, the ground east of the road rises to a low knoll. Moving to the army's rear via Mondel Road would have made the most sense given where the battery had seen action and where its guns were disabled.[44]

Poague's battery had run low on ammunition and had no choice but to travel back to the army's supply depot on the Shepherdstown Pike west of Lee's headquarters to refill its caissons. It is almost certain that the captain would have used local roads for this job because crossing the countryside involved the impossible task of having to pass through or around stone and rail fences. These considerations render it most likely that the younger Lee spotted his father along Mondel Road near the Reel farm.

Another well-known incident supports General Lee being on the Reel farm ridge throughout the fight for the sunken road, i.e., the working of two guns by Longstreet's staff after the collapse of D. H. Hill's line. Longstreet's subordinates were manning the pieces, part of Capt. Merritt B. Miller's 3rd Company of the

43 Harsh, *Taken*, 406.

44 Lee, Jr., *Recollections*, 77.

Washington Artillery, in an apple orchard on the Henry Piper farm when Col. Robert Chilton of Gen. Lee's staff rode up. "[W]here are the troops you are holding your line with?" he asked. Longstreet pointed to his two guns and to Col. John Rogers Cooke's 27th North Carolina Infantry regiment: "there they are; but that regiment hasn't a cartridge." The colonel's eyes "popped as though they would come out of his head," recalled Longstreet, and "he struck spurs to his horse and away he went to General Lee."[45]

It is clear from Chilton's language that Lee had sent the colonel to Longstreet in this moment of crisis. It suggests as well that Lee witnessed the collapse of Hill's line with his own eyes. Harsh disagrees, and instead posited the theory that Chilton's visit occurred after Lee returned to Cemetery Hill at noon. Once there, the general heard about the collapse of Hill's line and sent Chilton to investigate.[46]

Little of this scenario makes sense. Lee had already displayed a determination that morning to be present within sight of the heaviest fighting. He had collared stragglers behind Jackson's line and helped form a new defensive position anchored by artillery on the Reel-Hauser ridge. Multiple sources place Lee on the ridge in the hours before Hill's line broke, and none of them suggest that he moved from his position until around noon, when Colonel Walton met him on Cemetery Hill. Given this evidence and Lee's limited mobility because of the injuries to his hands, it seems more probable that the general personally witnessed the disintegration of Hill's command from the vicinity of the Reel and Hauser farms.

Determining exactly when all of this occurred is difficult because the sources are not clear on the hour. The best that can be done is estimate the time-frame based on events that occurred around the same moment. According to Ezra Carman, around 11:30 a.m., a section of Capt. Joseph Knap's Independent Battery

---

45 Longstreet, "The Invasion of Maryland," 669, and Sorrel, *Recollections*, 112. Several Confederate veterans publicly contradicted Longstreet's version of the abandoned guns event after the war, claiming that North Carolina officers and not the general's staff had manned them. A close reading of their accounts suggests, however, that they recalled a separate incident of an abandoned Napoleon located west of the Hagerstown Pike, which four men from the 14th North Carolina manned and fired at the Federals near the sunken road. See Thomas B. Beall, "Reminiscences About Sharpsburg," in *Confederate Veteran*, Vol. 1, No. 8 (Aug. 1893), 246; "Letters from Veterans" in *Confederate Veteran*, Vol. 3, No. 2 (Feb. 1895), 50; Comment by Thomas M. Murphree of the 6th Alabama in *Confederate Veteran*, Vol. 3, No. 1 (Jan. 1895), 11; and William H. Healy, "That Artillery At Sharpsburg," in *Confederate Veteran*, Vol. 3, No. 5 (May 1895), 131. Cooke allegedly replied to Longstreet's orders, "I am out of ammunition, but I will hold this position as long as one man can stand on his legs." *Fayetteville Observer*, Oct. 27, 1862.

46 Harsh, *Taken*, 405.

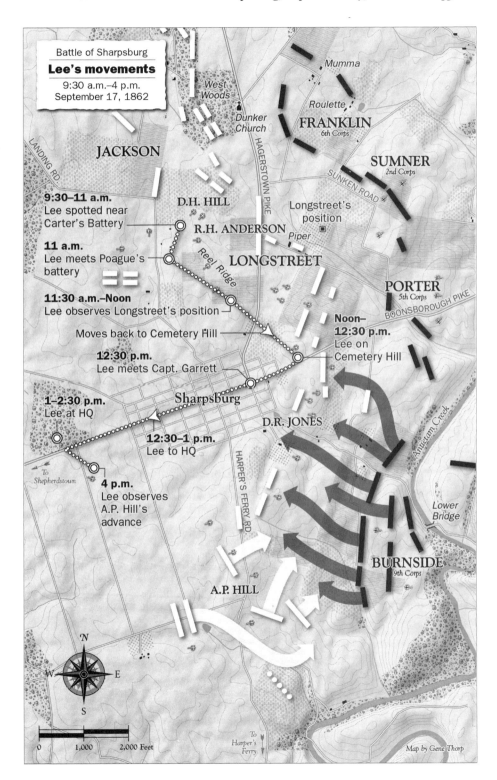

Battle of Sharpsburg
Lee's movements
9:30 a.m.–4 p.m.
September 17, 1862

West
Woods

Mumma

Roulette

Dunker
Church

FRANKLIN
6th Corps

JACKSON

LANDING RD.

SUMNER
2nd Corps

SUNKEN ROAD

HAGERSTOWN PIKE

9:30–11 a.m.
Lee spotted near
Carter's Battery

D.H. HILL

Longstreet's
position

R.H. ANDERSON

Piper

11 a.m.
Lee meets Poague's
battery

Reel Ridge

LONGSTREET

PORTER
5th Corps

BOONSBOROUGH PIKE

11:30 a.m.–Noon
Lee observes Longstreet's position

Moves back to Cemetery Hill

**Noon–
12:30 p.m.**
Lee on
Cemetery Hill

12:30 p.m.
Lee meets Capt. Garrett

Sharpsburg

Antietam Creek

D.R. JONES

1–2:30 p.m.
Lee at HQ

12:30–1 p.m.
Lee to HQ

*To
Shepherdstown*

HARPER'S FERRY RD.

*Lower
Bridge*

4 p.m.
Lee observes
A.P. Hill's
advance

BURNSIDE
9th Corps

A.P. HILL

N
W — E
S

0   1,000   2,000 Feet

*To
Harper's
Ferry*

Map by Gene Thorp

E, Pennsylvania Light Artillery, rolled up the Hagerstown Pike to the Dunker Church, where it faced a charge by Cooke's 27th North Carolina ordered by Longstreet. This event took place between 11:30 a.m. and noon, i.e., it occurred after D. H. Hill's line had crumbled, but around the same time that Longstreet's staff was working the section of Miller's guns. It is reasonable to conclude that Lee must have watched this from the Reel-Hauser ridge and not from Cemetery Hill, where an intervening hilltop blocked any view of Longstreet's (and most of Hill's) position.[47]

Lee probably also witnessed the collection and deployment of a so-called "Straggler's Brigade" by John Bell Hood around this time. Hood had marched his depleted division to a position near the Reel farm before McLaws pushed his division into the West Woods. Once there, Hood received orders (there is no record showing from whom) to form his men into a V-shaped picket line down which stragglers could be passed to a collection point. "In the course of two or three hours," recalled J. S. Johnston of the 11th Mississippi, "5000 men had been collected at this point. They were then formed into companies, regiments, and a brigade" and sent back into action as General Lee looked on "with bared head and [a] calm, but anxious expression, under the shade of an apple tree." That Lee would betray anxiety makes sense given the collapse of D. H. Hill's line in the sunken road.[48]

All of this probably occurred between 11:30 a.m. and noon, despite Johnston's estimate that the Straggler's Brigade returned to the front line about 4:00 p.m. Hood, for example, reported that his command, which had been responsible for assembling the Straggler's Brigade, returned to the front (Longstreet's line on the Hagerstown Pike) at noon. According to Johnston, thanks to Federal inactivity at this time, "nothing was required of this brigade but to remain as a reserve to

47 OR 19, 1:840; Sorrel, *Recollections*, 113; Long, *Memoirs*, 219; OR 19, 1:849. Carman, *The Maryland Campaign*, 2:315. A letter written by George McNeill of the Washington Artillery to Andrew Hero in May 1896 mentions that the men of Miller's battery spotted Longstreet on the field "near 12 o.c." NA, Antietam Battlefield Board Correspondence, Record Group 94, Records of the Adjutant General's Office, Longstreet Folder, Box 2. My thanks to Tom Clemens for the source.

48 Rev. J. S. Johnston, "A Reminiscence of Sharpsburg," in *SHSP* (1880), 8:528. Also see Historical Reminiscences of J. S. Johnston, 11th Mississippi Infantry, San Antonio, Texas. *The Daily Express*, Oct. 31, 1909, in Owen, McBride, and Allport, eds., *Texans at Antietam*, 242. Johnston's estimate of 5,000 men collected is surely an overstatement. Johnston reported that Lee commented at the time, "Men, I want you to go back on the line and show that the stragglers of the Army of Northern Virginia are better than the best troops of the enemy."

General Pryor, who occupied the line in their immediate front." The remnants of Pryor's brigade, part of Richard Anderson's division, had collected along the Hagerstown Pike following the retreat from the sunken road. Finally, Johnston described how Hood's sojourn behind the lines lasted several hours, putting its return to action within the period after the collapse of D. H. Hill's line.[49]

It is about this time, before he moved on to observe events elsewhere, that Lee ordered Jackson to deliver a counterattack against the Army of the Potomac's right flank. According to Harsh, Lee did not issue this order until between noon and 1:00 p.m., after he had ridden back to the left to meet with Jackson. This estimate is probably too late. There is no evidence that Lee returned to the Reel farm ridge once he departed from it just before noon. Moreover, as Lee himself noted in his August 1863 battle report, he sent the order to Jackson "while the attack on our center was progressing."[50] Other references in his report make it is clear that Lee was referring to the attack on the sunken road. For example, two pages earlier Lee wrote, "The attack on our left was speedily followed by one in heavy force on the center. This was met by part of Walker's division and the brigades of G. B. Anderson and Rodes." Lee noted shortly afterward, "While the attack on the center and left was in progress, the enemy made repeated efforts to force the passage of the [Rohrbach] bridge over the Antietam, opposite the right wing of General Longstreet."[51]

Longstreet's battle report, dated October 10, 1862, also supports and earlier time for Lee's order to Jackson to launch a counterattack:

> General Jackson soon moved off to our left for the purpose of turning the enemy's right flank. . . . As these movements were made, the enemy again threw forward his masses against my left. This attack was met by Walker's division, two pieces of Captain Miller's battery, of the Washington Artillery, and two pieces of Captain Boyce's battery, and was driven back in some confusion. An effort was made to pursue, but our line was too weak.

---

49 "My command was marched to the rear, ammunition replenished, and returned at 12m., taking position, by direction of the general commanding, in rear of the church, with orders to hold it." The 'general commanding' to whom Hood referred was Longstreet, not Lee. *OR* 19, 1:923. Also see Polley, *Hood's Texas Brigade*, 132-133. "The Texas Brigade was then ordered a short distance to the rear for a fresh supply of ammunition, and again *returned to the front about noon* [emphasis added] and found the woods near the church lately occupied by them, in possession of the enemy."

50 Harsh, *Taken*, 406; *OR* 19, 1:151.

51 *OR* 19, 1:149-150.

Colonel Cooke, of the Twenty-seventh North Carolina, very gallantly charged with his own regiment, but, his supply of ammunition being exhausted and he being unsupported, he was obliged to return to his original position in the line.[52]

John Walker's battle report supports the earlier time frame as well. "While I was with General Ransom's command, about 4.30 o'clock in the afternoon," recalled Walker,

an order was brought from General Longstreet directing General Ransom to advance and capture the enemy's batteries in his front. *Having been previously instructed* [emphasis added] by General Jackson to hold my position in the woods until General Stuart could turn the enemy's right and then to advance, I directed General Ransom to delay the execution of General Longstreet's order until I could see General Longstreet, in person, and confer with him on the subject. Upon my representations to him, he approved what I had done, and, while we were in conversation on the subject, General Jackson himself joined us, and informed us that *General Stuart had made the attempt spoken of* [emphasis added] but found it impracticable, as the enemy's right was securely posted on the Potomac and protected by heavy batteries of his reserve artillery.[53]

The testimony of Heros von Borcke, Jeb Stuart's chief of staff, is also worth considering. "[A]bout midday I was sent by General Stuart to our cavalry with orders that they should press forward, in corresponding movement with the infantry, up the bank of the Potomac," recalled von Borcke. Jackson wanted to Stuart to lead the attack and had forwarded Lee's order on to him. Stuart, in turn, issued the order to von Borcke. This is good evidence that that Lee transmitted his attack order before noon while he was still on the ridge behind Jackson's command. Lee likely conveyed his instructions to Jackson no later than 11:30 a.m., which was about the time that Longstreet was holding the army's broken center with two field pieces and a single North Carolina infantry regiment. Von Borcke also noted that Stuart sent him "with orders that [the cavalry] should press forward," implying that the horsemen had already collected and were prepared to move. Forming for an advance took time, which lends credence to the argument

---

52 OR 19, 1:840. The reference to Cooke confirms that Jackson had received orders to make the attack on the Federal right before noon.

53 Ibid., 1:916.

that Lee must have issued the attack order well before noon if Stuart's command, according to von Borcke, was ready to advance by midday.[54]

A Union army source also attests to Stuart initiating his attack around midday. Writing on September 22, 1862, only five days after the battle, Lt. Col. J. William Hofmann of the 56th Pennsylvania, commanding the Second Brigade in Abner Doubleday's First Division, testified as follows:

> about 11.30 o'clock, by order of General Doubleday, I moved the brigade to our front and left about 300 yards. . . . The brigade had been in this position *about half an hour* [emphasis added], when a large cavalry force was passing in rear of a narrow strip of wood, evidently attempting to attack us in flank; on the right a heavy body of infantry, much larger than my own, immediately followed.[55]

Hofmann's brigade occupied a position on the Federal right, which is precisely the place Lee had ordered Stuart to strike. The sight of a Federal super-battery numbering as many as 50 guns eventually stopped Stuart in his tracks, so no Confederate counterattack developed on that part of the field. Jackson, either on his own authority or in response to orders given to him by Lee during a mid-afternoon visit to army headquarters, ordered Stuart to test the enemy by directly engaging their artillery. William Poague attested to the failed attempt in his battle report: "Later in the day I was ordered, with my only remaining piece, to report to General Stuart on the left. Along with six or eight other guns, under the direction of Major Pelham, an attempt was made to dislodge the enemy's batteries, but failed completely, [we] being silenced in fifteen or twenty minutes by a most terrific fire from a number of the enemy's batteries."[56]

In summary, the evidence is that Lee gave Jackson his counterattack order before noon. When the attack proved impossible to carry out, Lee (or Jackson) ordered Stuart to shell the Federal line. When that failed, Lee set aside the idea of launching a counterattack that afternoon in favor of revisiting the subject the following day (September 18). Stuart found the Federal position too strong to

54 Von Borcke, *Memoirs*, 232.

55 *OR* 19, 1:236. Also see Clark, "The Battle of Sharpsburg," 91.

56 The estimate of the number of assembled Federal guns comes from Harsh, *Taken*, 442. *OR* 19, 1:1010.

assault on that day as well, forcing Lee to permanently abandon the idea of an attack against the Federal right.[57]

After ordering Jackson to launch a counterattack and his encounter with the Straggler's Brigade, General Lee departed the Reel-Hauser ridge for the last time. He had watched the battle for the West Woods and the sunken road rage in front of him there for nearly three hours—a period significantly longer than hour or less he had lingered atop Cemetery Hill. The Reel-Hauser ridge offer a better line of sight than Cemetery Hill for Lee to observe the attacks against his army's left and center and provided him with the opportunity to intervene directly in affairs at the tactical level, as his effort to arrange a counterattack demonstrates.

While D. H. Hill and James Longstreet struggled to maintain a defensive line in the Confederate center, Lee assisted them by collecting gun batteries on the heights behind Longstreet's position. Only a small number of Confederate infantry remained in the vicinity of the Reel farm. By noon, however, Lee had developed a powerful artillery position to anchor the army's center. This gun line may have helped deter further Federal attacks in that sector. In this sense, the Reel-Hauser ridge became an important part of the Army of Northern Virginia's defensive line during the battle, and it was Robert E. Lee who personally selected it during a moment of supreme crisis.

With the center of his line at least temporarily shored up, and plans in motion for Jackson and Stuart to counterattack on the left, Lee rode back to Cemetery Hill to observe the state of affairs on his army's right flank before returning to headquarters. What he saw from the heights east of Sharpsburg was anything but heartening. Around noon, Brig. Gen. Alfred Pleasonton, acting under orders from General McClellan, pushed cavalry and horse artillery across the creek to take up a position on the high ground several hundred yards east of Cemetery Hill. Lee had at his disposal only the small independent brigade of Brig. Gen. Shanks Evans and a handful of artillery pieces to meet this threat. At the same time, heavy firing continued off to the southeast around the Rohrbach Bridge, where Ambrose Burnside pressed his attack against Col. Henry Benning's two regiments of Georgia infantry defending the span.

About noon, Lee met Col. James Walton and Capt. William Owen of the Washington Artillery of New Orleans. "While standing with Col. Walton in Squires' battery, about noon, Gen. Lee walked over to us. One hand was in a sling,

---

57 Harsh, *Taken*, 441-444 describes Lee's efforts on September 18 in detail.

it not having recovered from the accident at the second Manassas; the other held his field-glass." Owen continued:

> He said, in his quiet way, 'Well, Colonel [Walton], what do you make of the enemy: what is he going to do?' The Colonel replied, 'They seem to be moving a battery more to our right.' At this moment a courier rode up, holding in his hand a dispatch, which he held out to the General, and, both of his hands being engaged, I took it from the courier and read it to him. It was as follows: 'The enemy is moving a six-gun battery to our right, evidently with the intention of covering with it their crossing.' It was signed 'Johnson, Engineer Officer.' 'Yes,' said the General, 'I see they are. Colonel, can you spare this young officer (Captain Owen) to ride for me? None of my staff are present.' Of course the Colonel said 'Yes,' and I modestly awaited my instructions, feeling considerable pride that I was about to do something for Gen. Lee. Turning to me the General said, 'Go to Gen. D. R. Jones, and tell him I wish that battery (Eshleman's)' — indicating with his field-glass the one he meant — 'moved farther to the right, to cover the lower ford, where the enemy will soon endeavor to cross. Let it be done at once.' Saluting, and springing upon my horse, I plunged down the ravine, and up the other side to the orchard. . . . [Later] I rode back to where I had left Gen. Lee, and, dismounting, reported 'the order had been obeyed.' He replied, 'I see it has. Thank you, *'Captain'*.'[58]

The sources are vague on Lee's movements this hour, but based on Owen's recollection, the general appears to have lingered on Cemetery Hill for about half an hour before making his way back to army headquarters on the west side of Sharpsburg. At least one witness, Capt. Thomas Garrett of the 5th North Carolina Infantry (a regiment that had broken and fled to the rear when D. H. Hill's brigades retreated from the north end of the field around 8:15 a.m.), met Lee in the town's streets after the general came off Cemetery Hill. Garrett had entered Sharpsburg to search for men from his command. After reporting this to Lee, the general "ordered [me] to rally all the stragglers I could, without regard to what command they belonged, and report with them to General Evans" atop Cemetery Hill. This exchange demonstrated Lee's concern about the weakness of his line opposite the Middle Bridge.[59]

58 Owen, *In Camp and Battle*, 151. Emphasis in the source.

59 Garrett described this incident as follows: "Seeing a regiment of the enemy coming up in the open field in our front and somewhat on the flank, and the breastwork turning where the right of the regiment rested in such a manner as to expose a few files of men of my regiment, I ordered these to deploy as flankers to the right and take shelter behind the trees. At this moment, and while directing this movement. Captain [T. P.] Thomson, Company G, came up

After his interaction with Captain Garrett, Lee proceeded to his headquarters where he found Brig. Gen. Wade Hampton, the commander of a brigade of cavalry, waiting for him. According to Carman, Hampton had "acted as rear-guard to McLaws in the march from Harper's Ferry and crossing [of] the Potomac" before reaching "the vicinity of Lee's headquarters about the middle of the forenoon" (approximately 10:00 a.m.) while Lee was on the Reel-Hauser ridge. Left without orders, and with no idea where his men should go, Hampton waited for Lee "until about 1 p.m.," when the general returned and immediately ordered Hampton to join Jeb Stuart's move against the Federal right, a directive indicating that Jackson had not yet reported the maneuver's failure to headquarters.[60]

Sending Hampton to the left instead of to the right also suggests that by 1:00 p.m. Lee had not learned of Burnside's and Cox's victory at the Rohrbach Bridge. The news would not be long in coming, and its arrival sent Lee scrambling for all the troops and artillery he could find. Stonewall Jackson and his aide, Lt. Henry Kyd Douglas, arrived at headquarters around this time, possibly to report the impossibility of launching a counter-stroke against the Federal right. A courier arrived with news. "Burnside's advance was reported," recalled Douglas, prompting Lee to ask Jackson for guns with an "absolutely reliable battery" to be sent to the army's right. Jackson "sent for Graham's section of Poague's Rockbridge Artillery," to reinforce the small number of defenders on the army's right flank.[61]

At Lee's prompting, Jackson also sent orders for the 21st Georgia "to report to General R. E. Lee's headquarters, on the Sharpsburg and Sheppardstown pike." James Nisbet, commander of the regiment, wrote later that upon "reporting to General Lee, whom I found viewing our right-field through his glasses, and giving orders to couriers as they arrived, I was ordered to form my Regiment across the pike, and halt all stragglers coming out of the town."[62]

By this time Lee was anxiously awaiting the arrival of Ambrose Powell Hill's Light Division, which he had ordered earlier that morning to make a forced march

---

to me, and in a very excited manner and tone cried out to me, 'They are flanking us! See, yonder's a whole brigade!' I ordered him to keep silence and return to his place. The men before this were far from being cool, but, when this act of indiscretion occurred, a panic ensued, and, despite the efforts of file-closers and officers, they began to break and run." *OR* 19, 1:1044.

60 Carman, *The Maryland Campaign*, 2:336-337.

61 Douglas, *I Rode with Stonewall*, 173.

62 Nisbet, *Four Years on the Firing Line*, 156.

to Sharpsburg from Harpers Ferry. Hill personally arrived at army headquarters ahead of his column around 2:30 p.m., soon after advance riders had alerted Lee about Hill's troops crossing the Potomac below Shepherdstown. Lee greeted Little Powell as he rode up: "General Hill I was never so glad to see you, you are badly needed, put your force in on the right as fast as they come up." Lee sent Hill to Brig. Gen. David R. "Neighbor" Jones, the senior commander on the right flank, for information on "the character of the ground as was necessary" for Hill to deploy his troops.[63]

After Hill rode off Lee began directing artillery, the one resource he had in relative abundance, to reinforce the army's right flank. This time, however, officers from the headquarters staff delivered the orders instead of Lee himself. As Capt. John Read, a Georgian in command of the Pulaski Artillery, recalled in his post-battle report, "about 3 p.m. . . . I was ordered by one of General Lee's staff to take my two rifle guns and report to him (Gen. Lee), who was in the woods on the left-hand side of the road this side of the town. I did so, and was ordered to take my guns and place them in a position so as to bear upon the enemy across some fields over on the right of the road."[64]

The axle of Read's three-inch Ordnance Rifle broke en route to his position, taking the gun out of action. His remaining 10-lb. Parrott Rifle continued firing as ordered. Colonel Stephen Dill Lee received similar instructions while returning through Sharpsburg from the army's ammunition depot on the Shepherdstown Pike west of Lee's headquarters: "About 3 p.m., the batteries having [been] refitted and replenished with ammunition," he recalled, "I again moved to the front with twelve guns, all that could be manned, and received orders from one of General Longstreet's aides to take position in front of the village of Sharpsburg, to the right and left of the turnpike, relieving Colonel Walton, of the Washington Artillery of New Orleans."[65]

---

63 White, *Robert E. Lee*, 222. "Couriers brought to Lee news of A. P. Hill's rapid approach from Harper's Ferry." Hill himself reported, "The head of my column arrived upon the battle-field of Sharpsburg, a distance of 17 miles, at 2.30 o'clock, and, re-porting in person to General Lee, he directed me to take position on our right." Carman, *The Maryland Campaign*, 2:463. Also see OR 19, 1:981: "Brig. Gen. D. R. Jones, commanding on our right, gave me such information as my ignorance of the ground made necessary."

64 According to Longstreet, in *From Manassas to Appomattox*, 261, "Batteries from all parts of our field drove to General Lee." See also, OR 19, 1:866-867.

65 OR 19, 1:845-846.

The hour had now reached 4:00 p.m., bringing with it the penultimate crisis faced by Lee's army that day. Burnside's and Cox's powerful attack was rolling up the hills toward Sharpsburg, pushing back Neighbor Jones's outnumbered Rebel defenders to the Harpers Ferry Road. General Lee continued directing guns and stragglers back into the fight from high ground on Sharpsburg's western limits and south of the Shepherdstown Pike, where he could see Jones's defensive line through the drifting haze of houses burning in town.[66]

Federal battle flags were beginning to appear on the high ground opposite the Confederate line when Jones himself arrived at headquarters with dire news that enemy troops had taken the town. Before Lee had an opportunity to respond, Capt. James R. Troup of Brig. Gen. Robert Toombs's staff rode up with a request for artillery. If more guns can be sent, pleaded Troup, General Toombs could push the enemy back across Antietam Creek. "What! Haven't the enemy got Sharpsburg?" asked the flabbergasted Jones, to which Troup responded "no, they had it, but have been driven out, and we have it." Lee ordered Troup to "take any guns he can find [for Toombs], and use them as he thinks best." Lee next sought Captain Squires of the Washington Artillery, whose command had fallen back to replenish its ammunition chests. Squires later claimed to have rallied as many as 1,000 stragglers he found in the rear near the depot, which may have been what brought him to Lee's attention. Whatever the case, Lee ordered Squires to report to Toombs with any rifled pieces he could find.[67]

Once Squires left to shore up the army's right flank, Lee peered to the southwest in anticipation of A. P. Hill's arrival, an act that suggests Jones may have informed Lee about the route Hill would take to reach the field. At some point after meeting Squires, who "found him on foot," Lee climbed once again into the saddle, although the identity of the horse he rode cannot be established. A section of rifled guns under the command of Lt. John A. Ramsay trundled up behind Lee, who noticed that Ramsay possessed a telescope. Ramsay's section had been idle near the

---

66 Sharpsburg "had several houses in full blaze" by this time according to Squires, "Boy Officer," 20.

67 Henry L. Benning, "Notes by General H. L. Benning on the Battle of Sharpsburg" in *SHSP*, Vol. 16 (1888), 395. Squires, "Boy Officer," 20. D. R. Jones never mentioned in his after-action report whether he encountered Lee mounted or dismounted. The assumption made here is that Lee was on foot at that time.

artillery depot most of the day waiting for ammunition for its two 10-lb. Parrott Rifles.[68]

Lee directed the artillery officer to use his telescope to identify troops he spotted approaching in the distance. Ramsay invited the general to use the glass himself, but unable to hold it steady with his injured hands, Lee declined. "What troops are those?" he asked, pointing to the Federal battle line near Harpers Ferry Road. Ramsay squinted through his glass and informed Lee that "they are flying the United States flag." Lee swung his hand to the right and asked Ramsay about the troops coming up from that direction. Ramsay looked again through his glass and answered that the men in question were "flying the Virginia and Confederate flags." "It is A. P. Hill, from Harper's Ferry," replied Lee, relieved at the last-minute arrival of his army's only available reinforcements.[69]

Lee instructed Ramsay to take position on the knoll and fire at the enemy troops he could see. Ramsay protested the order by explaining that doing so would draw Federal counter-battery fire onto their position, to which Lee responded, "never mind me." With that Ramsay commenced firing, helping to drive off the enemy infantry that Lee had pointed out to him. "Well done!" cheered the general, who told the artillerist to "elevate [his] guns and continue the fire until [A. P. Hill's] troops [came] near the line of fire, then change . . . position to the ridge on the right of the line and fire on the troops beyond the creek." After posting Ramsay's section, Lee rode off and soon encountered another set of guns procuring ammunition from the nearby depot. This battery, the 3rd Company of the Washington Artillery, included four Napoleons under Capt. Merritt B. Miller. Lee stopped the captain and ordered him to "an elevated and commanding position on the right and rear of the town, where General A. P. Hill had but just begun his attack."[70]

Lee remained in the vicinity of his headquarters for the balance of the day. The Ninth Corps' assault faltered under the blow Hill delivered against its exposed left flank and retreated toward Antietam Creek, ending the afternoon near the position originally held by Colonel Benning's Georgians. General Lee had been patrolling

---

68 Squires, "Boy Officer," 20.

69 Ramsay, "Additional Sketch Tenth Regiment: Light Batteries A, D, F, and I," in Clark, ed., *Histories of the Several Regiments and Battalions from North Carolina*, 1:575.

70 Ibid. Ramsay noted "General Lee then rode off," after their conversation, suggesting Lee had once again taken personal control of his horse. *OR* 19, 1:850.

the grounds near his encampment since about 1:00 p.m., rallying stragglers and sending artillery into the fight on the army's right flank. Much as he had done during the morning's crisis on the center-left, the general cobbled together an artillery position on the heights behind his lines to support the army's right flank and to provide a fallback position should one be required. A. P. Hill's arrival forestalled that need by solidifying the line and relieving the pressure exerted by the Federal Ninth Corps. Hill's division may have saved the day, but for many a long hour Robert E. Lee himself played an important role in blunting the enemy's attacks.

The fight at Sharpsburg was a very personal one for General Lee, who looked for every opportunity to control events on the field as they slipped toward chaos and a potentially war-ending defeat.

CONCLUSION

CONFEDERATE FAILURE IN MARYLAND

ᴍ

The End of the Beginning

"Now this is not the end. It is not even the beginning of the end.
But it is, perhaps, the end of the beginning."

— Winston Churchill, The Lord Mayor's Luncheon, Mansion House, London, Nov. 10, 1942

STUDENTS of history tend to think that our understanding of the past grows more complete with every generation, and to no subject is this belief more applicable than the American Civil War. Large numbers of books and articles about the war arrive every year, a portion of which deal with the Maryland Campaign; yet, we seem no closer to answering the question of why Robert E. Lee decided to fight a dangerous and, some have said, unnecessary battle at Sharpsburg on September 16-17, 1862. Facing down an enemy army roughly twice the size of his own, and with his own force weakened by straggling, Lee chose to fight without all his troops on the field and only a single, difficult route of retreat at his back. In a wartime career marked by episodes of extreme risk-taking, Lee's stand at Sharpsburg must be considered one of his most audacious acts, hazarding his army and perhaps even the Confederate cause itself to accomplish—what, exactly?

There is no widely accepted answer to this question. Is this because an answer is out of reach or because certain realities of the situation at the time have been lost over the years, rendering a clear understanding difficult? What might scholars of the Maryland Campaign be missing? Two persistent factors appear to be clouding the issue: a tendency to speculate on Lee's motives rather than to rely on the written evidence and a stubborn unwillingness to consider the secessionist dimensions of Lee's thinking.

Taking the latter subject first, the first chapter of this book demonstrates by using Lee's own words that he hoped a "military success" (i.e., a battlefield victory) would encourage Maryland's citizens to rise up and "recover their liberties." Based on letters he wrote to Jefferson Davis on September 7 and 12, and a comment he made to a Baltimore man that was reported in the *Philadelphia Inquirer*, it appears Lee developed this perspective after speaking with a number of secessionists in Frederick City. Lee then seems to have expressed his revised understanding of the situation in Maryland to at least one member of his headquarters staff, Armistead Long, who echoed the theme in his 1886 military biography of the general.[1]

Writing that as of noon on September 15 "Two courses now presented themselves . . . each of which involved results of the highest importance," Long explained how

> He (Lee) might either retire across the Potomac and form a junction, in the neighborhood of Shepherdstown, with the forces that had been employed in the reduction of Harper's Ferry, or maintain his position at Sharpsburg and give battle to a superior force. *By pursuing the former course the object of the campaign would be abandoned and the hope of co-operation from Maryland for ever relinquished.* The latter, although hazardous, if successful would be productive of results more than commensurate with the risk attending its execution. *Having a sympathy for the Marylanders, to whom he had offered his services, and a confidence in the bravery of his troops and the strength of his position, he adopted the latter course, and prepared to receive the attack of General McClellan* [emphasis added].[2]

Although Long may be accused of rank speculation because he did not cite any particular conversation with Lee, unlike Charles Marshall's postwar comments concerning the alleged "strategic dilemma" Lee faced prior to the Maryland operation, Long's remarks have the benefit of matching what Lee himself wrote to Jefferson Davis in his August 19, 1863, report on the Maryland Campaign. According to Long, Lee believed he had more to gain than to lose from fighting at Sharpsburg, including, most importantly, proving that his men stood ready to spill blood to help Marylanders reassert the liberties Confederates believed they had lost. At the same time, Lee understood the need to secure the support of

1   OR 19, 1:144.

2   Long, *Memoirs*, 216.

Maryland's people to pry the state from the Union, confiding to William Allan in a candid conversation on April 15, 1868, that his army alone could never hold the "hostile portions" of Northern territory it had occupied. Both Lee's own words and the observations of his military secretary make it clear that the general hoped by force of arms to achieve Maryland's secession from the union (i.e., a political objective) and yet this dimension of Lee's reasoning is routinely overlooked or dismissed as a motivating factor in his thinking.[3]

Also important is the fact that in a war often interpreted (either correctly or incorrectly—no judgment is offered here) as taking place between an aggressive North and a defensive South seeking only to be left in peace, Lee's political aims in Maryland represented a mortal threat to what remained of the United States after the Secession Winter of 1860-61. Moving north of the Potomac River to achieve a military victory that forced the Lincoln administration to sue for peace was one thing. Embarking on an offensive to pry Maryland out of the Union—per stated Confederate government war aims—threatened the remaining territorial integrity of the United States. In that sense, the political dimension of Lee's Maryland operation rendered it a direct attack on the United States, as opposed to an offensive movement intended to defend Virginia, which is how Lost Cause apologists came to portray the campaign.

Many complexities, legal, cultural, political, and otherwise, attend the interpretation of secession as treason and they are beyond the scope of this book. The Maryland Campaign appears to present a different issue altogether, particularly if Robert E. Lee's political objectives are considered. Having undertaken the invasion without explicit orders from President Davis (the Confederate president's sentiments in favor of it are another story), Lee's actions could have been considered an act of treason worthy of trial and execution once the war came to an end. Carrying an army north to encourage secession had nothing to do with the theoretical legality of secession itself as it had manifested in 1860-61. Instead, it had everything to do with leading an army onto United States soil specifically to excise a portion of the nation's territory. Pursuing such a radical objective could be one reason why Lee explained his rationale for the invasion to Davis in obtuse language, *ergo* as a way of avoiding an outright statement of his intentions, and why

---

3 See chapter one for a critique of the "strategic dilemma" thesis. Lee's phrasing in the April 1868 conversation is telling. Stating that there were "hostile portions" of the North implied that he thought there were portions of territory above the Potomac which were *not* hostile to the Confederacy. See Allan, "Memoranda," in Gallagher, ed., *Lee the Soldier*, 13.

once the effort had failed those who had encouraged it the most vehemently, such as Bradley Johnson, tried to cast the offensive operation in a purely defensive light. After all, they themselves shared culpability.

Studies of the Maryland Campaign have not always minimized the political dimensions of Lee's operation. As early as 1866, William Swinton concluded that "Aiming to raise the standard of revolt in Maryland, and rally the citizens of that State around the secession cause" led Lee to turn his columns north. Ten years later, the Comte de Paris argued that Lee "determined to accept battle on the soil he had invaded [because] the political causes which had rendered that invasion an imperative necessity did not admit of its being abandoned without trying the fortune of arms . . . [and because] the position chosen by Lee compensated to some extent for the numerical inferiority of his army." Lee believed the invasion of Maryland necessary, argued the Count, because he expected the state to rally to the Confederate cause and provide support for his troops.[4]

Tactical considerations during the campaign then sealed the decision in Lee's mind because the heights west of Antietam Creek provided his army with a formidable position it could defend against the pursuing Army of the Potomac. Francis Palfrey added to this calculation the influence of Lee's pride, writing in 1893 that given his "strong defensive position . . . Lee proceeded to form his men for the action which events had so forced upon him [and which he] could not avoid . . . without [a] loss of prestige." To this early generation of writers, honor-driven, tactically-informed politics provided the rationale upon which Lee based what may have been the most audacious military decision of his career—to confront a superior enemy force with a greatly depleted army in a location offering only one difficult route of retreat.[5]

Lee's influential biographer, Douglas Southall Freeman, did not think these reasons sufficient to explain the general's decision. Turning instead to unvarnished speculation, Freeman argued that Lee's low opinion of his opponent at Sharpsburg, George McClellan, must have also figured into the equation. Describing McClellan as "A cautious adversary who had never yet fought an offensive battle," wrote Freeman in 1934, Lee must have taken into account that his Army of Northern

---

4 Swinton, *Campaigns*, 224. Swinton also wrote, on page 195, "The theory of the invasion assumed that the presence of the Confederate army in Maryland would induce an immediate rising among the citizens of that State." Comte de Paris, *History of the Civil War in America*, 2:335.

5 Palfrey, *The Antietam and Fredericksburg*, 49.

Virginia had defeated a larger Federal army under John Pope only two weeks earlier.[6] Being both inexperienced and meek, McClellan commanded a smaller force than Pope, reasoned Freeman, so Lee must have thought his position along Antietam Creek less perilous than it would have been if another general commanded the Army of the Potomac at the time. Lee stood his ground, therefore, daring McClellan to attack him.

Never mind that "timid George" wrecked Lee's plans through a rapidly executed attack on Confederate positions atop South Mountain, or that after the war Lee judged McClellan "by all odds" to have been the most able opponent he had faced, or the fact that Lee never openly disparaged McClellan as a tactician.[7] To Freeman, it must have been Lee's doubts about McClellan's combat leadership that convinced the Southern commander to fight at Sharpsburg. Lacking definitive comments from Lee about McClellan, Freeman trod on shaky ground. The biographer did nevertheless share the Comte de Paris's conclusion that "A quick withdrawal in the face of his (Lee's) proclamation to the people of Maryland would mean the definite and *probably the permanent loss of that state to the Confederacy* [emphasis added]." It is this political dimension maintained by earlier generations that

6 Freeman, *R. E. Lee*, 2:381. Freeman likely picked up on a tendency to criticize McClellan that became common in Southern publications in the early 20th century. J. N. W., "Some Ex Cathedra Criticisms," in *Confederate Veteran*, Vol. 29, No. 8 (Aug. 1921), 317 wrote, for example, "Of the Sharpsburg battle, General Beauregard says: 'This is another very remarkable departure from the simple and important maxim of war, 'never to fight a battle in front of a defile or river.' It is evident that only the gallantry of our troops and the inaptitude of McClellan saved the army of the Confederacy from utter destruction.' Two rather important factors, after all, and the ones that determined General Lee to fight at Sharpsburg. It is idle to talk of what somebody other than McClellan would have done at Sharpsburg. If there had been any other, there would have been no battle there. Lee wasn't forced to fight on that side of the Potomac."

7 Lee Jr., *Recollections,* 416 and Long, *Memoirs*, 233. Even the questionable memory of John G. Walker after the war contains no hint of Lee showing disdain for McClellan's battlefield leadership when the two men conversed about the Union general. According to Walker, Lee said of McClellan "He is an able general but a very cautious one. His enemies among his own people think him too much so. His army is in a very demoralized and chaotic condition, and will not be prepared for offensive operations—or he will not think it so—for three or four weeks." See Walker, "Jackson's Capture of Harper's Ferry," 605-606. The closest Lee ever came to openly stating contempt for McClellan's combat leadership was his statement to Edward C. Gordon in Feb. 1868: "I went into Maryland to give battle, and could I have kept Gen. McClelland in ignorance of my position & plans a day or two longer, I would have fought and crushed him." Gordon, "Memorandum," in Gallagher, ed., *Lee the Soldier*, 27, Note 4. Upon visiting the Army of Northern Virginia, the Viscount Wolseley recalled Lee saying "In talking to me of all the Federal generals, Lee mentioned McClellan with most respect and regard." See Garnet Joseph Wolseley, "General Lee" in *MacMillan's Magazine*, Vol. 55 (Nov. 1886 to Apr. 1887), 328.

subsequent generations of scholars have forgotten in favor of other more elusive, and speculative, factors.

Stephen W. Sears played a formative role in changing the interpretive trajectory for modern readers. Writing fifty years after Freeman, Sears concluded "A major reason [Lee] stood and fought at Sharpsburg was his measured judgment that he was challenging a timid general heading an army demoralized by past defeats. That judgment was only half right." Sears meant by his latter sentence that Lee's appraisal of McClellan had been correct, not that the Federals opposing the Army of Northern Virginia were as demoralized as Lee had suspected. In stating this, Sears revealed more about his poor opinion of George McClellan than he did a clear understanding of Lee's decision-making process because Lee never uttered a documented condemnation of McClellan's battlefield leadership.[8]

Lee on the other hand believed that demoralization crippled the Federal army. He wrote of it to Jefferson Davis at the outset of the invasion and stated to William Allan in February 1868 that, had the circumstances differed in September 1862, he intended to attack McClellan, "hoping the best results from [the] state of my troops & those of the enemy."[9] In addition, Lee had expressed "amazement" to Lt. Col. Garnet Wolseley, the visiting Irish-British army officer, in October 1862, that "The disorganised mob under General Pope's command, whom he (Lee) had lately seen flying before his own victorious troops . . . had rallied under M'Clellan . . . and not

---

8 Sears, *Landscape*, 310. Longstreet, by contrast, did criticize McClellan, implying as well that Lee did not think him "capable of serious work." See Longstreet, *From Manassas to Appomattox*, 220. Also see comments offered by Longstreet in the *Richmond Times-Dispatch*, Nov. 12, 1911, stating: "General Lee had a certain respect for General McClellan, who had been his subordinate in the old engineers. But I judge that this feeling assumed somewhat the shape of patronage, like that of a father toward a son. He never feared any unexpected displays of strategy or aggressiveness on the part of McClellan and in dealing with him always seemed confident that on the Federal's part there would be no departure from the rules of war as laid down in the books. . . . Like General Lee, he was greatly learned in the theory and science of war: he knew how to fight a defensive battle fairly well. But in offensive tactics he was timid and vacillating and totally lacking in vigor."

9 Allan, "Memoranda," in Gallagher, ed., *Lee the Soldier*, 8. Longstreet, *From Manassas to Appomattox*, 211, continued to share this belief after the war, referring to McClellan's army as "somewhat demoralized." No less a figure than McClellan himself validated Lee's belief, writing in 1864 "It will be remembered that at the time I was assigned to the command of the forces for the defense of the National Capital, on the 2d day of September, 1862, the greater part of all the available troops were suffering under the disheartening influences of the serious defeat they had encountered during the brief and unfortunate campaign of General Pope. Their numbers were greatly reduced by casualties, their confidence was much shaken, and they had lost something of that *esprit de corps* which is indispensable to the efficiency of an army." See *OR* 19, 1:69.

only opposed a formidable front, but actually re-assumed the offensive." There is simply no indication in the sources that Lee believed McClellan to be as incompetent as historians and others have painted him. At the same time, the secessionist element of Lee's reasoning had by Stephen Sears's time all but disappeared in favor of open conjecture about the general's motives veiled as statements of fact.[10]

Joseph Harsh took up the subject some twenty years later in his three-volume examination of Confederate military strategy in 1862. Now, though, Harsh changed the interpretive trajectory by arguing that Lee had never intended to stand and fight at Sharpsburg in the first place. The battle, in Harsh's analysis, "derived not from a single decision, but from a series of decisions," that resulted in Lee being "boxed in [and forced to] . . . stand on the defensive."[11] Harsh's interpretation offered a more dynamic view of Lee's situation in the days before September 16-17, but, as the analysis in the sixth chapter of this study shows, there is no evidence that Lee ever sought to escape from the "box" into which he placed his army, nor that he engaged in any second-guessing in the days leading up to the fight itself. The "series of decisions" thesis promoted by Harsh simply does not hold up under scrutiny, and as for the issue of fomenting rebellion in Maryland, Harsh never considered this a fruitful line of inquiry so it remained absent from his analysis of Gen. Lee's motives.

Scott Hartwig, finally, wrote in 2012, "Unless some long-lost collection of papers is uncovered that contains Lee's rationale, the answer to this puzzle can only be an educated guess." Taking into account the possibility that the Rebel general may have sought to retain a foothold in Maryland from which he could launch an invasion of Pennsylvania, Hartwig also revisited the subject of Lee's September 8 proclamation to the people of Maryland as a possible motivating factor. "Perhaps [it was]," he concluded, "but it is doubtful that Lee risked his army for honor's sake . . . [he played] for far larger stakes than the tenuous support of Marylanders' hearts and minds."[12]

Hartwig's judgment here is partially correct. Lee did compete for larger stakes than Marylanders' hearts and minds. He tried at Sharpsburg to prove that his army, representing the Confederate States of America, stood ready to help Maryland's

---

10 Rawley, ed., *The American Civil War*, 31.

11 Harsh, *Taken*, 492.

12 Hartwig, *To Antietam Creek*, 519.

people "liberate" themselves from the shackles of Federal military control. This "inciting popular revolt" dimension of the Maryland Campaign rendered it very different from the second incursion north of the Potomac that Lee embarked upon nine months later, even though there were some strategic similarities.

A brief comparison of operations in 1862 and 1863 is instructive here given that several prominent officers from the Army of Northern Virginia discussed the subject after the war. For Armistead Long, the military goals of the Gettysburg Campaign echoed the 1862 operation in that Gen. Lee believed a defeat of Joseph Hooker "south of the Potomac, any where in the vicinity of Washington, [would allow] his shattered army . . . [to] find refuge within the defences of that city, as two Federal armies have previously done, and the fruits of victory would again be lost. But should we draw him far away from the defences of his capital, and defeat him on a field of our own choosing, his army would be irretrievably lost, and the victory would be attended with results of the utmost importance."[13]

Long elaborated on those potential results nine years later, writing "the Federal army, if defeated in a pitched battle, would be seriously disorganized and forced to retreat across the Susquehanna—an event which would give him (Lee) control of Maryland and Western Pennsylvania, and probably of West Virginia, while it would very likely cause the fall of Washington City and the flight of the Federal Government."[14]

Charles Marshall also suggested that Lee had military objectives in June 1863 akin to those he pursued in September 1862:

> As in the campaign of 1862, so again in the campaign of 1863 the desire to keep the enemy employed at a distance from Richmond, and the impossibility of maintaining his army near enough to Washington to accomplish this object without moving north of the Potomac, led to the invasion of Maryland and Pennsylvania. . . . I will not attempt to describe in detail the possible consequences of the defeat of McClellan in 1862, or of Meade in 1863, but it is safe to say that the defeat of either north of the Potomac would have been of vastly greater importance than an equal or greater success won in Virginia. A victory won in Maryland or in Pennsylvania, in 1863, might reasonably have been expected to have caused the

---

13 Armistead L. Long, "Letter to Rev. J. Wm. Jones, April 1877," in *SHSP*, Vol. 4, No. 1 (1877), 120.

14 Long, *Memoirs*, 269.

withdrawal of the Federal troops from the South West to defend the more important Federal interests which would in that event have been exposed.[15]

Walter Taylor concurred with Marshall's assessment, claiming that

General Lee determined to manoeuvre to draw [Hooker] from his impregnable position [on the Rappahannock] and if possible to remove the scene of hostilities beyond the Potomac. His design was to free the State of Virginia, for a time at least, from the presence of the enemy, to transfer the theatre of war to Northern soil, and, by selecting a favorable time and place in which to receive the attack which his adversary would be compelled to make on him, to take the reasonable chances of defeating him in a pitched battle; knowing full well that to obtain such an advantage there would place him in position to attain far more decisive results than could be hoped for from a like advantage gained in Virginia.[16]

Comparing these statements to comments written by the general himself shows that in September 1862 Lee sought to physically isolate Washington by cultivating Maryland's secession from the Union. After September 6 he refined this belief into a hypothesis that if he could fight and win a battle north of the Potomac it would encourage secessionists in Maryland to revolt in support of his army. By 1863, Lee understood that only his army, and not a popular uprising in Maryland, could accomplish the goal of isolating Washington by winning a battle in Pennsylvania. If Marylanders rose in rebellion after his army had triumphed, so much the better, but Lee assumed, based on his experience nine months earlier, that the sympathetic population of the Old Line State needed help. As he wrote to President Davis in October 1862, "Maryland is so tightly tied that I fear nothing but extraneous aid can relieve her."[17]

Openly stating this to Davis did not signal Lee's belief that the pro-Southern sympathies of Maryland's populace had been shaken. It suggested only that in his mind the Confederacy's friends in the state, situated as they were between fortified Washington, occupied Baltimore, and unionist Pennsylvania, remained at a geographic disadvantage. There is plenty of evidence to demonstrate that even

15 Maurice, ed., *Charles Marshall*, Chapter 9. Available online at https://leefamilyarchive.org /reference/books/marshall2/.

16 Walter Taylor, "Second Paper by Colonel Walter H. Taylor, of General Lee's Staff," in *SHSP*, Vol. 4, No. 1 (1877), 124-25. Also see "Letter from Gen. J. A. Early," in ibid., 56 for a similar perspective, but keep in mind Early's Lost Cause agenda.

17 OR 19, 2:644.

after Sharpsburg the general continued to think of Marylanders as potential allies. For example, on June 17, 1863, Lee entreated Gen. Richard Ewell to "repress marauding" in Maryland, taking only "what is necessary for the army & giv[ing] citizens of Maryland Confederate money or certificates." Similarly, on June 22, 1863, Lee ordered Maj. Gen. Stuart that "All supplies taken in Maryland must be by authorized staff officers for their respective departments, [and] by no one else. They will be paid for, or receipts for the same given to the owners." One day later, Lee wrote an order to Stuart instructing him to purchase tobacco in Maryland because "I can have nothing seized by the men."[18]

All of these statements are consistent with the opinion of circumstances in Maryland that Lee held at the end of the campaign in 1862, indicating that he wished his men to treat Marylanders sympathetically in order not to arouse anger against the Army of Northern Virginia. Isaac Trimble encouraged Lee to think in these terms as well, suggesting in Hagerstown on June 26, 1863, that the general send "a brigade to Baltimore to take that city, rouse Maryland, and thus embarrass the enemy." Lee, reported Trimble, thought enough of the fantastic plan that he wrote A. P. Hill "to ask if he could spare a brigade for that purpose." Hill replied that he could not and so the army's commander dropped the scheme.[19] Lee would continue to pursue a victory in Pennsylvania, hoping that in addition to shattering Union forces in the east it might offer the one long-shot possibility that still remained for the South to win the war—bringing Maryland into the Confederate fold.[20]

Historians have short memories. Having for nearly a century forgotten or discounted the secessionist dimensions of Lee's thinking in September 1862, they have relied instead on guessing the general's motives at Sharpsburg. This shift in perspective matters because the history people accept tends to be the history they

---

18 Dowdey and Manarin, eds. *Wartime Papers*, 518, 522-524, 526. Readers may also want to compare these orders from Lee to the harsher treatment of civilians in Pennsylvania documented in Robert J. Wynstra, *At the Forefront of Lee's Invasion: Retribution, Plunder, and Clashing Cultures on Richard S. Ewell's Road to Gettysburg* (Kent, OH, 2018).

19 Isaac R. Trimble, "The Campaign and Battle of Gettysburg," in *Confederate Veteran*, Vol. 25, No. 5 (May 1917), 210.

20 Fitzhugh Lee expressed a comparable opinion in 1877: "The knowledge that a decisive battle fought in Maryland or Pennsylvania would in all probability have given us the former State with large accessions to our ranks from a sympathizing population, while Washington, the capital of our opponents, would have necessarily fallen—a prize the moral effect of which cannot be overestimated." See "Letter from General Fitz Lee," in *SHSP*, Vol. 4, No. 1 (1877), 70.

read. One need recognize only the unfortunate influence of Stephen Sears's oft-repeated mischaracterization of George McClellan as slow, timid, and cautious in Maryland to realize this.[21] So it is with Robert E. Lee. Historians writing chronologically closer to the events had no difficulty citing Lee's belief that a Confederate victory at Sharpsburg could spark a rebellion in Maryland. They quoted the general's own words expressing that belief and fit them seamlessly into the stream of historical events.

Today, Lee's decision to fight at Sharpsburg is interpreted as an act of bravado, or defiance, or desperation, or a manifestation of spite for Gen. McClellan. Emotion and irrationality have become the accepted hallmarks of Lee's motives for fighting at Sharpsburg, which is ironic considering the general's reputation for cold, calculating aggressiveness. Lee rolled the dice at Sharpsburg and lost, but we cannot lose sight of the fact that the decision made sense to him at the time, just as it did to Stonewall Jackson, another icy military personality, whom Lee said agreed with it. There was nothing irrational or emotionally impulsive about Lee's actions. He based his decisions on the circumstances as he perceived them, what he believed he could gain at that moment, and on what he learned about Maryland after entering the state. In this sense, the first half of the campaign proved to be critically important for shaping what Robert E. Lee later thought he might be able to accomplish by fighting north of the Potomac.

Lee held a favorable impression of Maryland's people in early September that was also common in the ranks of his army. So much so, in fact, that he retained it even after the campaign had come to a disastrous close.[22] Yet by the time the guns

21 A more positive consensus is emerging on McClellan's performance during the Maryland Campaign. See, for example, Stotelmyer, *Too Useful to Sacrifice*; Rafuse, *McClellan's War*; and Thorp/Rossino, *The Tale Untwisted*.

22 For example, Lee ordered a cavalry raid into Pennsylvania on October 8, 1862, instructing Jeb Stuart: "Should it be in your power to supply yourself with horses or other necessary articles on the list of legal captures, you are authorized to do so." Stuart elaborated upon these orders in instructions of his own to his men, revealing in the process what were likely Lee's wishes that the Confederate cavalrymen respect the property of Maryland's citizens. "During the expedition into the enemy's country on which this command is about to engage, brigade commanders will make arrangements for seizing horses, the property of citizens of the United States, and all other property subject to legal capture, provided, that in no case will any species of property be taken except by authority, given in person or in writing, of the commander of brigade, regiment, or captain of company in the absence of his superior officers. . . . So much of this order as authorizes seizures of persons and property will not take effect until the command crosses the Pennsylvania line." See *OR* 19, 2:55-56. Of this raid, Maj. Henry B. McClellan recalled, "The terms of Stuart's orders were strictly enforced during the whole march. Nothing whatever was disturbed on the soil of Maryland; but when once the Pennsylvania line was

opened at Sharpsburg, the general's beliefs and those of his men had begun to diverge, opening a gulf that would grow wider with time. As Adam Kersh of the 52nd Virginia noted in a letter to his brother several weeks after the campaign "our boys are not very keen to go back to Maryland. They said it is not very wholesome there."[23]

Harrison Wells of the 13th Georgia echoed the sentiment, reporting in a letter to his fiancé Mollie on October 2 "There is not much feeling for the South in Maryland, and I don't care to enter the Union again (i.e., cross the Potomac). There are some few patriots in Maryland who appeared glad to see us, but they were 'few and far between.' Some of the women had Union Stars and Stripes hanging from their window and some would sing Union songs."[24]

The romanticized Confederate vision of how things might be in Maryland no longer animated those who had seen enough of the state to know that its people would never actively support the South. Lee's men endured enough taunts, jibes, and outward expressions of old-nation patriotism to conclude that Marylanders were, in their eyes, a miserable unionist lot. Above all, the expressions of friendship that Southern troops did receive could not outweigh the hard reality of the Rebel army's failed recruiting efforts. John Ryder Randall and Marylanders in the ranks had inspired visions of adding 20,000-50,000 soldiers to the Army of Northern Virginia. When those imaginary legions did not come, the dream of a sympathetic Maryland shattered against the hard reality of empty Confederate recruiting stations. Sharp-tongued Maryland women then sealed the unpleasant view of the state that Lee's men took with them back to Virginia.[25]

Acting as allies or antagonists according to their political inclinations, female Marylanders expressed themselves in word and deed, cementing forever after the unionist character of the state in the minds of Lee's men. Confederate sources

---

crossed, the seizure of horses was prosecuted with system and diligence. Six hundred men scoured the country on either side of the line of march, and as far as scouts could extend the country was denuded of its horses." See McClellan, *Life and Campaigns*, 140.

23 Letter of Adam W. Kersh to George P. Kersh, Oct. 14, 1862. Kersh Family Letters, Augusta County, Virginia Collection, Center for Digital History, University of Virginia, Charlottesville, VA. Available online at https://valley.lib.virginia.edu/VoS/personalpapers/sdocuments/augusta/p2kershletters.html.

24 Wells Letter, Oct. 2, 1862.

25 See Gallagher, "The Net Result of the Campaign Was in Our Favor," in Gallagher, ed., *The Antietam Campaign*, 3-43, for a recounting of various spiteful Southern reactions to the Maryland operation.

recount many anecdotes about the interaction between Maryland's women and their self-proclaimed Southern liberators. Sympathetic mothers and wives greeted Stonewall Jackson's command as it crossed the Potomac and ladies in Frederick provided Rebel troops with food, drink, and clothing. Women in Washington County set out roadside tables laden with coffee, fruit, and water for Confederate columns, and in Sharpsburg one particularly courageous young woman named Savilla Miller stood on her front stoop under fire all day on September 17 providing thirsty Confederates with refreshing sips of water from the ladle of her bucket.[26]

Lee's men recalled these women with gratitude, calling them friends and noting with fondness the occasions when they appeared on the roadside waving handkerchiefs or throwing smiles at the ragged columns marching by. These women represented the comforting Maryland on whose support Southern soldiers had counted when they entered the state. Even after the campaign came to a gory close one could still occasionally find stories in Southern newspapers describing the defiant spirit of "loyal" women in the Old Line State. One such account claimed, for example, that "Maryland women are as brave as any the sun ever shone on. They are the only noble spirits I saw who had not been crushed into a servile and cowardly submission to the despotism. Everywhere and always they were intensely Southern. . . . With such mothers Maryland must and shall be free."[27]

Other women, however, probably more numerous than their Southern-sympathizing counterparts, flew the United States' flag openly in the faces of Lee's men, brazenly pinched their noses at the oniony stench of sweat-soaked Confederate columns, and hurled bitter insults at the bedraggled troops. A hardened mountain woman with children huddled around her skirt even scolded Alabama soldiers during the fighting on South Mountain, calling them "thieves" as the bullets began to fly.[28]

Patriotic women in Frederick, Middletown, and Boonsboro pinned red, white, and blue ribbons to their bosoms, or threatened to poison any Southerner who dared to beg for something to drink on a hot day.[29] An elderly matron named

---

26 Douglas, *I Rode with Stonewall*, 170. Also see Kathleen A. Ernst, *Too Afraid to Cry: Maryland Civilians in the Antietam Campaign* (Mechanicsburg, PA, 1999), 212.

27 *Atlanta Southern Confederacy*, Nov. 20, 1862.

28 Priest, *Before Antietam*, 232-233.

29 By the time Rebel columns reached northern Washington County this harsh treatment by the fairer sex had transformed sentiment among some in the ranks into a deep suspicion of

Barbara Frietchie even became a symbol of Maryland's loyalty to the Union, although she could not rise from her bed when she was alleged to have called out for Stonewall Jackson to "shoot, if you must, this old gray head!"[30] Little did it matter that John Greenleaf Whittier's fanciful poem about Frietchie contained not an iota of truth. The grand old dame symbolized a grandmother's love for "freedom and union" around which Union men could rally.[31]

These displays of female anger, antagonism, and disgust appear to have made a more forceful impression on Lee's men than the acts of kindness performed by those who smiled and waved.[32] John Ryder Randall had promised that "mother" Maryland would "break the tyrant's chain" and be the "battle queen of yore." She was not dead, Randall had claimed, "nor deaf, nor dumb," but contrary to expectations she did not "spurn the Northern scum!" Lady Maryland did not breathe, burn, or rise in response to the Southern call. Naïve and desperate Confederates conditioned by propaganda masquerading as patriotic mythology, and hoping beyond hope to find military support in Maryland, learned instead that the state's women, far more than its men, openly disparaged them and spat on their offers of friendship. This reality encouraged a deep and abiding resentment in the ranks. Maryland's men could not openly express their opinions due to the fear of violence against them or the unfounded suspicion that they might be conscripted into the Confederate army. The state's women harbored no such reservations. In an era when women were considered to be the fragile, gentler sex, they could spew

---

even the women who took pity on them. The experience of Angela Davis, a former New Yorker living in Funkstown, Maryland, serves as a case in point. Writing that she "felt sorry" for the "Poor, brave, uncomplaining men," Davis placed "buckets of water at the front door with two or three new tin cups, out of which they constantly drank." Then "An officer rode up in front of the door and asked for a drink of water which one of the men gave him, at the same time saying, 'A Yankee lady is giving us the water.' To which the officer made answer, excitedly, 'If that is so, I won't drink a drop of it,' and dashing down the cup, he put spurs to his horse and rode off at a furious rate." Angela Kirkham Davis, "War Reminiscences: A Letter to My Nieces" in Washington County Historical Society, Hagerstown, MD.

30 John Greenleaf Whittier, "Barbara Frietchie," in Thomas R. Lounsbury, ed., *The Yale Book of American Verse* (New Haven, CT, 1912).

31 Johnson, "Address," 515; Douglas, *I Rode with Stonewall*, 151; Williams and McKinsey, *History of Frederick County Maryland*, 378-379; and W. Gordon McCabe, "The Real Barbara Frietchie," in *SHSP*, Vol. 27 (1899), 288.

32 Captain Henry King of McLaws's division, for example, recorded the following in his diary on September 10: "Considerable demonstration of welcome from the young ladies" of Frederick City. "Reached Middletown about 12 [midnight] . . . Union people—all women." Trimpi, ed., "Lafayette McLaws' Aide-de-Camp," 31.

venom at the invaders without fear of reprisal from men they derisively called "the chivalry."

Sharp-witted Rebel troops gave as good as they got, boldly exchanging barbs with their female detractors, but no evidence has been found of them laying hands on the women who treated them with such contempt—just the opposite, in fact. Stonewall Jackson tipped his cap to little girls waving U.S. flags at him while men in the ranks politely warned women wearing the national colors to remove themselves from sight lest some fool come along and insult them. Simply put, and strangely enough, the ladies of wartime Maryland, both for and against secession, became prominent voices of political opinion, a role that they could not play in times of peace. Unionist women came to define the Confederate experience in the state, expressing a wanton disdain for the secessionist cause that ultimately convinced Lee's men "Mother Maryland," as Randall styled it, did not care for them or want them within her bounds. This realization left the bitter taste of disappointment on Confederate tongues that their pens would pour out for decades to come.

By the time Gen. Lee's battered, but still defiant, army withdrew across the Potomac River, the dream of a Confederate Maryland lay in ruins. Stalwarts unwilling to accept the truth may have retained the hope that Maryland could still be persuaded to join the Southern cause, but soldiers in the Army of Northern Virginia knew it to be a delusion. They hissed when bands struck up *Maryland! My Maryland* and swore never again to be taken for fools as far as the Old Line State was concerned. As Georgia correspondent Peter Alexander put it in a report home on September 19, "The political effect upon Maryland of our retrograde movement must be highly injurious. We shall doubtless lose ground among [the] people, and it may be we shall have to make up our minds to loose the State itself."[33]

Long, difficult years of war remained to be fought before the conflict would finally come to an end; and in a war replete with turning points, the failure of Lee's campaign in Maryland is often considered one of the most important. Given the frequency of debate about the importance of pivotal moments in Civil War enthusiasts' circles, this is perhaps not the most instructive way to think about the campaign's barren results for the South.

It may be more fruitful to view the event as the shutting of a door that Confederate leaders and soldiers alike thought they could use to escape the gory cataclysm in which they found themselves entangled. Lee's defeat at Sharpsburg

---

33 *Atlanta Southern Confederacy*, Oct. 5, 1862.

shattered the dream of help that secessionist Maryland might offer. Unlike a dream, however, waking from the experience provided no respite for the sleeper. A nightmarish reality loomed over everything instead.

With no support coming from Maryland, the rebellious South stood forsaken against an opponent growing stronger and better organized while its own limited resources drained slowly away. The failed secessionist dream heralded the end of the beginning for the Confederacy. While the misty residue of that dream might obscure this reality for some time, the demise of hope for Maryland's support brought the South materially closer to its ultimate ruination—a fate hinted at by the beginning of the end at Gettysburg and Vicksburg nine months later.

Appendix A

Sketches of the
Army of Northern Virginia's Potomac River Crossing

T HE second chapter of this study includes three illustrations of the Army of Northern Virginia's crossing of the Potomac River into Maryland during the period from September 4-7, 1862. The northward movement of Robert E. Lee's army ranks as one of the Civil War's most momentous events, but like most incidents at the time there is no photographic record of it. With portable camera technology still in its infancy, wartime publications relied instead on skilled artists to sketch impressions of historic happenings for the public. Two such artists working for *Harper's Weekly* magazine, Alfred R. Waud and Thomas Nast, drew depictions of the Confederate army's Potomac River crossing in the same month it occurred, while a third artist named Allen C. Redwood created his own image of the event for the publishers of *The Century Magazine* in 1887.

Each of these drawings provides a unique perspective on the Rebel army's entry into Maryland and over the years publishers have made extensive use of them as interior illustrations or as jacket covers for their books. To date, however, no analysis of the drawings' accuracy has been conducted. Indeed, more often than not the images appear without any accompanying details concerning which of the Rebel army's Potomac crossing points they purport to show. The lack of contextual background for the drawings raises questions about the extent to which they should be trusted as historical sources. Do they convey details about the Rebel army's crossing that add to our understanding of the event, or might we be better off thinking of them as realistic-looking, albeit contrived, war art similar to Francisco Goya's paintings of the French Imperial Army's occupation of Spain under Napoleon Bonaparte? This brief analysis examines each drawing in the order of its production, with the goal being to describe what the image shows, explore the context in which it was produced, and evaluate how accurate its content might be.

Alfred Waud's Nearly Forgotten Sketch

Alfred R. Waud created his sketch of the Army of Northern Virginia's Potomac River crossing first. An intrepid illustrator born in London, England on October 2, 1828, Waud found employment in early 1862 as a sketch artist with *Harper's Weekly*. He was assigned to cover Federal military operations and traveled through Virginia drawing events until the calamitous defeat of John Pope's army at the Battle of Second Manassas in late August of that year. Caught up in the chaos surrounding the Federal retreat, Waud quickly found himself trapped behind Confederate lines. However, instead of attempting to return to Washington on the south side of the Potomac River, he decided to trail the Confederate army north through Leesburg, Virginia.

According to a September 7 report sent by Alfred Pleasonton, the Army of the Potomac's cavalry commander, to Maj. Gen. George McClellan, Waud traveled through Leesburg before crossing with James Longstreet's command into Maryland on September 6 at White's Ford.[1] 1st Virginia Cavalry troopers screening the right (eastern) flank of Lee's army apprehended Waud soon thereafter, which resulted in a fanciful drawing of them that a notation in the artist's diary says he finished September 7. Waud produced his drawing of Lee's army crossing the Potomac on September 8, although he later captioned the image "Previous to Antietam. Rebels crossing the Potomac. Union scouts in foreground."[2]

Waud sketched his original in pencil, but an unidentified individual, perhaps another artist at *Harper's Weekly*, later rendered it as a black-and-white watercolor painting. Oddly enough, only Waud's sketch of the 1st Virginia Cavalry appeared in *Harper's* on September 27, 1862. His river sketch seems to have been forgotten and might have been lost forvever had the estate of banking mogul John Pierpont Morgan, Sr. not donated a collection of Civil War era drawings to the Library of Congress that included Waud's image.[3]

Even though Waud crossed the Potomac with Longstreet's men, there are aspects of his image which make it clear he chose not to depict that particular event. The first of these is the mountainous terrain in the background. There are no hills near White's Ford that approach the height shown by Waud. The same is true of the crossing points used by Jeb Stuart's cavalry farther south of the ford, specifically Conrad's Ferry (known after the war as White's Ferry) and Edwards' Ferry. The setting for the crossing is therefore a work of imagination, with Waud depicting the Confederate columns in a romanticized landscape of

---

1   OR 19, 2:200.

2   Alfred R. Waud Diary, Sept. 4 to Oct. 31, 1862. Folder 31, MSS 106. Williams Research Center. The Historic New Orleans Collection. New Orleans, LA.

3   See notes accompanying the Library of Congress online record for Waud's drawing. Waud, Alfred R., Artist. Previous to Antietam. Rebels crossing the Potomac. Union scouts in foreground. United States Maryland Virginia Potomac River Antietam, 1862. Available online at www.loc.gov/item/2004660339/.

wooded hills sloping down dramatically to the river. He may have been attempting to depict the Catoctin Mountain range, but there is no evidence to confirm that.

Whatever the case might have been, Waud clearly relied on details he learned from Rebel horsemen in Maryland to help compose his image. For example, the bright moon hanging in the upper-center of the drawing is accurate for the crossing made by some of Jeb Stuart's men. Wade Hampton's cavalry brigade forded on the "clear moonlit night" of September 5, a fact Waud could only have known if he learned it from the Rebels in Leesburg or those he met on the Maryland side of the river. In addition, Conrad's Ferry is located close to the Ball's Bluff battlefield, something Rebel troopers likely mentioned to orient Waud, which could explain why he incorporated the impression of wooded hills south of the Rebel column. All together, the presence of these hills and the moonlit night suggest that Waud tried to capture the sight of Confederate cavalry traversing the river at Conrad's Ferry. He did not witness the crossing with his own eyes, however, making the sketch more an informed artistic portrayal than a reliable depiction of the event itself.

Nast's Propaganda Drawing

Thomas Nast's drawing appeared in the September 27, 1862, issue of *Harper's Weekly* and, like Waud's image, it is a combination of fact and fiction. The German-born Nast resided in New York City, which suggests he drew his image based on contemporary reports of Confederate operations in Maryland. Several of the details in Nast's depiction are interesting in that they clearly reflect information which appeared in newspapers at the time. The first of these details is the pontoon bridge in the center-rear of the image. Nast did not assign a location to his drawing, writing in his caption that it showed "The Rebel Army Crossing the Fords of the Potomac for the Invasion of Maryland."

The September 27 issue of *Harper's Weekly*, likely based on a report that appeared in the *Philadelphia Inquirer* on September 9, mentioned a Union army pontoon bridge that the Rebels had captured on the Peninsula and placed at Noland's Ferry for artillery and supply wagons (see chapter two for details). Engineers with the Army of Northern Virginia did not assemble the bridge until a couple of days after the initial Rebel crossing, however, so Nast's drawing clearly conflated how he imagined the initial crossing must have looked with news about it that came out several days later.

Another detail worth mentioning is the men on the left side of the drawing waving their hats. Contemporary reports circulating in Maryland and Pennsylvania noted how a portion of the population sympathetic to the Southern cause greeted Lee's army with some enthusiasm. The available evidence presented in chapter four also hints that the closer to the Potomac a community sat the more likely its inhabitants were to support the Confederacy. Nast probably heard stories along these lines, leading him to show local sympathizers emerging from their hiding places to greet the arriving Rebel cavalry and point it north toward Frederick City.

The presence of Confederate cavalry in the column's vanguard is a final detail to consider. Reports from Federal observers on nearby Sugarloaf Mountain noted the presence of the horsemen on the canal berm as early as the morning of September 5. Frederick County residents also spotted riders in advance of the main Rebel force, men who most likely belonged to Lige White's border cavalry from Loudoun County, Virginia. These outriders approached Frederick City ahead of the main column, with the first rider to appear in Frederick announcing that "he belonged to White's company of border cavalry, and was the advance of Lee's army that would soon be up."[4] Nast surely learned details like these from reports about the Confederate incursion spreading north in September.

Curiously, Nast's sketch also depicts the crossing taking place by moonlight. Appearing like wraiths out of the darkness, Rebel troopers approach the Maryland shoreline in a swarm. There is menace in their appearance, reflecting the panic experienced by unionists in Maryland upon hearing of the Army of Northern Virginia's approach. Here Nast seems to have chosen to incorporate details about Wade Hampton's cavalry crossing at Conrad's Ferry on the night of September 5. Depicting the Southern army's river crossing at night, even though it took place over a number of days and nights, struck an ominous tone that would have resonated with Nast's anxious Northern audience. His image contained elements of fact, but the vocally pro-Union, anti-slavery Nast nevertheless used the subject to communicate fear of the ragged horde of Rebel troops that had descended on Maryland. This fact renders his drawing both a simple illustration and a complex piece of propaganda.

Redwood's Postwar Reminiscence

Born in Lancaster, Virginia, on June 19, 1844, Allen Christian Redwood is the only artist of the three examined here to have fought in the war. Redwood's pre-war connections to Maryland ran deep, perhaps firing in him a special interest in Confederate military operations in the state. The 17-year-old Redwood attended schools in Baltimore, Maryland, and Brooklyn, New York, before enlisting in the 55th Virginia infantry regiment when the war broke out. Following a number of engagements, Redwood found himself taken prisoner during the Battle of Second Manassas and sent to a prison camp for several months. His capture in August 1862 meant that Redwood missed the Maryland Campaign before he was exchanged in time to fight at Chancellorsville and Gettysburg. A wound

---

4 OR 19, 2:186. "Signal officer of Banks' corps reports from Sugar Loaf Mountain: The enemy crossed at Noland's Ferry last evening. The river is easily fordable at that point. Saw about 2,000 of the enemy on this side, scattered along from the aqueduct to Noland's Ferry. Think they are cavalry. Saw two guns in position on opposite side of the river, at Noland's Ferry." Army surgeon Dr. Charles E. Goldsborough quoted in the *National Tribune*, Oct. 1886. Available online at www.civilwarmed.org/explore/bibs/onevast hospital/occupied/.

received in the latter engagement knocked him out of action for a second time, but he eventually became well enough to rejoin the Army of Northern Virginia and serve out the remainder of the war.

Redwood made numerous sketches of the things he witnessed during the conflict, including the crossing of the Potomac by Lee's army in 1863 en route to Pennsylvania. It is apparently this experience that he drew upon when making his sketch of Stonewall Jackson's men crossing at White's Ford. Three elements of the sketch's content and one detail about its context make this evident. The first element is a difference between what the image purports to show and how the White's Ford crossing is described in the historical sources. The sources cited in chapter two state that Jackson's men waded the ford in ranks of four with arms locked or hands held to ensure no man drowned during the passage. The men in Redwood's drawing are not crossing in an organized column. Admittedly, the organization of Jackson's command could have broken down as the crossing went on, but in Redwood's case he was not present when the event occurred so he could not have known about it.

The second element is the column's disappearance into the distance. It is a dead giveaway that Redwood did not draw what comrades might have told him about 1862, but rather what he recalled from his own experience traversing the Potomac during the Gettysburg Campaign in 1863. When Jackson's column reached Maryland in September 1862 it took a hard left up the towpath of the Chesapeake and Ohio Canal before crossing the canal via a makeshift bridge at Lock No. 26. Redwood's drawing shows the Rebel column moving straight up the hillside in the distance from the river.

Additionally, and this is the third revealing element, the equipment carried by the men does not match the stripped-down appearance of Jackson's troops in the Confederate army's first northern offensive. As is explained in chapter five, according to Frank Mixson of the 1st South Carolina Volunteers, before reaching the Potomac the troops received orders "to leave all their baggage" behind. "On this trip," noted Mixson, "we had nothing but a haversack, canteen, and a blanket or oil cloth besides the accoutrements gun, cartridge box, and scabbard." The men in Redwood's drawing are exceptionally well-equipped for a Rebel column in September 1862, the month when the ramshackle state of Lee's army reached its nadir. Several men are carrying bulging knapsacks and one man on the far left waiting to enter the river is sporting the widely-hated white leggings that most troops quickly discarded in 1861. Although possible, it is unlikely that by the time of the Maryland Campaign any seasoned member of Jackson's hard-marching command would have still worn shoe gaiters, unless perhaps he intended to weather constant ribbing by his sharp-tongued comrades.[5]

5 Mixson, *Reminiscences*, 26.

As for the drawing's context, Redwood probably made the sketch at the request of his friend and student, Sophia Herrick. Redwood met Herrick after the war when she worked as an associate editor of the *Southern Review* magazine. She subsequently joined Scribner's publishing house and worked as an assistant editor for *The Century Magazine* until her retirement in 1906.[6] Redwood was one of the many artists that The Century Company retained to produce illustrations for their series on Civil War events and his work is featured in the multi-volume *Battles and Leaders of the Civil War* series that first appeared in 1884.

Volume 2 contains Redwood's White's Ford drawing on page 621 as an illustration for the "Stonewall Jackson in Maryland" article by Henry Kyd Douglas. Its appearance in the earlier volume suggests Redwood made the sketch specifically for that subject. When the third volume appeared, he submitted an altered version of the same drawing (see page 250) captioned "Confederates at a Ford." His changes in the image are confirmed by the presence of the soldier wearing the white gaiters in both drawings. Redwood's drawing in the third installment, however, shows the man standing in a slightly different pose. In short, Redwood's sketch is neither historically accurate nor drawn from memory. He never made it to Maryland in 1862, so he relied on his memory of events for the Gettysburg Campaign in 1863 and applied those details to his depiction of the White's Ford crossing in 1862.

Drawings of the September 1862 Potomac Crossing: Accurate or Fanciful?

None of the sketches examined here can be considered authentic depictions of the events themselves. The best that can be said about the drawings is that each shows Confederate columns at different crossing points, those being Conrad's Ferry (Waud), Noland's Ferry (Nast), and White's Ford (Redwood). Simmering tensions in Maryland raised fears in Washington and elsewhere north of the Mason-Dixon Line that the populace would rise in revolt and join the Rebel war effort once Lee's army appeared in the state. Confederate Southerners hoped that exactly this sort of event would come to pass, bringing "downtrodden" Maryland into the secessionist fold.

Waud's and Nast's images convey a sense of the drama and foreboding that attended the arrival of Robert E. Lee's men north of the Potomac River while Redwood's drawing presents a more straightforward, although idealized, portrait. Each image served a purpose intended at the time, but none of them captured the events as they occurred. The best that can be said about the sketches is that they fit neatly within the genre of Civil War art akin to the modern-day depictions produced by Mort Künstler, Don Troiani, Keith Rocco, and others. The drawings are evocative as illustrations and they were useful as propaganda, but relevant as depictions of the actual historical events they are not.

---

6   Robert Bain, Joseph Flora, and Louis Rubin, eds., *Southern Writers: A Biographical Dictionary* (Baton Rouge, LA, 1979), 223.

Appendix B

Did William Nelson Pendleton Lose Special Orders No. 191?

T HE third chapter of this study posits the hypothesis that a Confederate officer lodging at the farm of Elias Luckett Delashmutt, Jr. during the Army of Northern Virginia's stay near Frederick City may have been responsible for losing a copy of Robert E. Lee's Special Orders No. 191. A potential candidate and a man who might have known the Delashmutt family is Brig. Gen. William Nelson Pendleton, the commander of the Army of Northern Virginia's Reserve Artillery and former Rector of All Saints' Episcopal Church in Frederick from 1847 to 1853.

Pendleton noted in a letter to his wife dated September 10, 1862, that his command left Leesburg early in the morning on September 7. Most of the artillery forded the Potomac in the wake of Longstreet's column and "About twelve that night . . . reached the Arcadia farm," which was an older name for the Best farm where Lee had arranged his headquarters. "After reporting to General Lee, Monday morning (September 8)," Pendleton continued, "I spent the day in calling on my old friends in Frederick." He then alluded to having learned the army's upcoming movements from Lee. "To-day we go farther inward," he added, "I must not indicate where lest my letter fail and give some clue where I would not have information gotten. Suffice it that General Lee seems well to understand what he is about."[1]

This comment makes it clear that Lee informed Pendleton on September 8 of the army's pending operations outlined in Special Orders No. 191, although it is unknown if Lee had a copy of the orders given to his Reserve Artillery chief. The assumption made here, based on two points, is that he did. First, in his analysis of the orders, Joseph Harsh identified eleven potential copies being made (if a copy for Pendleton is included in this

---

1 Susan P. Lee, *Memoirs of William Nelson Pendleton* (Philadelphia, PA, 1893), 211.

total). Second, most of the copies have been accounted for, except for the one presumably given to William Pendleton.

Questions have been raised about the copies given to Jeb Stuart and Lafayette McLaws. The copy for Stuart is irrelevant because by the time the orders were distributed on September 9, Stuart had already returned to his headquarters in Urbana several miles southeast of Frederick City. The copy for McLaws is also not pertinent because the general received his copy at his headquarters via courier on the evening of September 9. The third chapter of this study demonstrates that McLaws's command occupied an area straddling the Monocacy River southeast of the B&O Railroad junction and Best's Grove. Captain Henry King of McLaws's staff confirmed this vicinity in his diary entry of September 7, writing that he returned from a visit to Frederick "about dark [riding] some 5 miles to our H'd Qrs," which implies a location one mile beyond Lee's headquarters, which was located four miles from Frederick. McLaws's headquarters, like Stuart's, lay in the *opposite* direction from where the men with the 27th Indiana eventually found the lost copy of S.O. No. 191.[2]

This leaves only the copy of the orders potentially given to William Pendleton. Pendleton traveled from Best's Grove to the home of friends in Frederick City immediately after visiting Lee's headquarters on September 8. The route he took to town is unknown, but the discovery of the lost copy of the Lee's orders between Frederick and Best's Grove is in the direction Pendleton traveled, opening the possibility that he may have dropped it en route. Historian Wilbur D. Jones reasonably suggests that the out-of-the-way place where the orders were lost may be attributable to the carrier of the document stepping off the road to heed the call of nature. If that man was William Pendleton, then he could have let the document bearing the precious cigars slip from his pocket while he was in the process of relieving himself.[3]

This scenario is a realistic option in Pendleton's case because, as he had reported in a letter to his wife dated August 31, 1862, "Again I am writing to you from a bed, and this time I am in it as an invalid. Not much, I hope, only the crisis of a diarrhoea *of some two weeks' duration* [emphasis added], rendered worse by hard effort to catch up with General Lee." A little more than one week later, after the army had moved into Maryland, Pendleton appears to have fallen ill for a second time. "Pretending to be sick," is how Capt. James A. Blackshear mockingly described the general in his diary on September 8, adding how Pendleton lodged "at a house as usual" while the army rested near Frederick City. Could the house referred to by Blackshear have been the Delashmutt home? Pendleton suffered from

---

2   Harsh, *Sounding the Shallows*, 160-162. Von Borcke, *Memoirs*, 199. Lafayette McLaws, "The Maryland Campaign: An Address Delivered before the Confederate Veterans Association of Savannah, Ga.," (1896) in McLaws Papers, Collection Number 00472, Folder 30. Southern Historical Collection, The Wilson Library, University of North Carolina at Chapel Hill; Trimpi, ed., "Lafayette McLaws' Aide-de-Camp," 30.

3   Jones, "Who Lost the Lost Orders," 11.

malaria he contracted before the war. The disease can flare-up for extended periods often accompanied by uncontrollable diarrhea. If such an episode caught the ailing Pendleton returning from Lee's headquarters, finding a secluded spot behind a locust tree (the location where the orders were found, according to George W. Welch) makes sense. In addition, there was no reason for a courier from Lee's headquarters to be carrying a copy of the orders beyond the location where it was found because there is no evidence that any Confederate unit camped there.[4]

Although the lost copy of the orders was addressed to D. H. Hill, it may have also been originally dated September 8, suggesting that while initially made out to the North Carolinian, the orders were not actually sent to him because he had already received a copy from Jackson. The evidence shows that Hill began acting on those orders by moving George Burgwyn Anderson's brigade toward the army's rear on September 8. Because the orders were to be distributed officially on September 9, Col. Robert Chilton appears to have scratched out the September "8" date on the copy initially intended for Hill and replaced it with a "9." After doing this he could have simply handed the copy to Pendleton because Section VII of the orders covered the operations of both the Reserve Artillery and D. H. Hill's command.

Finally, there is the matter of the cigars. Harvey Hill smoked a pipe, not cigars, although in wartime he may have made an occasional exception if there was a scarcity of pipe tobacco. William Pendleton's penchant for smoking is unknown.[5]

Pendleton visited Lee's headquarters to receive orders. He reported himself sick, and would have had to stop along the way if he experienced a bout of diarrhea. He traveled to Frederick, which gave him a chance to drop the orders between Lee's headquarters and the city—especially if he was lodging at the Delashmutt farm.

In short, the circumstances point to William Pendleton more than to any other individual as being the man who lost the orders, if Lee indeed had a copy of S.O. No. 191 given to his Reserve Artillery chief.

Finally, if Pendleton did drop or otherwise lose the orders, it would have been consistent with his well-known reputation for incompetence.[6]

4 Lee, *Memoirs*, 209. Blackshear Diary, Sept. 8, 1862. Affidavit of George W. Welch, Jul. 24, 1906 in Datzman, "Who Found Lee's Lost Dispatch?" MNBP.

5 At Sharpsburg "I saw Gen. Hill on horse guiding the troops with stoic indifference, smoking his short pipe, while shot and shell plowed up the ground around him." Frank H. Venn, "That Flag of Truce at Antietam," in *Confederate Veteran*, Vol. 4, No. 12 (Dec. 1896), 389. After the war Hill expressed a mild disdain for those who used tobacco, writing "Of a numerous staff, we thought him to be the most habitually cheerful who used nor spirits, nor tobacco, nor coffee, nor tea." See Daniel Harvey Hill, "Hints to Parents," in *The Land We Love*, Vol. I (Charlotte, NC, 1866), 199.

6 Robert K. Krick, "A Stupid Old Useless Fool," in *Civil War Times* (June 2008).

Appendix C

Confederate Straggling to Avoid Entering Maryland

ALTHOUGH most of the sources examined for this study contain comments supporting Lee's decision to enter Maryland, there is evidence to suggest that some men in the Army of Northern Virginia questioned crossing the Potomac out of concern about "invading" Northern soil. These comments appear to have been made by men whose regiments, and the brigades to which they were attached, did not include Maryland soldiers.

For example, two of the five sources containing such comments are from men who served with the 2nd South Carolina and the 15th South Carolina. Lieutenant Colonel Franklin Gaillard of the former regiment called crossing the Potomac "simply ridiculous" in a letter home, while the mortally wounded Lt. Col. George W. James of the 3rd South Carolina Battalion commented to Charles Walcott of the 21st Massachusetts on the day after the Battle of South Mountain that the commander of the 15th South Carolina, Col. William DeSaussure, had refused to cross the Potomac because his men "had enlisted to defend the South and not to invade the North."[1]

The third source is 2nd Lt. Garland S. Ferguson from Company F of the 25th North Carolina in Robert Ransom's brigade, who wrote this in his history of the regiment:

When it was first made known to the men by General Lee's order that the army was to cross the Potomac there was a considerable murmur of disappointment in ranks. The men said they had volunteered to resist invasion and not to invade, some did not believe it right

---

1 Harsh, *Sounding the Shallows*, 153. These two regiments (the 2nd South Carolina and 15th South Carolina) belonged to brigades comprised of either a mix of South Carolinians and Georgians (the 15th South Carolina served with Thomas Drayton's brigade) or entirely of South Carolinians (the 2nd South Carolina served with Joseph Kershaw's brigade).

to invade Northern territory, others thought that the same cause that brought the Southern army to the front would increase the Northern army, still others thought the war should be carried into the North; thus the men thought, talked and disagreed.[2]

The fourth source is a man named Isaac Hirsch who enlisted with the 30th Virginia, a regiment assigned to Col. Van Manning's mixed brigade of Virginians, North Carolinians, and Arkansans. "I don't like to invade anybodys country," he wrote in his diary on September 5. Hirsch mustered in with a regiment raised around Spotsylvania, Virginia, far from the influence of the Maryland men who flooded across the Virginia state line in 1861 to join the Confederate forces being formed by Thomas J. Jackson.[3]

The fifth source is a civilian named Rev. Joseph C. Stiles who traveled with the army and wrote after the Maryland Campaign that "a large number [of men] hung back and would not cross the river."[4] Historian Joseph Harsh astutely points out that, despite raising concens about the Potomac crossing, none of the men mentioned above dropped out of the ranks to remain in Virginia.

There is abundant evidence to show that those holding convictions sufficient to fight for the Confederate cause generally believed Maryland to be a Federally occupied Southern state, meaning complaints about invading "Northern" soil would have made little sense at the time. It is nevertheless worth noting that none of the men who wrote the comments mentioned above served in units containing large numbers of Maryland soldiers. This suggests that pro-Potomac crossing sentiment may have been stronger in units exposed to Marylanders who constantly preached to their comrades about secessionist sentiment in their homeland. A few of the men in regiments not containing Marylanders, or not exposed to them by association in a brigade setting, may have held different opinions, leading to some of Lee's troops to remain behind in Virginia.

Beyond this, however, there seems to be little evidence of unwillingness to "invade" Northern territory by crossing the Potomac. More work is required on this subject to clarify the extent of such opinion within the Army of Northern Virginia and the number of Confederate soldiers who might have remained in the Old Dominion based on their convictions.

---

2 Clark, ed., *Histories of the Several Regiments and Battalions from North Carolina*, 2:296. Apart from a company of Virginia artillerists, Old North Staters comprised practically all of the 25th North Carolina.

3 Harsh, *Sounding the Shallows*, 153.

4 Ibid.

APPENDIX D

The Contrabands of Harpers Ferry

THE story of Maj. Gen. Thomas J. 'Stonewall' Jackson's victory at Harpers Ferry on September 15, 1862, is well-known. Capturing more than 12,000 Federal troops at a cost of just over 300 killed and wounded, Jackson achieved a major Confederate triumph shortly before the larger clash at Sharpsburg on September 16-17. Less well-known is the fact that Jackson's men also seized thousands of refugee slaves who had taken shelter with Col. Dixon Miles's command at Harpers Ferry. No official Confederate report on the Harpers Ferry operation made mention of these prisoners, to whom Northerners and Southerners alike referred during the war as "contrabands" due to their legal status as property. Fortunately for posterity, the *Richmond Dispatch* covered their capture and transportation to the Confederate capital in some detail, mentioning the prisoners for the first time in an article that appeared on September 18, 1862. "The whole garrison . . . surrendered on Sunday morning," wrote the *Dispatch*, noting how "our forces captured about one thousand negroes." Seven additional reports then appeared in the *Dispatch* and the *Richmond Enquirer* over the next five days outlining the story of what happened to these unfortunate human spoils of war after they fell into Rebel hands.[1]

Following the Federal garrison's surrender, Jackson assigned Maj. Gen. Ambrose Powell Hill to parole enemy soldiers and collect captured property for transportation to the rear. Hill commenced these tasks on September 15, and by September 16 thousands of Union prisoners began the long march from Harpers Ferry to Frederick, Maryland, and points beyond. At the same time, some of Hill's men scoured the town for all the black individuals they could find, rounding them up for transfer south. A witness to these events

---

1 *Richmond Dispatch*, Sept. 18, 20, 22, 23, and 24, 1862. Also see two reports in the *Richmond Enquirer*, Sept. 23, 1862.

named Abba Goddard described them in her journal: "Every nook, cranny, barn, and stye has been searched and men, women, and little children in droves have been carried off . . . our hospital laundresses, and our men servants, without a word of warning, were seized upon" and taken. An unidentified Rebel major even tried to seize the black men employed by Federal regiments, rather than let them go with the column of parolees heading to Frederick.[2]

This attempt to separate the blacks led to a confrontation between the major and Col. William H. Trimble of the 60th Ohio. Trimble had secured a pass for the black non-combatants in his regiment, but when they tried to leave town the Confederate major attempted to separate them from the column. Trimble pulled his sidearm in response and compelled the Rebel officer to step aside at gunpoint, saving the black personnel in his command from being seized.[3]

According to the *Richmond Dispatch*, by September 20 Hill had collected as many as 2,500 people, many of whom were marched to Winchester, Virginia, along with the guns, ammunition, and other materiel captured at Harpers Ferry. Additional details of the operation began to appear in the *Dispatch* by September 22, which reported that "a large number of contrabands . . . had taken refuge with the Yankee thieves . . . [including] negroes [that] belonged to citizens of Jefferson and adjoining counties. A letter before us states that one gentleman from Clarke [County], who had lost 31 negroes, found 28 of them in this lot." Subsequent reports on September 23 and 24 also noted that the contrabands were captured "slaves" and "negroes, whom the Yankees had stolen."[4]

According to a report that appeared in Southern newspapers, some of these individuals returned to their masters. "I met to-day hundreds of negroes taken at Harper's Ferry going home with their owners," wrote the report's author from Winchester, Virginia, under the pseudonym ACCOMAC. "Most of them seemed in fine spirits, singing 'Carry me back to Old Virginia,' & c." Major Andrew Wardlaw of the 14th South Carolina had a similar personal experience while enjoying the hospitality of the Bell family, who "were delighted to see the Southern Army [and] had fifteen negroes at Harpers Ferry." No fewer than "1200 negroes were captured & restored to their owners," confided Wardlaw to his diary, including the helpful "Mrs. Bell [who] got 10 of hers."[5]

2   *OR* 19, 1:981; Dennis E. Frye, *Harpers Ferry Under Fire: A Border Town in the American Civil War* (Virginia Beach, VA, 2012), 102.

3   Hartwig, *To Antietam Creek*, 564-565.

4   *Richmond Enquirer*, Sept. 23, 1862 and *Richmond Dispatch*, Sept. 24, 1862.

5   *The Southern Banner*, Oct. 1, 1862. Diary of Andrew B. Wardlaw, Sept. 14 and 15, 1862 in South Carolina Vertical File, ANBL. My thanks to Steven Stotelmyer for providing me with this source.

Still other contrabands ended up being confiscated by the Confederate army rather than returned to their owners. According to the *Richmond Dispatch* on September 24, this occurred because their "masters propose to offer them for sale in Richmond, not deeming them desirable servants after having associated with the Yankees."[6]

That same day, the *Dispatch* noted, "Two car loads of negroes arrived in this city yesterday by the Central Railroad." According to A. P. Hill's campaign report, the men responsible for completing this task belonged to Col. Edward L. Thomas's brigade. Hill recorded that he "remained at Harper's Ferry until the morning of the 17th . . . at 6.30 a.m., I received an order from General Lee to move to Sharpsburg. Leaving Thomas, with his brigade, to complete the removal of the captured property, my division was put in motion at 7.30 a.m."[7] A wealthy planter before the war, Thomas commanded four regiments of Georgia troops (the 14th, 35th, 45th, and 49th). The evidence suggests it was these men who oversaw the transfer of the contrabands from Harpers Ferry to Richmond.

There is evidence that others in the Army of Northern Virginia knew about these events at Harpers Ferry.[8] For instance, Col. Francis H. Smith of the 9th Virginia wrote to Gov. John Letcher of Virginia on September 16 (in a letter that appeared in the *Dispatch*) that the Federal garrison at Harpers Ferry had surrendered unconditionally, including "10,000 men, with all the arms, fifty pieces of artillery, ammunition, 100 wagons, quartermaster and commissary stores, and many cars, some of which were loaded [with] 600 negroes" among those seized. Smith's regiment belonged to Lewis Armistead's brigade of Richard H. Anderson's division, Longstreet's command.[9]

The 9th Virginia passed through Harpers Ferry on the way to Sharpsburg. It did not, however, participate in the processing and removal of prisoners and materiel after the Federal garrison's surrender. Thus, Smith either saw for himself or received word from others that a significant number of black individuals had been captured.[10]

---

6 *Richmond Dispatch*, Sept. 24, 1862.

7 Ibid.; *OR* 19, 1:981.

8 Word also traveled through the civilian populace, as noted by Joseph Addison Waddell, a former newspaper editor and wartime clerk in the army quartermaster's office in Staunton, Virginia: "Maj Yost has just arrived from Harper's Ferry. He says that . . . Gen. Jackson . . . had captured at Harper's Ferry 11,000 prisoners and 1500 negroes, 50 pieces of artillery, all their ammunition, commissary and Quartermaster's stores." Diary of Joseph Addison Waddell, Sept. 17, 1862. Augusta County, Virginia Collection, Center for Digital History, University of Virginia, Charlottesville, VA. Available online at https://valley.lib.virginia.edu/papers/AD1500.

9 Harsh, *Sounding the Shallows*, 42.

10 A commissary sergeant with the 13th Georgia, part of Alexander Lawton's brigade in Jackson's command, also wrote home about the event, informing his fiancé that after Jackson had compelled the Federals "to surrender on the 15th September . . . We took 11.700 prisoners

A brief mention of "1000 negroes" captured at Harpers Ferry also made it into the local newspaper of Camden, South Carolina, in late September 1862, proving that many civilians in the South far from the front learned about the event.[11]

The matter-of-fact language used in the article suggests their capture raised no special interest. This remarkable incident demonstrates how, in addition to fighting a war for independence, Robert E. Lee's men also enforced standing Southern property laws concerning captured contrabands. The removal and sale of the Harpers Ferry captives would prove to be a foreshadowing of events to come when, during the Gettysburg Campaign, Richard Ewell's Second Corps seized and shipped south black men, women, and children in Pennsylvania without regard for their legal status.[12]

& small arms, 76 cannons, 3000 'contrabands' and many stores of all kinds." Wells Letter, Oct. 2, 1862.

11 *Camden Confederate*, Sept. 26, 1862.

12 See Robert J. Wynstra, *At the Forefront of Lee's Invasion: Retribution, Plunder, and Clashing Cultures on Richard S. Ewell's Road to Gettysburg* (Kent, OH, 2018).

Appendix E

When Did Lafayette McLaws Reach Sharpsburg on September 17, 1862?

ONE of the more vexing puzzles related to the Battle of Sharpsburg is determining when Lafayette McLaws reached Robert E. Lee's headquarters with his division and that of Richard H. Anderson. The treatment of this subject offered in the seventh chapter of this study relies on the time estimate provided by McLaws himself in the campaign report he submitted on October 20, 1862, and a letter to John Bell Hood on May 31, 1863. The former states plainly, "On the morning of the 17th, about sunrise, the head of my column reached the vicinity of General Lee's headquarters near Sharpsburg," while the latter notes, "My division arrived in the vicinity of Sharpsburg just after day light on the morning of the 17th."[1]

Brigadier General Joseph Brevard Kershaw, a brigade commander in McLaws's division, agreed with this arrival time in the battle report he filed on October 9, 1862, observing that his command arrived "at Sharpsburg at daylight on Wednesday morning, September 17."[2] Because McLaws's and Kershaw's reports were written within weeks of the fighting, they have been relied upon in this study to determine the time when McLaws's command came up, which looked to be between 5:50 and 6:00 a.m.

This interpretation differs from that offered by historian Joseph Harsh in *Taken at the Flood*, which argues that McLaws arrived as early as 4:30 a.m. on September 17.[3] Harsh relied on comments made by McLaws 34 years after the war. "Upon [the] call of General

---

1 OR 19, 1:857; Oeffinger, ed., *A Soldier's General*, 182.

2 OR 19, 1:865.

3 Harsh, *Taken*, 368-369.

Lee," wrote the aging general, "I resumed the march at 12 at night and crossing the river by fording, guided by the light of torches, reached the vicinity of Sharpsburg *before sunrise* [emphasis added] on the 17th, in person to General Lee [and] was directed by him to hold my division in reserve, subject to his orders only."[4]

McLaws repeated this claim more than once, stating in a talk he gave before a group of Confederate veterans in Savannah, Georgia, that he

> began the march again shortly after midnight in response to an urgent call from Gen. Lee, and crossing the ford before daylight reached the vicinity of where, I afterwards found, was Gen. Lee's headquarters, with the head of the column, *before sunrise* [emphasis added] on the 17th. At this early hour there was not a gun being fired, nor were there any noticeable indications that a battle had been fought, nor that one was imminent, and I returned toward my column, meeting Gen. Longstreet, who, with his staff, was coming from the rear. I received orders from him to send Gen. Anderson's division direct down the road to the hill beyond Sharpsburg, where he would receive orders. He informed me that Gen. Lee was in a bunch of woods just in his rear, and I rode to it, and found Gen. Lee dressing for the day.[5]

In addition, as historian Tom Clemens explains in his annotated edition of the volume on the battle by Ezra Carman, McLaws wrote to Carman in the last few years before he died describing a similar chronology. These letters, along with McLaws's insistence that his command reached Sharpsburg before sunrise, convinced Harsh that the Georgian had come up well in advance of daybreak, providing more than enough time for his command to play a key role in the contest.[6]

Postwar testimony about wartime events is often riddled with inventions as participants seek to "correct the record" of their performance, or address accusations leveled against them. This is particularly true concerning Lafayette McLaws, who was criticized by Confederate veterans and Lost Cause advocates, including William Allan and John Esten Cooke, that slow marching on his part had probably cost Lee's army a victory at Sharpsburg. Even during the war itself, the Rev. Nicholas A. Davis, a chaplain with the 4th

---

4 See Lafayette McLaws, "The Capture of Harper's Ferry," in *The Philadelphia Weekly Press*, Vol. XXXI, (Philadelphia, PA, 1888). McLaws Papers, Collection Number 00472, Folder 30 "Addresses and Articles on Civil War Battles." Southern Historical Collection, The Wilson Library, University of North Carolina at Chapel Hill. Available online at https://finding-aids.lib.unc.edu/00472/.

5 McLaws, "The Maryland Campaign."

6 Carman, *The Maryland Campaign*, 2:184. McLaws died in 1894. Harsh, *Taken*, 566, note 86. Harsh wrote of McLaws, "His positive assertion that the battle had not commenced places his arrival at between 4:00 and 5:00." This estimate is entirely Harsh's as McLaws himself never stated such a thing.

Texas, published a pamphlet on John Bell Hood's command stating (incorrectly) that McLaws's division arrived behind the West Woods at 10:30 a.m.[7]

McLaws took affront to this statement and wrote Hood about it in the spring of 1863. "I find that the pamphlet has been industriously circulated," he observed, "and as I have been attacked it has become a necessity for me to defend myself. I dislike very much to be drawn into newspaper notoriety nothing is so repugnant to my sense of propriety as a military man." Hood responded to McLaws that he had "never read the book, and regret[ted] it was published." Writing further, Hood stated, "I gave my opinion [in my battle report] that [with] your arrival by 8 or 8 ½ A. M. I believe our victory would have been complete, on the left . . . I had been fighting since sunrise that morning, and my ammunition was exhausted an hour and a half before your arrival."[8]

One can easily see how a proud officer like McLaws, raised in an age of chivalric Southern culture, would choose to offer a version of the events that demonstrated his timely arrival and which, conveniently, placed responsibility for his time of arrival squarely on the shoulders of Robert E. Lee. After all, if McLaws was up and waiting in the rear for Lee's orders to advance, and only arrived on the field after receiving orders by Lee, then blame for shaping the course of events rested with the Confederate commander and not with Lafayette McLaws.

Fortunately, McLaws revealed in another portion of his 1863 letter to Hood how he had unintentionally combined the two events, i.e., his arrival in Sharpsburg ahead of his

---

7 Tom Clemens observes that "McLaws must have been stung by the criticism as he offered several documents to defend his actions, and Carman's defensive tone suggests he believed McLaws." See Carman, *The Maryland Campaign*, 2:184, Note 20. Criticism of McLaws may have originated in a statement penned by Robert E. Lee to Jefferson Davis on September 18, 1862: "Early next morning ... large masses of the Federal troops that had crossed the Antietam above our position assembled on our left and threatened to overwhelm us. They advanced in three compact lines. The divisions of Generals McLaws, R. H. Anderson, A. P. Hill, and [John G.] Walker *had not arrived the previous night, as I had hoped* [emphasis added] and were still beyond the Potomac." *OR* 19, 1:141. Walker arrived on September 16 with Jackson's division, not on the morning of September 17. Evidence provided by war correspondent Peter Alexander demonstrates the patent unfairness of postwar criticism of McLaws. Writing to his newspaper from Sharpsburg on the evening of September 16 Alexander noted, "Jackson recrossed the river this morning, and reached this place this afternoon. McLaws came up later, and will move into position early to-morrow." This statement suggests that word of McLaws's approach circulated among the ranks before September 17, meaning the general's command was close enough to join the battle the next morning. See *Savannah Republican*, Sept. 26, 1862. Allan, *The Army of Northern Virginia in 1862*, 380, also credited McLaws with crossing the Potomac at daybreak, although he falsely estimated the Georgian's arrival on the field at 10:00 a.m. Davis, *Campaign from Texas to Maryland*, 90.

8 Oeffinger, ed., *A Soldier's General*, 183. Davis formally apologized for his mistake in a letter to McLaws dated Jul. 30, 1863; Ibid., 275. Here Hood inadvertently confirmed the arrival of McLaws's command behind the West Woods around 9:00 a.m. because Hood's division fell back ninety minutes earlier at 7:30.

division and the arrival of the division itself, in his October 1862 report. Writing that his division arrived "in the vicinity of Sharpsburg just after day light," McLaws added shortly thereafter, "My Command crossed the [Potomac] river before day light . . . *I rode ahead* [emphasis added] and went into and beyond the town of Sharpsburg looking for Genl Lee or some one from whom to receive information and directions, but saw but one or two persons about the place. When returning I met Genl Longstreet & staff going to the front and he told me where Genl Lee was. [E]verything at that time was perfectly still. I did not hear a gun or sound denoting the vicinity of a battlefield."[9]

In other words, the 4:00 to 5:00 a.m. estimate for McLaws's arrival in Sharpsburg offered by Harsh is perfectly legitimate, but only for the general himself. It appears not to be correct regarding the arrival of his division, the head of which did not reach the vicinity of Lee's headquarters until near 6:00 a.m. on the morning of September 17. It is easy to see how McLaws garbled the order of events, which in turn led Harsh to conclude that his division arrived just west of Sharpsburg as early as 4:30 a.m.

Relying on contemporaneous documents can help sort out these kinds of complicated scenarios, but there is confusion in this instance as well. Take, for example, the diary entries of Capt. Henry King, Maj. Gen. McLaws's aide-de-camp. According to editor Helen Trimpi, King mailed the torn-out pages of his diary to his sister in two sections, "one section on September 21—four days after Sharpsburg—and another on September 26 from near Martinsburg immediately after the campaign ended."[10]

King's diary pages provide a source for the events even closer in time to their occurrence than the reports of McLaws and Kershaw. Even so, the chronology described in them is not clear. According to King, McLaws's division

Marched in the dark and crossed the Potomac again at the ford below Shepherdstown—about 2 ½ or 3 [a.m.]. *Reached near Sharpsburg about 4 ½ or 5* [emphasis added]—the battle begun as soon as light enough. Anderson's Div. partly with Longstreet. We at first as reserve. Witnessed the battle from a hill—extended firing over a long semicircular line around Sharpsburg. Rode around to Hospitals—wounded coming in. Met Gen. Ripley wounded. Orders came to move to the front & left to Jackson! Marched nearly a mile. ... Severe battle going on—our forces contending for a wood in our front. Moved forward— referred to Gen. Hood for knowledge of the ground, order on the left from centre. . . . The Division came up in fine stile and formed line of battle beautifully. Momentous hour! (It was before 8 A.M.) Gen. McLaws made his dispositions speedily . . . Officers com'dg Brigades and Regts. Spoke a few words of fire to their men, and onward moved the line

9 Oeffinger, ed., *A Soldier's General*, 182-183.

10 Trimpi, ed., "Lafayette McLaws' Aide-de-Camp," 23.

without a waver. In less than five minutes the dropping fire of skirmishers turned into a roar of musketry and our men drove the enemy through the wood gallantly.[11]

King's diary mentions reaching Sharpsburg between 4:30 and 5:00 a.m., but it does not clarify if this is when the captain himself, a member of McLaws's staff, accompanied his chief on the ride ahead to town or if it was when the division reached Sharpsburg.

There is good reason to doubt King's memory of the details and especially his estimate of the hour when McLaws's division went into action. The sources cited in the seventh chapter herein, both Federal and Confederate, demonstrate that McLaws began his assault on the West Woods shortly after 9:00 a.m. King, on the other hand, reckoned that the attack jumped off before 8:00 a.m. This error suggests that King had no good way of keeping time, or that he flat-out guessed when events occurred. The latter seems increasingly possible if the time of his meeting the wounded Roswell Ripley is taken into account. Hit in the throat by a spent bullet sometime between 7:00 and 8:15 a.m., Ripley retired to the rear, where King found him after arriving at Sharpsburg. The location where King met the general is not known, but King does describe riding to a place that sounds very much like Cemetery Hill, which suggests he was not present when McLaws received Lee's orders. Therefore, if King's estimate for the West Woods attack is off by an hour, and cannot be trusted, how much faith should be put in his estimate for the arrival of McLaws's column at Lee's headquarters?[12]

It is important in this regard to keep in mind the simplicity of using daylight as a chronological marker. Like McLaws, King had been awake for much of the night. Anyone experiencing a loss of sleep can attest to the debilitating loss of orientation when it comes to the time of day. The only event that makes a definite impression upon a sleep-deprived person is the rising of the sun. Both McLaws's and Kershaw's reports specify that their column reached Sharpsburg about sunrise. Neither man strove to provide the exact moment when he arrived, believing it sufficient to state that it occurred at daybreak. Michael Hubbert of the 13th Mississippi, a regiment in William Barksdale's brigade, McLaws division, offers a case in point. Hubbert estimated "our Division crossed the Potomac at daybreak." His memory relied on the arrival of daylight as reference point. Hubbert did not write that the division crossed the Potomac at 5:53 a.m. He wrote "daybreak."[13]

11 Ibid., 38-39.

12 See Allan, *The Army of Northern Virginia in 1862*, 380, for a brief discussion of the difficulties that exist estimating when Ripley's brigade went into action on the morning of September 17, 1862.

13 Diary of Michael Hubbert cited in Harsh, *Taken*, 567, Note 86.

King, by contrast, attempted to be precise, which raises suspicions about his accuracy. Certainly, he could have glanced down at his pocket watch at that moment, but if King was so meticulous when he reached Lee's headquarters, why did he later botch the time estimate of McLaws's attack so badly? The likeliest explanation is that King recorded his estimate of the division's arrival time in his diary late on September 17 after a night of lost sleep and a long day of battle. That estimate proved to be too early by roughly one hour. His estimate of the time for the West Woods assault then proved to be early by that same span.

In summary, I believe that Joseph Harsh estimated McLaws's command arrived in Sharpsburg between 4:30 and 5:00 a.m. on September 17 after being misled by the Georgian's garbled statements. The letter to John Bell Hood penned by McLaws in 1863 makes it clear that while he may have personally arrived in Sharpsburg before 5:00 a.m., his division and that of R. H. Anderson did not reach Gen. Lee's headquarters until around 6:00 a.m.

Appendix F

Special Orders No. 191
Hd. Qrs. Army of Northern Va., Sept. 9, 1862

I. The citizens of Fredericktown being unwilling, while overrun by members of this army, to open their stores, in order to give them confidence, and to secure to officers and men purchasing supplies for benefit of this command, all officers and men of this army are strictly prohibited from visiting Fredericktown except on business, in which case they will bear evidence of this in writing from division commanders. The provost-marshal in Fredericktown will see that his guard rigidly enforces this order.

II. Major Taylor will proceed to Leesburg Va., and arrange for transportation of the sick and those unable to walk to Winchester, securing the transportation of the country for this purpose. The route between this and Culpepper Court-House east of the mountains will no longer be travelled. Those on the way to this army already across the river will move up promptly; all others will proceed to Winchester collectively and under command of officers, at which point, being the general depot of this army, its movements will be known and instructions given by the commanding officer regulating further movements.

III. The army will resume its march to-morrow, taking the Hagerstown road. General Jackson's command will form the advance and, after passing Middletown, with such portions as he may select, take the route toward Sharpsburg, cross the Potomac at the most convenient point, and by Friday morning take possession of the Baltimore and Ohio Railroad, capture such of the enemy as may be at Martinsburg, and intercept such as may attempt to escape from Harper's Ferry.

IV. General Longstreet's command will pursue the main road as far as Boonsborough, where it will halt, with reserve, supply and baggage trains of the army.

V. General McLaws, with his own division and that of R.H. Anderson, will follow General Longstreet. On reaching Middletown will take the route to Harper's Ferry, and by Friday morning possess himself of the Maryland Heights and endeavor to capture the enemy at Harper's Ferry and vicinity.

VI. General Walker, with his division, after accomplishing the object in which he is now engaged, will cross the Potomac at Cheek's Ford, ascend its right bank to Lovettsville, take possession of Loudon Heights, if practicable by Friday morning, Key's Ford on his left, and the road between the end of the mountain and the Potomac on his right. He will, as far as practicable, co-operate with Generals McLaws and Jackson, and intercept the enemy.

VII. General D. H. Hill's division will form the rear guard of the army, pursuing the road taken by the main body. The reserve artillery, ordinance, and supply trains &c., will precede General Hill.

VIII. General Stuart will detach a squadron of cavalry to accompany the commands of Generals Longstreet, Jackson, and McLaws, and with the main body of the cavalry, will cover the route of the army, bringing up all stragglers that may have been left behind.

IX. The commands of Generals Jackson, McLaws, and Walker, after accomplishing the objects for which they have been detached, will join the main body of the army at Boonsborough or Hagerstown.

X. Each regiment in the march will habitually carry its axes in the regimental wagons, for use of the men at their encampments to procure wood & c.

By command of General R. E. Lee:

R. H. Chilton
Assistant Adjutant-General

Bibliography

Newspapers

Alabama Beacon

Alexandria Gazette

Athens Watchman

Atlanta Southern Confederacy

Baltimore American

Baltimore Sun

Camden [SC] *Confederate*

Cecil [MD] *Whig*

Columbus [GA] *Sun*

Cumberland [MD] *Civilian and Telegraph*

Davenport [IA] *Daily Gazette*

Edgefield [SC] *Advertiser*

Fayetteville [NC] *Observer*

Frederick Examiner

Frederick News Post

Harper's Weekly

Hudson [WI] *North Star*

Jacksonville [AL] *Republican*

Middletown [MD] *Valley Register*

Mobile Advertiser and Register

National Tribune

New Albany [IN] *Weekly Ledger*

New York Herald

New York Tribune

New York World

Philadelphia Inquirer

Philadelphia Ledger

Richmond Times-Dispatch

Richmond Examiner

Rockingham Register and Virginia Advertiser

Savannah Republican

Southern Recorder

The Columbus [GA] *Daily Sun*

The Rome [GA] *Weekly Courier*

Valley News Echo

Washington Republican

Maps and Atlases

Bond, Isaac. *Map of Frederick County, MD*. Baltimore, MD: E. Sachse & Co., 1858.

Lake, D. J. *Atlas of Frederick County, Maryland*. Philadelphia, PA: C. O. Titus & Co., 1873.

Archival Collections

Beidelman, George Washington. Musselman Library Digital Collections. Gettysburg College. Gettysburg, PA.

Blackshear, James Appleton. Diary. Manuscript Collection No. 302, Stuart A. Rose Manuscript, Archives, and Rare Book Library, Emory University. Atlanta, GA.

Coleman, Clayton G. Civil War Letters, 1862-1863. Collection #MS-0021, Virginia Military Institute Archives. Lexington, VA.

Davis, Angela Kirkham. War Reminiscences: A Letter to My Nieces. Washington County Historical Society, Hagerstown, MD.

DeRossett William L. Collected Papers. North Carolina State Archives. Raleigh, NC.

Garber Family Letters, Augusta County, Virginia Collection. Center for Digital History, University of Virginia. Charlottesville, VA.

Heirs, William A. Letter. Alabama Vertical File. Antietam National Battlefield Library. Keedysville, MD.

Hotchkiss Family Letters, Augusta County, Virginia Collection, Center for Digital History, University of Virginia. Charlottesville, VA.

Joyner Family Papers #4428, Folder 9, Southern Historical Collection, The Wilson Library. University of North Carolina. Chapel Hill, NC.

Kersh Family Letters. Augusta County, Virginia Collection, Center for Digital History, University of Virginia. Charlottesville, VA.

Leach, Calvin. Diary and Letters. Southern Historical Collection, The Wilson Library. University of North Carolina. Chapel Hill, NC.

McClellan, George Brinton. Collected Papers. Library of Congress. Washington, DC.

McLaws, Lafayette. McLaws Papers. Southern Historical Collection, The Wilson Library. University of North Carolina. Chapel Hill, NC.

Rockwell, Elihu H. Civil War Letters of E. H. Rockwell. Frederick Historical Society. Frederick, MD.

Schuler, Michael. Diary. Miscellaneous Manuscript Collection, Manuscript Division. Library of Congress. Washington, DC.

Shinn, James W. Diary. Edwin Augustus Osborne Papers. Southern Historical Collection, The Wilson Library. University of North Carolina. Chapel Hill, NC

Waddell, Joseph A. Diary. Augusta County, Virginia Collection, Center for Digital History, University of Virginia. Charlottesville, VA.

Wardlaw, Andrew B. Diary. South Carolina Vertical File. Antietam National Battlefield Library. Keedysville, MD.

Waud, Alfred R. Papers and Diary, Folder 31, MSS 106. Williams Research Center. The Historic New Orleans Collection. New Orleans, LA.

Wells, Harrison. Collected Papers #5422-z, Southern Historical Collection, The Wilson Library. University of North. Chapel Hill, NC.

Unpublished Manuscripts

Datzman, Richard C. "Who Found Lee's Lost Dispatch?" Lost Orders File. Antietam National Battlefield Library. Keedysville, MD.

Diehl, George W. "A True Confederate Soldier: Col. Elijah Viers White." Thomas Balch Library. Leesburg, VA.

Fritz, Karen Elizabeth. "Voices in the Storm: Confederate Rhetoric, 1861-1865." Louisiana State University Historical Dissertations and Theses (1995).

Hagood, James R. "Memoirs of the First South Carolina Regiment of Volunteer Infantry in the Confederate War for Independence from April 12, 1981 to April 10, 1865." University of South Carolina. South Caroliniana Library. Columbia, SC.

Hotchkiss, Jedediah. "Field Notes on Sharpsburg Battle Field. Dec. 7, 1894." Library of Congress Geography and Map Division. Washington, DC.

Humphreys, Benjamin Grubb. "Unpublished Autobiography." Mississippi Department of Archives and History. Jackson, MS.

Markell, Catherine Susannah Thomas. "Diary: Frederick, Maryland in Peace and War, 1856-1864." Frederick Historical Society. Frederick, MD.

Quynn, William R., ed. "The Diary of Jacob Engelbrecht, 1840-1882, Vol. III." Frederick Historical Society. Frederick, MD.

Schaeffer, Ann R. L. "Records of the Past: Ann R. L. Schaeffer Civil War Diary, September 4–23, 1862." Transcribed by Kira Vaughan. Frederick Historical Society. Frederick, MD.

Stewart, Vaughn M. "Bailey G. McClellan and His Civil War." Antietam National Battlefield Library, Keedysville, MD (1977).

Published Primary Sources

Alexander, Edward Porter. *Military Memoirs of a Confederate: A Critical Narrative.* New York, NY: Charles Scribner's Sons, 1907.

Allan, William. *The Army of Northern Virginia in 1862*. Boston, MA: Houghton Mifflin, 1892.

——. "Memoranda of Conversations with General Robert E. Lee." *Lee the Soldier*. Gary W. Gallagher, ed. Lincoln, NE and London: University of Nebraska Press, 1996.

——. "First Maryland Campaign." *Southern Historical Society Papers*, Vol. 14 (1886).

Andrews, Welburn J. *Sketch of Company K. 23rd South Carolina Volunteers, in the Civil War, from 1862-1865*. Richmond, VA: Whittet & Shepperson, Printers, 1909.

Andrews, William H. *Footprints of a Regiment: A Recollection of the 1st Georgia Regulars*. Atlanta, GA: Longstreet Press, 1992.

——. "Hardships of Georgia Regulars." *Confederate Veteran*, Vol. 17, No. 5 (May 1909).

Atkisson, George B. "Charlie 'Recruit' to Troup Artillery." *Confederate Veteran*, Vol. 19, No. 11 (November 1911).

Avery, A. C. "On the Life and Character of Lieut.-General D. H. Hill." *Southern Historical Society Papers*, Vol. 21 (1893).

Baltimorean. "Great War Song Was Cheap." *Confederate Veteran*, Vol. 16, No. 5 (May 1908).

Bartlett, Napier. *Military Record of Louisiana*. New Orleans, LA, 1875.

——. *A Soldier's Story of the War*. New Orleans, 1874.

Baylor, George. *Bull Run to Bull Run or Four Years in the Army of Northern Virginia*. Richmond, VA: B. F. Johnson Publishing Company, 1900.

Beale, George W. "Maryland Campaign: The Cavalry Fight at Boonsboro Graphically Described." *Southern Historical Society Papers*, Vol. 25 (1897).

Beale, R. L. T. *History of the Ninth Virginia Cavalry*. Richmond, VA: B. F. Johnson Publishing, 1899.

Beall, Thomas B. "Reminiscences About Sharpsburg." *Confederate Veteran*, Vol. 1, No. 8 (August 1893).

Beck, Brandon, ed. *Third Alabama! The Civil War Memoirs of Brigadier General Cullen Battle, CSA*. Tuscaloosa, AL: University of Alabama Press, 2000.

Benning, Henry L. "Notes by General H. L. Benning on the Battle of Sharpsburg." *Southern Historical Society Papers*, Vol. 16 (1888).

Bernard, George. *War Talks of Confederate Veterans*. Dayton, OH: Morningside Press, 1981.

Betts, Alexander D. *Experience of a Confederate Chaplain, 1861-1865*. Piedmont, SC: No Publisher, 1904.

Blackford, William W. *War Years With Jeb Stuart*. New York, NY: Charles Scribner's Sons, 1945.

Booth, George W. *Personal Reminiscences of a Maryland Soldier in the War Between the States*. Baltimore, MD: Fleet-McGinley & Company, 1898.

Bosbyshell, Oliver C. *The 48th PA in the War*. Philadelphia, PA: Avil Printing Company, 1895.

Brooks, Ulysses. R. ed. *Stories of the Confederacy*. Columbia, SC: The State Company, 1912.

Brown, Edmund R. *The Twenty-Seventh Indiana Volunteer Infantry in the War of the Rebellion 1861 to 1865*. Monticello, IN: No Publisher, 1899.

Buck, Samuel D. *With the Old Confeds: Actual Experiences of a Captain in the Line*. Gaithersburg, MD: Butternut Press, 1983.

Buel, Clarence C. & Johnson, Robert U., eds. *Battles and Leaders of the Civil War*. 3 Vols. New York, NY: The Century Co., 1884-1888.

Caldwell, James F. J. *The History of a Brigade of South Carolinians Known First as "Gregg's" and Subsequently as "McGowan's Brigade."* Philadelphia, PA: King & Baird, 1866.

Carman, Ezra A. *The Maryland Campaign of September 1862: Volume 1, South Mountain.* Thomas G. Clemens, ed. El Dorado, CA: Savas Beatie, 2010.

Carraway, D. F. "Lieutenant General A. P. Hill: Some Reminiscences of the Famous Virginia Commander." *Southern Historical Society Papers*, Vol. 19 (1891).

Chamberlayne, John H. *Ham Chamberlayne – Virginian Letters and Papers of an Artillery Officer in the War for Southern Independence, 1861-1865.* Richmond, VA: Dietz Printing Co. 1932.

Charles, Robert K. "Brief Sketch of the First Maryland Campaign." *Confederate Veteran*, Vol. 14, No. 2 (February 1906).

Clark, Walter, ed. *Histories of the Several Regiments and Battalions from North Carolina in the Great War.* Wendell, NC: Broadfoot Publishing, 1982.

———. "The Battle of Sharpsburg—Personal Incidents." *The Wake Forest Student*, Vol. 17, No. 2 (November 1897).

Cockrell, Monroe F., ed., *Gunner With Stonewall: Reminiscences of William T. Poague.* Jackson, TN: McCowat-Mercer, 1957.

Colgrove, Silas. "The Finding of Lee's Lost Orders." *Battles and Leaders of the Civil War*, Vol. 2. Robert Underwood Johnson and Clarence Clough Buel, eds. New York, NY: The Century Company, 1885.

Cooke, John Esten. *Stonewall Jackson: A Military Biography.* New York, NY: D. Appleton and Company, 1866.

———. *The Life of Stonewall Jackson: From Official Papers, Contemporary Narratives, and Personal Acquaintance.* New York, NY: Ayres & Wade, 1863.

Cox, Jacob D. *Military Reminiscences of the Civil War, Vol. 1: April 1861-November 1863.* New York, NY: Charles Scribner's Sons, 1900.

Cummings, Cully C. "Mississippi Boys at Sharpsburg." *Confederate Veteran*, Vol. 5, No. 1 (January 1897).

Curran, Robert E., ed. *John Dooley's Civil War: An Irish American's Journey in the First Virginia Infantry Regiment.* Knoxville, TN: The University of Tennessee Press, 2012.

Cutrer, Thomas W., ed. *Longstreet's Aide: The Civil War Letters of Major Thomas J. Goree.* Charlottesville, VA: University Press of Virginia, 1995.

Dabney, Robert L. *Life and Campaigns of Lieut.-Gen. Jackson.* New York, NY: Blelock, 1866.

Daniel, Frederick S. *Richmond Howitzers in the War: Four Years Campaigning with the Army of Northern Virginia.* Richmond, VA: No Publisher, 1891.

Davis, Jefferson. "Robert E. Lee." *The North American Review*, Vol. 150, No. 398 (January 1890).

Davis, Nicholas A. *Campaign From Texas to Maryland.* Richmond, VA: Office of the Presbyterian Committee, 1863.

Dickert, D. Augustus. *History of Kershaw's Brigade.* Dayton, OH: Morningside Books, 1973.

Dinkins, James. *1861 to 1865: Personal Recollections and Experiences in the Confederate Army.* Dayton, OH: Morningside Press, 1975.

———. "The Griffith-Barksdale-Humphrey Brigade, and Its Campaigns." *Southern Historical Society Papers*, Vol. 32 (1904).

Douglas, Henry K. *I Rode With Stonewall*. Chapel Hill, NC: University of North Carolina Press, 1940.

Dowdey, Clifford & Manarin, Lewis H., eds. *The Wartime Papers of R. E. Lee*. Boston, MA: Little Brown & Co., 1961.

Dozier, Graham T., ed. *A Gunner in Lee's Army: The Civil War Letters of Thomas Henry Carter*. Chapel Hill, NC: The University of North Carolina Press, 2014.

Dunaway, Wayland F. *Reminiscences of a Rebel*. New York, NY: The Neale Publishing Company, 1913.

Durkin, Joseph T., ed. *John Dooley Confederate Soldier, His War Journal*. Washington, DC: Georgetown University Press, 1945.

Early, Jubal A. *Autobiographical Sketch and Narrative of the War Between the States*. Philadelphia, PA: Lippincott, 1912.

——. *A Memoir of the Last Year of the War for Independence in the Confederate States of America*. Toronto, ON: Lovell & Gibson, 1866.

——. "Letter from Jubal A. Early." *Southern Historical Society Papers*, Vol. 7 (1879).

Giles, Valerius C. *Rags and Hope: The Recollections of Val C. Giles, Four Years with Hood's Brigade, Fourth Texas Infantry*. New York, NY: Coward-McCann, 1961.

Ebert, Valerius. "Letter from Mrs. Frietchie's nephew." *Southern Historical Society Papers*, Vol. 7 (1879).

Edwards, W. H. *A Condensed History of Seventeenth Regiment S.C.V. From Its Organization to the Close of the War*. Columbia, SC: R. L. Bryan Co., 1906.

Eggleston, George. *A Rebel's Recollections*. Bloomington, IN: Indiana University Press, 1959.

Evans, Clement A., ed. *Confederate Military History*. 12 Vols. Atlanta, GA: Confederate Publishing Company, 1899.

Evans, Robert G., ed., *The 16th Mississippi Infantry: Civil War Letters and Reminiscences*. Jackson, MS: University Press of Mississippi, 2002.

Folsom, James M. *Heroes and Martyrs of Georgia*. Baltimore, MD: Butternut and Blue, 1995.

Fonerden, Clarence A. *A Brief History of the Military Career of Carpenter's Battery*. New Market, VA: Henkel & Co., 1911.

Forsyth, Charles. *History of the 3d Alabama Regiment, C.S.A.* Montgomery, AL: Confederate Publishing Co., 1866.

Gallagher, Gary, ed. *Fighting For the Confederacy: The Personal Recollections of General Edward Porter Alexander*. Chapel Hill, NC: University of North Carolina Press, 1989.

Goldsborough, William W. *The Maryland Line in the Confederate States Army*. Baltimore, MD: Kelly, Piet & Co., 1869.

Goldsmith, Washington L. "Crucial Test for General S. D. Lee." *Confederate Veteran*, Vol. 3, No. 5 (May 1895).

Gordon, John B. *Reminiscences of the Civil War*. New York, NY: Charles Scribner's Sons, 1904.

Govan, Gilbert E. & Livingood, James W., eds. *The Haskell Memoirs*. New York, NY: G. P. Putnam's Sons, 1960.

Hamilton, J. G. De Roulhac, ed. *The Papers of Randolph A. Shotwell*. 3 Vols. Raleigh, NC: The North Carolina Historical Commission, 1929-1936.

Hassler, William H., ed. *The Civil War Letters of William Dorsey Pender to Fanny Pender.* Chapel Hill, NC: University of North Carolina Press, 1962.

Haynes, Draughton S. *Field Diary of a Confederate Soldier.* Darien, GA: Ashantilly Press, 1963.

Healy, William H. "That Artillery At Sharpsburg." *Confederate Veteran,* Vol. 3, No. 5 (May 1895).

Hill, Daniel Harvey. "The Lost Dispatch." *The Land We Love,* Vol. IV. Charlotte, NC: Hill, Irwin & Co., 1868.

———. "The Lost Dispatch—Letter from General D.H. Hill." *Southern Historical Society Papers,* Vol. 13 (1885).

Hood, John B. *Advance and Retreat: Personal Experiences in the United States and Confederate States Armies.* New Orleans, LA: Hood Orphan Memorial Fund, 1880.

Hopkins, Luther W. *From Bull Run to Appomattox: A Boy's View.* Baltimore, MD: Fleet-McGinley & Company, 1908.

Hough, Franklin B. *History of Duryee's Brigade During the Campaign in Virginia Under Gen. Pope and in Maryland Under Gen. McClellan in the Summer and Autumn of 1862.* Albany, GA: J. Munsell, 1864.

Hubbs, G. Ward, ed. *Voices from Company D: Diaries by the Greensboro Guards, Fifth Alabama Infantry Regiment.* Athens, GA: University of Georgia Press, 2003.

Hughes, William E., ed. *The Civil War Papers of Lt. Colonel Newton T. Colby, New York Infantry.* Jefferson, NC: McFarland & Company, 2003.

Hunter, Alexander. "A High Private's Account of the Battle of Sharpsburg." *Southern Historical Society Papers,* Vol. 10 (1882).

Hurst, Marshall B. *History of the Fourteenth Alabama Vols.* Richmond, VA: No Publisher, 1863.

Huyette, Miles C. *The Maryland Campaign and the Battle of Antietam.* Buffalo, NY: The Hammond Press, 1915.

Imboden, John D. "Incidents of the Battle of Manassas." *The Century Magazine,* Vol. 30 (1885).

Johnson, Bradley T. "Address on the First Maryland Campaign." *Southern Historical Society Papers,* Vol. 12 (1884).

———. "Heroic and Patriotic Marylanders. *Confederate Veteran,* Vol. 2, No. 9 (September 1894).

Johnson, William A. "The Capture of Harper's Ferry." *Confederate Veteran,* Vol. 5, No. 6 (June 1897).

Johnston, David E. *The Story of a Confederate Boy.* Ann Arbor, MI: University Microfilms, 1972.

Johnston, J. S. "A Reminiscence of Sharpsburg." *Southern Historical Society Papers,* Vol. 8 (1880).

Kittrell, Warren. *History of the Eleventh Georgia Volunteers.* Richmond, VA: Smith, Bailey & Co., 1863.

Lang, David. "Civil War Letters of Colonel David Lang." *Florida Historical Quarterly,* Vol. LIV (1976).

Ledford, P. L. *Reminiscences of the Civil War, 1861-1865.* Thomasville, NC: News Print House, 1909.

Lee, Fitzhugh. *General Lee.* New York, NY: D. Appleton and Company, 1898.

———. "Letter from General Fitz Lee." *Southern Historical Society Papers,* Vol. 4 (1877).

Lee, Laura E. *Forget-Me-Nots of the Civil War, A Romance Containing Original Letters of Two Confederate Soldiers.* St. Louis, MO: A. R. Fleming Printing Co., 1909.

Lee, Robert E., Jr. *Recollections and Letters of General Robert E. Lee.* New York, NY: Archibald, Constable & Co., Ltd., 1904.

Lee, Susan P. *Memoirs of William Nelson Pendleton*. Philadelphia, PA: Hess Publications, 1893.

Long, Armistead L. *Memoirs of Robert E. Lee*. New York, NY: J. M. Stoddart and Company, 1886.

Longstreet, James. *From Manassas to Appomattox*. Bloomington, IN: Indiana University Press, 1960.

———. "The Invasion of Maryland." *Battles and Leaders of the Civil War*, Vol. 2. Robert Underwood Johnson and Clarence Clough Buel, eds. New York, NY: The Century Company, 1885.

McCarthy, Carlton. *Contributions To A History of the Richmond Howitzer Battalion*. Baltimore, MD: Butternut and Blue, 2000.

———. *Detailed Minutiae of Soldier Life in the Army of Northern Virginia, 1861-1865*. Richmond, VA: B. F. Johnson Publishing Co., 1899.

McClellan, Henry B. *The Life and Campaigns of Major-General J. E. B. Stuart*. Boston, MA: Houghton, Mifflin and Company, 1885.

———. *Campaigns of Stuart's Cavalry*. Edison, NJ: Blue and Gray Press, 1993.

McClendon, William A. *Recollections of War Times by an Old Veteran While Under Stonewall Jackson and Lieut. General James Longstreet*. Montgomery, AL: The Paragon Press, 1909.

McDaniel, J. J. *Diary of the Battles, Marches and Incidents of the Seventh S. C. Regiment*. No Publisher, 1862.

McDonald, Archie P., ed. *Make Me a Map of the Valley: The Civil War Journal of Stonewall Jackson's Topographer*. Dallas, TX: Southern Methodist University Press, 1973.

McLaws, Lafayette. "The Maryland Campaign." Savannah, GA: Confederate Veterans Association, 1896.

———. "The Capture of Harper's Ferry." *The Philadelphia Weekly Press*, Vol. XXXI (1888).

McMurray, Richard, ed. *Footprints of a Regiment: A Recollection of the 1st Georgia Regulars*. Atlanta, GA: Longstreet Press, 1992.

Maurice, Frederick, ed. *An Aide-de-Camp of Lee: Being the Papers of Colonel Charles Marshall*. Boston, MA: Little, Brown and Co., 1927.

Mills, George H. "Supplemental Sketch Sixteenth Regiment." *Histories of the Several Regiments and Battalions from North Carolina*, Vol. 4. Walter Clark, ed. Goldsboro, NC: Nash Brothers, Book and Job Printers, 1901.

Mixson, Frank M. *Reminiscences of a Private*. Columbia, SC: The State Company, 1910.

Moore, Frank, ed. *The Rebellion Record: A Diary of American Events*. 8 Vols. New York, NY: G. P. Putnam, 1864.

Moore, Edward A. *The Story of a Cannoneer Under Stonewall Jackson*. New York, NY: The Neale Publishing Company, 1907.

Moore, Robert A. & Silver, J. W., eds. *A Life for the Confederacy, as Recorded in the Pocket Diaries of Pvt. Robert A. Moore. Co. G. 17th Mississippi Regiment, Confederate Guards, Holly Springs, Mississippi*. Wendell, NC: Broadfoot Publishing Company, 1987.

Morgan, William H. *Personal Reminiscences of the War of 1861-5*. Lynchburg, VA: J. P. Bell Company, 1911.

Morrison, Joseph G. "Jackson at Harper's Ferry." *Philadelphia Weekly Press*, Dec. 22, 1883.

Myers, Frank M. *The Comanches: A History of White's Battalion, Virginia Cavalry*. Baltimore, MD: Kelly, Piet, & Co., Publishers, 1871.

Neese, George. *Three Years in the Confederate Horse Artillery*. New York, NY: The Neale Publishing Company, 1911.

Nisbet, James C. *Four Years on the Firing Line*. Chattanooga, TN: The Imperial Press, 1914.

Oeffinger, John C., ed. *A Soldier's General: The Civil War Letters of Major General Lafayette McLaws*. Chapel Hill, NC: The University of North Carolina Press, 2002.

Otey, William Mercer. "The Story of Our Great War." *Confederate Veteran*, Vol. 7, No. 8 (August 1899).

Owen, William M. *In Camp and Battle with the Washington Artillery*. Boston, MA: Ticknor and Company, 1885.

Park, Robert E. *Sketch of the Twelfth Alabama Infantry of Battle's Brigade, Rodes' Division, or Early's Corps of the Army of Northern Virginia*. Richmond, VA: W. M. Ellis Jones, Book and Job Printer, 1906.

Parks, Leighton. *Turnpikes and Dirt Roads*. New York, NY: Charles Scribner's Sons, 1927.

———. "What a Boy Saw of the Civil War." *The Century Magazine*, Vol. 70, No. 2 (1905).

Philpot, G. B. "A Maryland Boy in the Confederate Army." *Confederate Veteran*, Vol. 24, No. 7 (July 1916).

Polley, Joseph B. *A Soldier's Letters to Charming Nellie*. New York, NY: The Neale Publishing Company, 1908.

———. *Hood's Texas Brigade: Its Marches, Its Battles, Its Achievements*. Dayton, OH: Morningside Bookshop [Press?], 1976.

Ramsay, John A. "Additional Sketch Tenth Regiment. Light Batteries A, D, F and I." *Histories of the Several Regiments and Battalions from North Carolina*, Vol. 1. Walter Clark, ed. Goldsboro, NC: Nash Brothers, Book and Job Printers, 1901.

Rawle, William B. *History of the Third Pennsylvania Cavalry in the American Civil War, 1861-1865*. Philadelphia, PA: Franklin Printing Company, 1905.

Rawley, James A. *The American Civil War: An English View. The Writings of Field Marshal Viscount Wolseley*. Mechanicsburg, PA: Stackpole Books, 2002.

Ray, Neill W. "Sixth Regiment." *Histories of the Several Regiments and Battalions from North Carolina in the Great War, 1861-'65*, Vol. 1. Walter Clark, ed. Goldsboro, NC: Nash Brothers, Book and Job Printers, 1901.

Reese, James. "Private Soldier Life—Humorous Features." *Confederate Veteran*, Vol. 16, No. 4 (April 1908).

Robson, John S. *Reminiscences of the Civil War*. Durham, NC: The Educator Co. Printers and Binders, 1898.

Schiller, Herbert N. *A Captain's War: The Letter and Diaries of William H. S. Burgwyn 1861-1865*. Shippensburg, PA: White Mane Publishing Co., 1994.

Sheeran, James B. *Confederate Chaplain*. Milwaukee, WI: The Bruce Publishing Company, 1960.

Sieburg, Evelyn R. & Hansen II, James E., eds. *Memoirs of a Confederate Staff Officer From Bethel to Bentonville*. Shippensburg, PA: White Mane Books, 1998.

Skock, George & Perkins, Mark W., eds. *Lone Star Confederate: A Gallant and Good Soldier of the Fifth Texas Infantry*. College Station, TX: Texas A&M University Press, 2003.

Sloan, John A. *Reminiscences of the Guilford Grays*. Washington, DC: R. O. Polkinhorn, Printer, 1883.

Smith, James P. "With Stonewall Jackson in the Army of Northern Virginia." *Southern Historical Society Papers*, Vol. 43 (1920).

Smith, N. S. "Additional Sketch Thirteenth Regiment." *Histories of the Several Regiments and Battalions from North Carolina*, Vol. 1. Walter Clark, ed. Goldsboro, NC: Nash Brothers, Book and Job Printers, 1901.

Smith, William A. *The Anson Guards, Company C, Fourteenth Regiment North Carolina Volunteers 1861-1865*. Wendell, NC: Broadfoot Publishing, 1978.

Sorrell, G. Moxley. *Recollection of a Confederate Staff Officer*. New York, NY: The Neale Publishing Company, 1905.

Steiner, Lewis H. *Report of Lewis H. Steiner, Inspector of the Sanitary Commission Containing a Diary Kept During the Rebel Occupation of Frederick, MD, and an Account of the Operations of the U.S. Sanitary Commission During the Campaign in Maryland, September, 1862*. New York, NY: Anson D. F. Randolph, 1862.

Stevens, John W. *War Reminiscences*. Powhatan, VA: Derwent Books, 1982.

Stiles, Robert. *Four Years Under Marse Robert*. New York, NY: The Neale Publishing Company, 1904.

Stocker, Jeffery, ed. *From Huntsville to Appomattox: R. T. Coles's History of the 4th Alabama Infantry, C. S. A., Army of Northern Virginia*. Knoxville, TN: University of Tennessee Press, 1996.

Styple, William B., ed. *Writing and Fighting the Confederate War: The Letters of Peter Wellington Alexander*. Kearny, NJ: Belle Grove Publishing Co., 2002.

Squires, Charles W. "The 'Boy Officer' of the Washington Artillery, Part 1." *Civil War Times Illustrated*, Vol. XIV, No. 2 (May 1975).

Taylor, Michael W., ed. *To Drive the Enemy from Southern Soil: The Letters of Col. Francis Marion Parker and The History of the 30th Regiment North Carolina Troops*. Dayton, OH: Morningside Press, 1998.

Taylor, Walter H. *Four Years with General Lee*. New York, NY: D. Appleton and Company, 1878.

———. *General Lee: His Campaigns in Virginia, 1861-1865 with Personal Reminiscences*. Norfolk, VA: Nusbaum Book and News Company, 1906.

Terrill, J. Newton. *Campaign of the Fourteenth Regiment New Jersey Volunteers*. New Brunswick, NJ: Daily Home News Press, 1884.

Thomas, Henry W. *History of the Doles–Cook Brigade, Army of Northern Virginia, C. S. A.* Atlanta, GA: The Franklin Printing and Publishing Co., 1903.

Tilberg, Frederick. *Antietam*. Washington, DC: National Park Service, 1960.

Tower, R. Lockwood, ed. *Lee's Adjutant: The Wartime Letters of Colonel Walter Herron Taylor 1862-1865*. Columbia, SC: University of South Carolina Press, 1995.

Trimble, Isaac R. "The Campaign and Battle of Gettysburg." *Confederate Veteran*, Vol. 25, No. 5 (May 1917).

Trimpi, Helen, ed. "Lafayette McLaws' Aide-de-Camp: The Maryland Campaign Diary of Captain Henry Lord Page King." *Civil War Regiments: A Journal of the American Civil War*, Vol. 6, No. 2 (1998).

Trout, Robert J., ed. *With Pen and Saber: The Letters and Diaries of J. E. B. Stuart's Staff Officer*. Harrisburg, PA: Stackpole Books, 1995.

Turner, Charles W., ed. *Captain Greenlee Davidson, C.S.A. Diary and Letters, 1851-1863*, Verona, VA: McClure Press, 1975.

Turner, V. E. & Wall, H. C. "Twenty-Third Regiment." *Histories of the Several Regiments and Battalions from North Carolina in the Great War, 1861-'65*, Vol. 2. Walter Clark, ed. Goldsboro, NC: Nash Brothers, Book and Job Printers, 1901.

U. S. House of Representatives. *Report of the Joint Committee on the Conduct of the War.* 3 Parts. Washington, DC: Government Printing Office, 1863.

U. S. War Department. *The War of the Rebellion: A Compilation of the Official Records of the Union and Confederate Armies.* 128 vols. Washington, DC: Government Printing Office, 1880-1901.

Venn, Frank H. "That Flag of Truce at Antietam." *Confederate Veteran*, Vol. 4, No. 12 (December 1896).

Von Borcke, Heros. *Memoirs of the Confederate War for Independence.* Gaithersburg, MD: Butternut & Blue, 1985.

Walbrook, D. Swank, ed. *Sabres, Saddles, and Spurs.* Shippensburg, PA: Burd Street Press, 1998.

Walcott, Charles F. *History of the Twenty-First Regiment Massachusetts Volunteers.* Boston, MA: Houghton Mifflin and Co., 1882.

Walker, John G. "Jackson's Capture of Harper's Ferry." *Battles and Leaders of the Civil War*, Vol. 2. Robert Underwood Johnson and Clarence Clough Buel, eds. New York, NY: The Century Company, 1885.

———. "Sharpsburg." *Battles and Leaders of the Civil War*, Vol. 2. Robert Underwood Johnson and Clarence Clough Buel, eds. New York, NY: The Century Company, 1885.

White, Thomas H. "About The Shelling of Leesburg." *Confederate Veteran*, Vol. 21, No. 1 (January 1913).

Williams, Jonathan Whitehead. *His Life and Times with the 5th Alabama, C.S.A. Company "D" Greensboro Guards.* Greensboro, AL: No Publisher, 1903.

Wilson, Gary, ed. "The Diary of John S. Tucker: Confederate Soldier from Alabama." *The Alabama Historical Quarterly*, Vol. XLII, No. 1 (Spring 1981).

Wise, George. *History of Seventeenth Virginia Infantry.* Baltimore: Kelly, Piet & Co., 1870.

———. *Campaigns and Battles of the Army of Northern Virginia.* New York, NY: The Neale Publishing Company, 1916.

Wolseley, Garnet J. "General Lee." *MacMillan's Magazine*, Vol. 55 (November 1886 to April 1887).

Wood, James H. *The War: "Stonewall" Jackson: His Campaigns and Battles, the Regiment as I Saw Them.* Cumberland, MD: Eddy Press Corporation, 1910.

Wood, William. *Reminiscences of Big I.* Jackson, TN: McCowen-Mercer Press, 1956.

Worsham, John. *One of Jackson's Foot Cavalry.* New York, NY: The Neale Publishing Company, 1912.

Young, Charles P. "History of Crenshaw Battery." *Southern Historical Society Papers*, Vol. 31 (1903).

Secondary Works

Abbott, Eleanor D. *A Sketch of Barbara Fritchie, Whittier's Heroine.* Frederick, MD: Frederick News Post Publishing Co., 1921.

Andrews, J. Cutler. *The South Reports the Civil War*. Princeton, NJ: Princeton University Press, 1970.

Armstrong, Jr., Marion V. *Unfurl Those Colors! McClellan, Sumner, and the Second Army Corps in the Antietam Campaign*. Tuscaloosa, AL: The University of Alabama Press, 2008.

Armstrong, Richard L. *19th and 20th Virginia Cavalry*. Lynchburg, VA: H. E. Howard, 1994.

Bolcik, Paul, Davis, Erik, and Heberton IV, Craig. "Confederates in Frederick: New Insights on a Famous Photo." *Battlefield Photographer: The Journal of the Center for Civil War Photography*. Vol. 16, No. 1 (April 2018).

Bridges, Hal. *Lee's Maverick General: Daniel Harvey Hill*. Lincoln, NE: University of Nebraska Press, 1961.

Chambers, Lenoir. *Stonewall Jackson*. 2 Vols. New York, NY: William Morrow, 1959.

Collins, Joseph V. *Battle of West Frederick, July 7, 1864: Prelude to Battle of Monocacy*. Xlibris, 2011.

Cooling, B. Franklin. *Monocacy: The Battle that Saved Washington*. Shippensburg, PA: White Mane Publishing, 1997.

Davis, James A. *51st Virginia Infantry*. Lynchburg, VA: H. E. Howard, 1984.

Delaplane, Edward S. "General Early's Levy on Frederick." *The 100th Anniversary of the Battle of Monocacy*. Frederick, MD: Frederick County Civil War Centennial, 1964.

Driver, Jr., Robert J. & Ruffner, Kevin C. *1st Battalion Virginia Infantry, 39th Battalion Virginia Cavalry, and 24th Battalion Virginia Partisan Rangers*. Lynchburg, VA: H. E. Howard, 1996.

Dyer, Frederick H. *A Compendium of the War of the Rebellion*. 3 Vols. New York, NY: T. Yoseloff, 1959.

Ernst, Kathleen A. *Too Afraid to Cry: Maryland Civilians in the Antietam Campaign*. Mechanicsburg, PA: Stackpole Books, 1999.

Fain, J. Tyree. "Robert E. Lee—Maurice." *Tennessee Historical Magazine*, Vol. 8, No. 3 (October 1924).

Fellman, Michael. *The Making of Robert E. Lee*. New York, NY: Random House, 2000.

Freeman, Douglas Southall. *R. E. Lee: A Biography*. 4 Vols. New York, NY: Charles Scribner's Sons, 1934.

——. *Lee's Lieutenants*. 3 Vols. New York, NY: Charles Scribner's Sons, 1942-1944.

Frye, Dennis E. *Harpers Ferry Under Fire: A Border Town in the American Civil War*. Virginia Beach, VA: The Donning Company, 2012.

Gallagher, Gary W., ed. *Lee the Soldier*. Lincoln, NE: University of Nebraska Press, 1996.

——., ed., *The Antietam Campaign*. Chapel Hill, NC: University of North Carolina Press, 1999.

Gordon, Paul and Rita. *Frederick County, Maryland: Never the Like Again*. Frederick, MD: The Heritage Partnership, 1995.

——. *Frederick County, Maryland: A Playground of the Civil War*. Frederick, MD: The Heritage Partnership, 1994.

Harsh, Joseph L. *Taken at the Flood: Robert E. Lee and Confederate Strategy in the Maryland Campaign of 1862*. Kent, OH and London: The Kent State University Press, 1999.

——. *Sounding the Shallows: A Confederate Companion for the Maryland Campaign of 1862*. Kent, OH and London: The Kent State University Press, 2000.

——. *Confederate Tide Rising: Robert E. Lee and the Making of Southern Strategy, 1861-1862*. Kent, OH and London: The Kent State University Press, 1998).

Hartwig, D. Scott. *To Antietam Creek: The Maryland Campaign of September 1862*. Baltimore, MD: The Johns Hopkins Press, 2012.

———. "From the Crossroads: White Lies." *America's Civil War* (November 2018).

Johnson, Thomas C. *Life and Letters of Robert Lewis Dabney*. Richmond, VA: Whittet & Shepperson, 1903

Jones, Jr., Wilbur D. "Who Lost the Lost Orders? Stonewall Jackson, His Courier, and Special Orders No. 191." *Civil War Regiments: A Journal of the American Civil War*. Vol. 5, No. 3 (1997).

Kleese, Richard B. *23rd Virginia Cavalry*. Lynchburg, VA: H. E. Howard, 1996.

Knott, Steven W. "Lee at Antietam: Strategic Imperatives, the Tyranny of Arithmetic, and a Trap Not Sprung." *Army History*, No. 95 (Spring 2015).

Koleszar, Marilyn B. *Ashland, Bedford, and Taylor Virginia Light Artillery*. Lynchburg, VA: H. E. Howard, 1994.

Krick, Robert K. "A Stupid Old Useless Fool." *Civil War Times* (June 2008).

———. "Postwar Dinner Guests Dished and Debated Confederate Heroes." *America's Civil War* (September 2019)

Lewis, David J. *Frederick War Claim: Evidence and Argument in Support of Bill to Refund Ransom Paid by the Town of Frederick, During the Civil War, to Save Said Town and Union Military Supplies from Destruction*. Frederick, MD: No Publisher, No Date.

Lowry, Terry D. *26th Battalion Virginia Infantry*. Lynchburg, VA: H. E. Howard, 1991.

McCabe, W. Gordon. "The Real Barbara Frietchie." *Southern Historical Society Papers*, Vol. 27 (1899).

McNeely, Patricia G., *et al. Knights of the Quill: Confederate Correspondents and their Civil War Reporting*. West Lafayette, IN: Purdue University Press, 2010.

McPherson, James M. *Crossroads of Freedom: Antietam*. New York, NY: Oxford University Press, 2002.

Macaluso, Gregory J. *Morris, Orange, and King William Artillery*. Lynchburg, VA: H. E. Howard, 1991.

Martenet, Simon J. & Bond, Isaac. *Martenet and Bond's Map of Montgomery County*. Baltimore, MD, 1865.

Martin, David G. *The Fluvanna Artillery*. Lynchburg, VA: H. E. Howard, 1992.

Maurice, Frederick. *Robert E. Lee the Soldier*. Boston, MA: Houghton Mifflin, 1925.

Menuet, Robert W. "Corporal Barton W. Mitchell and the Lost Orders." *America's Civil War*. (September 2007).

Miller, William J. *Mapping for Stonewall: The Civil War Service of Jed Hotchkiss*. Washington, DC: Elliott & Clark Publishing, 1993.

Murfin, James V. *The Gleam of Bayonets: The Battle of Antietam and the Maryland Campaign of 1862*. New York, NY: Bonanza Books, 1965.

Nicholas, Richard L. & Servis, Joseph. *Powhatan, Salem, and Courtney Henrico Artillery*. Lynchburg, VA: H. E. Howard, 1997.

Nolan, Alan T. *Lee Considered: General Robert E. Lee and Civil War History*. Chapel Hill, NC: The University of North Carolina Press, 1991.

Owen, Joe, McBride, Philip, and Allport, Joe. *Texans at Antietam: A Terrible Clash of Arms, September 16–17, 1862*. Fonthill Media, 2017.

Palfrey, Francis W. *The Antietam and Fredericksburg*. New York, NY: Charles Scribner's Sons, 1893.

Palmer, Michael A. *Lee Moves North: Robert E. Lee on the Offensive*. New York, NY: John Wiley & Sons, 1998.

Paris, Louis-Philippe-Albert d'Orleans, Comte de. *History of the Civil War in America*. 4 Vols. Trans. Louis F. Tasistro. Philadelphia, PA: J. H. Coates & Co., 1876.

Platteborze, Peter L. "Crossroads of Destiny: Lew Wallace, the Battle of Monocacy, and the Outcome of Jubal Early's Drive on Washington, D.C." *Army History*, No. 61 (Spring 2005).

Pollard, Edward A. *The Lost Cause: A New Southern History of the War of the Confederates*. New York, NY: E. B. Treat & Co., 1866.

Priest, John Michael. *Before Antietam: The Battle for South Mountain*. Shippensburg, PA: White Mane Publishing, 1992.

Pryor, Elizabeth Brown. *Reading the Man: A Portrait of Robert E. Lee Through His Private Letters*. New York, NY: Penguin Books, 2007.

Rafuse, Ethan S. *McClellan's War: The Failure of Moderation in the Struggle for the Union*. Bloomington, IN: Indiana University Press, 2005.

Rankin, Thomas M. *23rd Virginia Infantry*. Lynchburg, VA: H. E. Howard, 1985.

Reese, Timothy J. *High-Water Mark: The 1862 Maryland Campaign in Strategic Perspective*. Baltimore, MD: Butternut and Blue, 2004.

———. *Sealed with Their Lives: The Battle of Crampton's Gap, Burkittsville, MD, Sept. 14, 1862*. Baltimore, MD: Butternut and Blue, 1998.

Reimer, Terry. *One Vast Hospital: The Civil War Hospital Sites in Frederick, Maryland, after Antietam*. Frederick, MD: The National Museum of Civil War Medicine, 2001.

Robertson, Jr., James I. *4th Virginia Infantry*. Lynchburg, VA: H. E. Howard, 1982.

———. *Stonewall Jackson: The Man, The Soldier, The Legend*. New York, NY: Macmillan Library Reference, 1997.

Schildt, John W. *The Twelfth Corps at Antietam*. Brunswick, MD: E Graphics, 2012.

Sears, Stephen W. *Landscape Turned Red: The Battle of Antietam*. Boston, MA: Mariner Books, 1983.

———. "The Twisted Tale of the Lost Order." *North and South Magazine*, Vol. 5, No. 7 (October 2002).

Sherlock, Scott M. "The Lost Order and the Press." *Civil War Regiments: A Journal of the American Civil War*, Vol. 6, No. 2 (1998).

Sherwood, W. Cullen & Nicholas, Richard L. *Amherst Artillery, Albemarle Artillery, and Sturdivant's Battery*. Lynchburg, VA: H. E. Howard, 1996.

Simpson, Harold B. *Gaines' Mill to Appomattox: Waco & McLennan County in Hood's Texas Brigade*. Texian Press: Waco, TX, 1988.

Spaulding, Brett W. *Last Chance for Victory: Jubal Early's 1864 Maryland Invasion*. Thomas Publications, 2010.

Stotelmyer, Steven R. *Too Useful to Sacrifice: Reconsidering George B. McClellan's Generalship in the Maryland Campaign from South Mountain to Antietam*. El Dorado, CA: Savas Beatie, 2019.

Swinton, William. *Campaigns of the Army of the Potomac*. New York, NY: Charles Scribner's Sons, 1866.

Thomas J. C. Williams and Folger McKinsey, *History of Frederick County, Maryland.* 2 Vols. Baltimore, MD: Regional Publishing Co., 1997 and 2003.

Thorp, Gene M. and Rossino, Alexander B. *The Tale Untwisted: George McClellan and the Discovery of Lee's Lost Orders, September 13, 1862.* El Dorado, CA: Savas Beatie, 2019.

Thorp, Gene, M. "In Defense of McClellan at Antietam: A Contrarian View." *The Washington Post* (September 7, 2012).

Toomey, Daniel C. *The Civil War in Maryland.* Baltimore, MD: Toomey Press, 1983.

Unrau, Harlan D. *Historic Resource Study: Chesapeake & Ohio Canal.* Hagerstown, MD: National Park Service, 2007.

Wallace, Jr., Lee A. *5th Virginia Infantry.* Lynchburg, VA: H. E. Howard, 1988.

——. *The Richmond Howitzers.* Lynchburg, VA: H. E. Howard, 1993.

——. White, Henry A. *Robert E. Lee.* New York, NY: Fred DeFau & Co., 1897.

Wiley, Bell Irvin. *The Life of Johnny Reb: The Common Soldier of the Confederacy.* Garden City, NY: Doubleday & Co., 1943.

Williams, N. Mahony. *Frederick Directory, City Guide, and Business Mirror.* Vol. 1. Frederick, MD, 1859.

Worthington, Glenn H. *Fighting for Time: The Battle of Monocacy.* Shippensburg, PA: Burd Street Press, 1985.

Index

Alexander B. Rossino received his B.A. from Canisius College, in Buffalo, NY, and his Ph.D. in History from Syracuse University. He worked at the U.S. Holocaust Memorial Museum from 1994 to 2003 and is the author of numerous scholarly articles. His first book, *Hitler Strikes Poland: Blitzkrieg, Ideology, and Atrocity*, is an acclaimed history of racial-political policies implemented by the Third Reich during its 1939 invasion of Poland.

His interest in the American Civil War dates from childhood. He is the author of the highly acclaimed *Six Days in September,* a novel on Lee's Army in Maryland, 1862 (2017), *The Tale Untwisted: George McClellan and the Discovery of Lee's Lost Orders, September 13, 1862*, and the forthcoming *The Guns of September*, a novel on McClellan's Army in Maryland, 1862.

For more information about Alex and his work, please visit him online at www.facebook.com/alexander.rossino.33, and read his outstanding and informative blog posts at www.alexanderrossino.com.